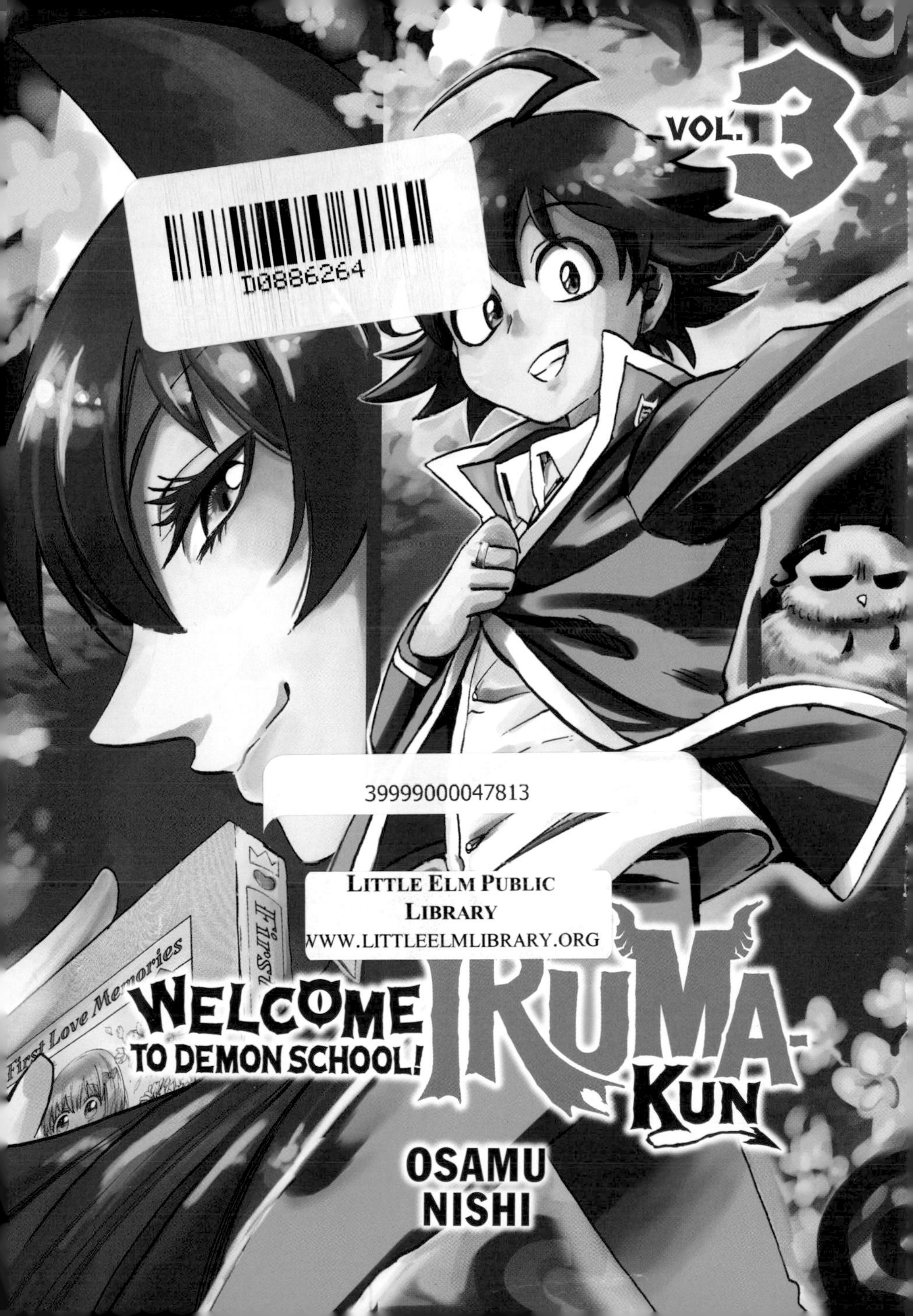
VOL. 3
First Love Memories
WELCOME TO DEMON SCHOOL! IRUMA-KUN
OSAMU NISHI

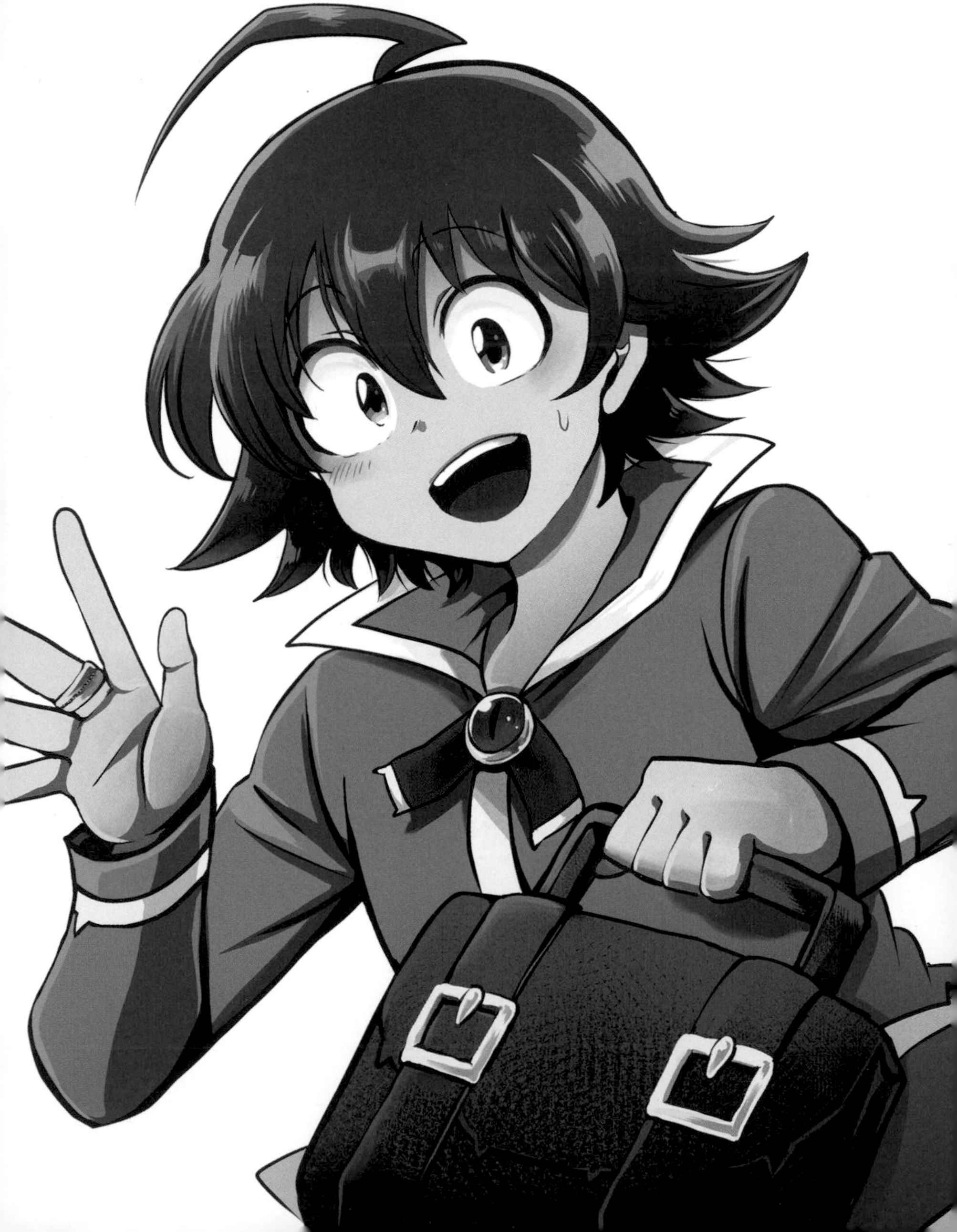

OSAMU NISHI PRESENTS

I JOINED A SPORTS CLUB WHEN I
WAS IN ELEMENTARY SCHOOL.

MY PHYSICAL STRENGTH
HAS PROBABLY ONLY DECLINED
SINCE THEN.

EVEN DEMONS HAVE THINGS
THEY'RE GOOD AND BAD AT.
WHEN YOU SPLIT THEM UP
BASED ON THEIR TALENTS,
IT'S A LOT LIKE DIVIDING
REAL SCHOOL CLASSES.

THE ONE DEMON I DON'T EVER
WANT TO BE FRIENDS WITH IS
ANDRAS. HE'S JUST TOO SCARY.

& STORY

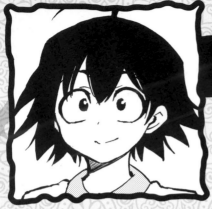

IRUMA SUZUKI

A kindhearted but extreme pushover. He just can't seem to turn down anyone who makes a request of him, and he's extremely skilled at avoiding danger. He hopes he can hide his identity as a human and live a peaceful life while at demon school.

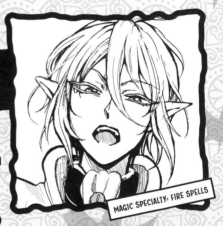

MAGIC SPECIALTY: FIRE SPELLS

ALICE ASMODEUS

A demon hailing from a family known as authorities on destruction and virtue. He got the highest scores on the entrance exam, making him the top first-year. He lost his temper after Iruma upstaged him during the entrance ceremony, but when Iruma defeated him in battle, Alice accepted his loss and swore fealty to Iruma.

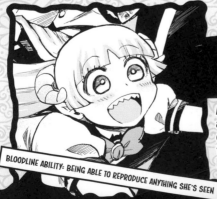

BLOODLINE ABILITY: BEING ABLE TO REPRODUCE ANYTHING SHE'S SEEN

CLARA VALAC

An energetic and cheerful demon girl. She's rowdy and doesn't know the meaning of "calm." Because of this, many avoid and ostracize her. She was touched by Iruma's kindness and became one of his best friends as a result.

CHARACTERS

KALEGO

An extremely strict teacher at Babyls. Kalego despises dealing with the inconsiderate Sullivan, and he also detests Iruma. But a particular incident in class resulted in Iruma summoning Kalego and making him his familiar.

SULLIVAN

A doting demon and the Chair-Demon of Babyls, who has made Iruma his grandson. Not only is his love for Iruma bottomless, but his actual powers as a demon may also be just as limitless...

AMERI AZAZEL

The beautiful and proud student council president who deduces Iruma is human. But after Iruma begins reading to her from *First Love Memories*, a shojo manga from the human world, they develop a close friendship.

THE STORY SO FAR

As an extreme pushover, Iruma Suzuki was sold off for a pretty penny to a demon by his good-for-nothing parents. Fortunately, what awaited him in the netherworld was a kindhearted demon named Sullivan, whose only wish was for Iruma to become his grandson. Iruma is showered with love and sent to the demon school, Babyls, where despite his best efforts to avoid attention, he is constantly in the spotlight. Before long, the student council president Ameri begins to suspect that Iruma must be human. But once Iruma starts reading her the shojo manga *First Love Memories*, the two develop a friendship that pursuades Ameri to shelve her investigation into his true identity. However, Ameri soon chastises Iruma for his lack of ambitions. Iruma resolves to shoot for the stars at the Execution Cannonball showdown to learn about the importance of working hard for his own sake, and successfully ranks up to Bet! What new challenges will he take on next?!

WELCOME TO DEMON SCHOOL! IRUMA-KUN
CONTENTS

FIRST SERIALIZED IN SHONEN CHAMPION COMICS #31-40 IN 2017.

IT'S THE TABLE OF CONTENTS!

ASK ME!

ASK ME!

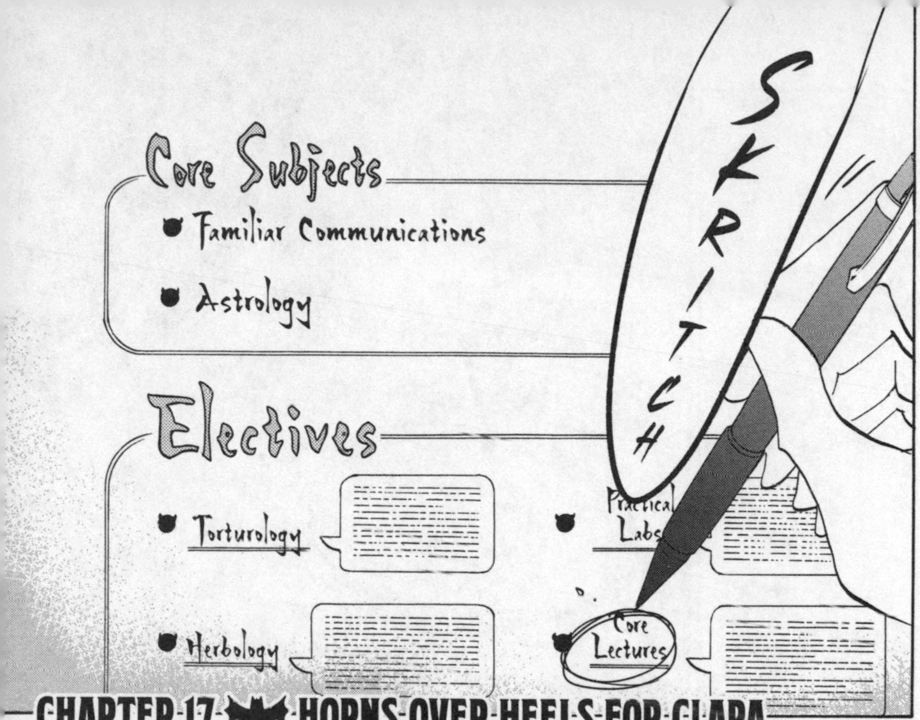
SKRITCH
Core Subjects
Familiar Communications
Astrology
Electives
Torturology
Practical Labs
Herbology
Core Lectures

CHAPTER 17 HORNS OVER HEELS FOR CLARA

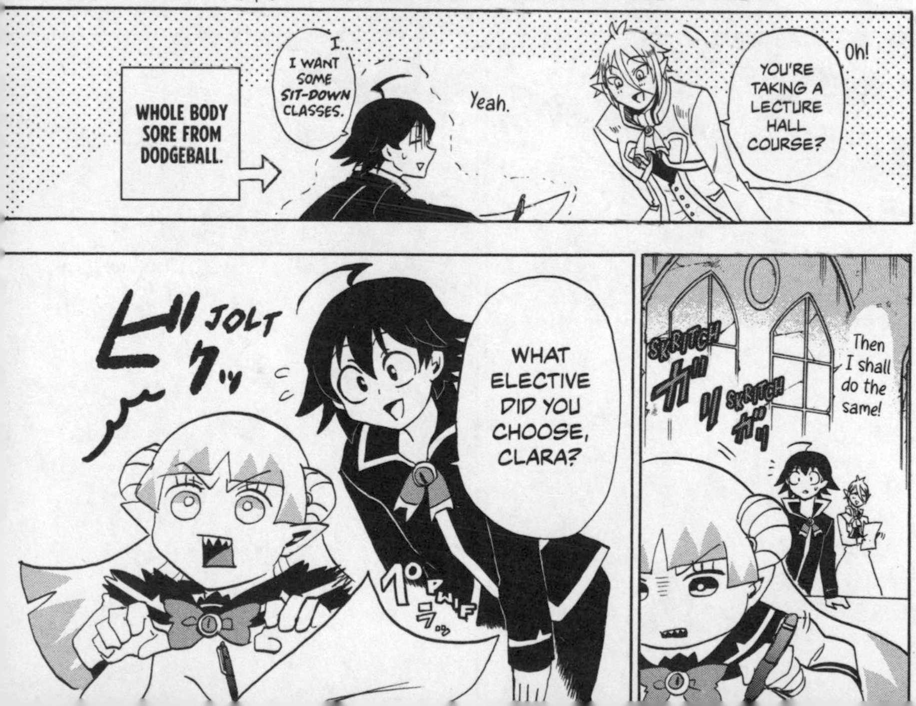
Oh!
YOU'RE TAKING A LECTURE HALL COURSE?
Yeah.
I... I WANT SOME SIT-DOWN CLASSES.
WHOLE BODY SORE FROM DODGEBALL.
SKRITCH
SKRITCH
Then I shall do the same!
WHAT ELECTIVE DID YOU CHOOSE, CLARA?
JOLT
PWIF

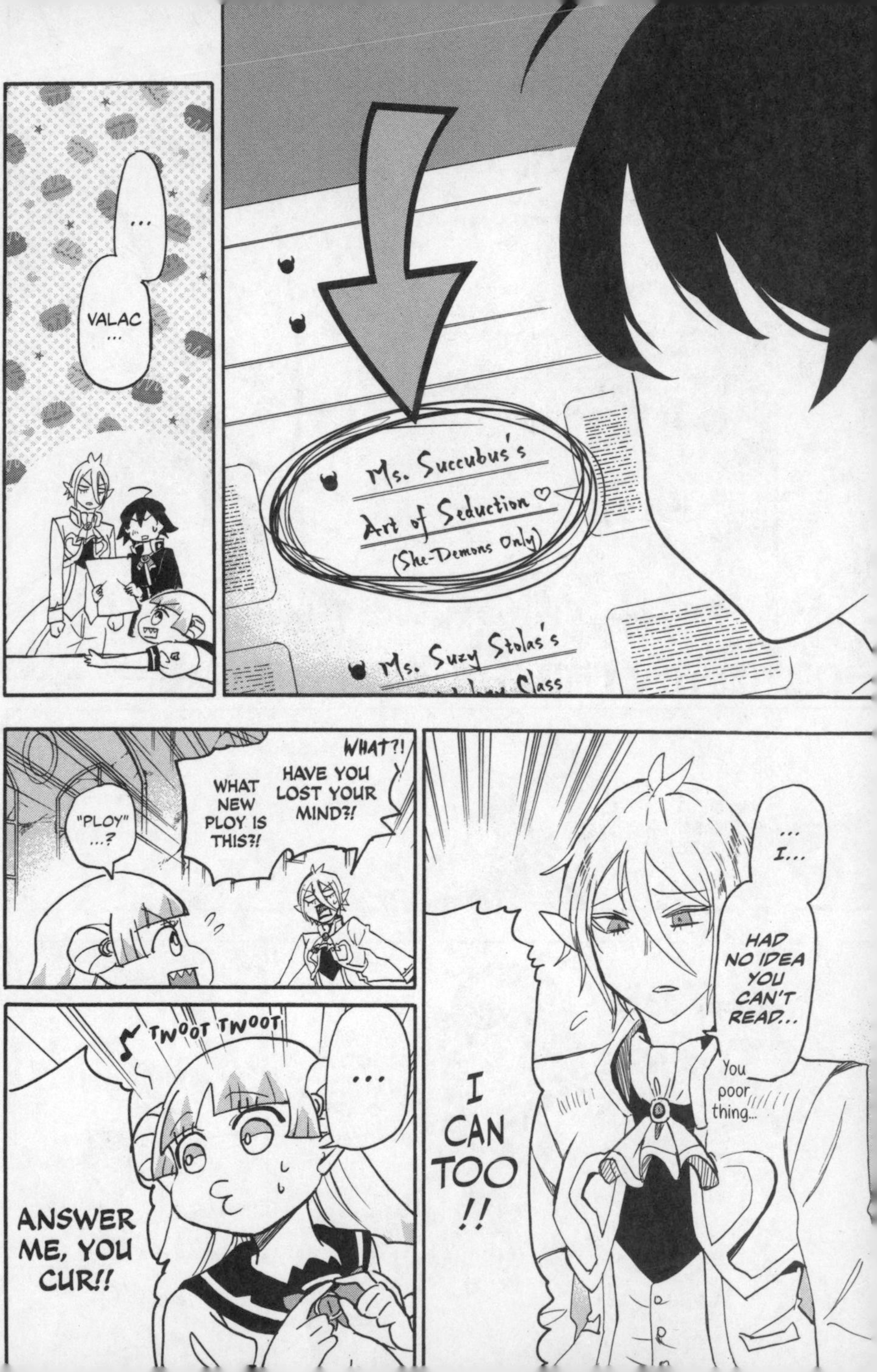
Ms. Succubus's
Art of Seduction ♡
(She-Demons Only)
Ms. Suzy Stolas's
Class
...
VALAC ...
... I...
HAD NO IDEA YOU CAN'T READ...
You poor thing...
I CAN TOO !!
WHAT?!
HAVE YOU LOST YOUR MIND?!
WHAT NEW PLOY IS THIS?!
"PLOY" ...?
TWOOT TWOOT
...
ANSWER ME, YOU CUR!!

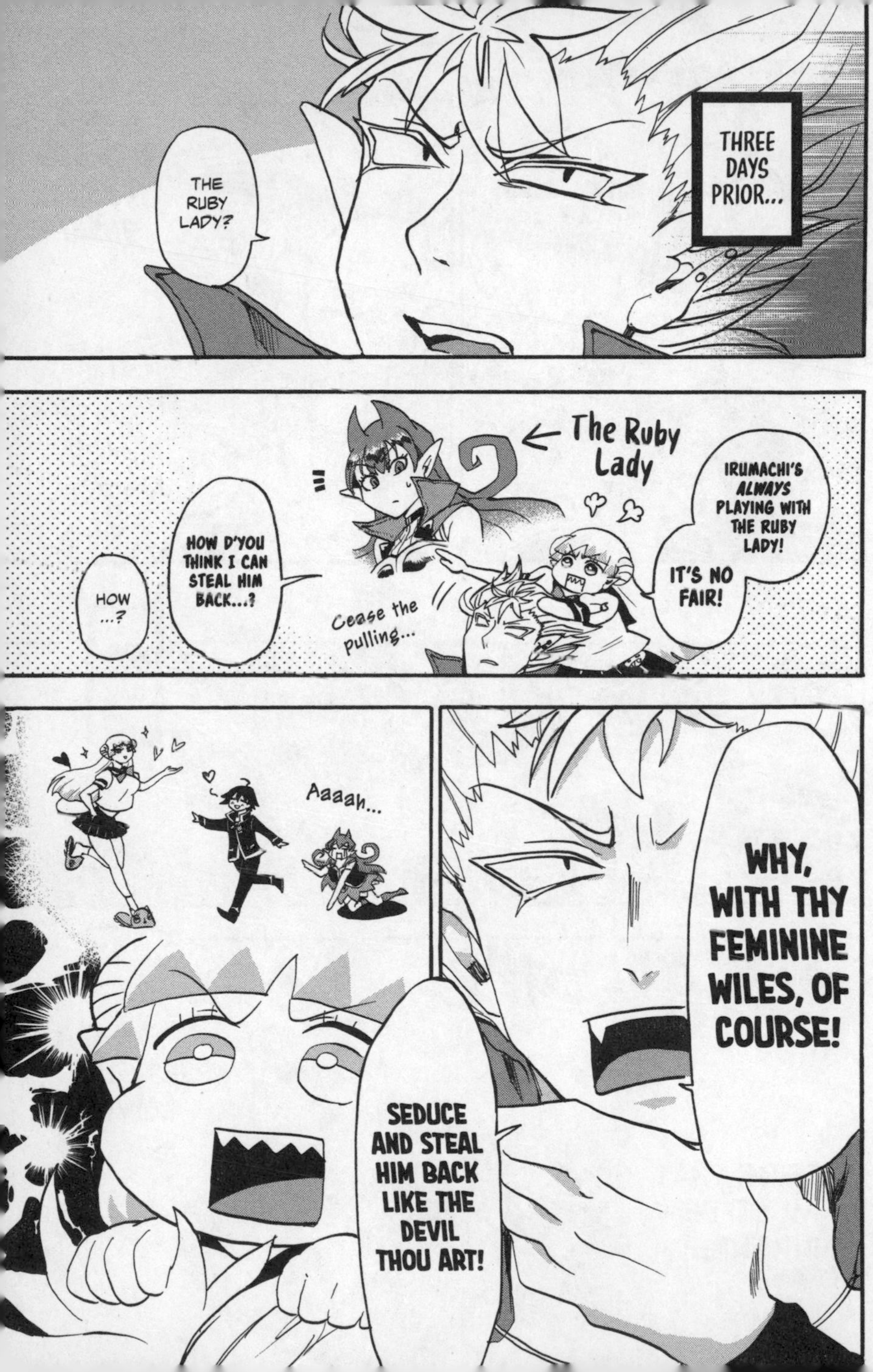
THREE DAYS PRIOR...
THE RUBY LADY?
IRUMACHI'S *ALWAYS* PLAYING WITH THE RUBY LADY!
IT'S NO FAIR!
The Ruby Lady
Cease the pulling...
HOW D'YOU THINK I CAN STEAL HIM BACK...?
HOW ...?
WHY, WITH THY FEMININE WILES, OF COURSE!
SEDUCE AND STEAL HIM BACK LIKE THE DEVIL THOU ART!
Aaaah...

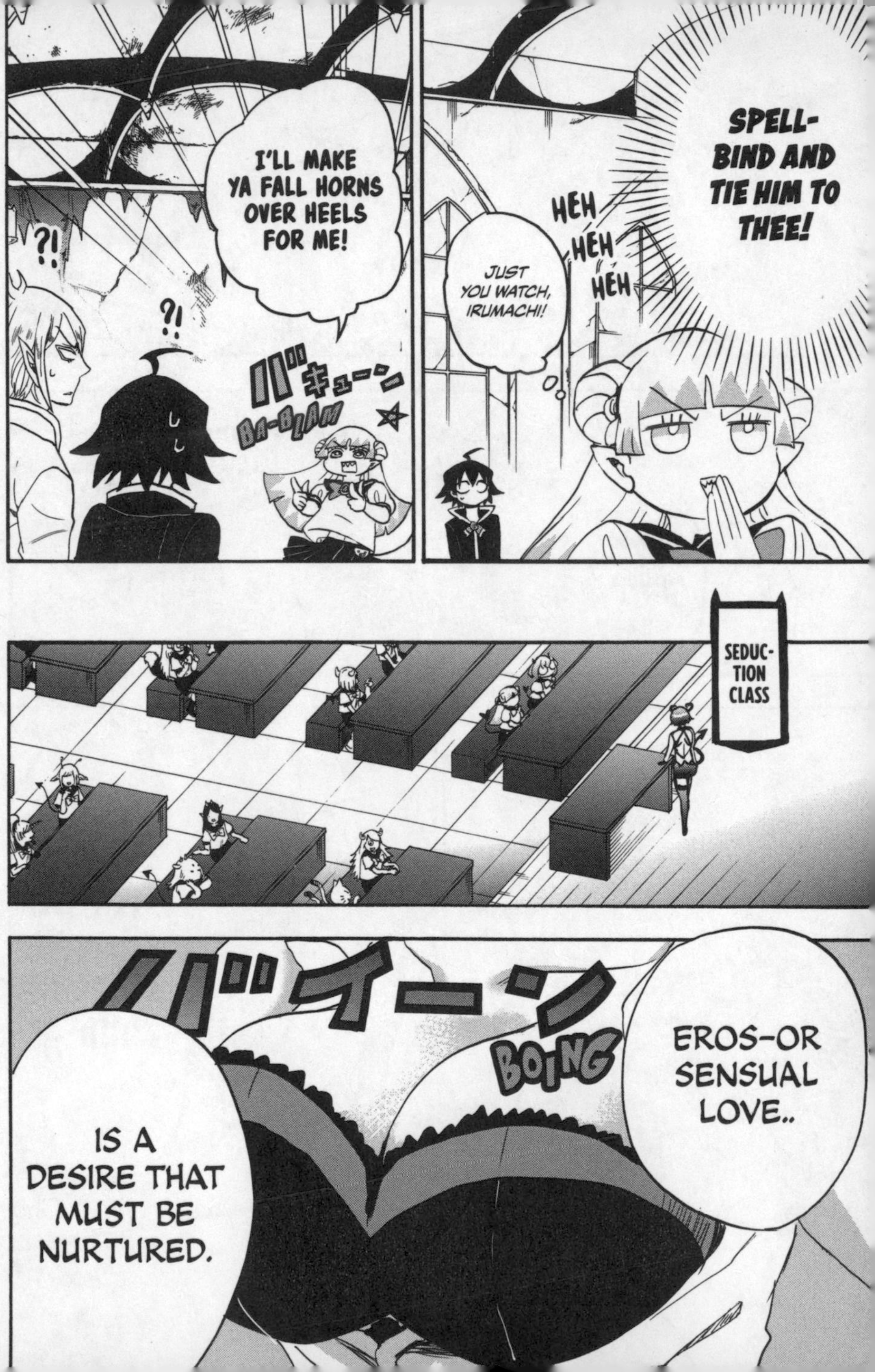
SPELL-BIND AND TIE HIM TO THEE!
HEH HEH HEH
JUST YOU WATCH, IRUMACHI!
I'LL MAKE YA FALL HORNS OVER HEELS FOR ME!
バキューン
BA-BLAM
?!
?!
SEDUCTION CLASS
バイーン
BOING
EROS—OR SENSUAL LOVE..
IS A DESIRE THAT MUST BE NURTURED.

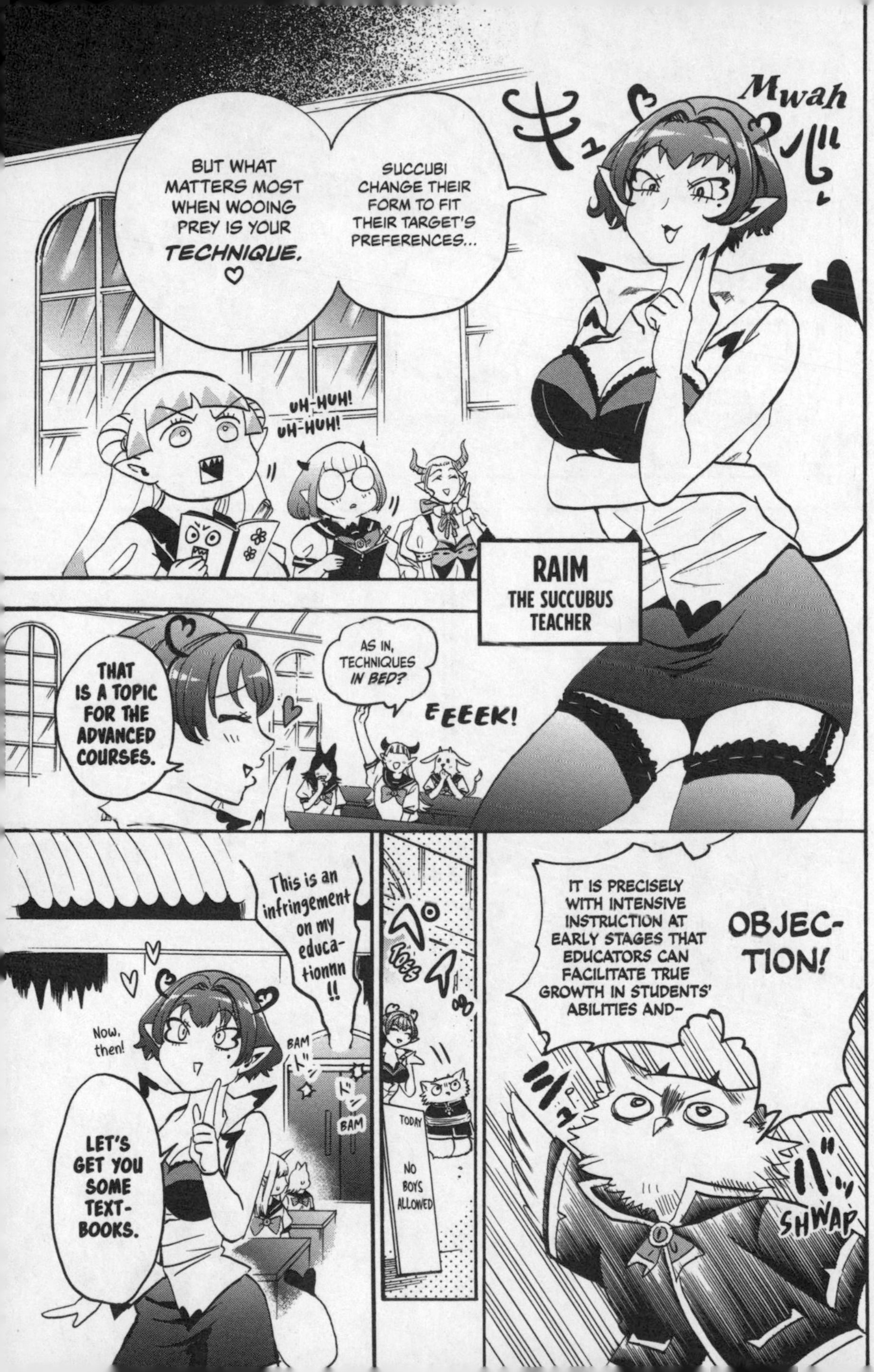
Mwah
SUCCUBI CHANGE THEIR FORM TO FIT THEIR TARGET'S PREFERENCES...
BUT WHAT MATTERS MOST WHEN WOOING PREY IS YOUR TECHNIQUE. ♡
UH-HUH! UH-HUH!
RAIM THE SUCCUBUS TEACHER
AS IN, TECHNIQUES IN BED?
EEEEK!
THAT IS A TOPIC FOR THE ADVANCED COURSES.
OBJEC-TION!
IT IS PRECISELY WITH INTENSIVE INSTRUCTION AT EARLY STAGES THAT EDUCATORS CAN FACILITATE TRUE GROWTH IN STUDENTS' ABILITIES AND-
SHWAP
TOSS
BAM
BAM
TODAY
NO BOYS ALLOWED
This is an infringement on my educa-tionnn !!
Now, then!
LET'S GET YOU SOME TEXT-BOOKS.

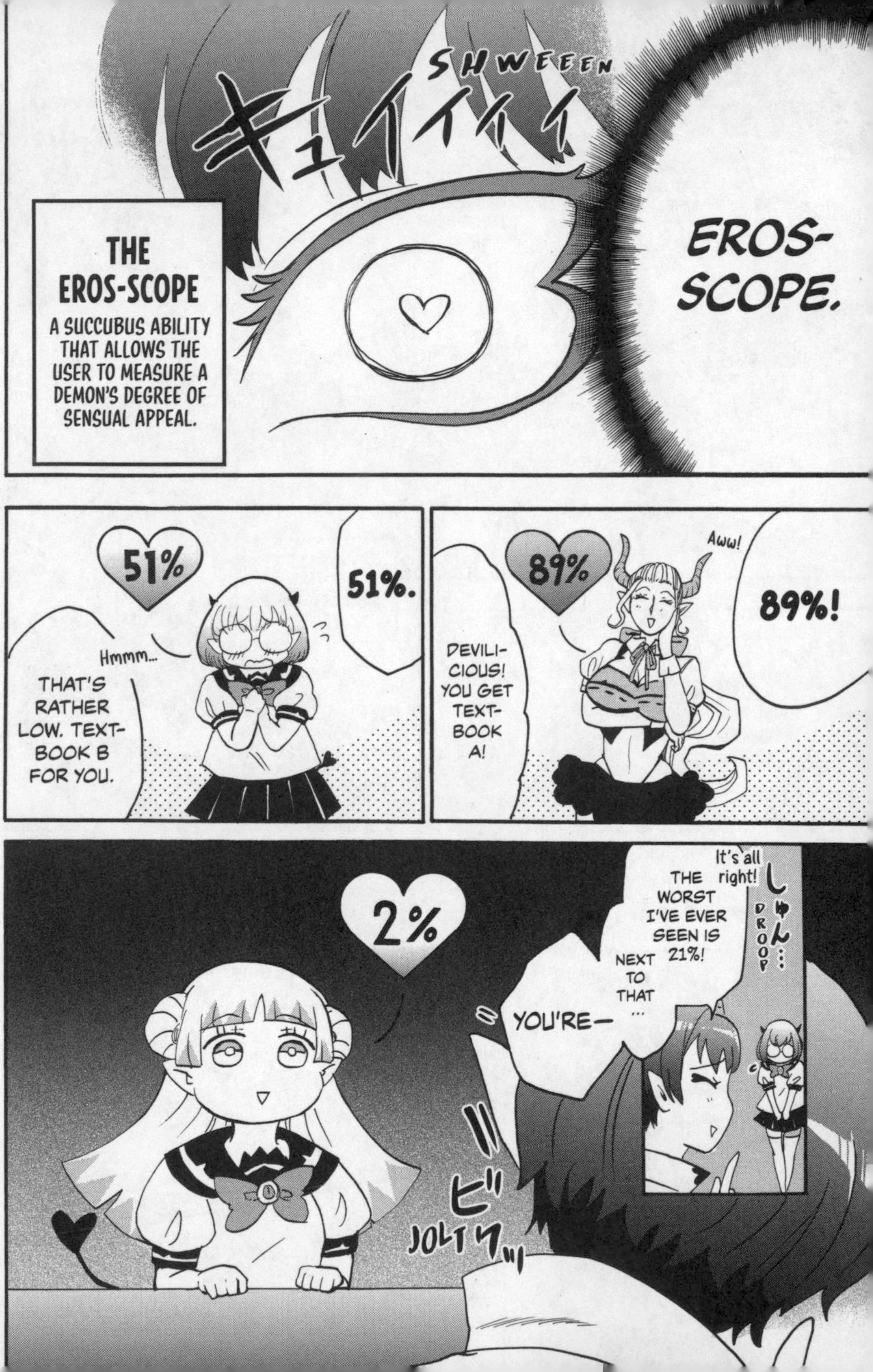
キュイイイ SHWEEEN
EROS-SCOPE.
THE EROS-SCOPE
A SUCCUBUS ABILITY THAT ALLOWS THE USER TO MEASURE A DEMON'S DEGREE OF SENSUAL APPEAL.
89%
Aww!
89%!
DEVILICIOUS! YOU GET TEXTBOOK A!
51%
51%.
Hmmm...
THAT'S RATHER LOW. TEXTBOOK B FOR YOU.
しゅん… DROOP
It's all right!
THE WORST I'VE EVER SEEN IS 21%!
NEXT TO THAT ...
YOU'RE—
2%
ビクッ JOLT

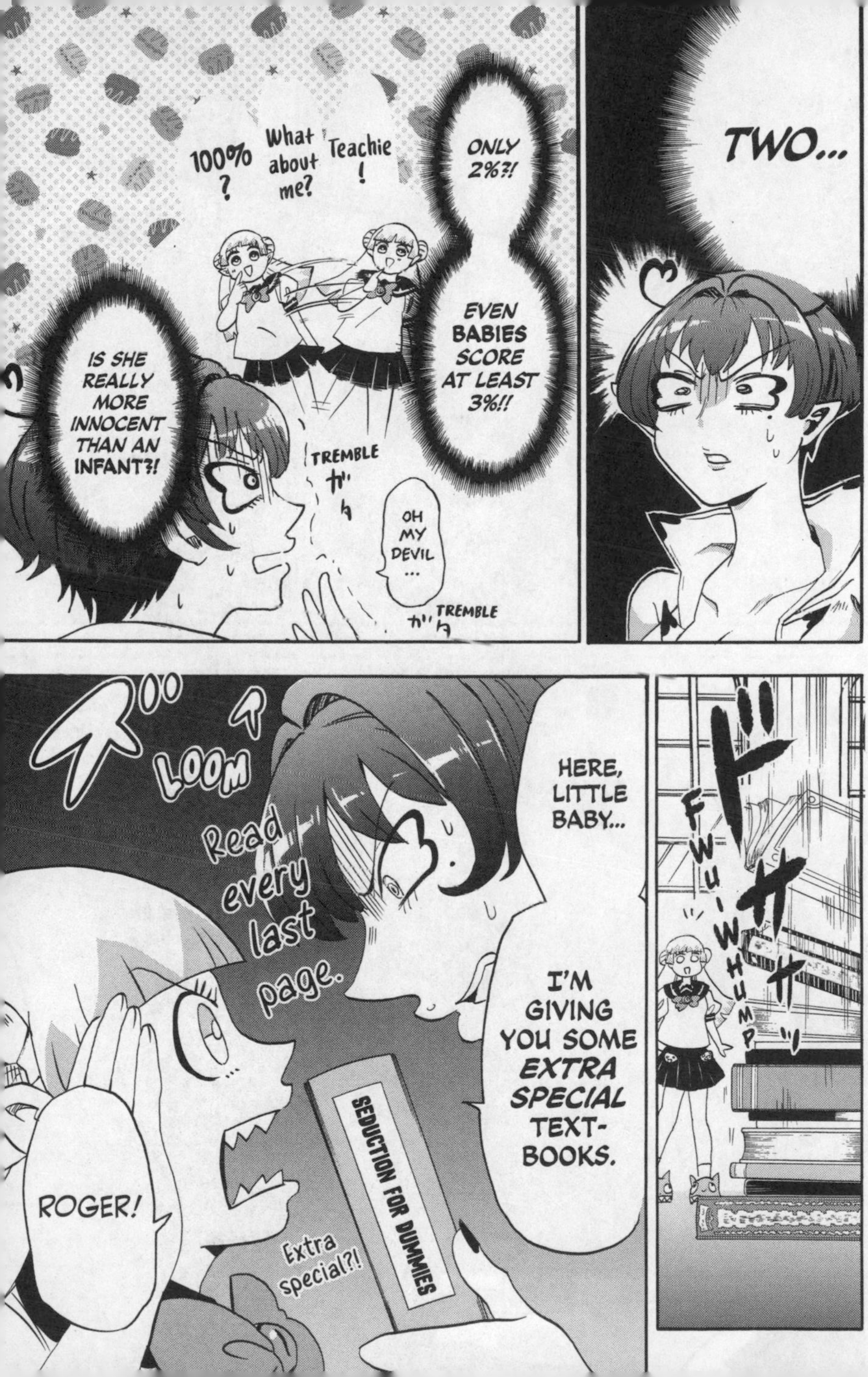
TWO...
ONLY 2%?!
EVEN BABIES SCORE AT LEAST 3%!!
Teachie!
What about me?
100%?
IS SHE REALLY MORE INNOCENT THAN AN INFANT?!
TREMBLE
OH MY DEVIL...
TREMBLE
FWU-WHUMP
HERE, LITTLE BABY...
I'M GIVING YOU SOME EXTRA SPECIAL TEXT-BOOKS.
LOOM
Read every last page.
SEDUCTION FOR DUMMIES
Extra special?!
ROGER!

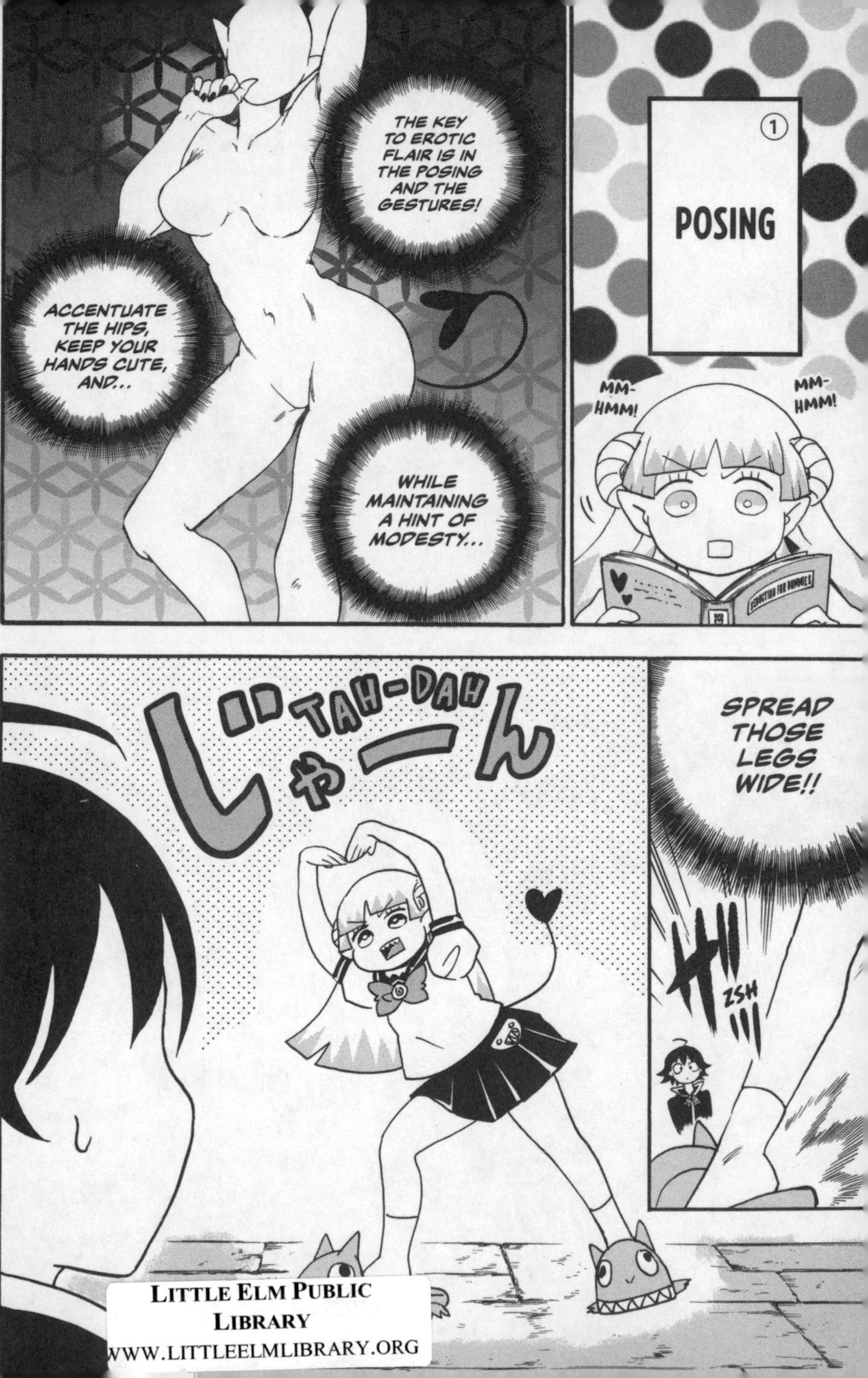
1
POSING
MM-HMM!
MM-HMM!
SEDUCTION FOR DUMMIES
THE KEY TO EROTIC FLAIR IS IN THE POSING AND THE GESTURES!
ACCENTUATE THE HIPS, KEEP YOUR HANDS CUTE, AND...
WHILE MAINTAINING A HINT OF MODESTY...
SPREAD THOSE LEGS WIDE!!
ZSH
じゅーん
TAH-DAH

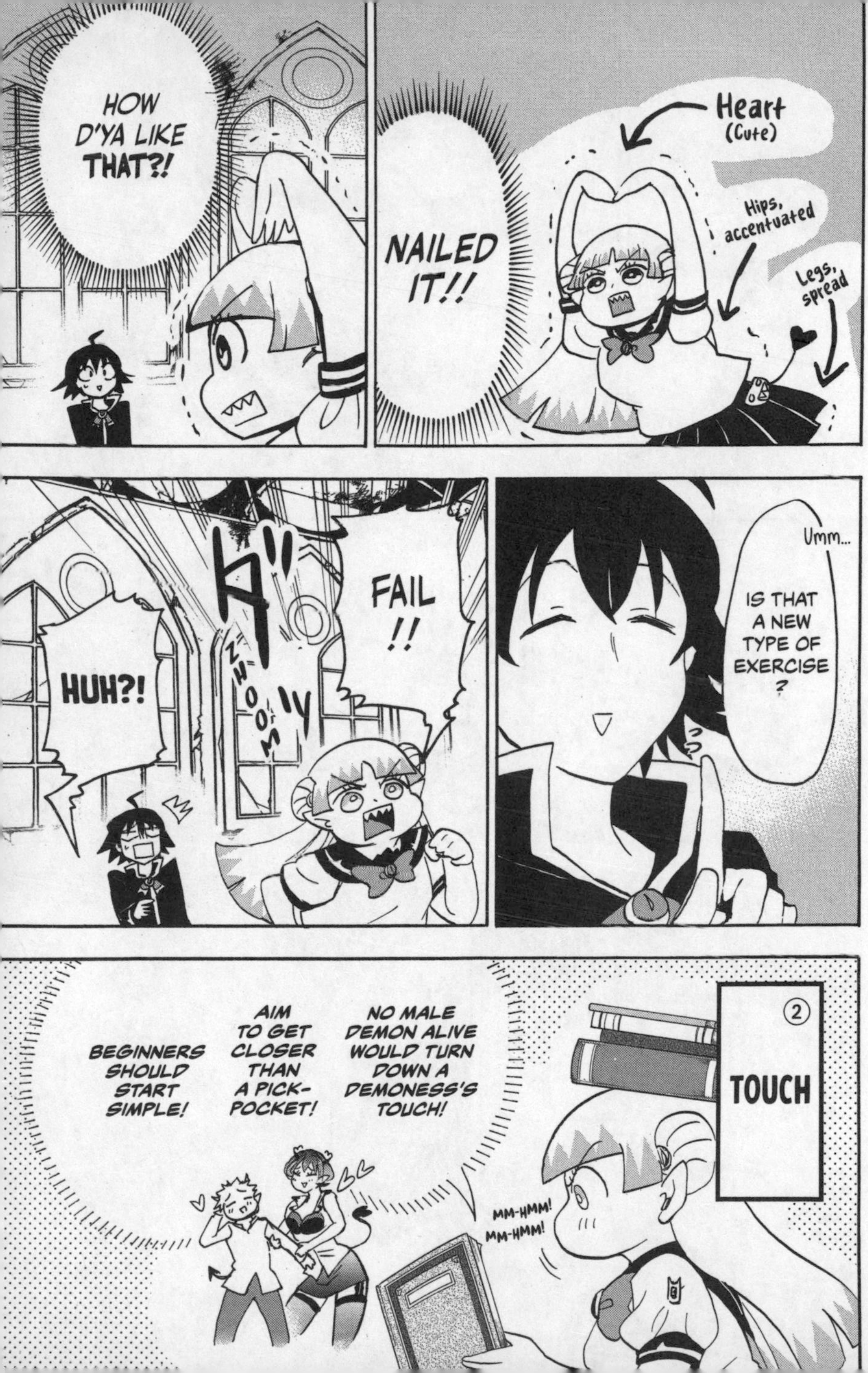
NAILED IT!!
Heart (Cute)
Hips, accentuated
Legs, spread
HOW D'YA LIKE THAT?!
Umm...
IS THAT A NEW TYPE OF EXERCISE?
FAIL!!
ZHOOM
HUH?!
② TOUCH
NO MALE DEMON ALIVE WOULD TURN DOWN A DEMONESS'S TOUCH!
AIM TO GET CLOSER THAN A PICK-POCKET!
BEGINNERS SHOULD START SIMPLE!
MM-HMM! MM-HMM!

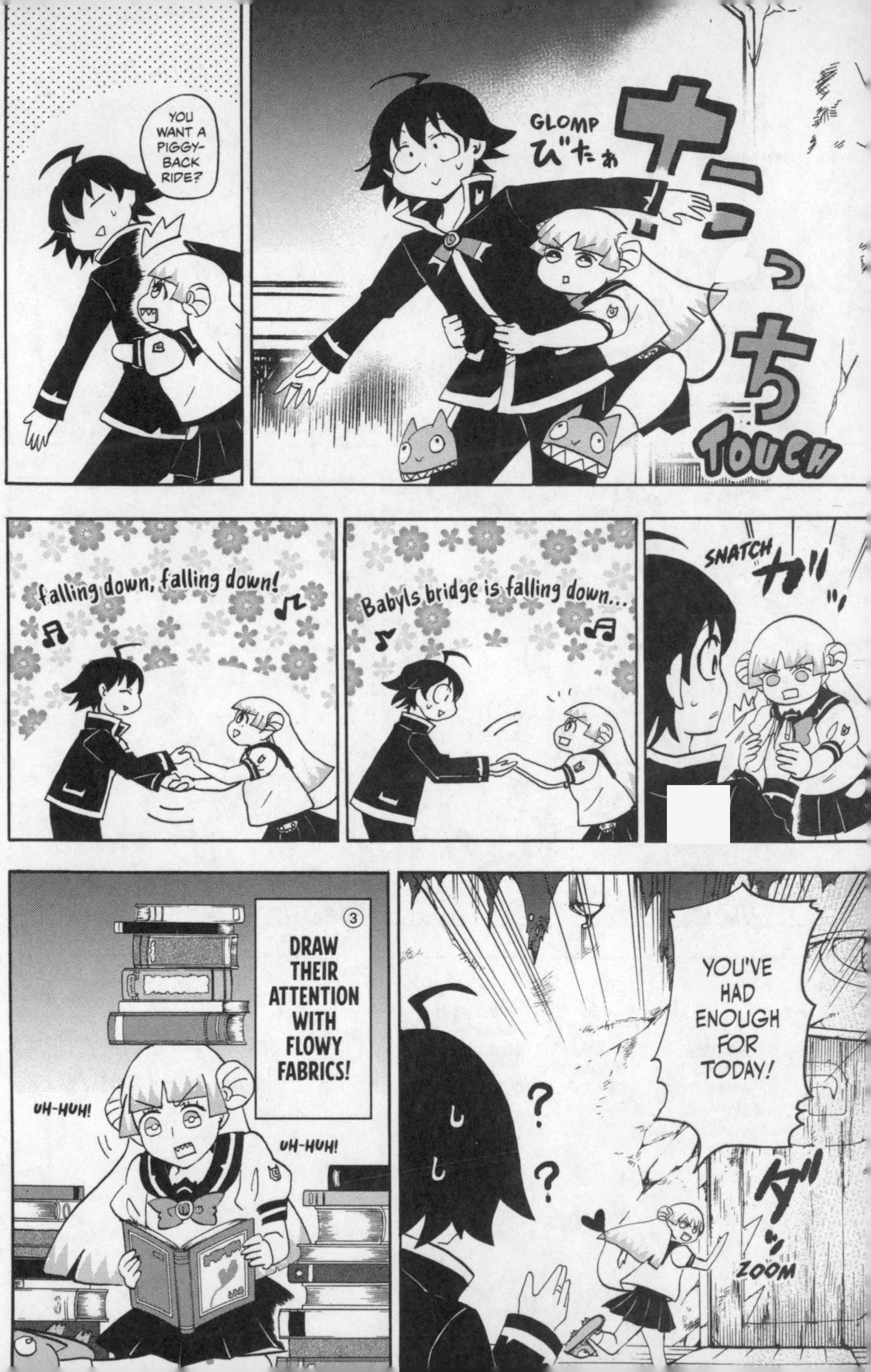
GLOMP
びたぁ
TOUCH
YOU WANT A PIGGY-BACK RIDE?
SNATCH
ガッ
Babyls bridge is falling down...
falling down, falling down!
YOU'VE HAD ENOUGH FOR TODAY!
?
?
ダッ
ZOOM
③
DRAW THEIR ATTENTION WITH FLOWY FABRICS!
UH-HUH!
UH-HUH!

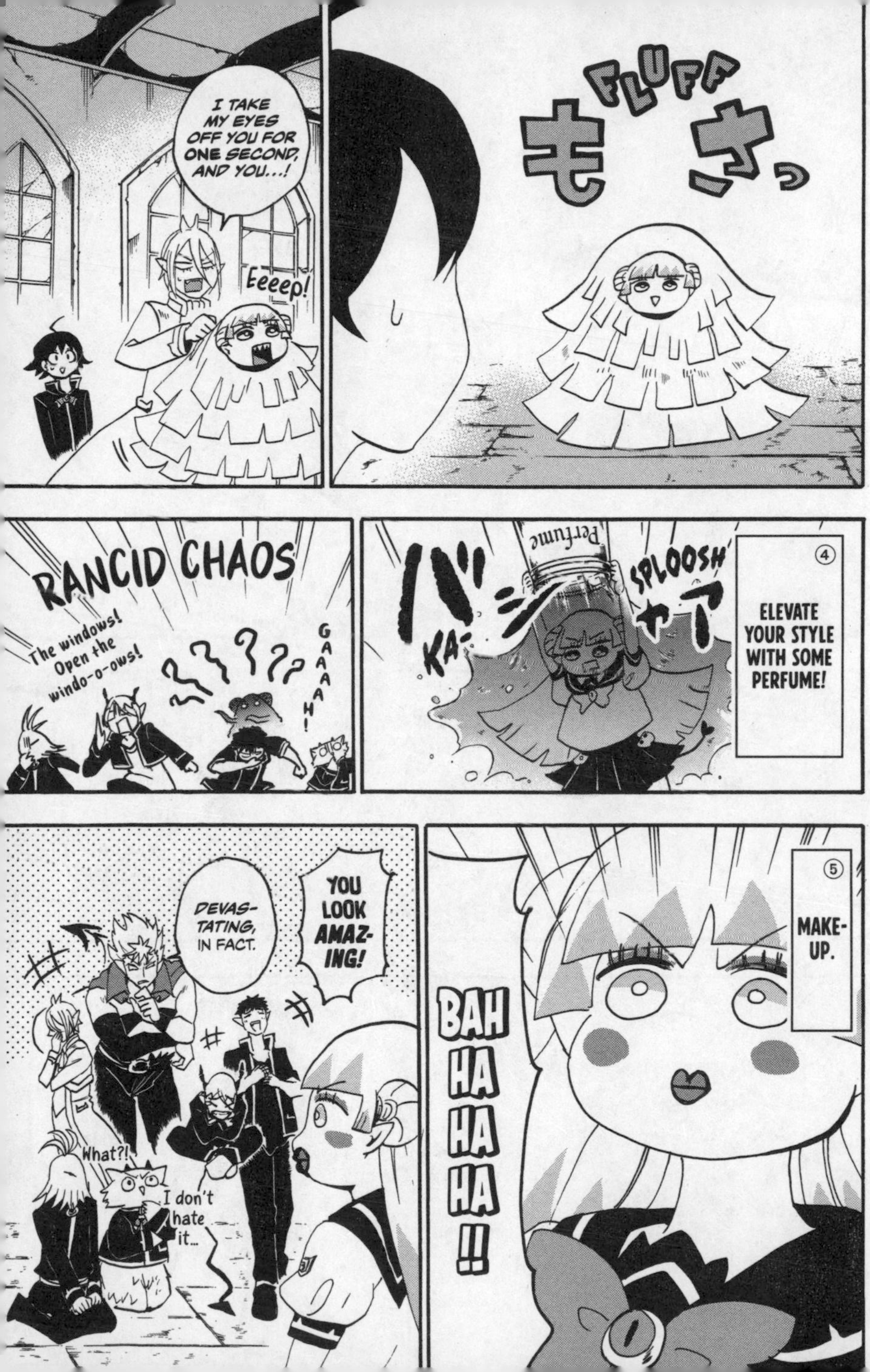
FLUFF
もさっ
I TAKE MY EYES OFF YOU FOR ONE SECOND, AND YOU...!
Eeeep!
④
ELEVATE YOUR STYLE WITH SOME PERFUME!
Perfume
バ
KA-
SPLOOSH
ャア
RANCID CHAOS
The windows! Open the windo-o-ows!
GAAAAH!
⑤
MAKE-UP.
BAHHAHAHAHA!!
YOU LOOK AMAZ-ING!
DEVAS-TATING, IN FACT.
What?!
I don't hate it...

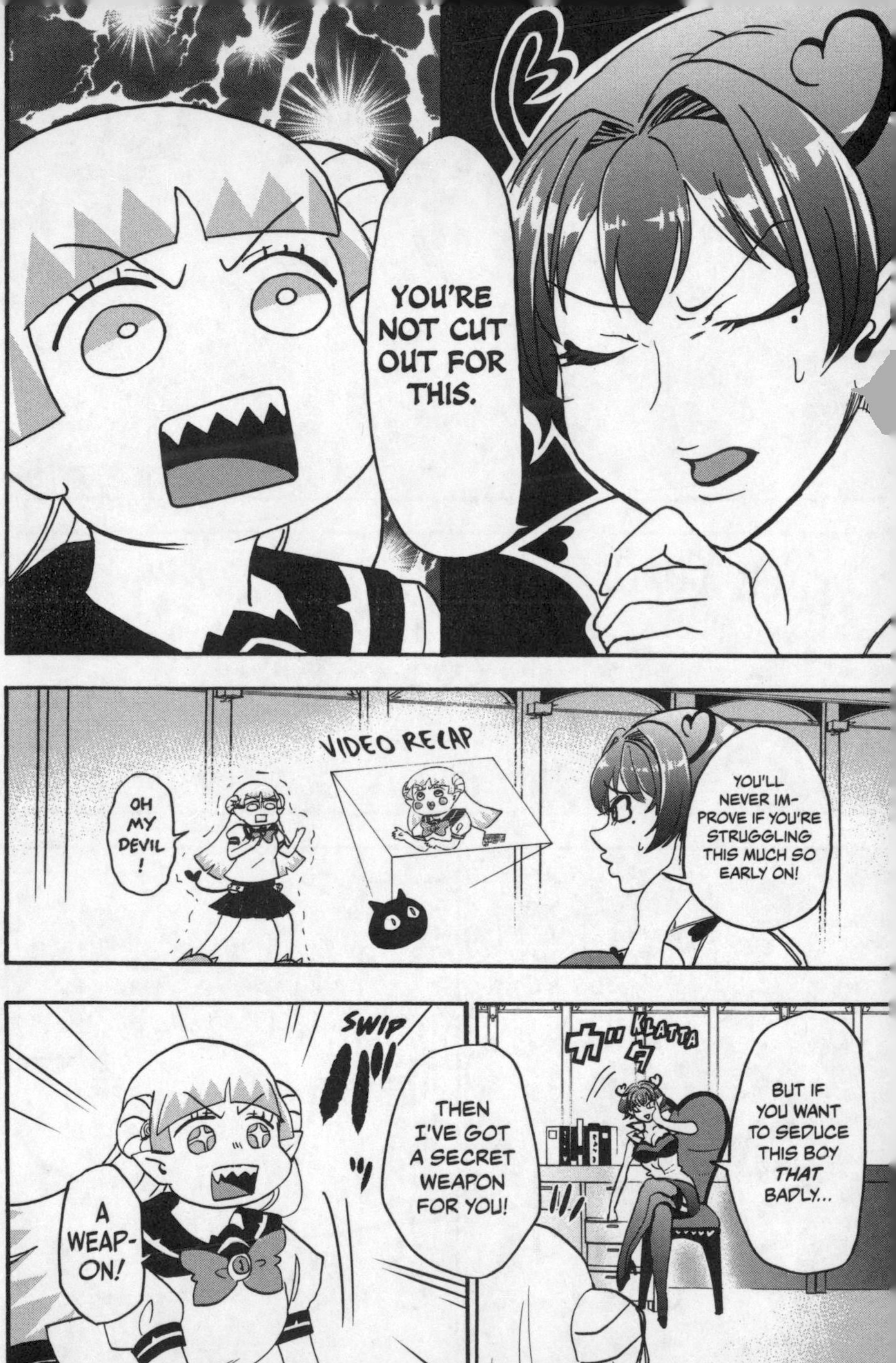
YOU'RE NOT CUT OUT FOR THIS.
YOU'LL NEVER IM-PROVE IF YOU'RE STRUGGLING THIS MUCH SO EARLY ON!
VIDEO RECAP
OH MY DEVIL!
BUT IF YOU WANT TO SEDUCE THIS BOY *THAT* BADLY...
KLATTA
SWIP
THEN I'VE GOT A SECRET WEAPON FOR YOU!
A WEAP-ON!

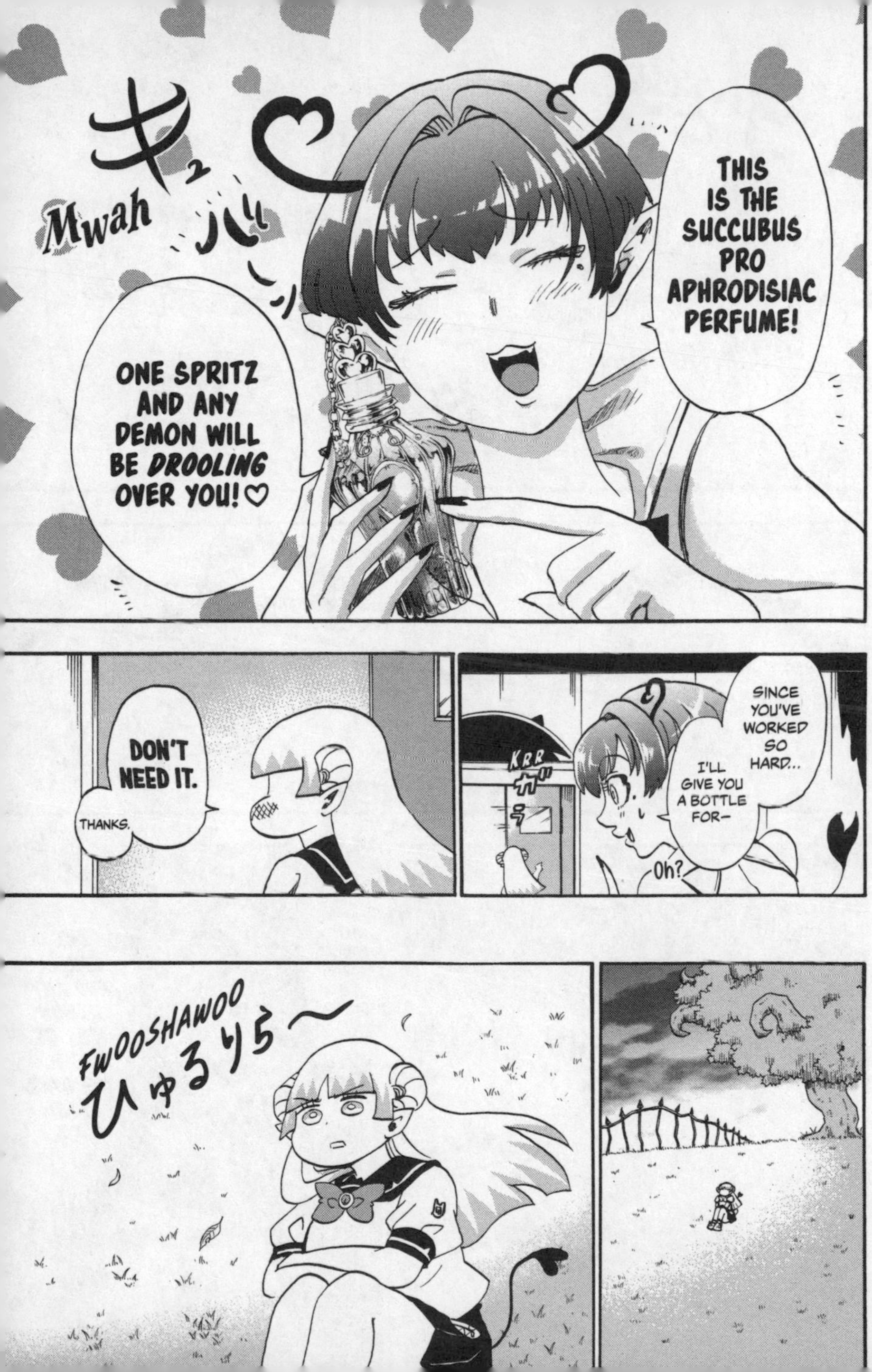
THIS IS THE SUCCUBUS PRO APHRODISIAC PERFUME!
Mwah
ONE SPRITZ AND ANY DEMON WILL BE DROOLING OVER YOU! ♡
SINCE YOU'VE WORKED SO HARD...
I'LL GIVE YOU A BOTTLE FOR—
KRR
Oh?
DON'T NEED IT.
THANKS.
FWOOSHAWOO
ひゅるりら～

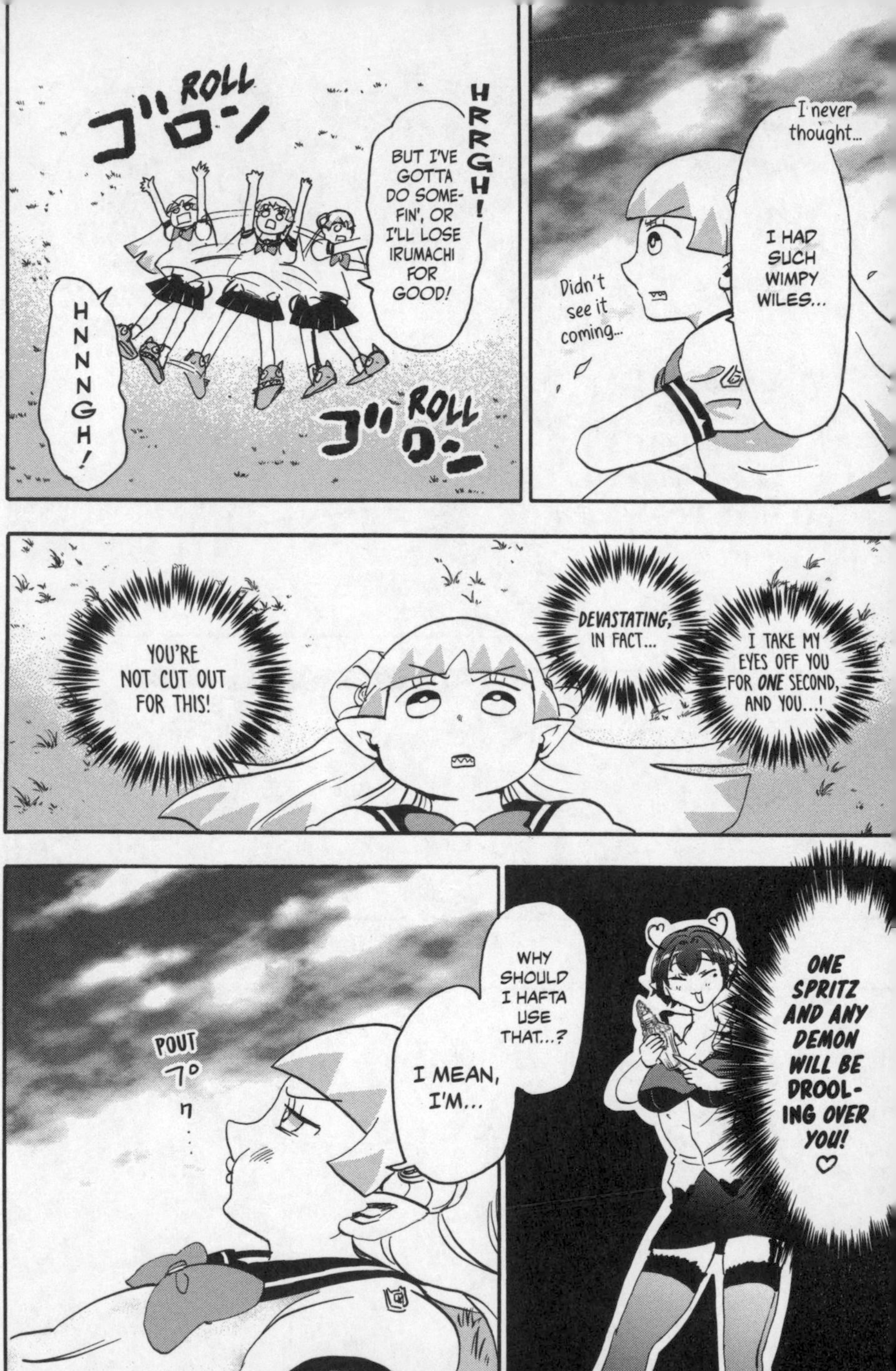

I never thought...
I HAD SUCH WIMPY WILES...
Didn't see it coming...
HRRGH!
BUT I'VE GOTTA DO SOME-FIN', OR I'LL LOSE IRUMACHI FOR GOOD!
ROLL
HNNNGH!
ROLL
I TAKE MY EYES OFF YOU FOR ONE SECOND, AND YOU...!
DEVASTATING, IN FACT...
YOU'RE NOT CUT OUT FOR THIS!
ONE SPRITZ AND ANY DEMON WILL BE DROOL-ING OVER YOU! ♡
WHY SHOULD I HAFTA USE THAT...?
I MEAN, I'M...
POUT

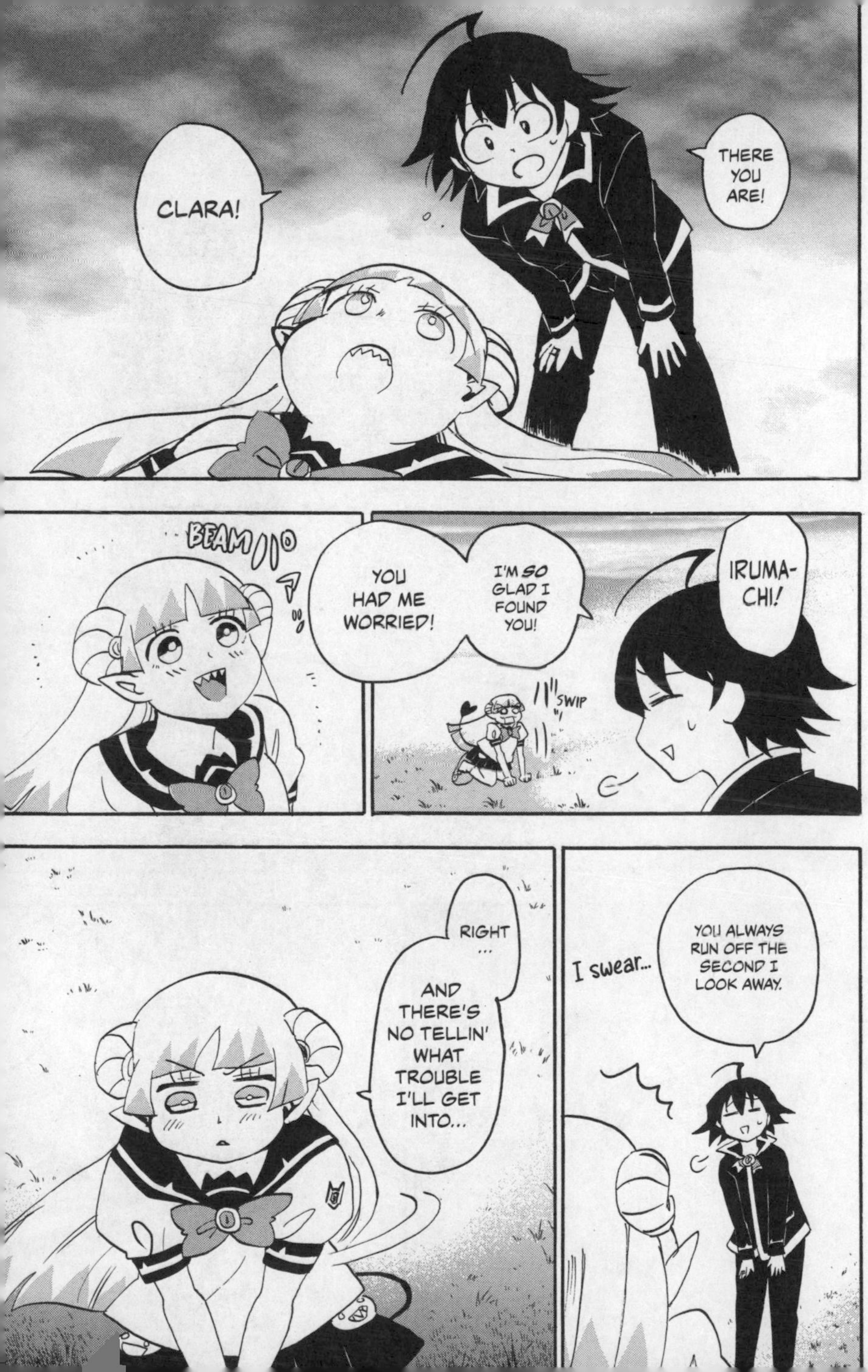
THERE YOU ARE!
CLARA!
IRUMA-CHI!
I'M SO GLAD I FOUND YOU!
YOU HAD ME WORRIED!
SWIP
BEAM
YOU ALWAYS RUN OFF THE SECOND I LOOK AWAY.
I swear...
RIGHT...
AND THERE'S NO TELLIN' WHAT TROUBLE I'LL GET INTO...

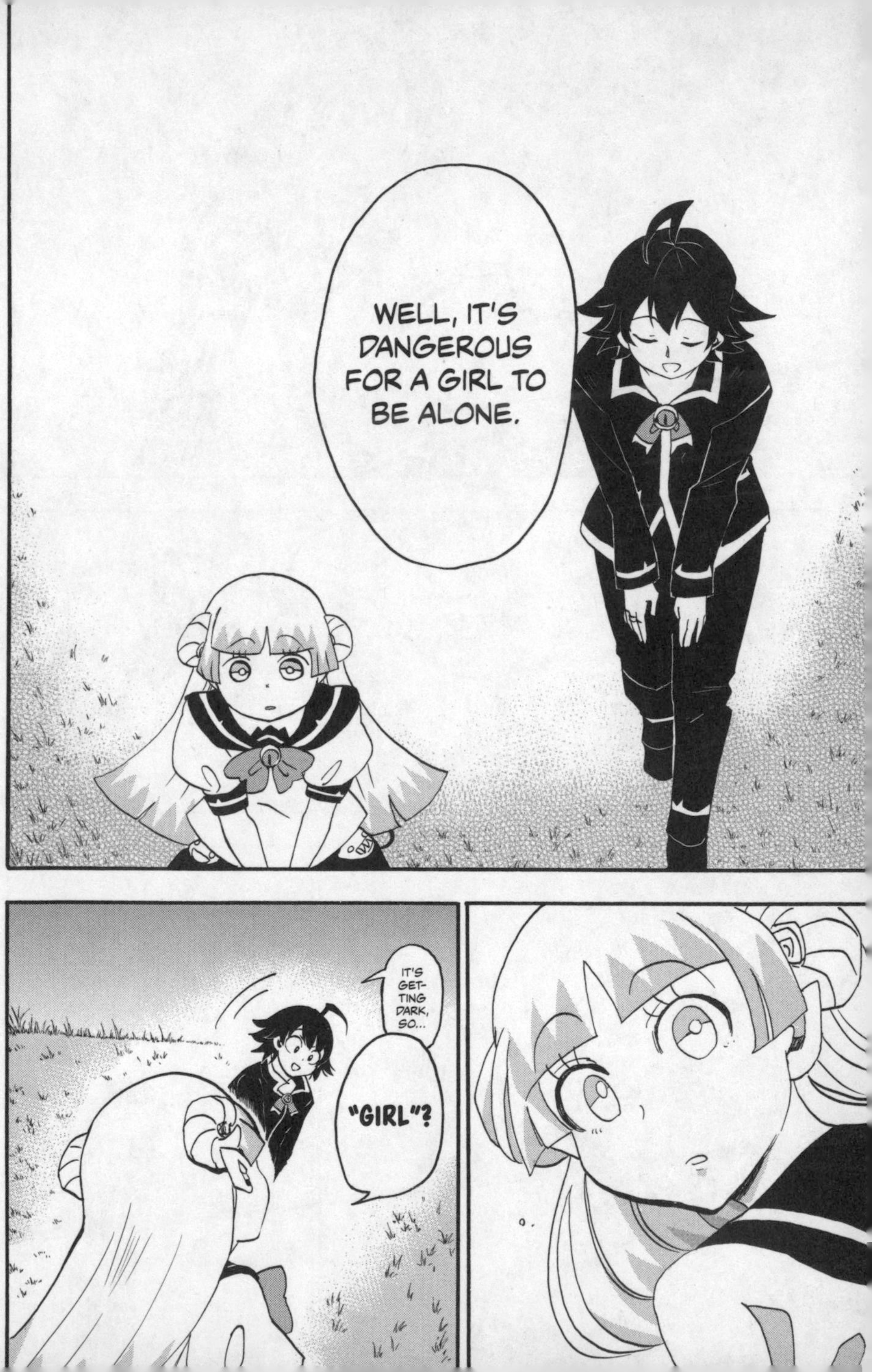
WELL, IT'S DANGEROUS FOR A GIRL TO BE ALONE.
IT'S GET-TING DARK, SO...
"GIRL"?

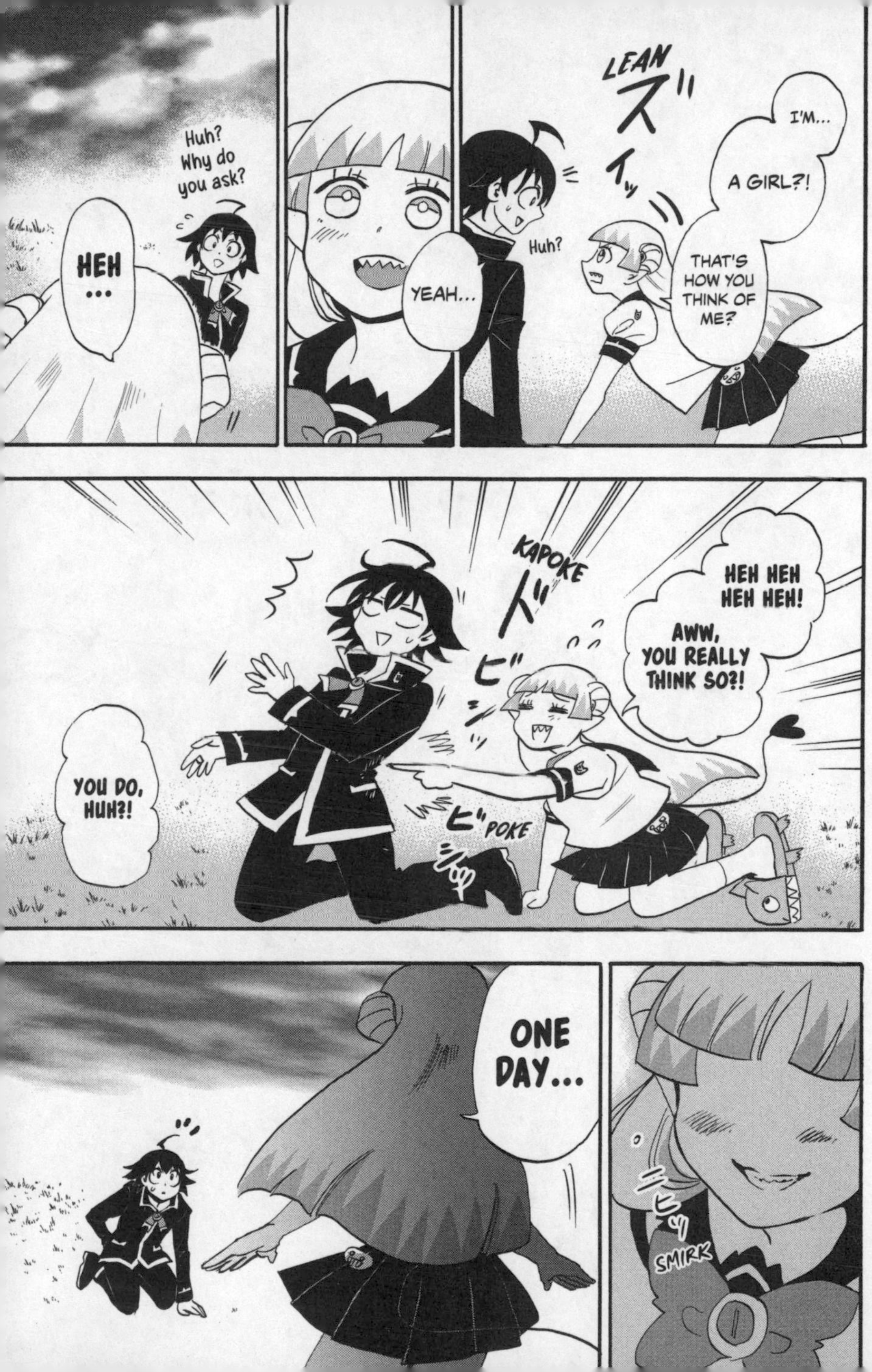
I'M...
A GIRL?!
LEAN
ズイッ
THAT'S HOW YOU THINK OF ME?
Huh?
YEAH...
Huh? Why do you ask?
HEH ...
HEH HEH HEH HEH!
AWW, YOU REALLY THINK SO?!
KAPOKE
ド
POKE
YOU DO, HUH?!
ニヒッ
SMIRK
ONE DAY...

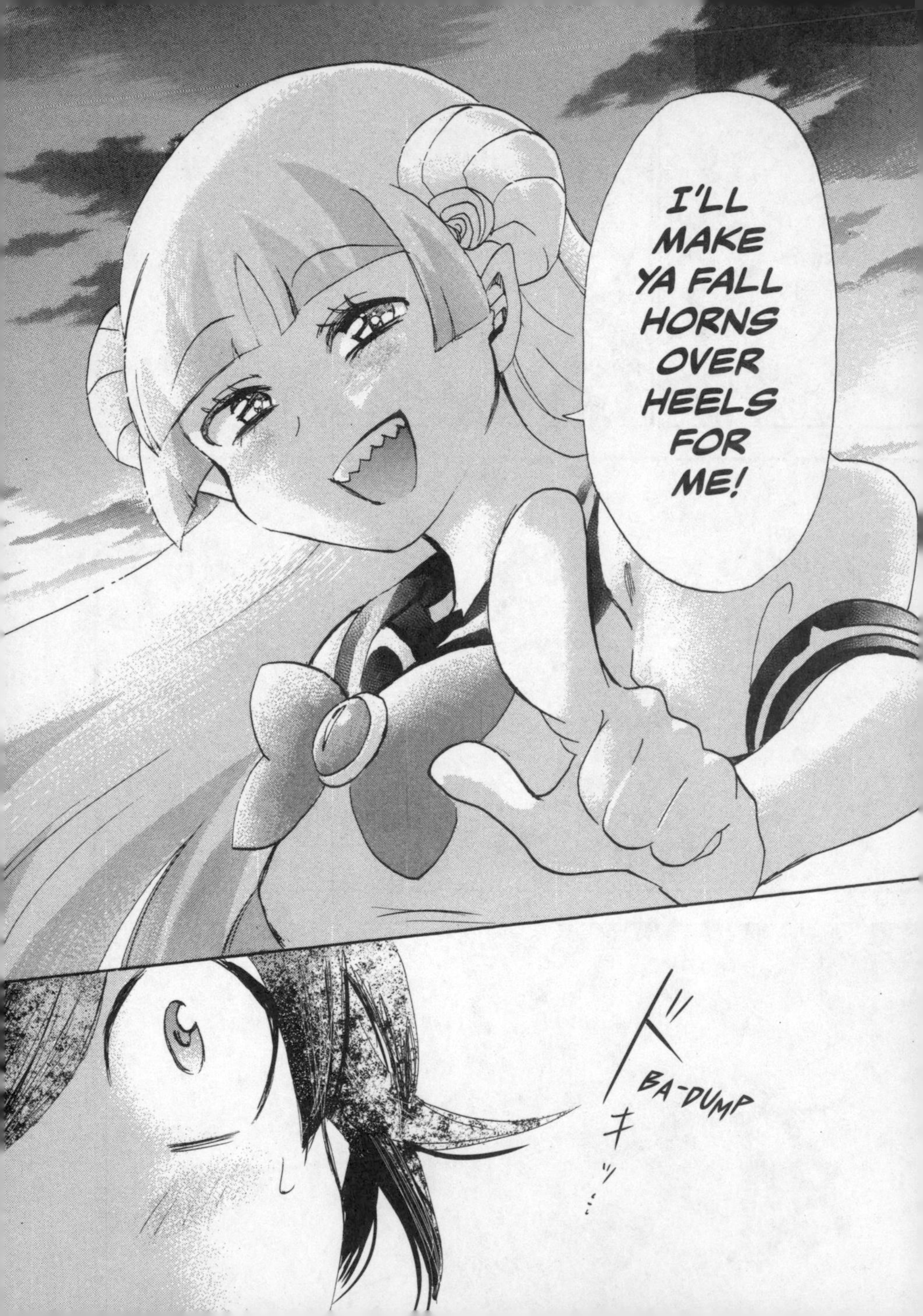
I'LL MAKE YA FALL HORNS OVER HEELS FOR ME!
ドキッ…
BA-DUMP

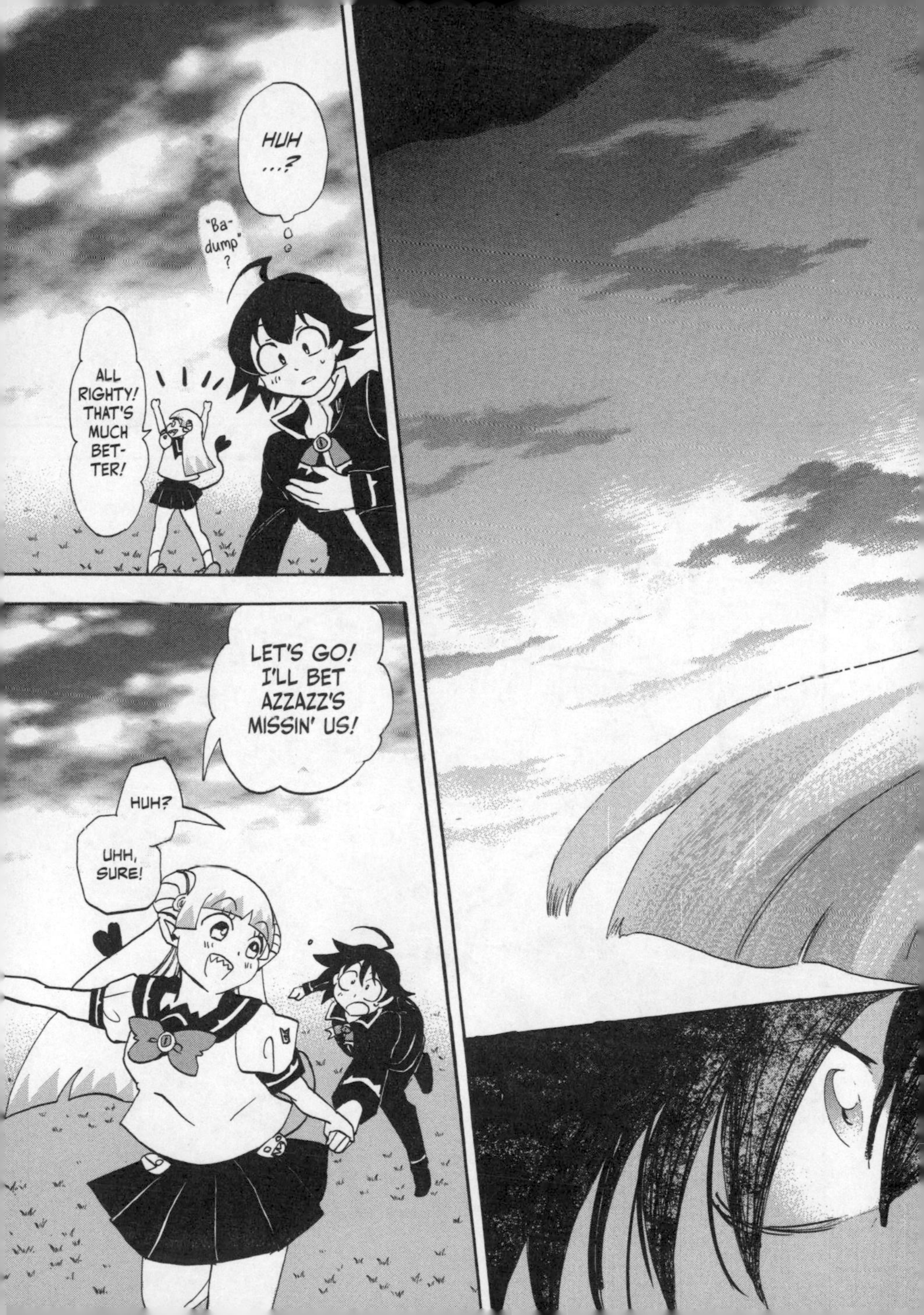
HUH ...?
"Ba-dump"?
ALL RIGHTY! THAT'S MUCH BET-TER!
LET'S GO! I'LL BET AZZAZZ'S MISSIN' US!
HUH?
UHH, SURE!

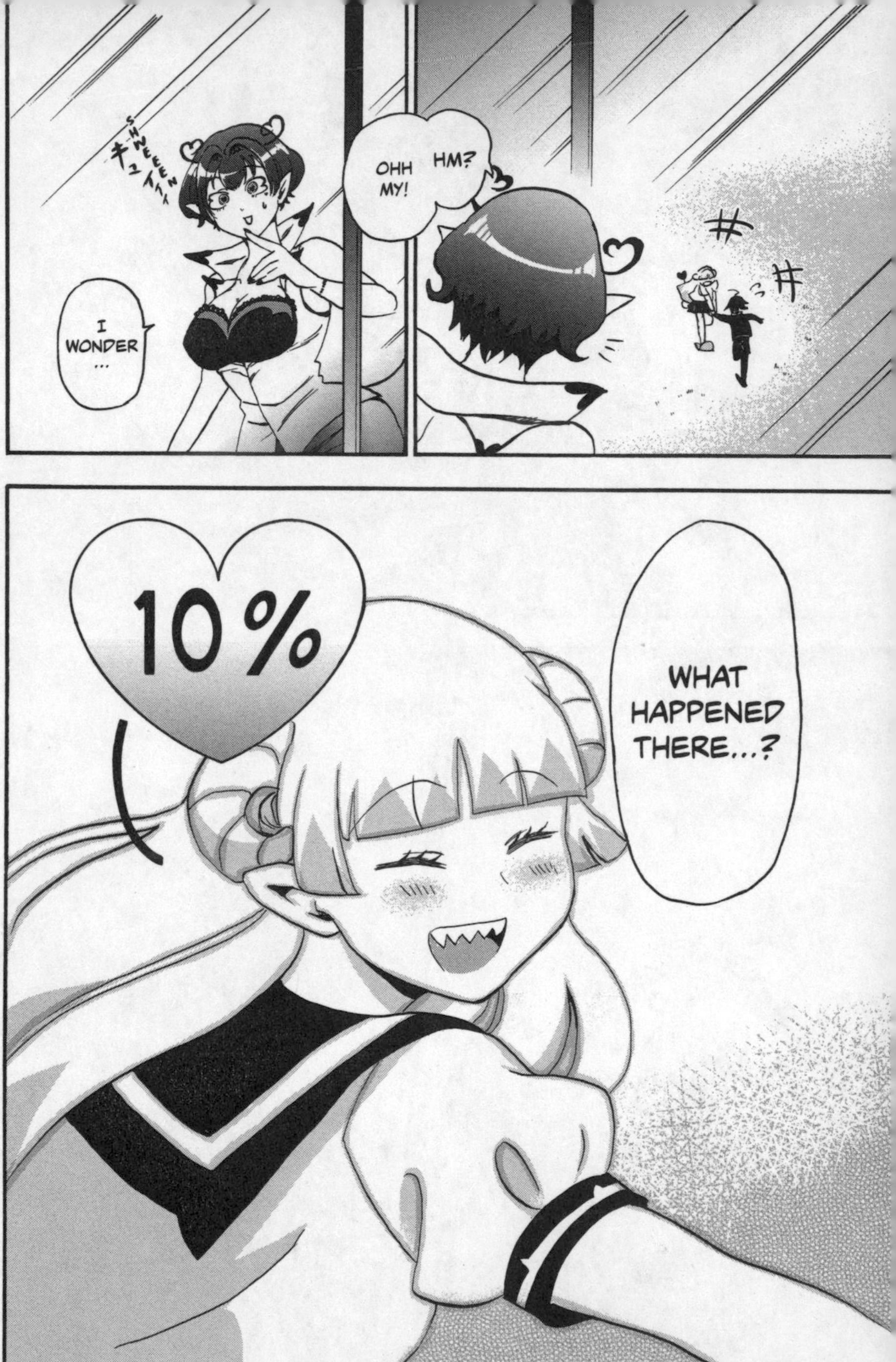
HM?
OHH MY!
SHWEEEN
I WONDER...
WHAT HAPPENED THERE...?
10%

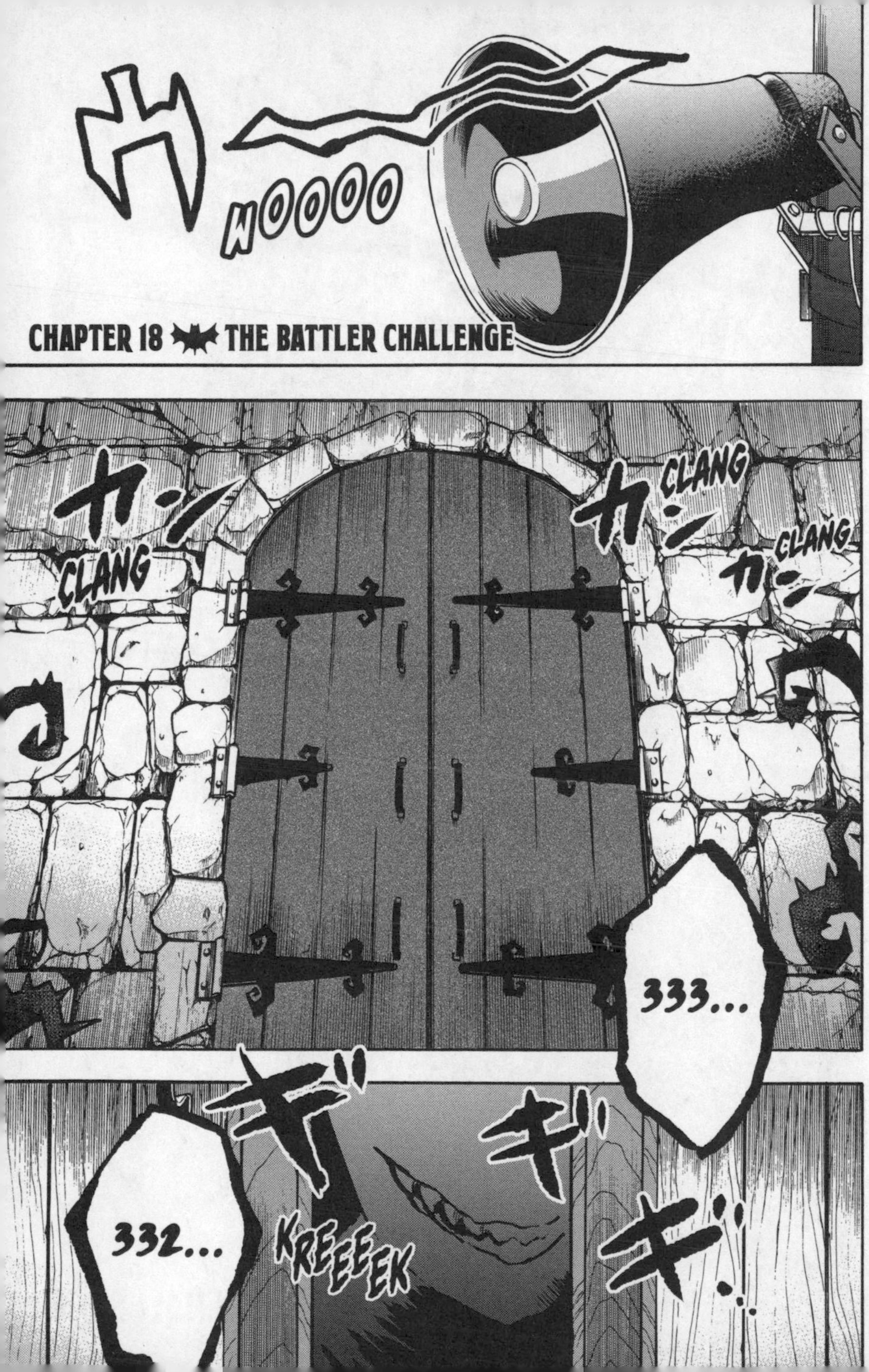
WOOOO
CHAPTER 18 THE BATTLER CHALLENGE
CLANG
CLANG
CLANG
333...
KREEEK
332...

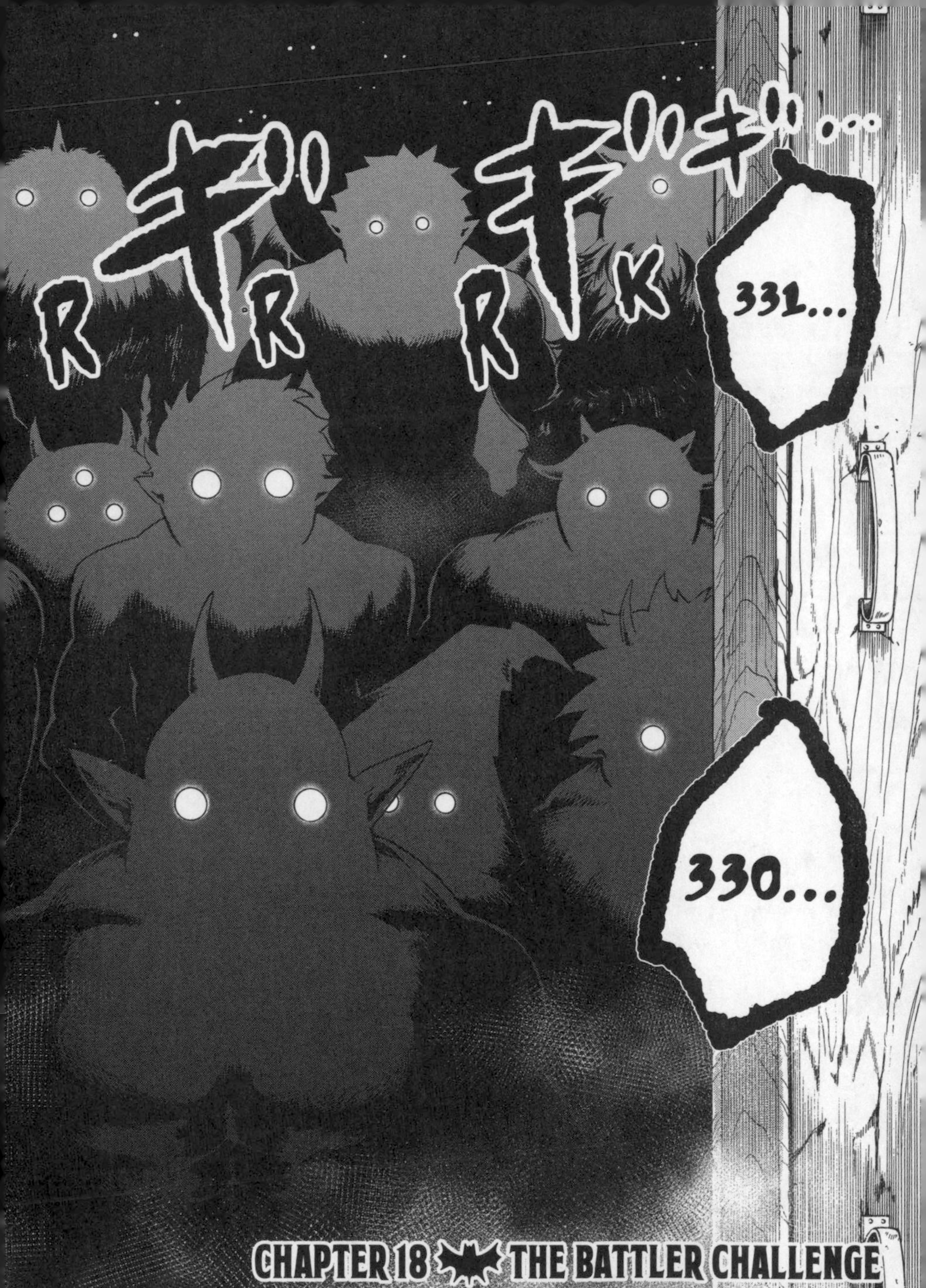
331...
330...
ギギギ…
RRRK

CHAPTER 18 THE BATTLER CHALLENGE

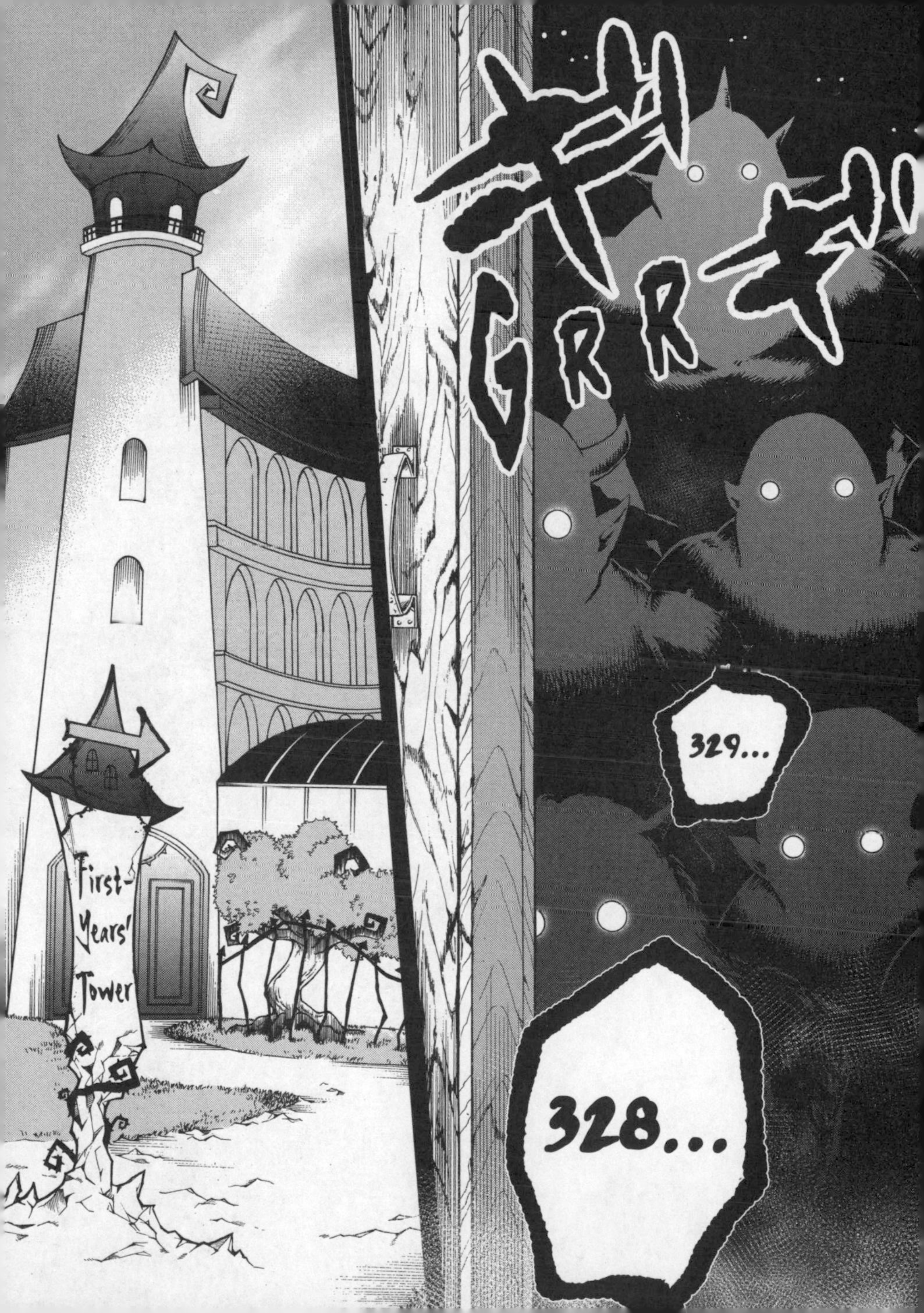
GRRR
329...
328...
First-Years' Tower

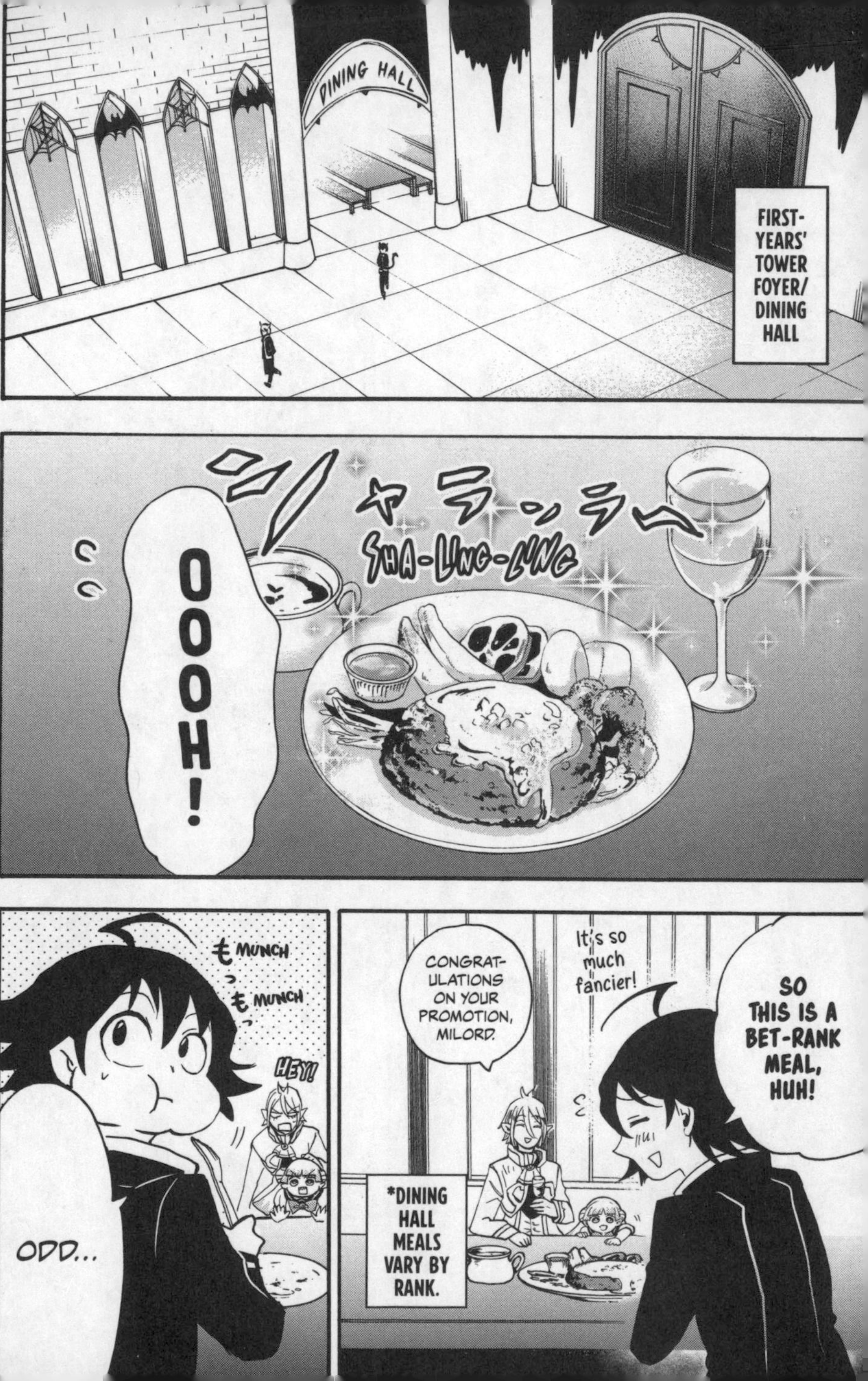
DINING HALL
FIRST-YEARS' TOWER FOYER/ DINING HALL
SHA-LING-LING
OOOOH!
SO THIS IS A BET-RANK MEAL, HUH!
It's so much fancier!
CONGRATULATIONS ON YOUR PROMOTION, MILORD.
*DINING HALL MEALS VARY BY RANK.
MUNCH
MUNCH
HEY!
ODD...

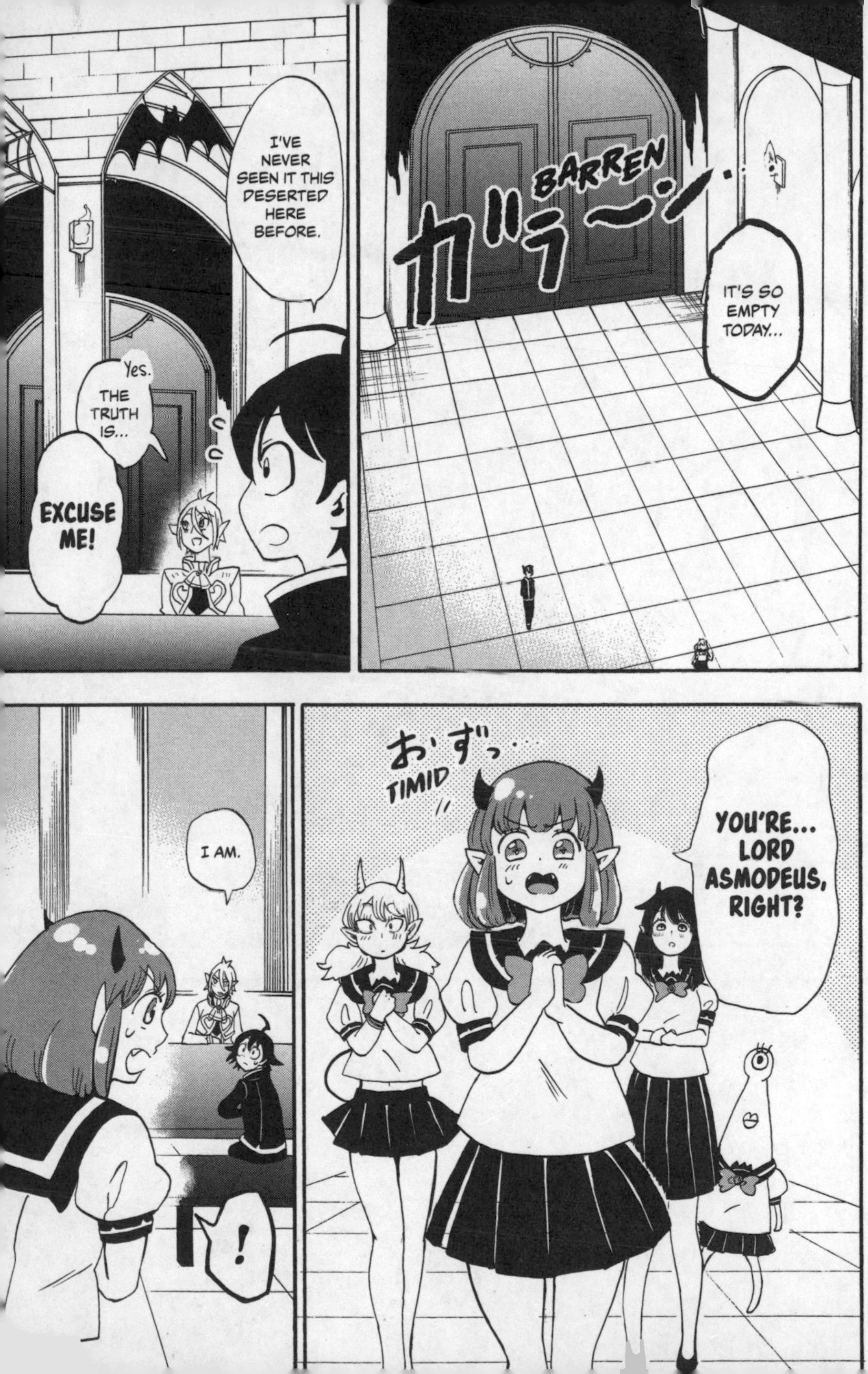
カラ～ン…
BARREN
IT'S SO EMPTY TODAY...
I'VE NEVER SEEN IT THIS DESERTED HERE BEFORE.
Yes. THE TRUTH IS...
EXCUSE ME!
おずっ…
TIMID
YOU'RE... LORD ASMODEUS, RIGHT?
I AM.
!

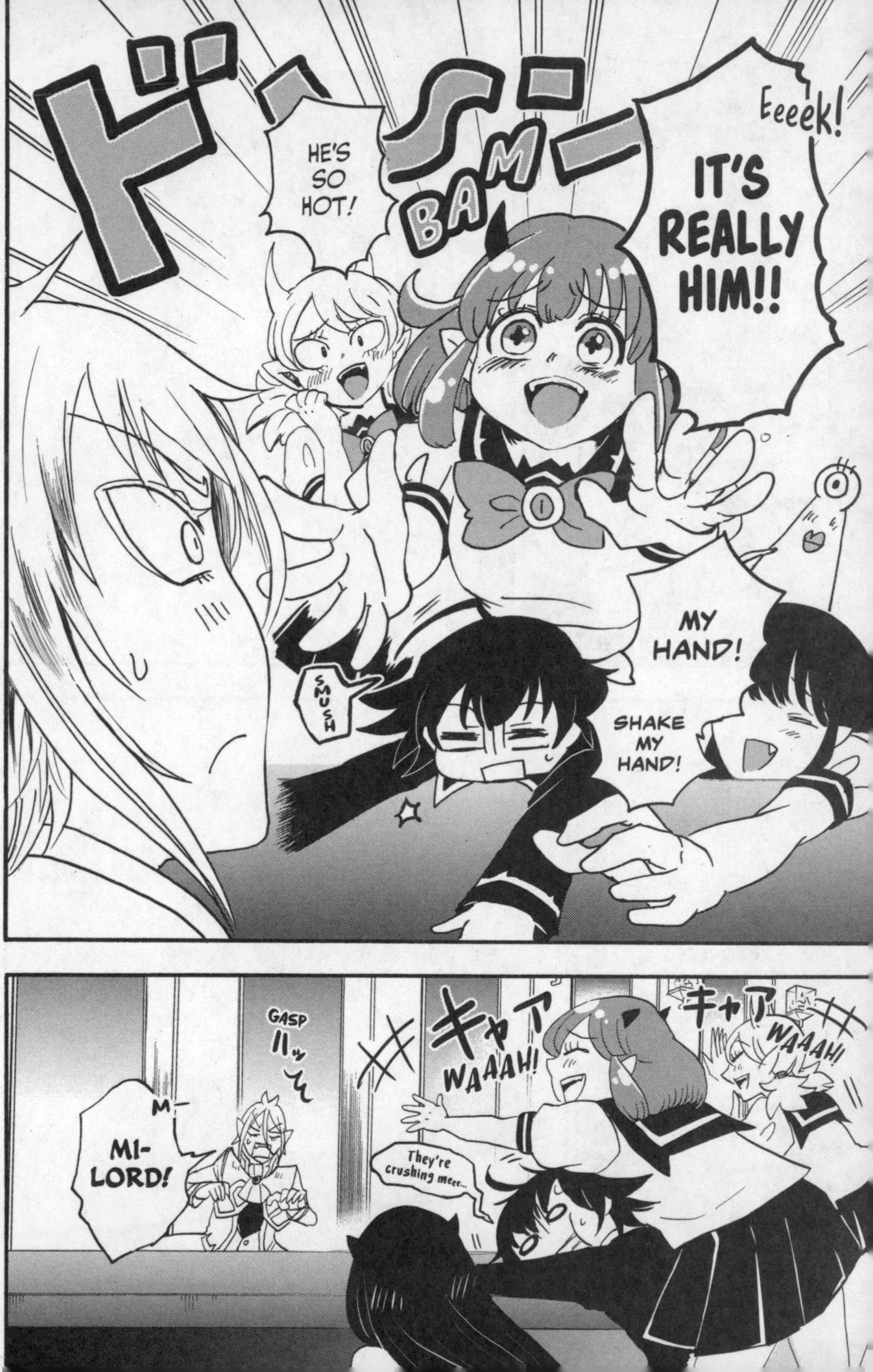
Eeeek!
IT'S REALLY HIM!!
ドーン
BAM
HE'S SO HOT!
MY HAND!
SHAKE MY HAND!
SMUSH
キャア
WAAAH!
キャア
WAAAH!
They're crushing meee...
GASP
ハッ
M—
MI-LORD!

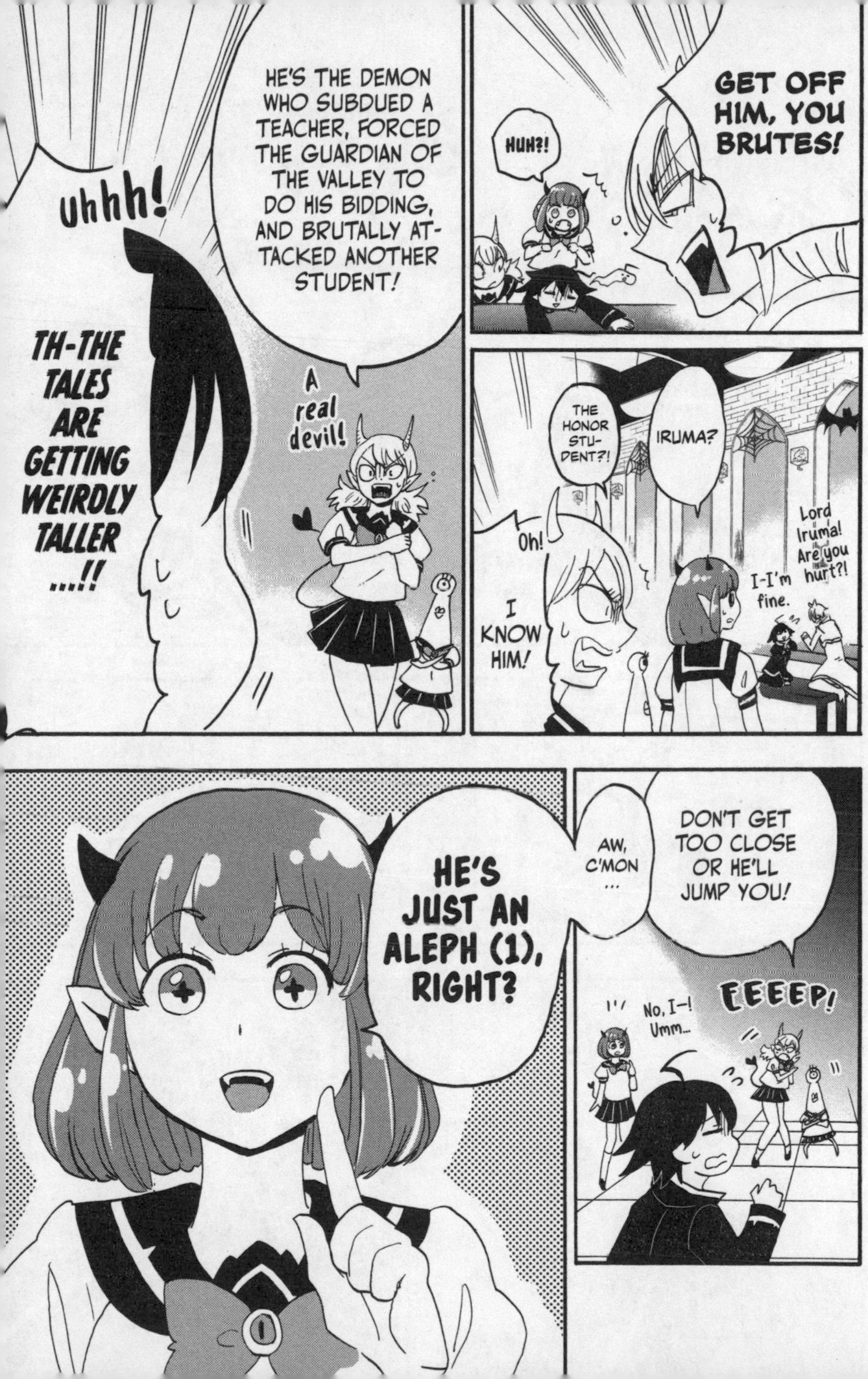
GET OFF HIM, YOU BRUTES!
HUH?!
IRUMA?
THE HONOR STU-DENT?!
Lord Iruma! Are you hurt?!
I-I'm fine.
Oh!
I KNOW HIM!
HE'S THE DEMON WHO SUBDUED A TEACHER, FORCED THE GUARDIAN OF THE VALLEY TO DO HIS BIDDING, AND BRUTALLY AT-TACKED ANOTHER STUDENT!
A real devil!
uhhh!
TH-THE TALES ARE GETTING WEIRDLY TALLER ....!!
DON'T GET TOO CLOSE OR HE'LL JUMP YOU!
AW, C'MON ...
EEEEP!
No, I—! Umm...
HE'S JUST AN ALEPH (1), RIGHT?

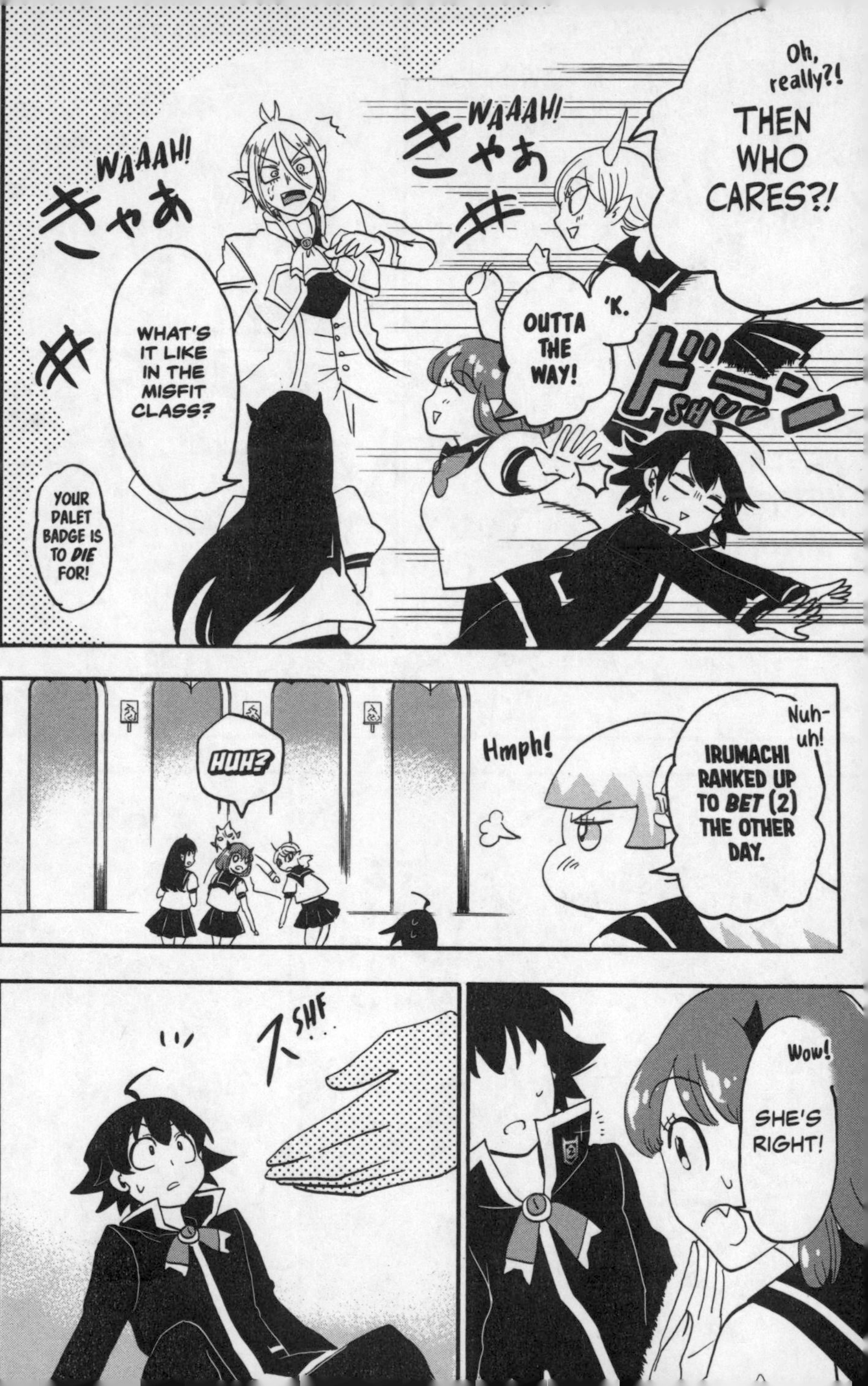
Oh, really?!
THEN WHO CARES?!
WAAAH!
きゃあ
'K.
OUTTA THE WAY!
WAAAH!
きゃあ
WHAT'S IT LIKE IN THE MISFIT CLASS?
YOUR DALET BADGE IS TO *DIE* FOR!
Nuh-uh!
IRUMACHI RANKED UP TO *BET* (2) THE OTHER DAY.
Hmph!
HUH?
Wow!
SHE'S RIGHT!
SHF

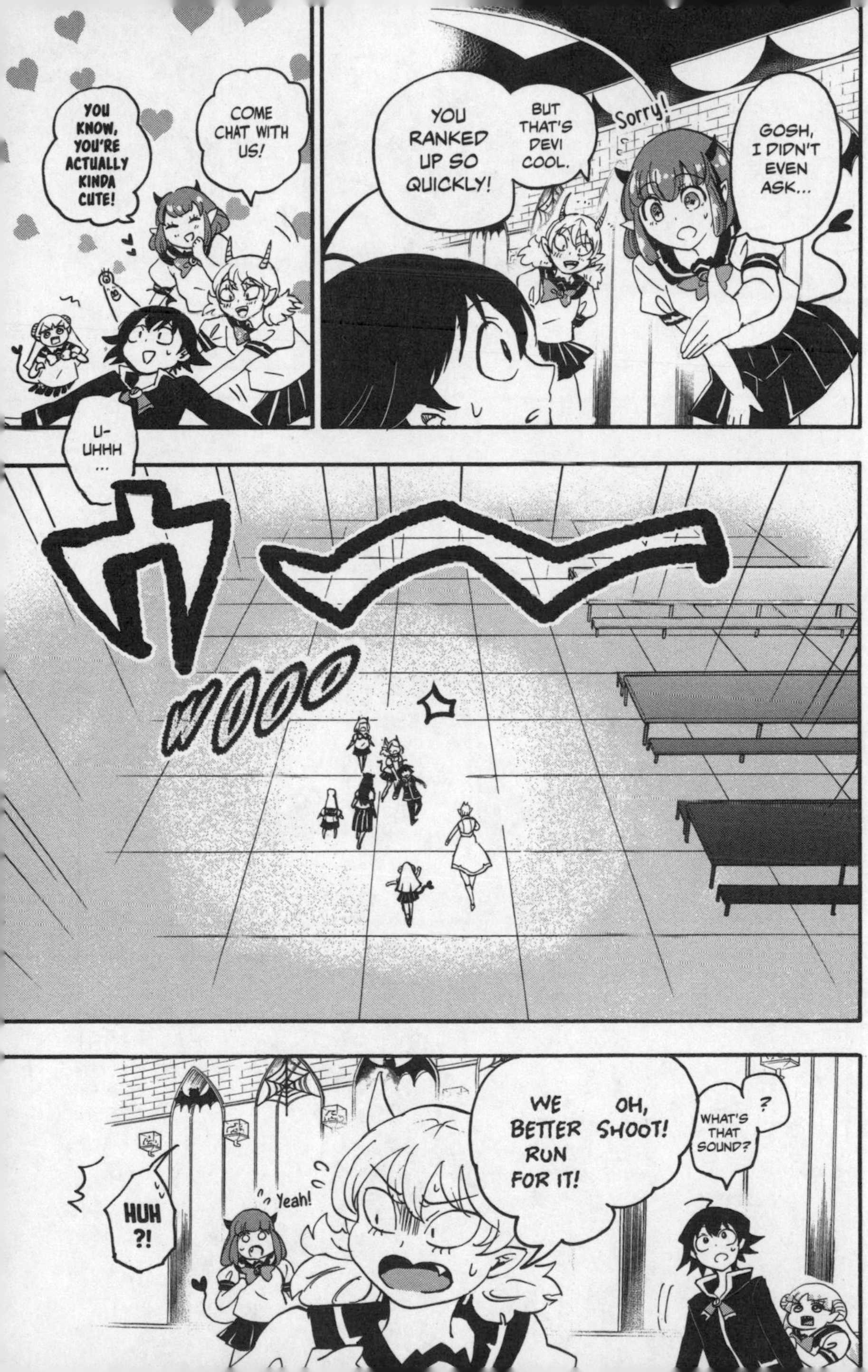
GOSH, I DIDN'T EVEN ASK...
Sorry!
BUT THAT'S DEVI COOL.
YOU RANKED UP SO QUICKLY!
COME CHAT WITH US!
YOU KNOW, YOU'RE ACTUALLY KINDA CUTE!
U-UHHH ...
WOOOO
WHAT'S THAT SOUND?
?
OH, SHOOT!
WE BETTER RUN FOR IT!
Yeah!
HUH ?!

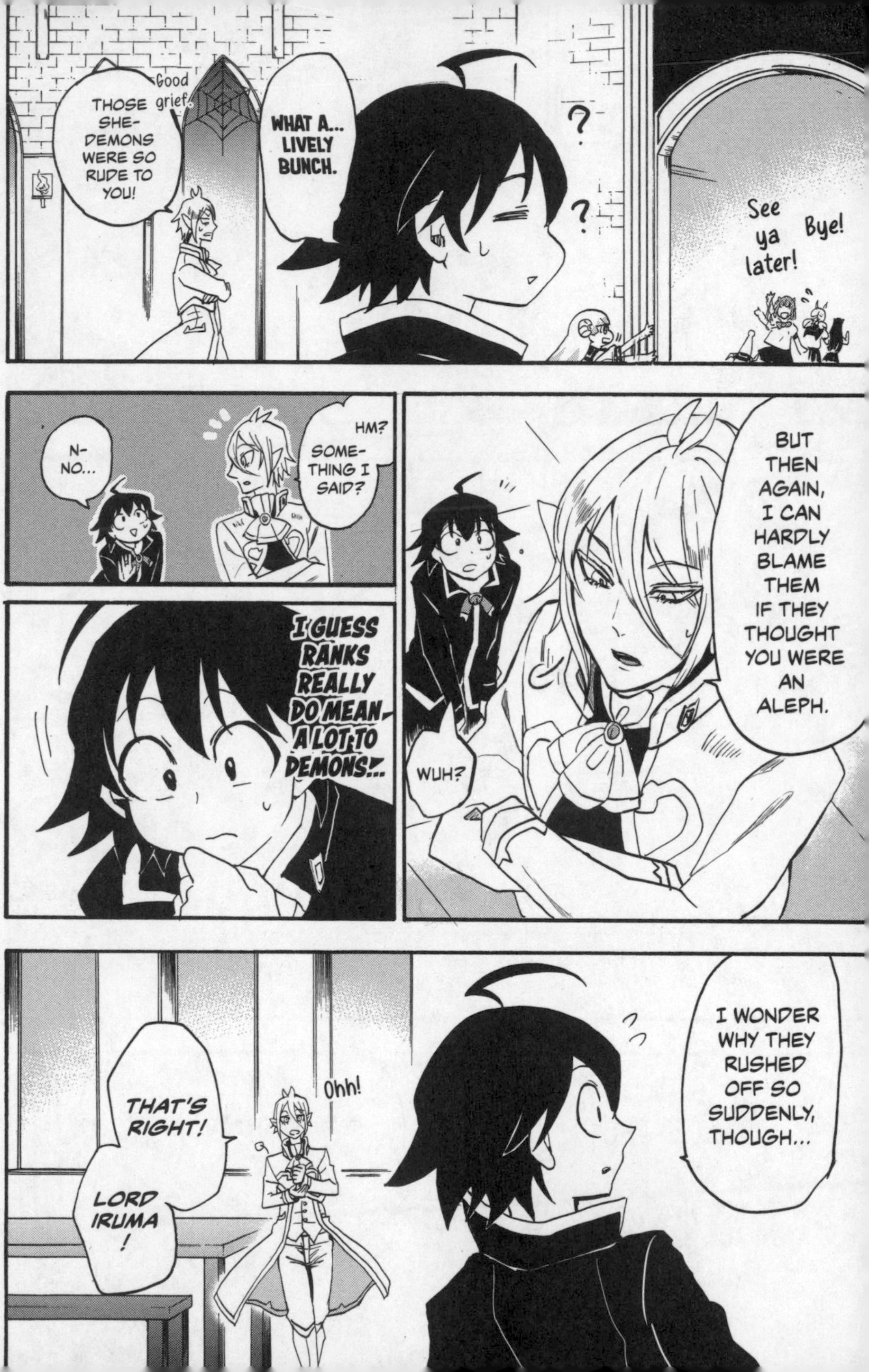
Bye!
See ya later!
?
?
WHAT A... LIVELY BUNCH.
Good grief.
THOSE SHE-DEMONS WERE SO RUDE TO YOU!
BUT THEN AGAIN, I CAN HARDLY BLAME THEM IF THEY THOUGHT YOU WERE AN ALEPH.
WUH?
HM? SOMETHING I SAID?
N-NO...
I GUESS RANKS REALLY DO MEAN A LOT TO DEMONS...
I WONDER WHY THEY RUSHED OFF SO SUDDENLY, THOUGH...
Ohh!
THAT'S RIGHT!
LORD IRUMA!

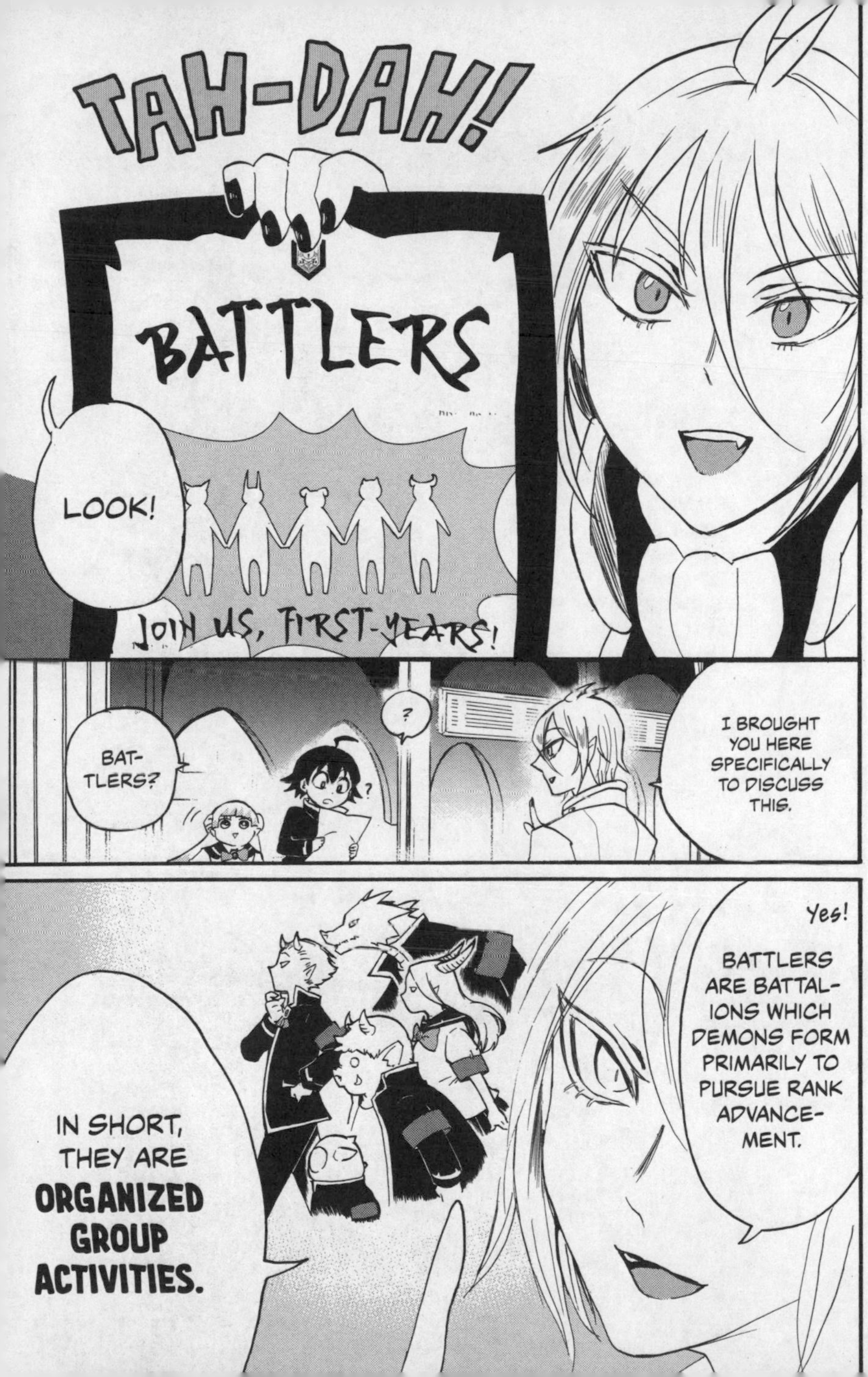
TAH-DAH!
BATTLERS
JOIN US, FIRST-YEARS!
LOOK!
I BROUGHT YOU HERE SPECIFICALLY TO DISCUSS THIS.
?
BAT-TLERS?
Yes!
BATTLERS ARE BATTAL-IONS WHICH DEMONS FORM PRIMARILY TO PURSUE RANK ADVANCE-MENT.
IN SHORT, THEY ARE ORGANIZED GROUP ACTIVITIES.

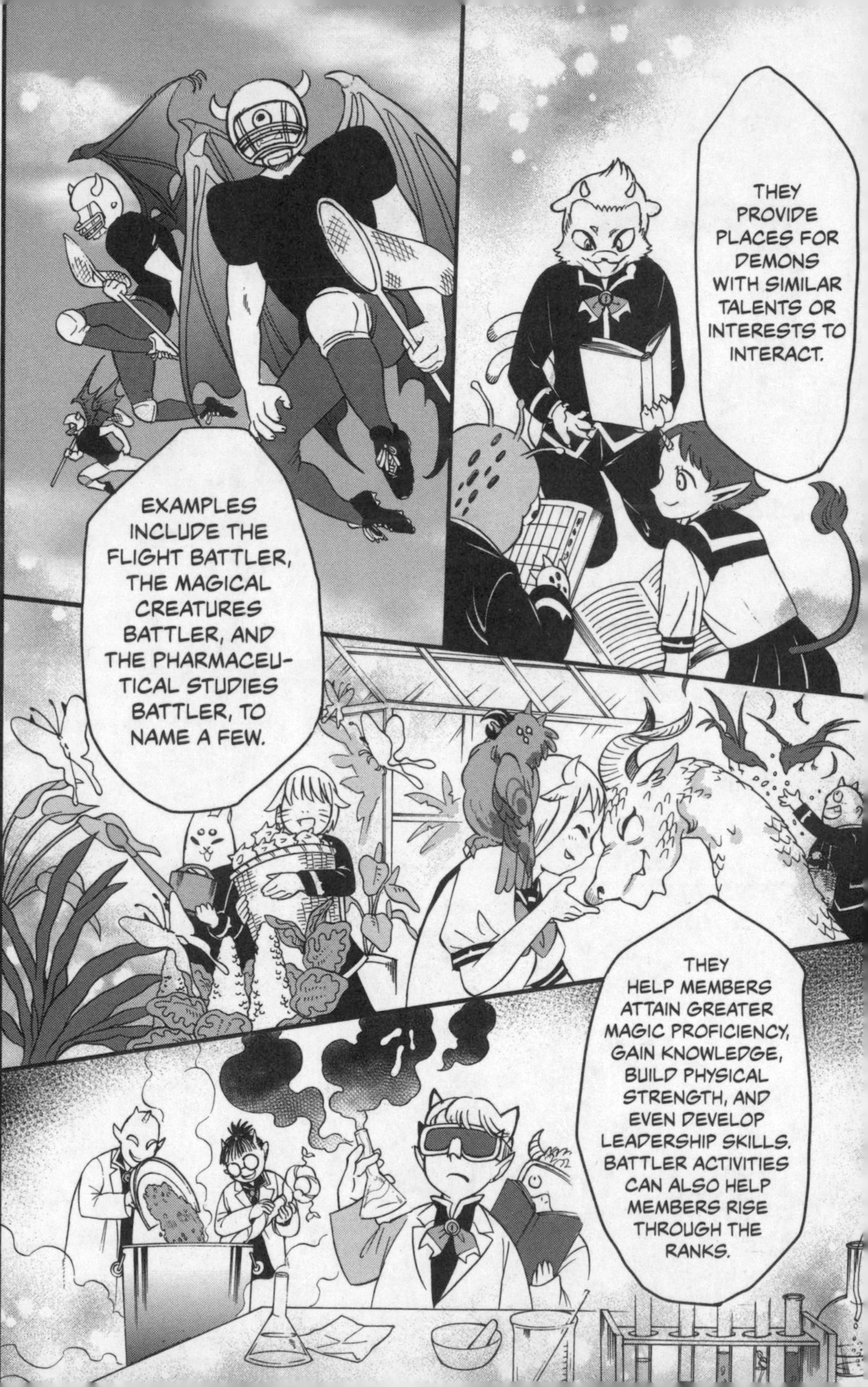
THEY PROVIDE PLACES FOR DEMONS WITH SIMILAR TALENTS OR INTERESTS TO INTERACT.
EXAMPLES INCLUDE THE FLIGHT BATTLER, THE MAGICAL CREATURES BATTLER, AND THE PHARMACEU-TICAL STUDIES BATTLER, TO NAME A FEW.
THEY HELP MEMBERS ATTAIN GREATER MAGIC PROFICIENCY, GAIN KNOWLEDGE, BUILD PHYSICAL STRENGTH, AND EVEN DEVELOP LEADERSHIP SKILLS. BATTLER ACTIVITIES CAN ALSO HELP MEMBERS RISE THROUGH THE RANKS.

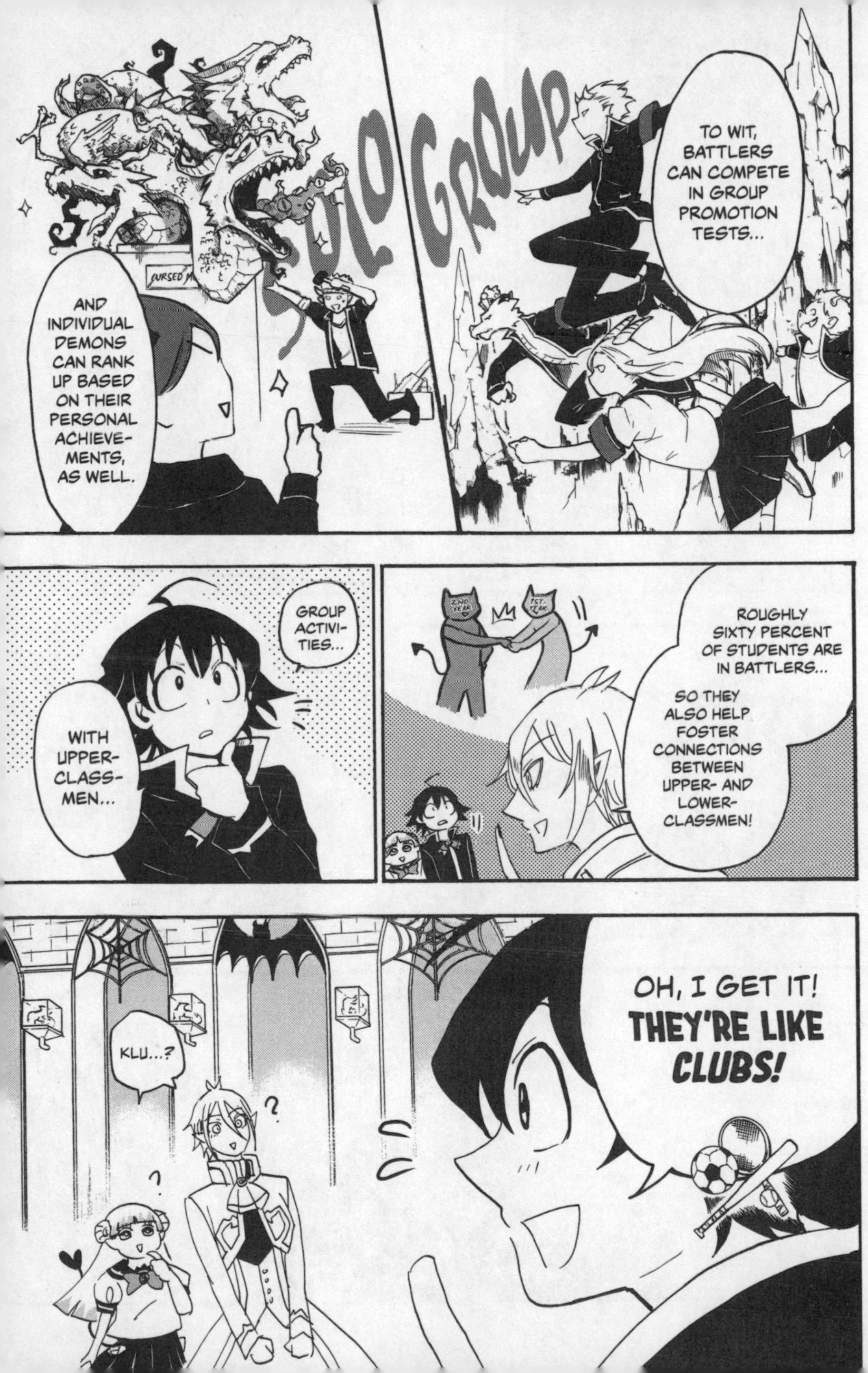

GROUP
TO WIT, BATTLERS CAN COMPETE IN GROUP PROMOTION TESTS...
SOLO
AND INDIVIDUAL DEMONS CAN RANK UP BASED ON THEIR PERSONAL ACHIEVEMENTS, AS WELL.
2ND YEAR
1ST YEAR
ROUGHLY SIXTY PERCENT OF STUDENTS ARE IN BATTLERS...
SO THEY ALSO HELP FOSTER CONNECTIONS BETWEEN UPPER- AND LOWER-CLASSMEN!
GROUP ACTIVITIES...
WITH UPPERCLASSMEN...
OH, I GET IT! THEY'RE LIKE CLUBS!
KLU...?

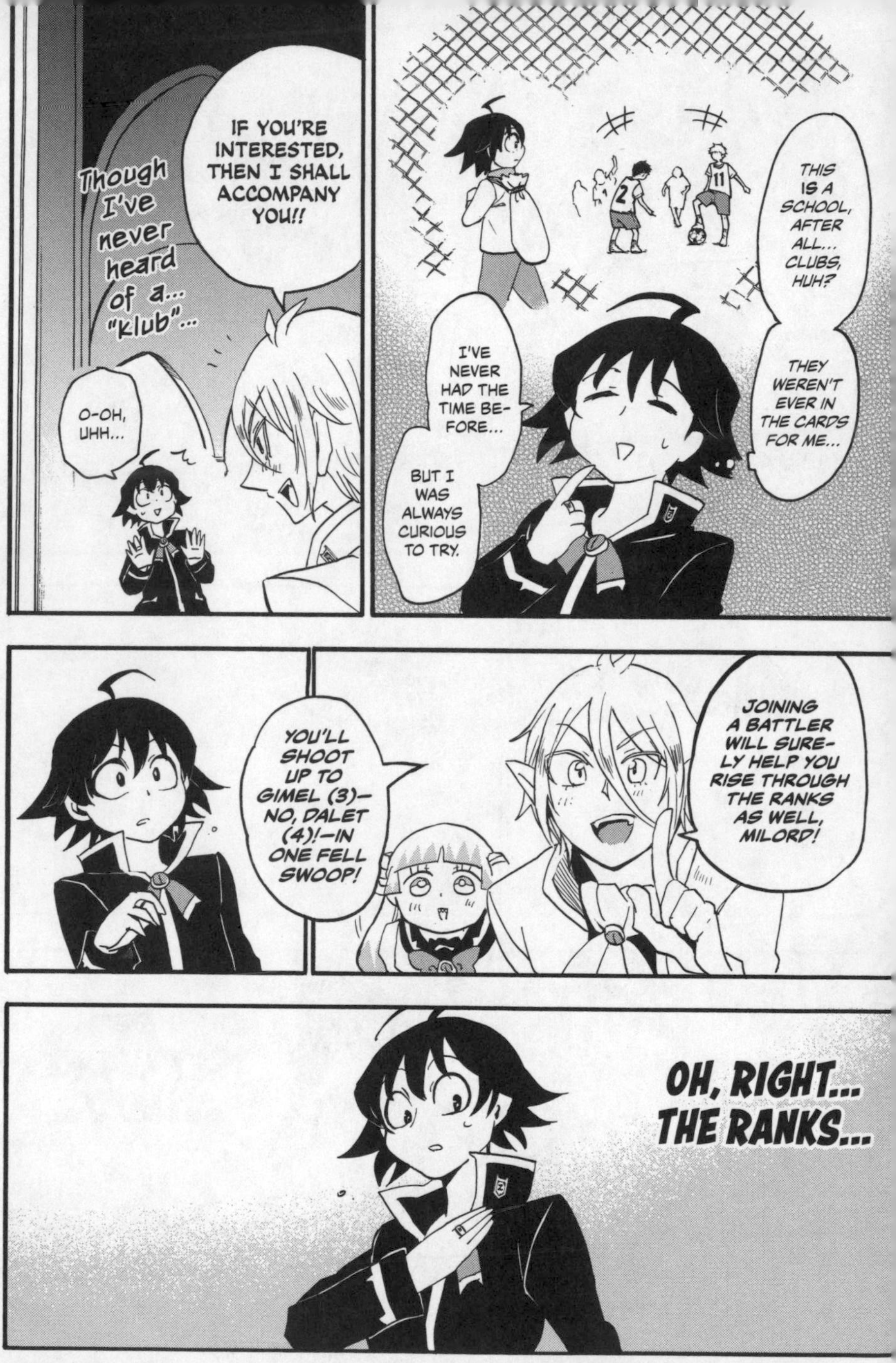
THIS IS A SCHOOL, AFTER ALL... CLUBS, HUH?
THEY WEREN'T EVER IN THE CARDS FOR ME...
I'VE NEVER HAD THE TIME BEFORE...
BUT I WAS ALWAYS CURIOUS TO TRY.
IF YOU'RE INTERESTED, THEN I SHALL ACCOMPANY YOU!!
Though I've never heard of a... "klub"...
O-OH, UHH...
JOINING A BATTLER WILL SURELY HELP YOU RISE THROUGH THE RANKS AS WELL, MILORD!
YOU'LL SHOOT UP TO GIMEL (3)—NO, DALET (4)!—IN ONE FELL SWOOP!
OH, RIGHT... THE RANKS...

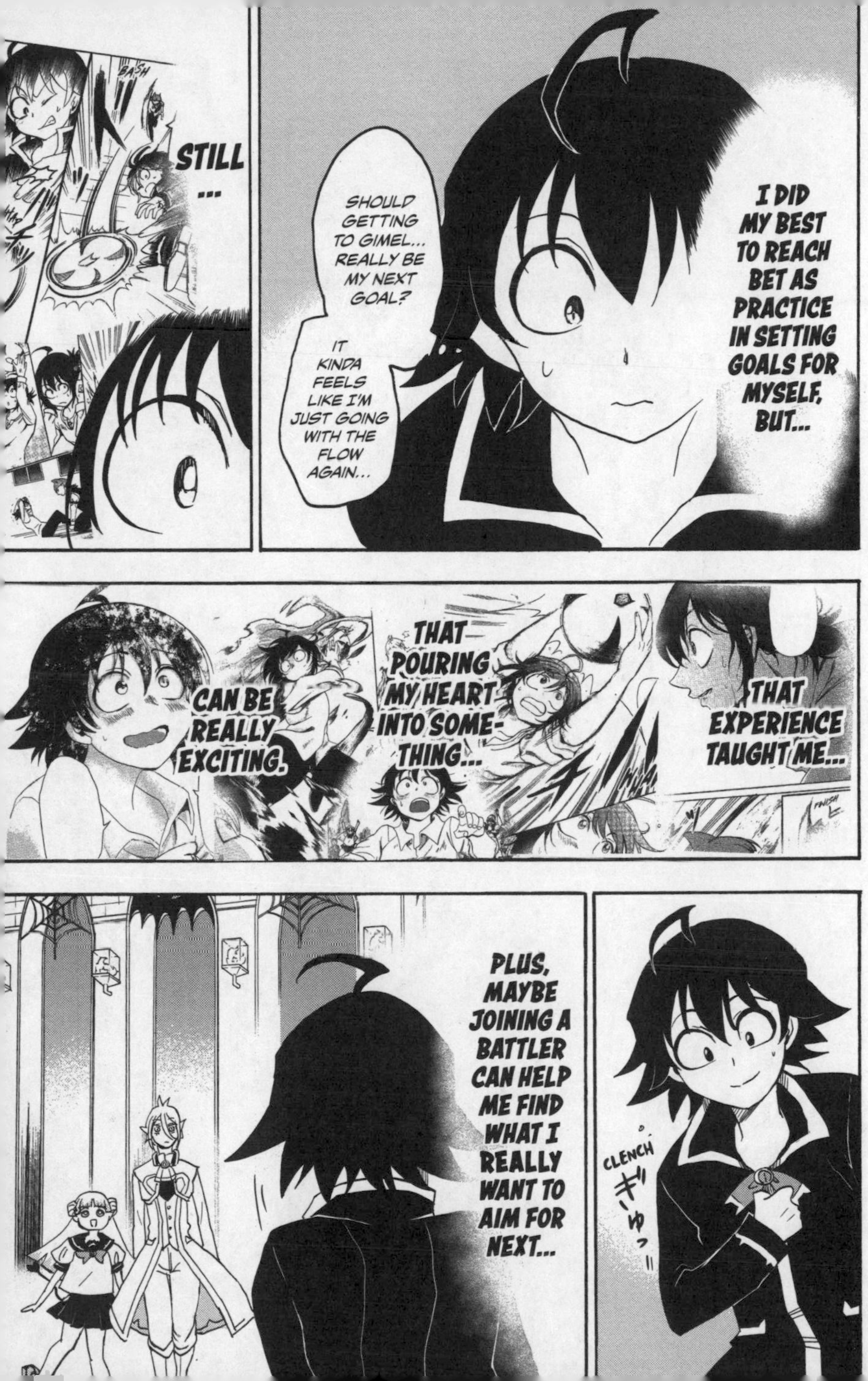
I DID MY BEST TO REACH BET AS PRACTICE IN SETTING GOALS FOR MYSELF, BUT...
SHOULD GETTING TO GIMEL... REALLY BE MY NEXT GOAL?
IT KINDA FEELS LIKE I'M JUST GOING WITH THE FLOW AGAIN...
BASH
STILL ...
THAT EXPERIENCE TAUGHT ME...
FINISH
THAT POURING MY HEART INTO SOME-THING...
CAN BE REALLY EXCITING.
CLENCH
ぎゅっ
PLUS, MAYBE JOINING A BATTLER CAN HELP ME FIND WHAT I REALLY WANT TO AIM FOR NEXT...

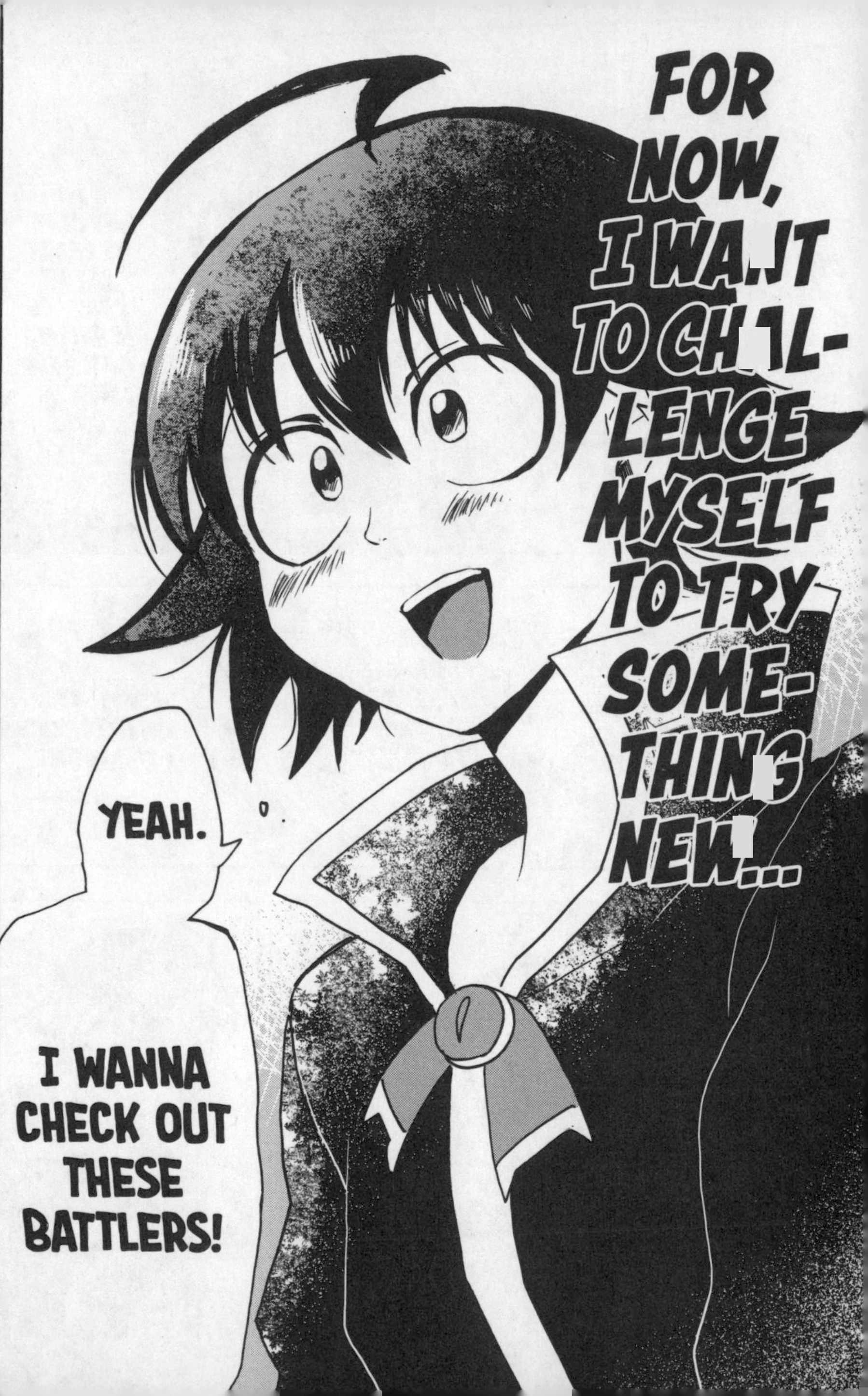
FOR NOW, I WANT TO CHALLENGE MYSELF TO TRY SOMETHING NEW...
YEAH.
I WANNA CHECK OUT THESE BATTLERS!

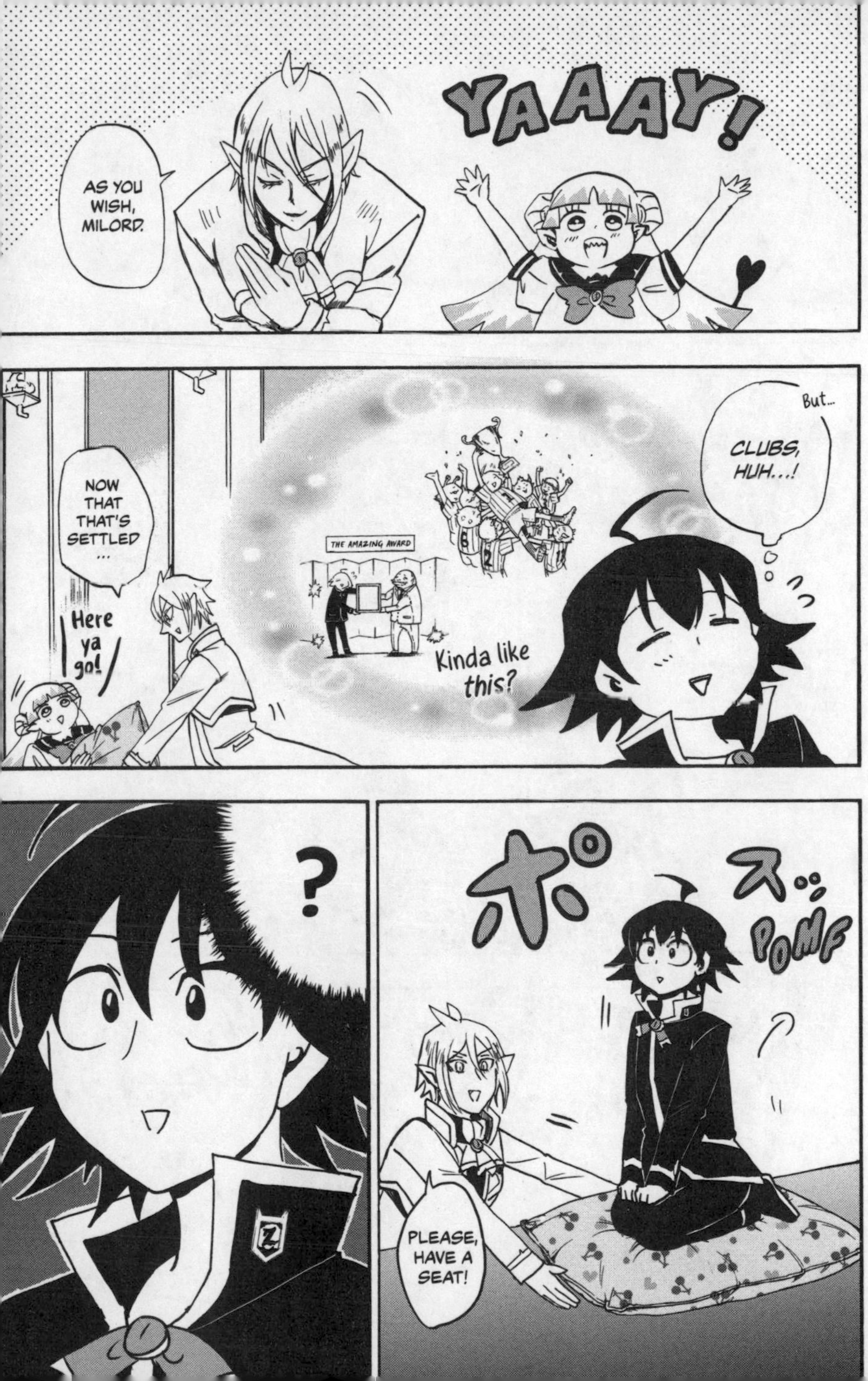
YAAAY!
AS YOU WISH, MILORD.
But...
CLUBS, HUH...!
Kinda like this?
THE AMAZING AWARD
NOW THAT THAT'S SETTLED...
Here ya go!
ポ
ス
POMF
PLEASE, HAVE A SEAT!
?

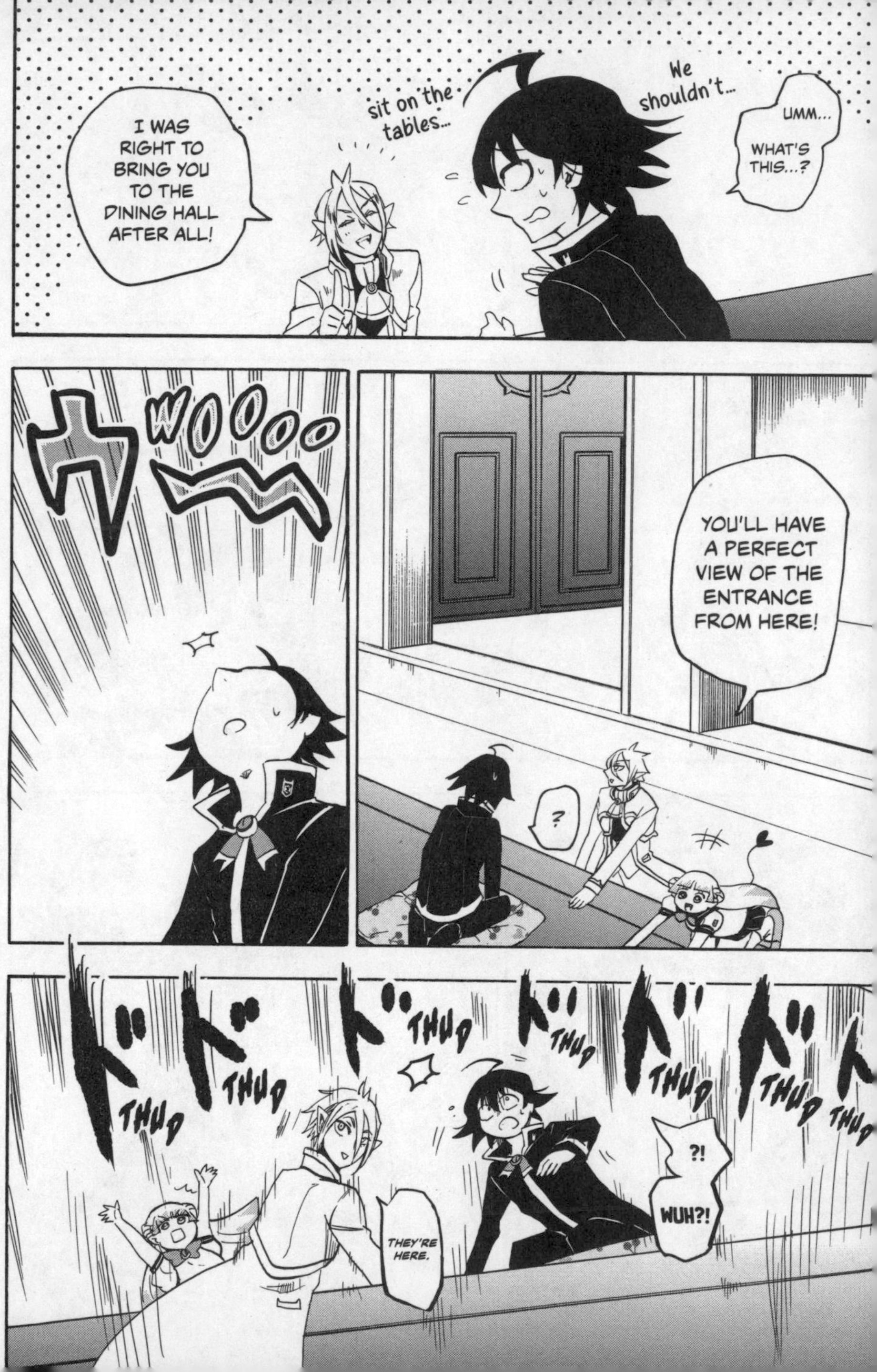

UMM... WHAT'S THIS...?
We shouldn't... sit on the tables...
I WAS RIGHT TO BRING YOU TO THE DINING HALL AFTER ALL!
YOU'LL HAVE A PERFECT VIEW OF THE ENTRANCE FROM HERE!
?
WOOooo
THUD THUD THUD THUD THUD THUD THUD THUD
?!
WUH?!
THEY'RE HERE.

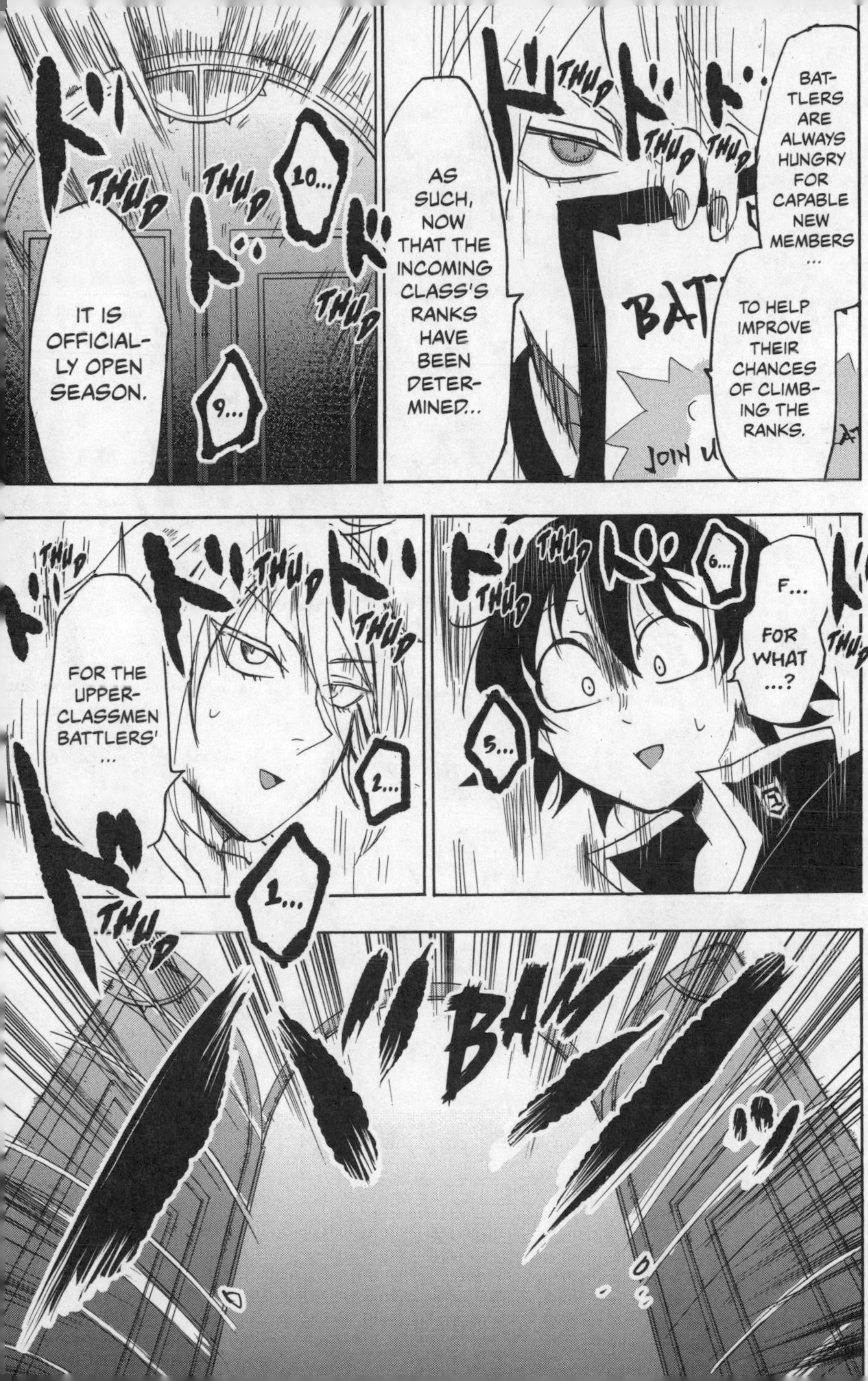
THUD
BATTLERS ARE ALWAYS HUNGRY FOR CAPABLE NEW MEMBERS...
TO HELP IMPROVE THEIR CHANCES OF CLIMBING THE RANKS.
BAT
JOIN U
THUD
AS SUCH, NOW THAT THE INCOMING CLASS'S RANKS HAVE BEEN DETERMINED...
THUD
10...
THUD
IT IS OFFICIALLY OPEN SEASON.
9...
THUD
6...
F... FOR WHAT...?
5...
THUD
THUD
FOR THE UPPERCLASSMEN BATTLERS'...
2...
1...
THUD
BAM

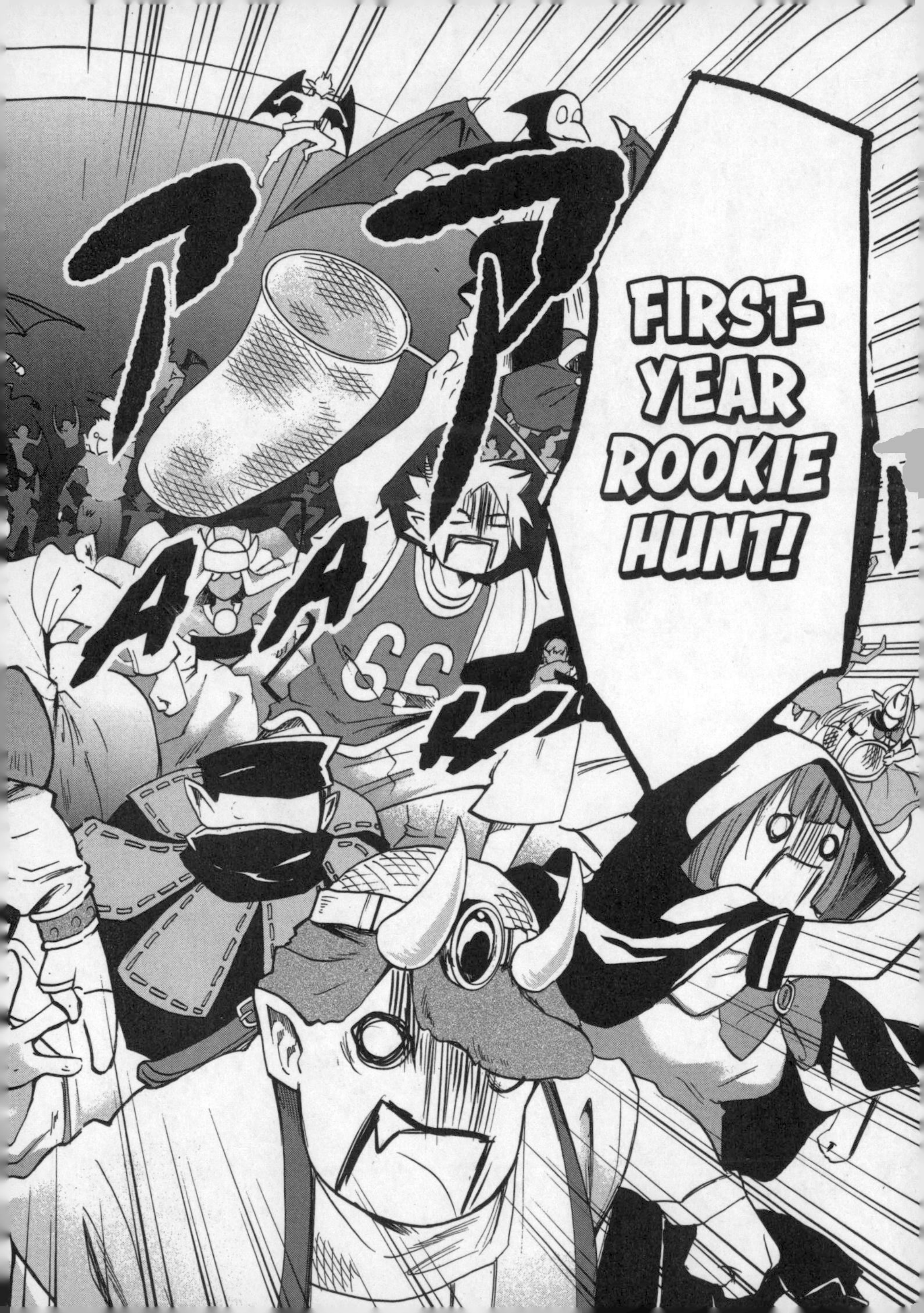
FIRST-YEAR ROOKIE HUNT!
AAAH

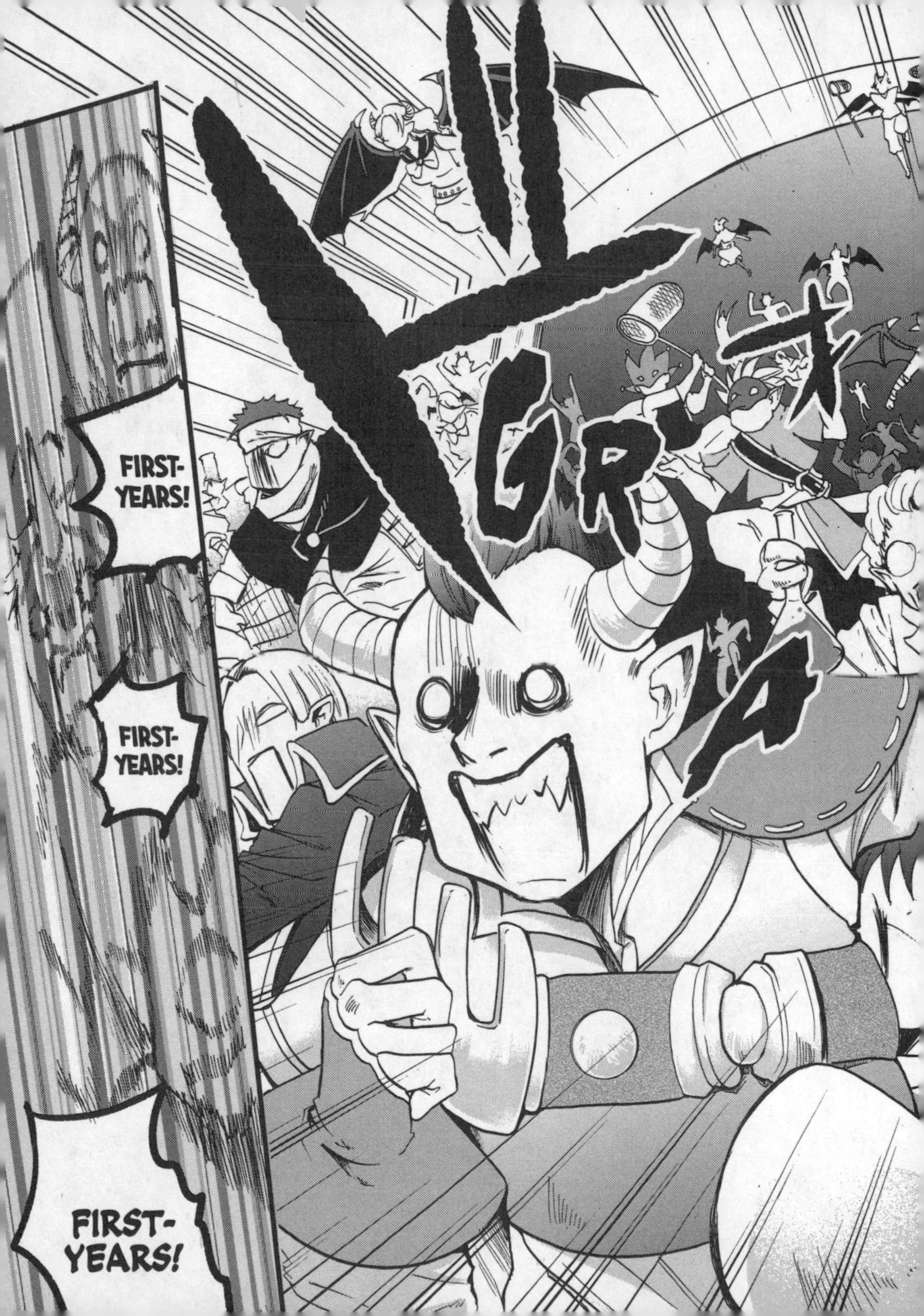
GRA
FIRST-YEARS!
FIRST-YEARS!
FIRST-YEARS!

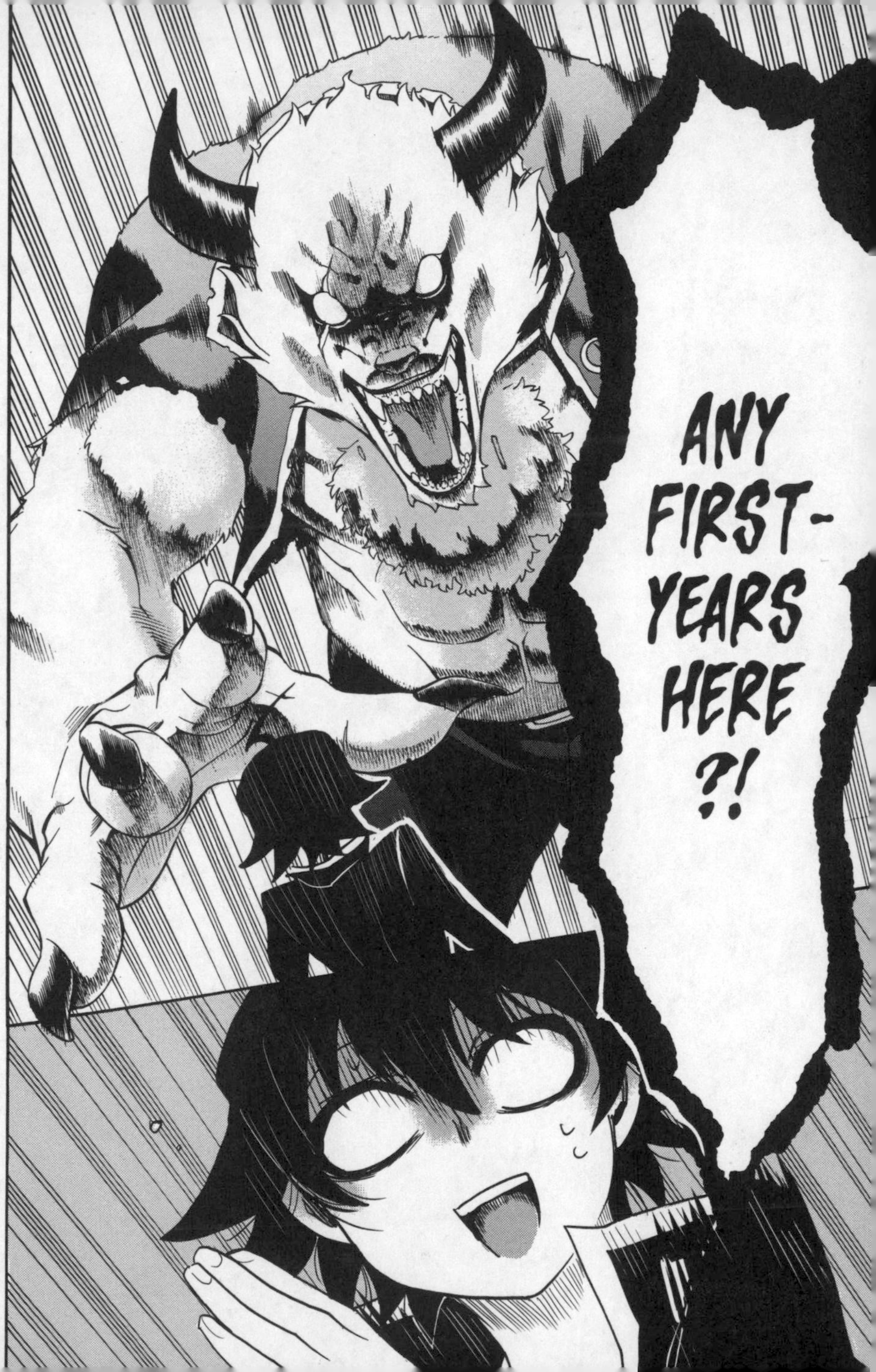
ANY FIRST-YEARS HERE?!

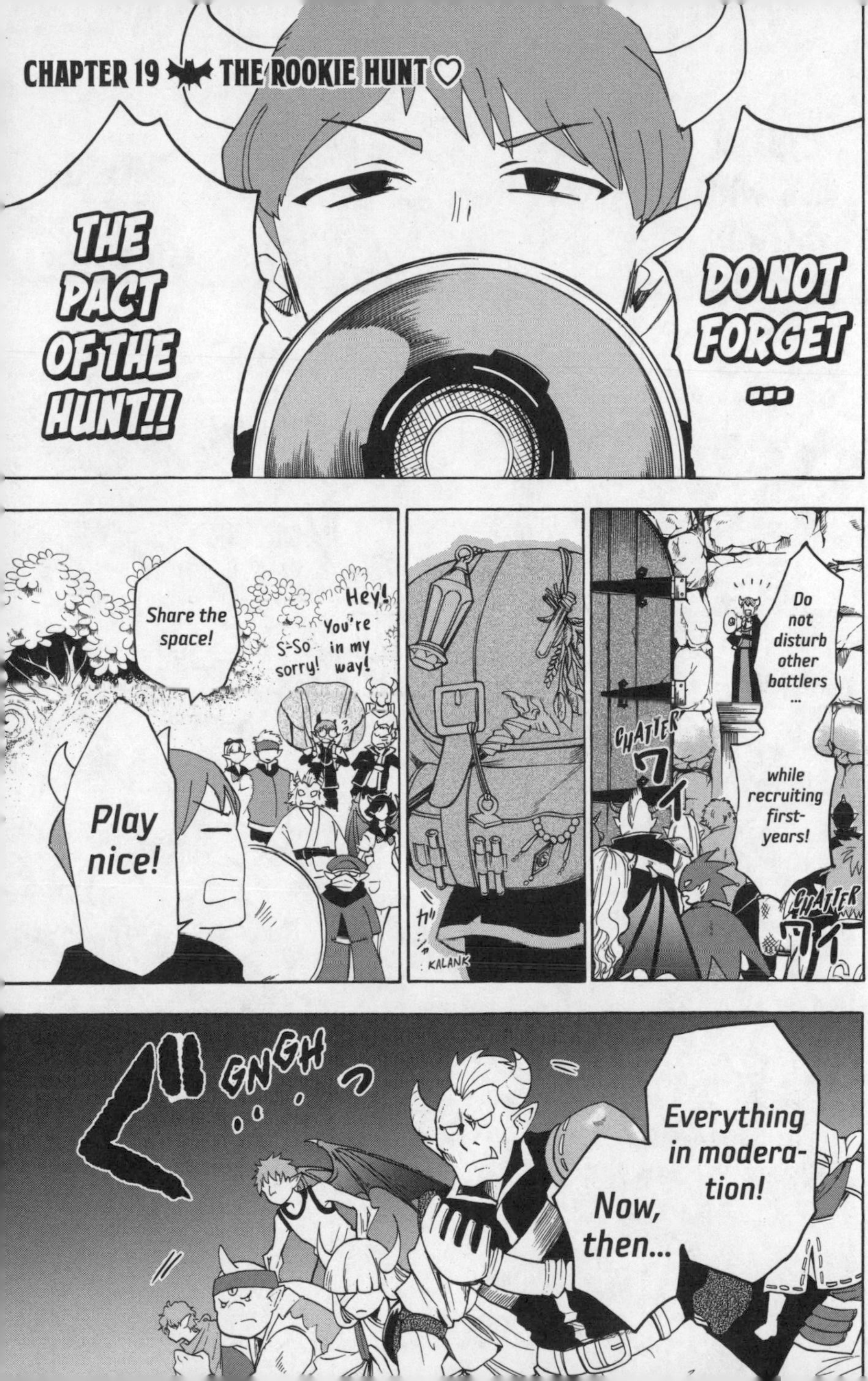
CHAPTER 19 THE ROOKIE HUNT ♡
DO NOT FORGET ...
THE PACT OF THE HUNT!!
Do not disturb other battlers ...
while recruiting first-years!
CHATTER
CHATTER
KALANK
Share the space!
Hey! You're in my way!
S-So sorry!
Play nice!
Everything in moderation!
Now, then...
GNGH

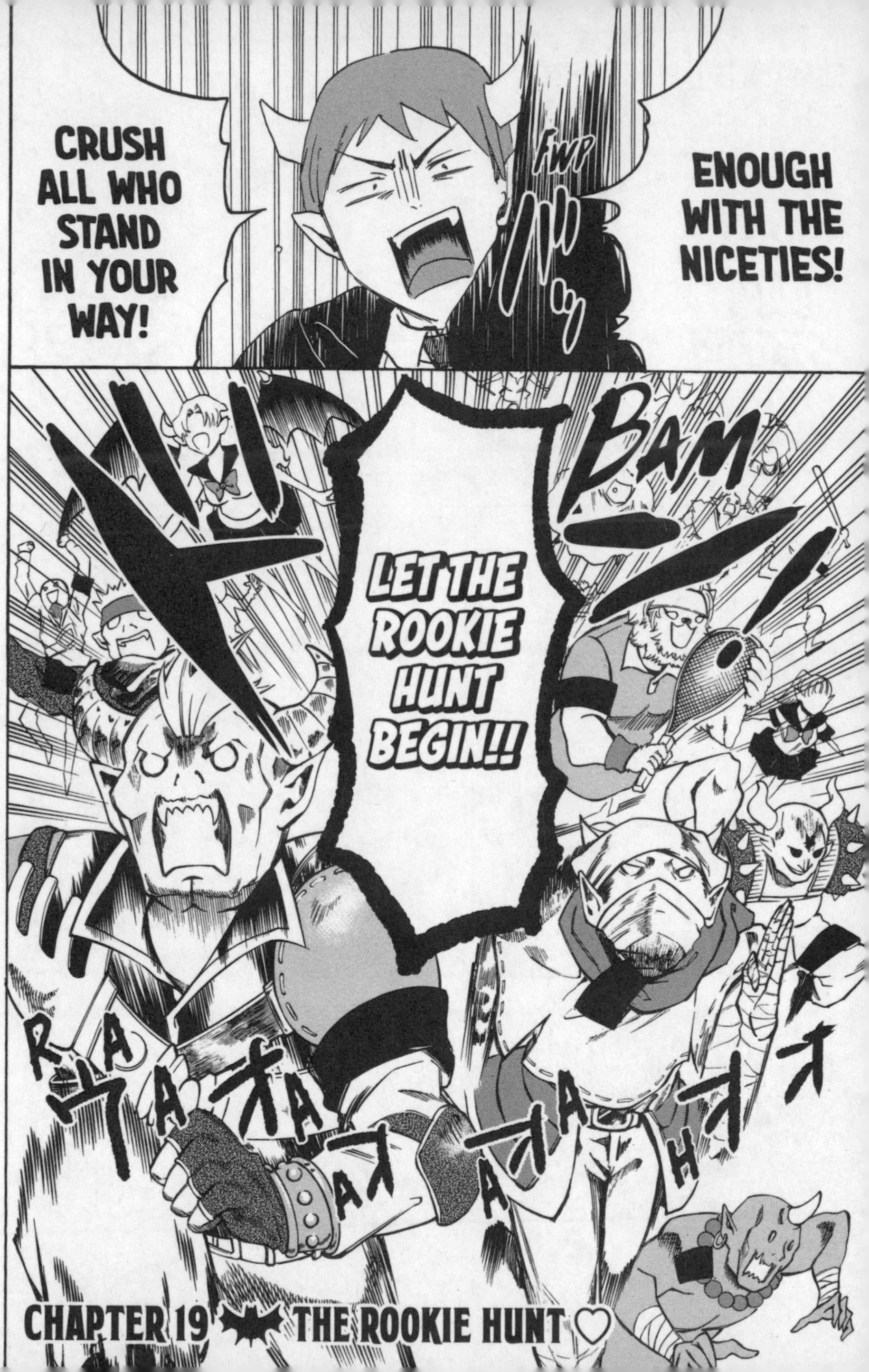
ENOUGH WITH THE NICETIES!
FWP
CRUSH ALL WHO STAND IN YOUR WAY!
BAM
LET THE ROOKIE HUNT BEGIN!!
RAAAAAAH

CHAPTER 19 THE ROOKIE HUNT ♡

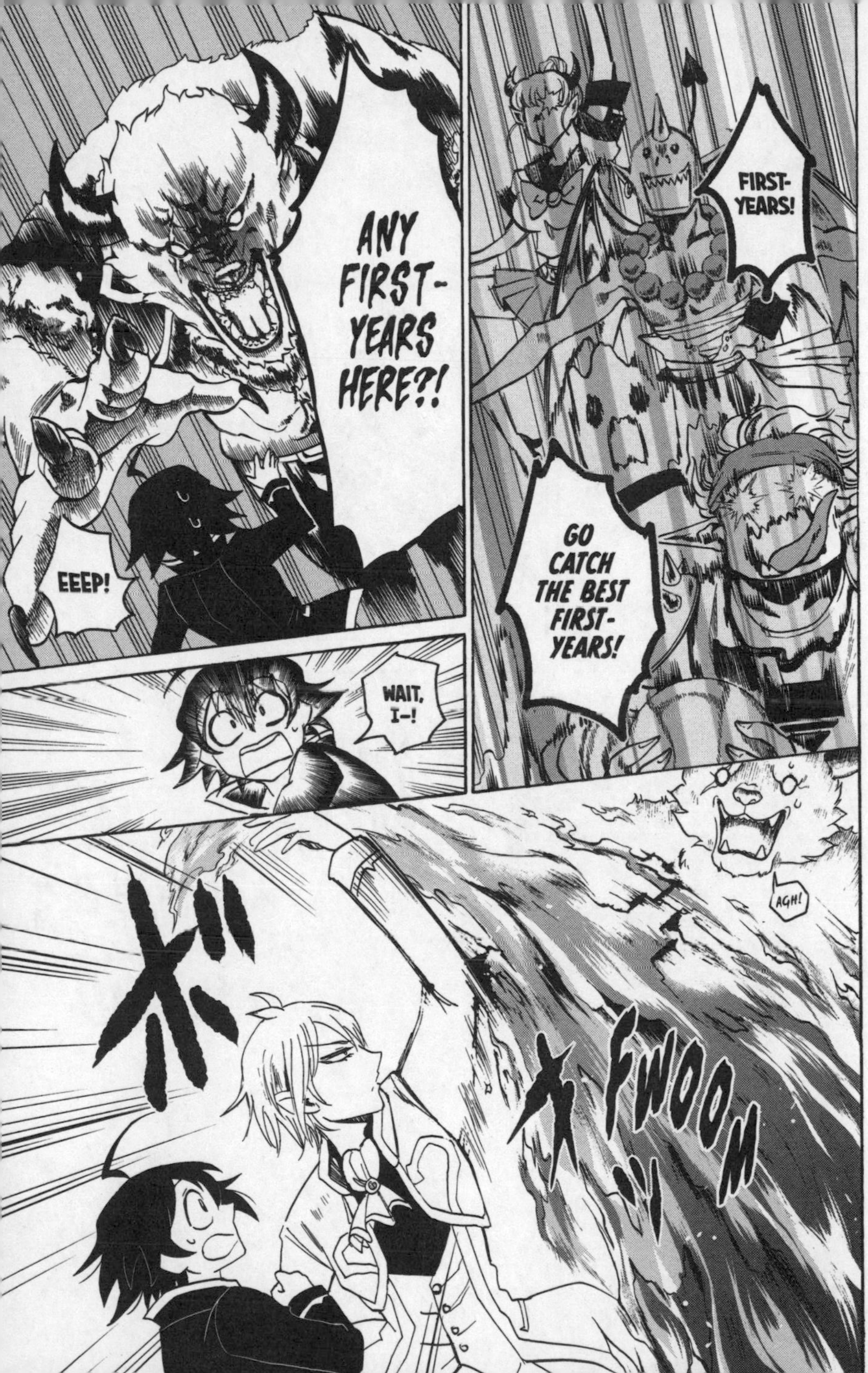
FIRST-YEARS!
GO CATCH THE BEST FIRST-YEARS!
ANY FIRST-YEARS HERE?!
EEEP!
WAIT, I-!
AGH!
FWOOM

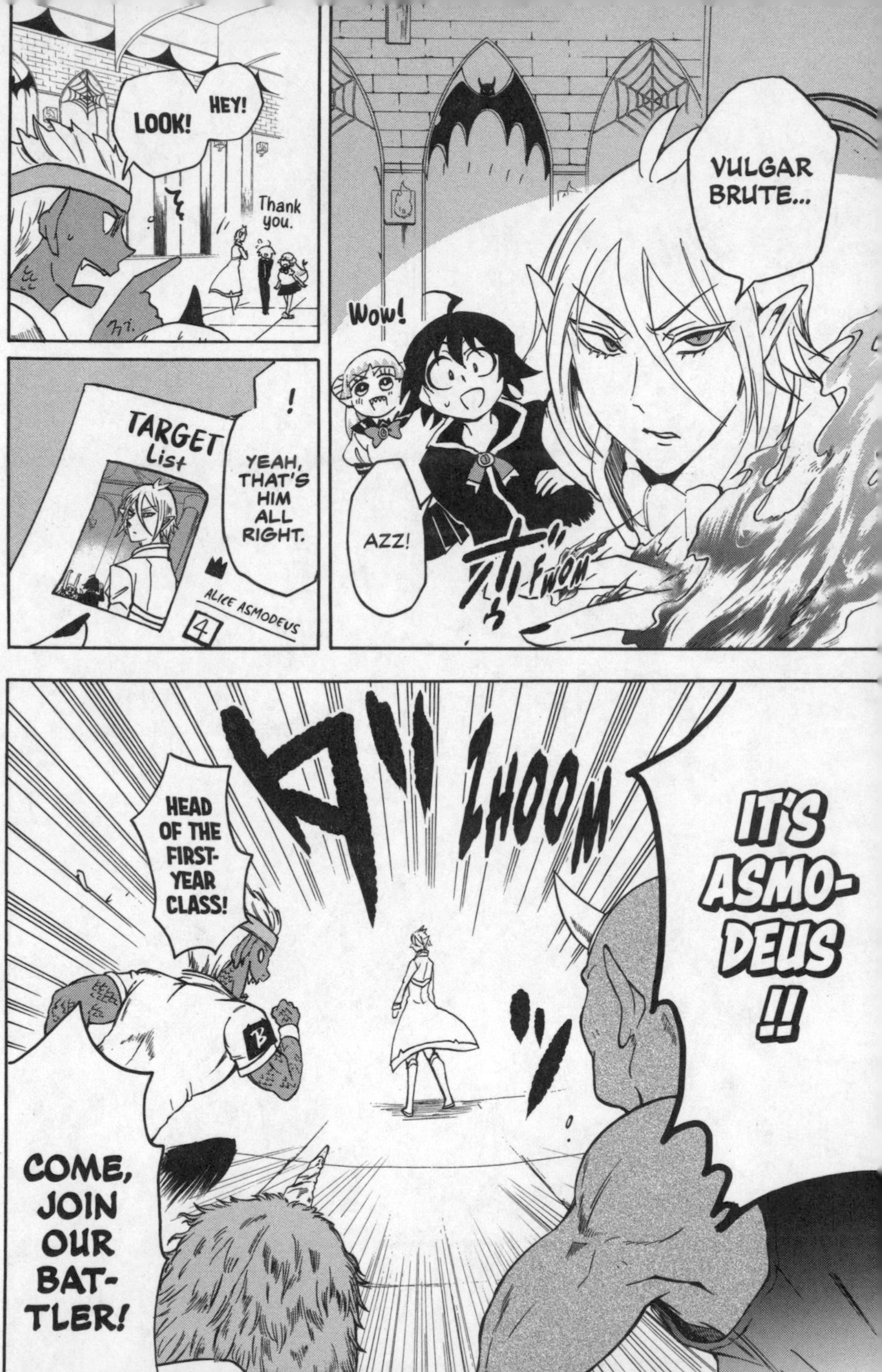
VULGAR BRUTE...
Wow!
AZZ!
FWOM
HEY!
LOOK!
Thank you.
TARGET List
!
YEAH, THAT'S HIM ALL RIGHT.
ALICE ASMODEUS
4
ZHOOM
IT'S ASMO-DEUS !!
HEAD OF THE FIRST-YEAR CLASS!
COME, JOIN OUR BAT-TLER!

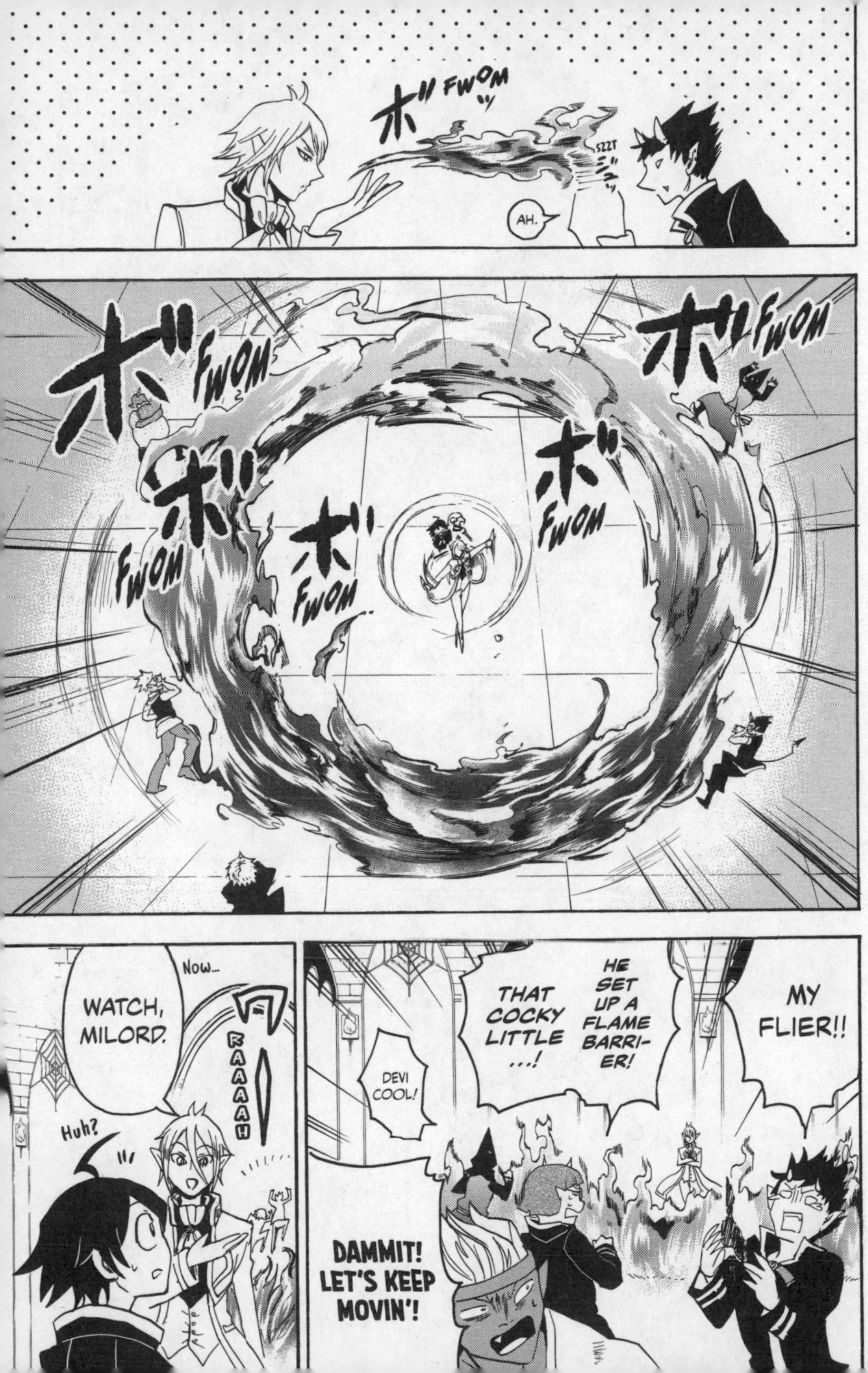
ボッ FWOM
SZZT
AH.
ボッ FWOM
ボッ FWOM
ボッ FWOM
ボッ FWOM
ボッ FWOM
MY FLIER!!
HE SET UP A FLAME BARRIER!
THAT COCKY LITTLE ...!
DEVI COOL!
DAMMIT! LET'S KEEP MOVIN'!
Now...
WATCH, MILORD.
RAAAAAH
Huh?

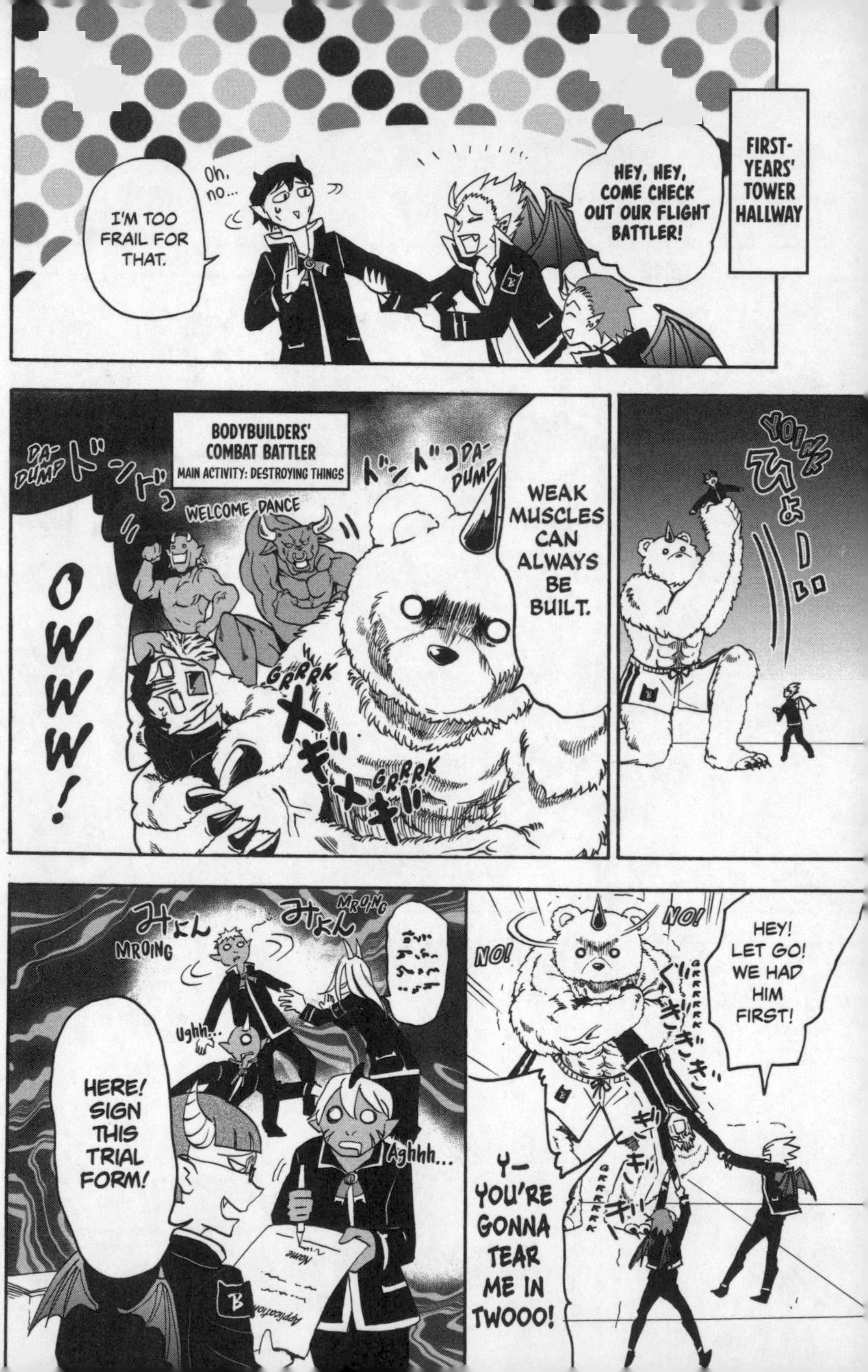
FIRST-YEARS' TOWER HALLWAY
HEY, HEY, COME CHECK OUT OUR FLIGHT BATTLER!
Oh, no...
I'M TOO FRAIL FOR THAT.
YOINK
ひょい
BODYBUILDERS' COMBAT BATTLER
MAIN ACTIVITY: DESTROYING THINGS
WEAK MUSCLES CAN ALWAYS BE BUILT.
DA-DUMP ドンドコ
DA-DUMP ドンドコ
WELCOME DANCE
OWWWW!
GRRRK メキ
GRRRK メキ
HEY! LET GO! WE HAD HIM FIRST!
NO!
NO!
GRRRRRK
Y- YOU'RE GONNA TEAR ME IN TWOOO!
MROING みょん
MROING みょん
Ughh...
HERE! SIGN THIS TRIAL FORM!
Aghhh...
Name
Application

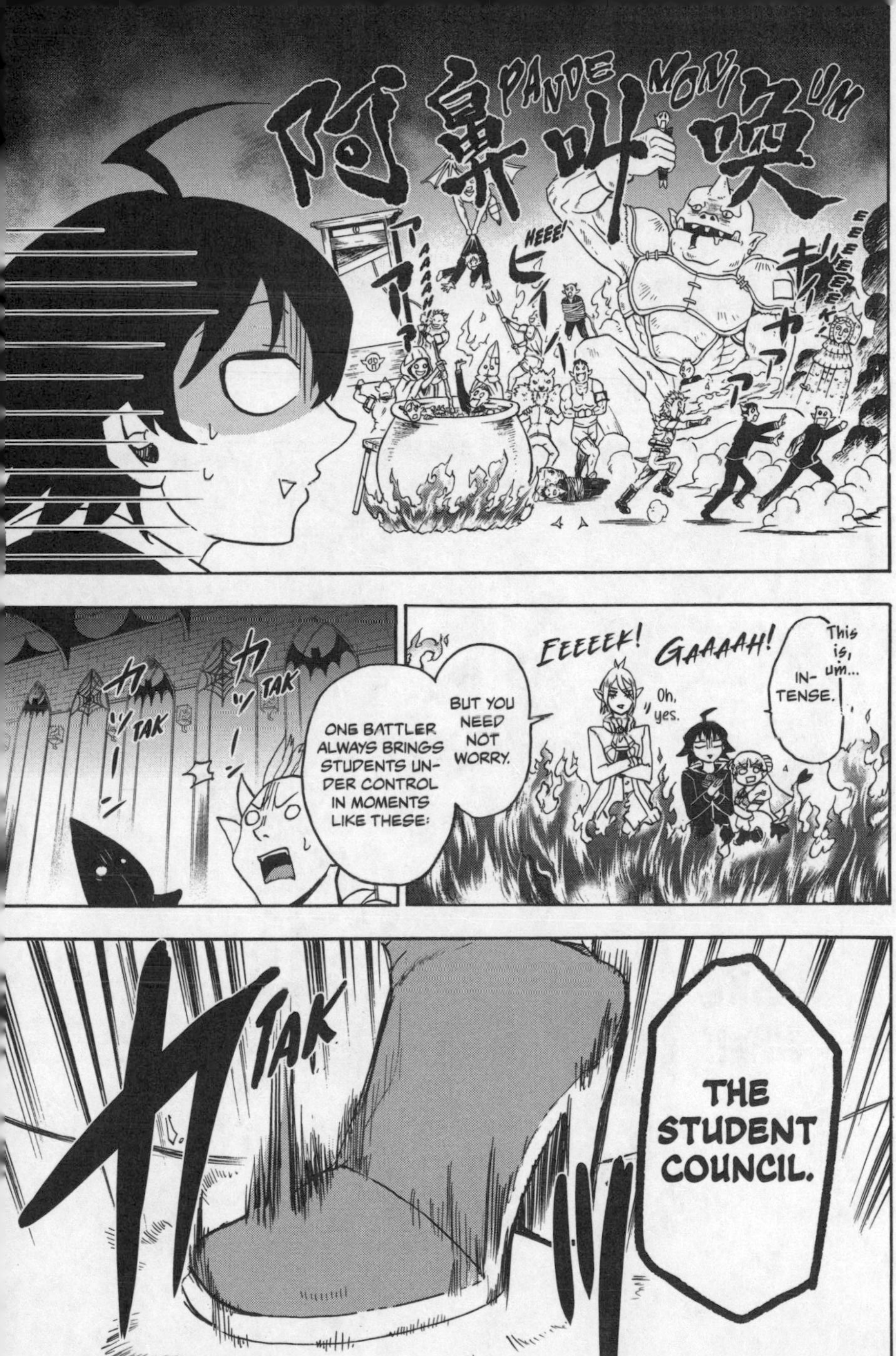

阿鼻叫喚
PANDEMONIUM
EEEEEEEEK!
HEEE!
AAAAAH!
GAAAAH!
EEEEEK!
This is, um... IN-TENSE.
Oh, yes.
BUT YOU NEED NOT WORRY.
ONE BATTLER ALWAYS BRINGS STUDENTS UN-DER CONTROL IN MOMENTS LIKE THESE:
TAK
TAK
THE STUDENT COUNCIL.
TAK

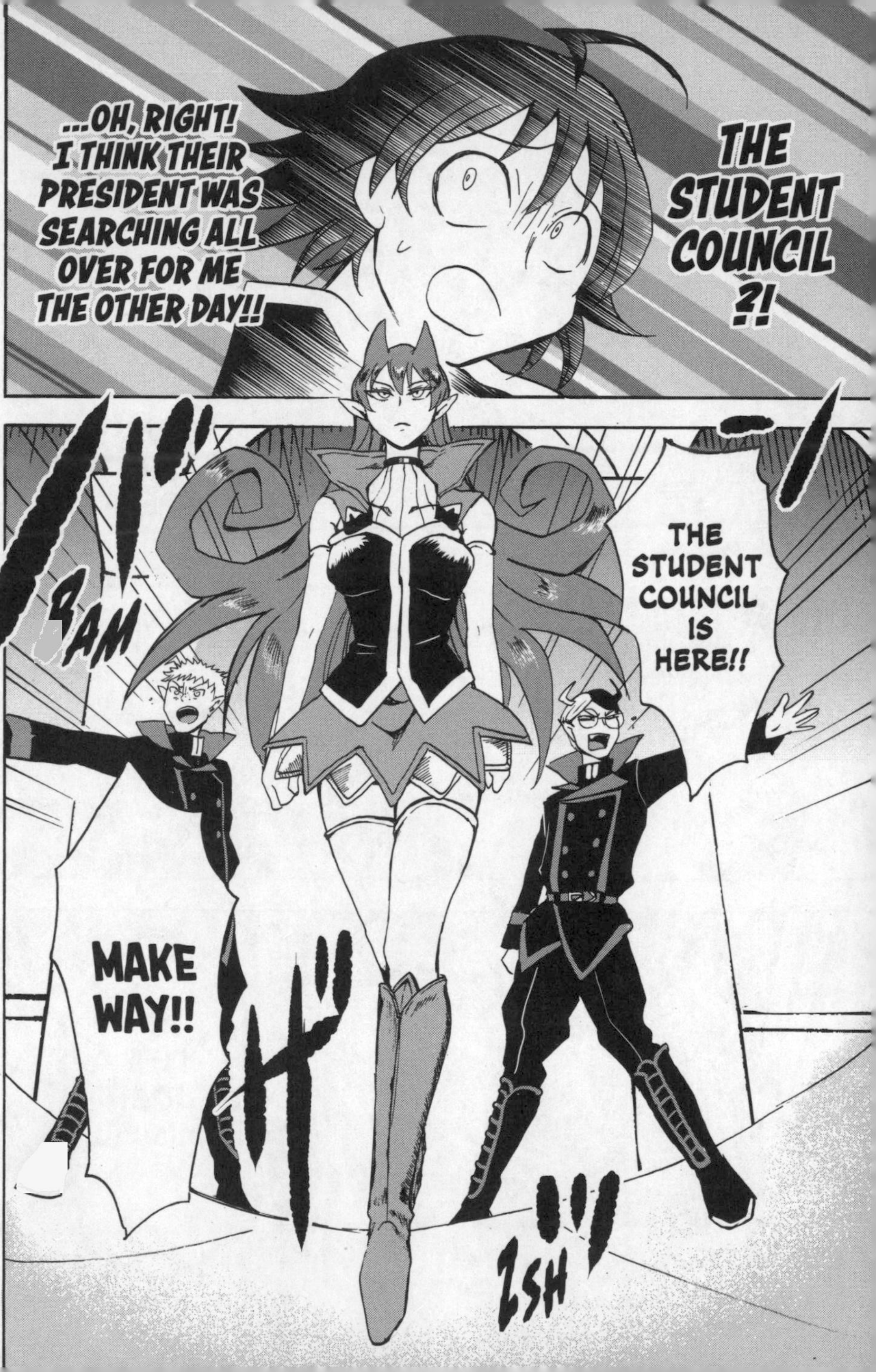
THE STUDENT COUNCIL ?!
...OH, RIGHT! I THINK THEIR PRESIDENT WAS SEARCHING ALL OVER FOR ME THE OTHER DAY!!
THE STUDENT COUNCIL IS HERE!!
BAM
MAKE WAY!!
ZSH

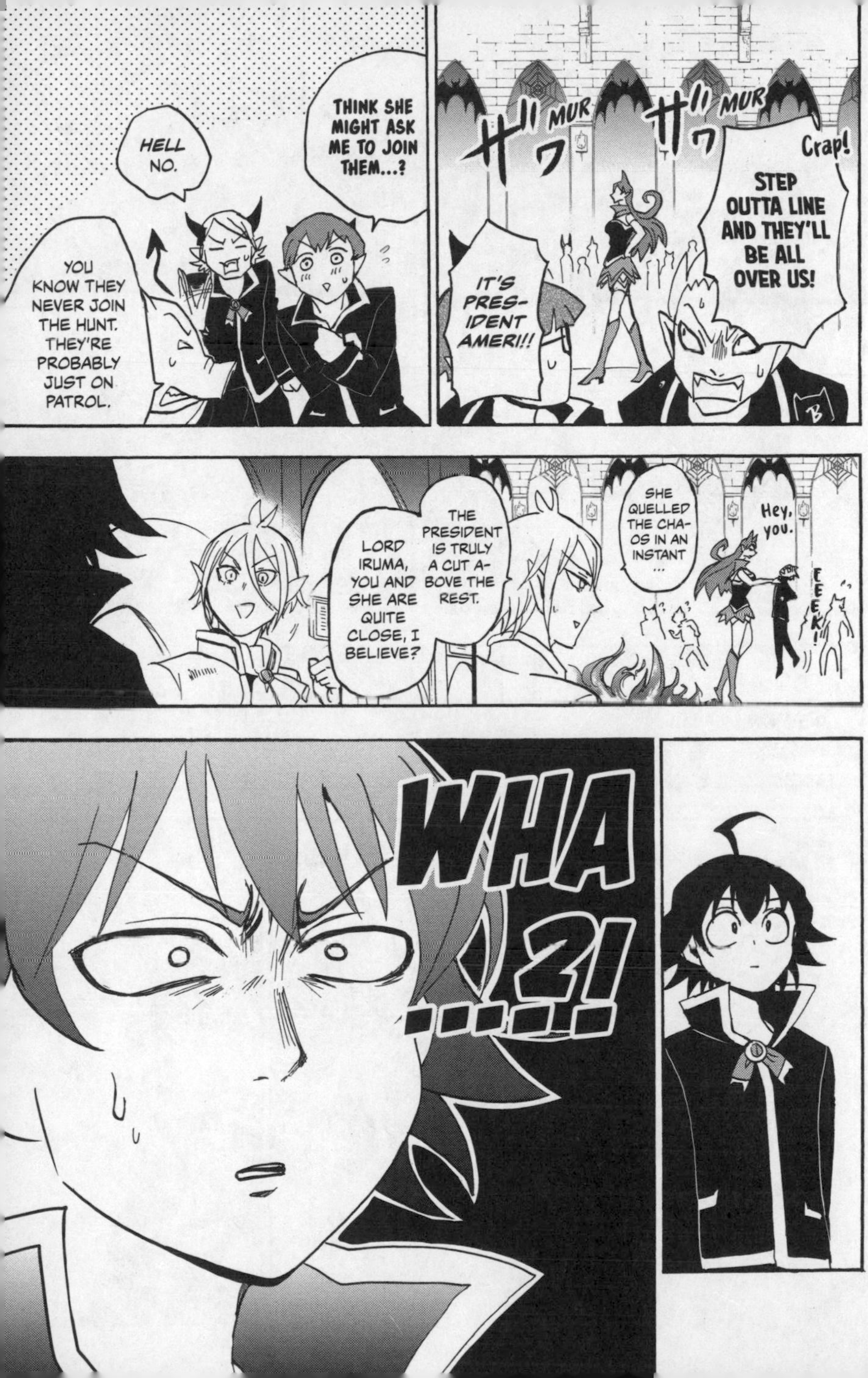

ザワ MUR
ザワ MUR
Crap!
STEP OUTTA LINE AND THEY'LL BE ALL OVER US!
IT'S PRES-IDENT AMERI!!!
THINK SHE MIGHT ASK ME TO JOIN THEM...?
HELL NO.
YOU KNOW THEY NEVER JOIN THE HUNT. THEY'RE PROBABLY JUST ON PATROL.
Hey, you.
EEEK!
SHE QUELLED THE CHA-OS IN AN INSTANT...
THE PRESIDENT IS TRULY A CUT A-BOVE THE REST.
LORD IRUMA, YOU AND SHE ARE QUITE CLOSE, I BELIEVE?
WHA...?!

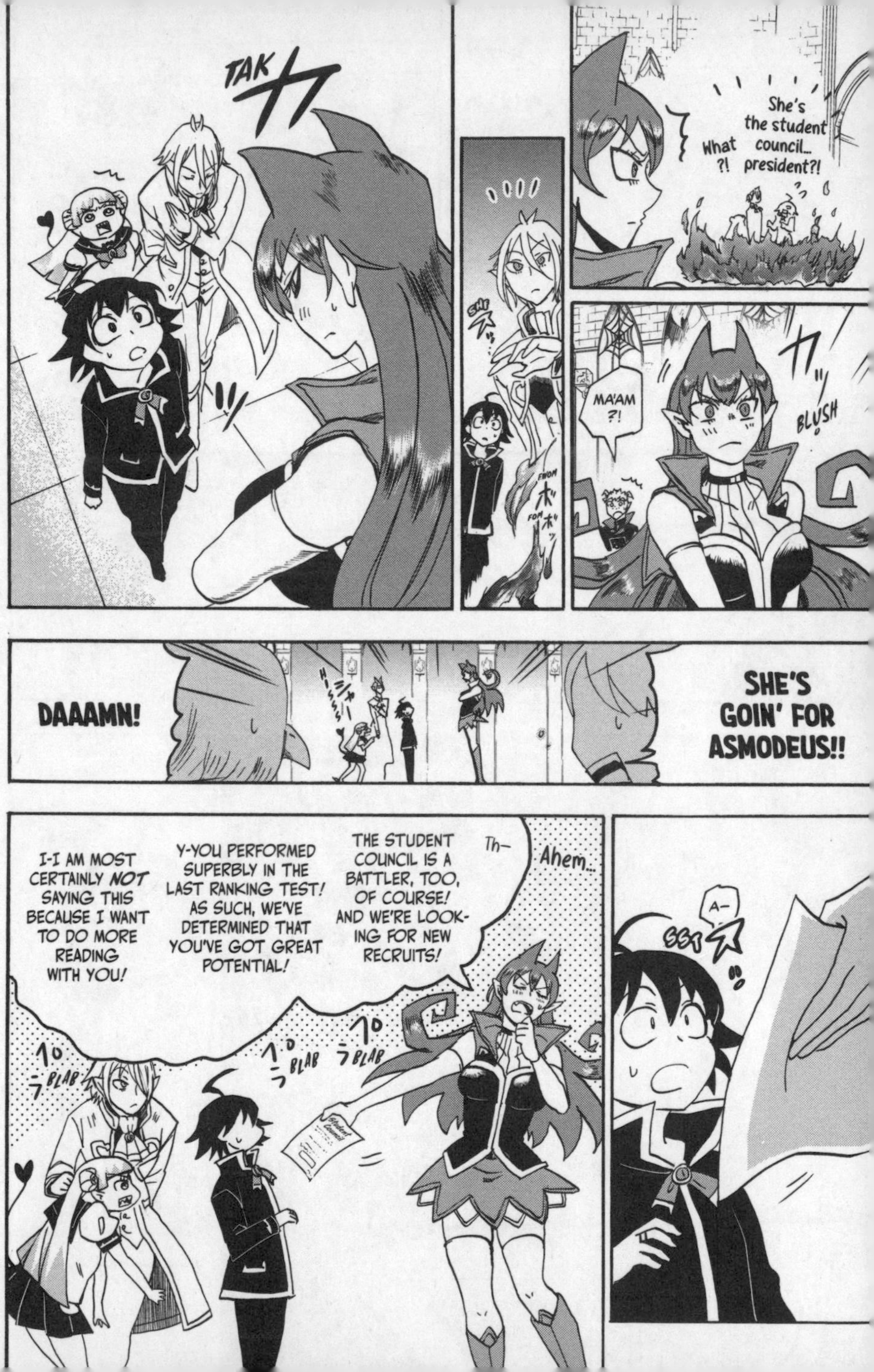
She's the student council... president?!
What ?!
MA'AM ?!
BLUSH
SHI
FWOM
FOM
TAK
SHE'S GOIN' FOR ASMODEUS!!
DAAAMN!
A–
Ahem...
Th–
THE STUDENT COUNCIL IS A BATTLER, TOO, OF COURSE! AND WE'RE LOOKING FOR NEW RECRUITS!
Y-YOU PERFORMED SUPERBLY IN THE LAST RANKING TEST! AS SUCH, WE'VE DETERMINED THAT YOU'VE GOT GREAT POTENTIAL!
I-I AM MOST CERTAINLY ***NOT*** SAYING THIS BECAUSE I WANT TO DO MORE READING WITH YOU!
BLAB
BLAB
BLAB
Student Council

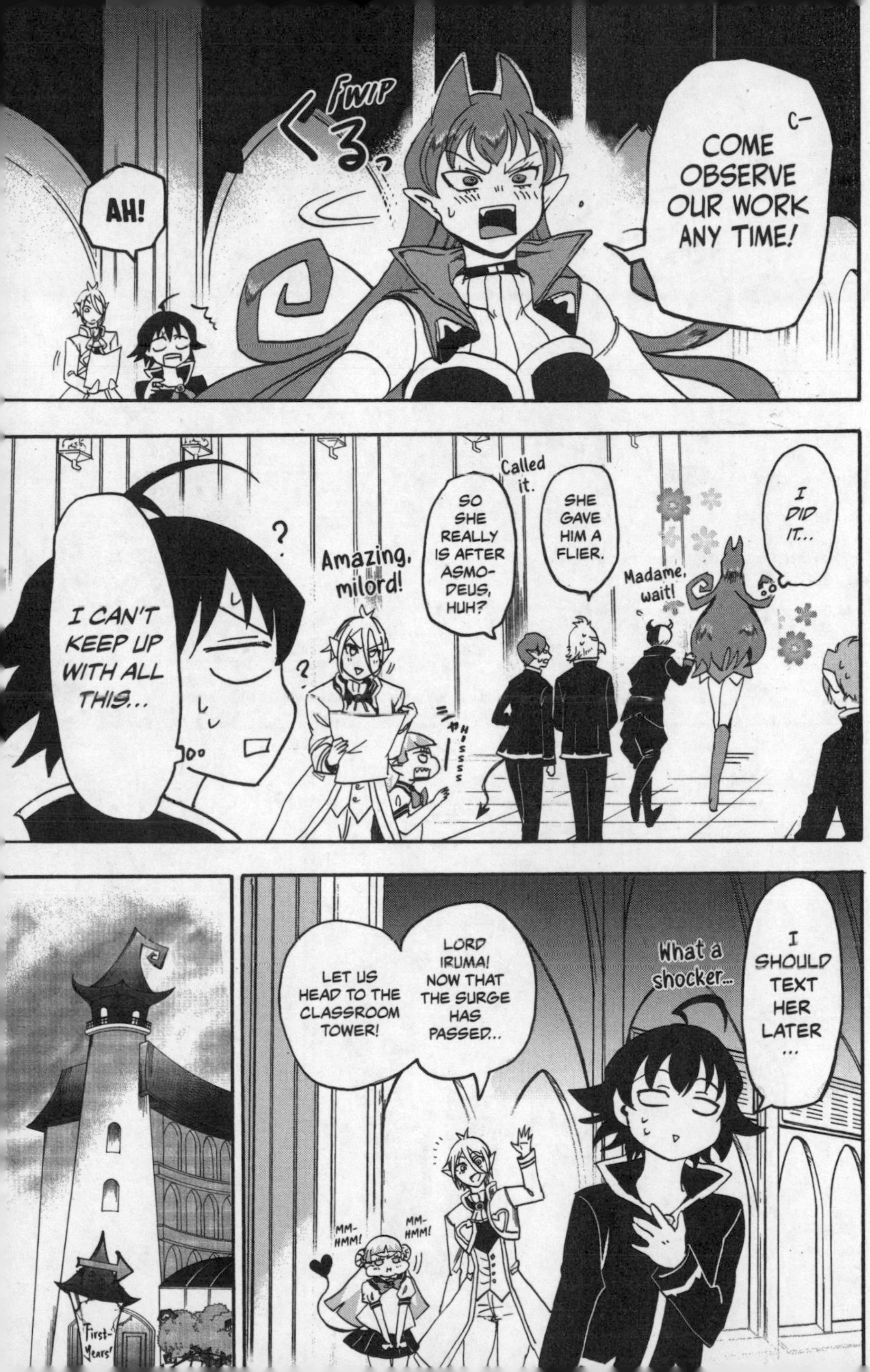
C—
COME OBSERVE OUR WORK ANY TIME!
FWIP
AH!
I DID IT...
Madame, wait!
SHE GAVE HIM A FLIER.
Called it.
SO SHE REALLY IS AFTER ASMODEUS, HUH?
Amazing, milord!
HISSSS
I CAN'T KEEP UP WITH ALL THIS...
I SHOULD TEXT HER LATER...
What a shocker...
LORD IRUMA! NOW THAT THE SURGE HAS PASSED...
LET US HEAD TO THE CLASSROOM TOWER!
MM-HMM!
MM-HMM!
First-Years'

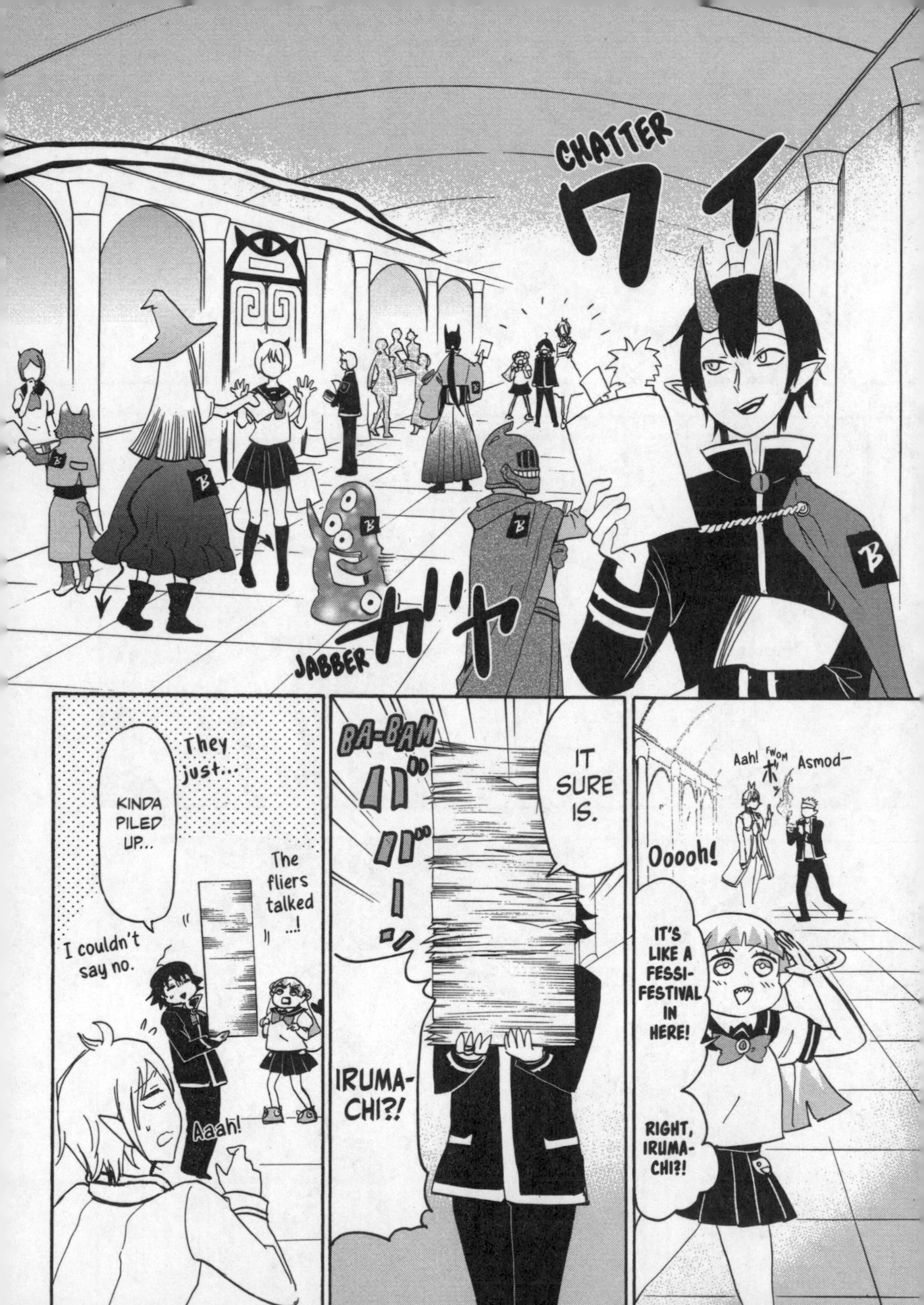
CHATTER
ワイ
ガヤ
JABBER
Aah!
FWOM
ボッ
Asmod-
Ooooh!
IT'S LIKE A FESSI-FESTIVAL IN HERE!
RIGHT, IRUMA-CHI?!
IT SURE IS.
BA-BAM
IRUMA-CHI?!
They just...
KINDA PILED UP...
I couldn't say no.
The fliers talked...!
Aaah!

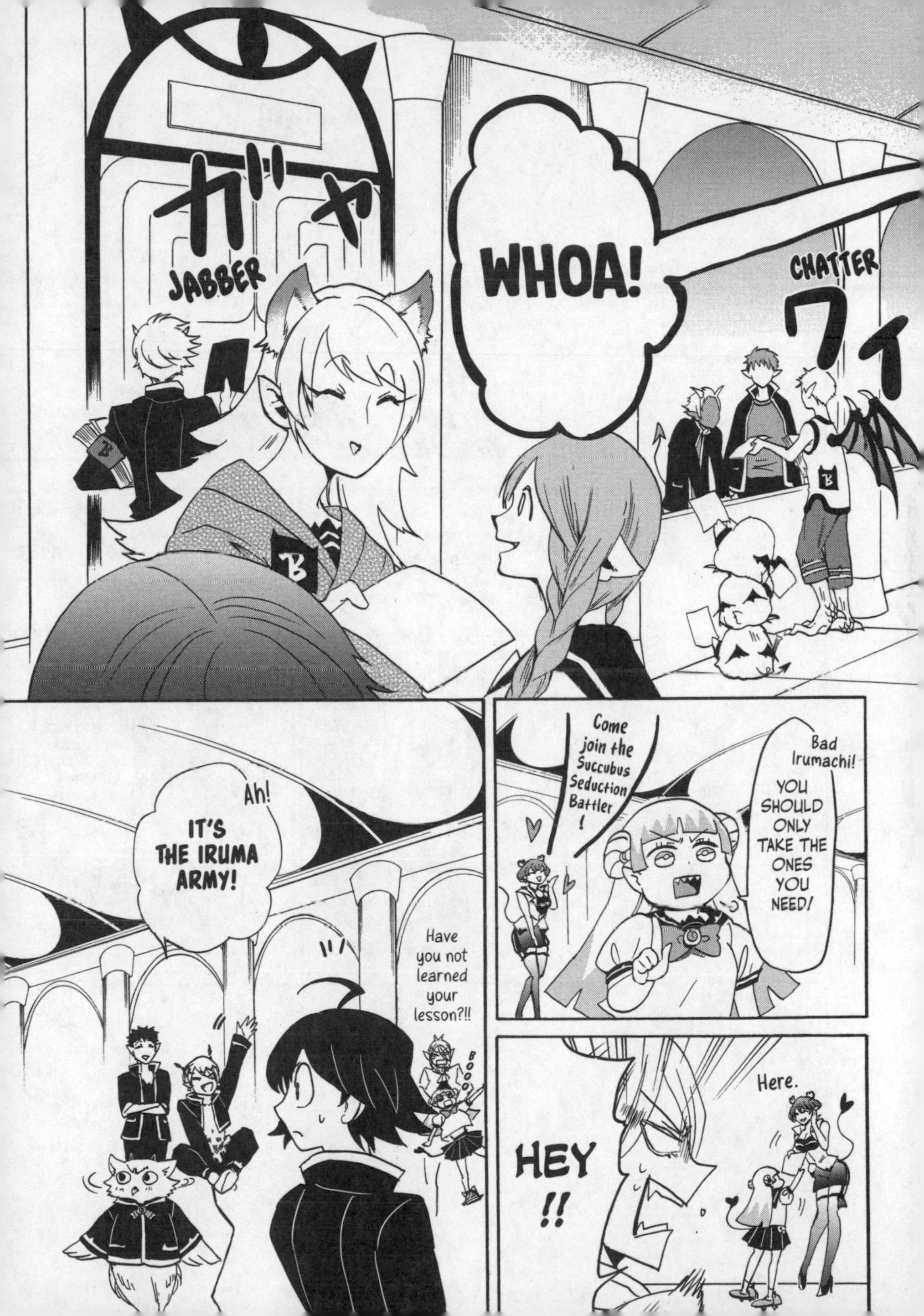
CHATTER
ワイ
WHOA!
ガヤ
JABBER
Bad Irumachi! YOU SHOULD ONLY TAKE THE ONES YOU NEED!
Come join the Succubus Seduction Battler!
Here.
HEY !!
Ah! IT'S THE IRUMA ARMY!
Have you not learned your lesson?!!
BOOO

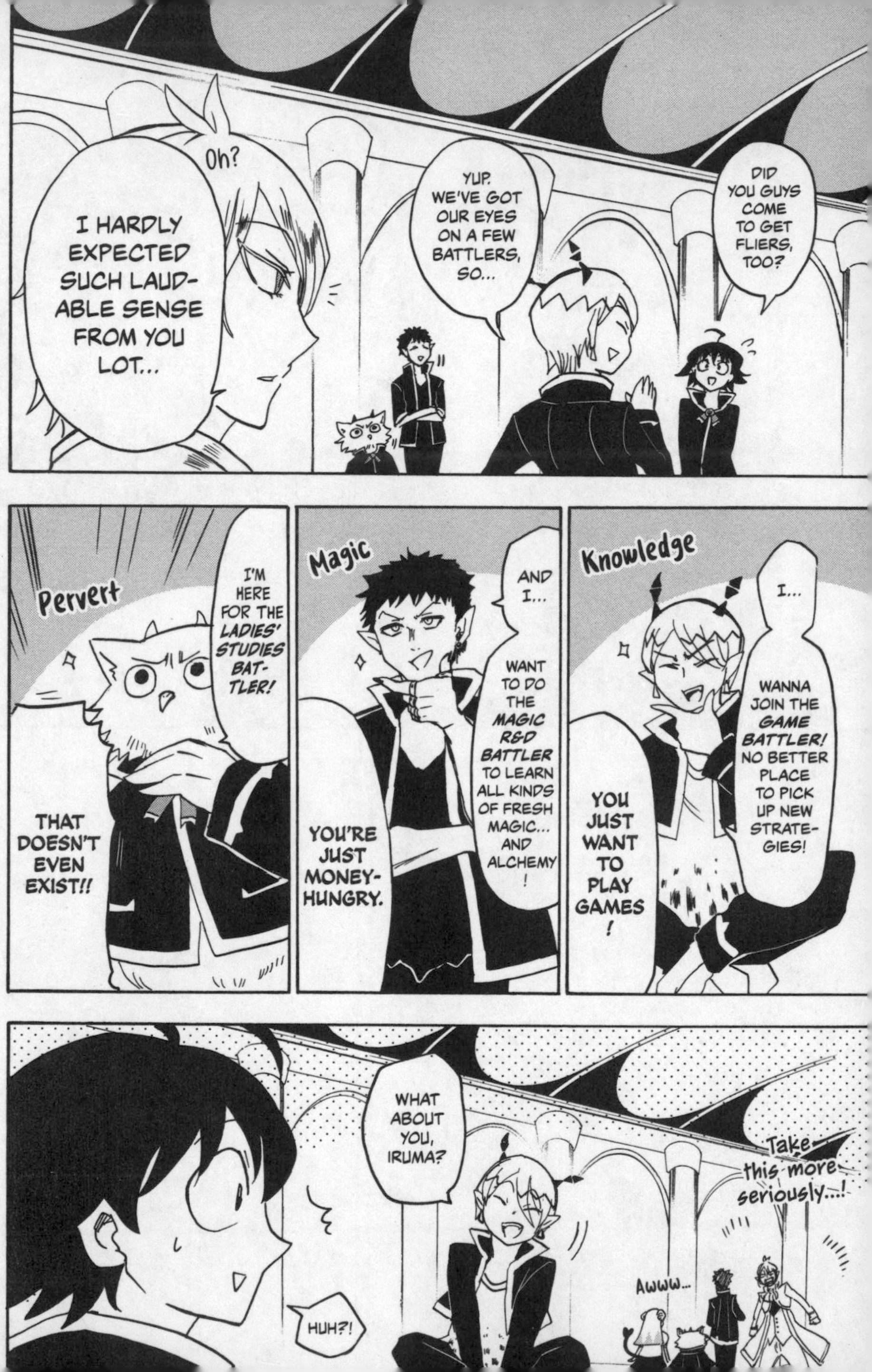
DID YOU GUYS COME TO GET FLIERS, TOO?
YUP. WE'VE GOT OUR EYES ON A FEW BATTLERS, SO...
Oh?
I HARDLY EXPECTED SUCH LAUD-ABLE SENSE FROM YOU LOT...
Knowledge
I...
WANNA JOIN THE GAME BATTLER! NO BETTER PLACE TO PICK UP NEW STRATE-GIES!
YOU JUST WANT TO PLAY GAMES!
Magic
AND I...
WANT TO DO THE MAGIC R&D BATTLER TO LEARN ALL KINDS OF FRESH MAGIC... AND ALCHEMY!
YOU'RE JUST MONEY-HUNGRY.
Pervert
I'M HERE FOR THE LADIES' STUDIES BAT-TLER!
THAT DOESN'T EVEN EXIST!!
WHAT ABOUT YOU, IRUMA?
Take this more seriously...!
Awww...
HUH?!

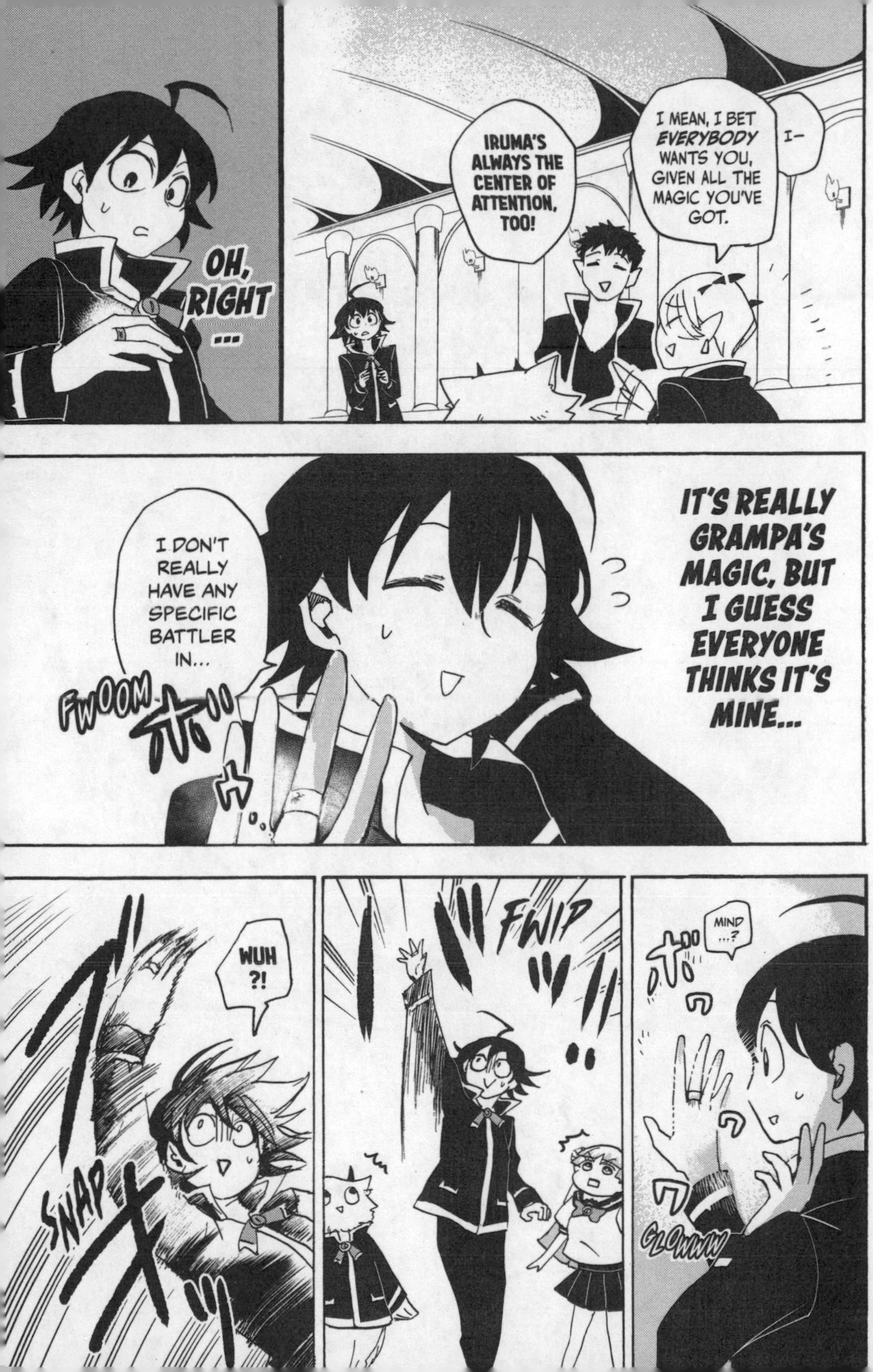
I—
I MEAN, I BET EVERYBODY WANTS YOU, GIVEN ALL THE MAGIC YOU'VE GOT.
IRUMA'S ALWAYS THE CENTER OF ATTENTION, TOO!
OH, RIGHT ...
IT'S REALLY GRAMPA'S MAGIC, BUT I GUESS EVERYONE THINKS IT'S MINE...
I DON'T REALLY HAVE ANY SPECIFIC BATTLER IN...
FWOOM
MIND ...?
GLOWWW
FWIP
WUH ?!
SNAP

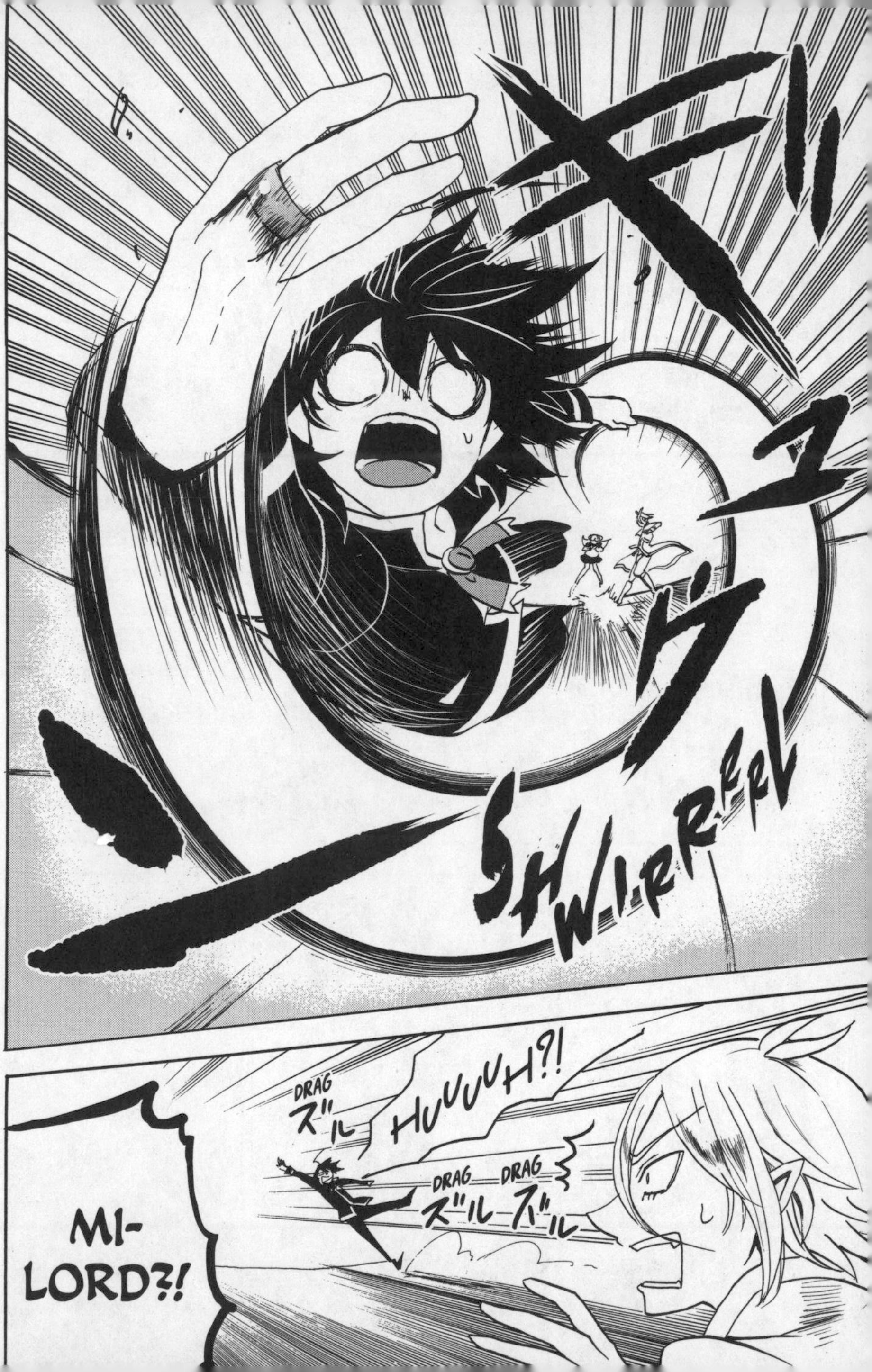
SHWIRRRRL
DRAG
ズル
HUUUUH?!
DRAG
ズル
DRAG
ズル
MI-
LORD?!

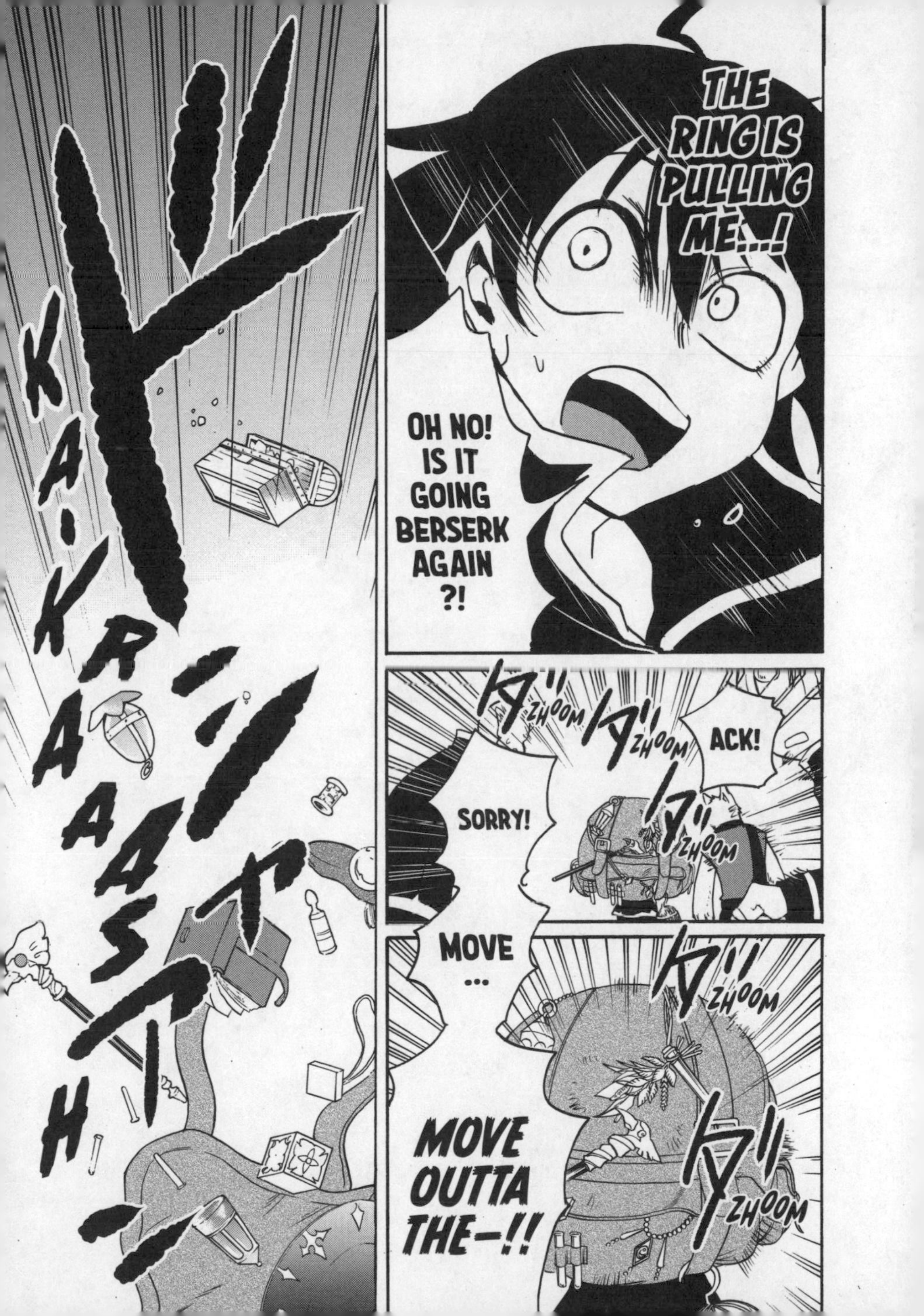
THE RING IS PULLING ME...!
OH NO! IS IT GOING BERSERK AGAIN?!
ACK!
ZHOOM
ZHOOM
ZHOOM
SORRY!
ZHOOM
MOVE ...
ZHOOM
MOVE OUTTA THE—!!
KA-KRAAAASH!

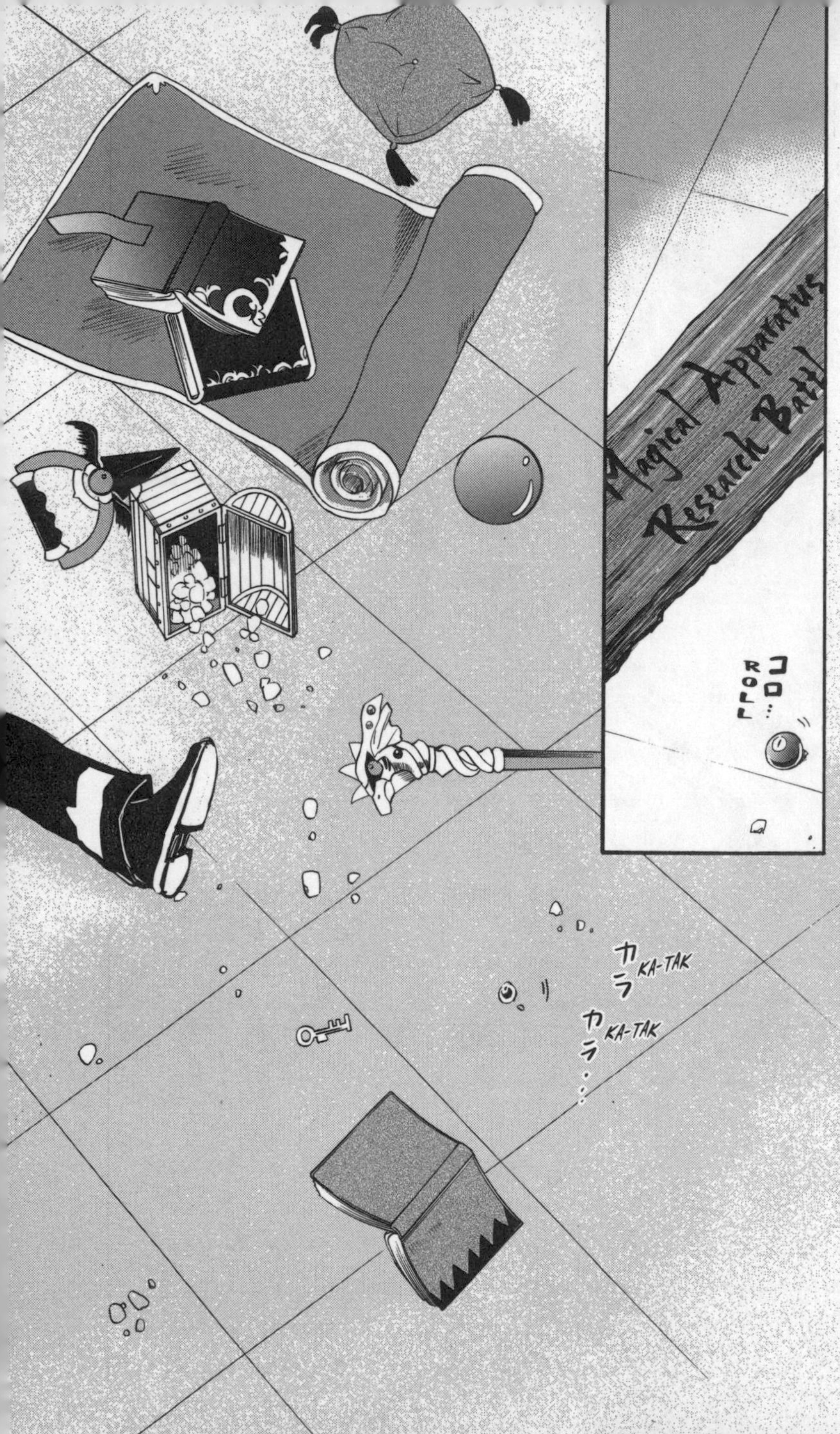
Magical Apparatus Research Batt
コロ… ROLL
カラ KA-TAK
カラ… KA-TAK

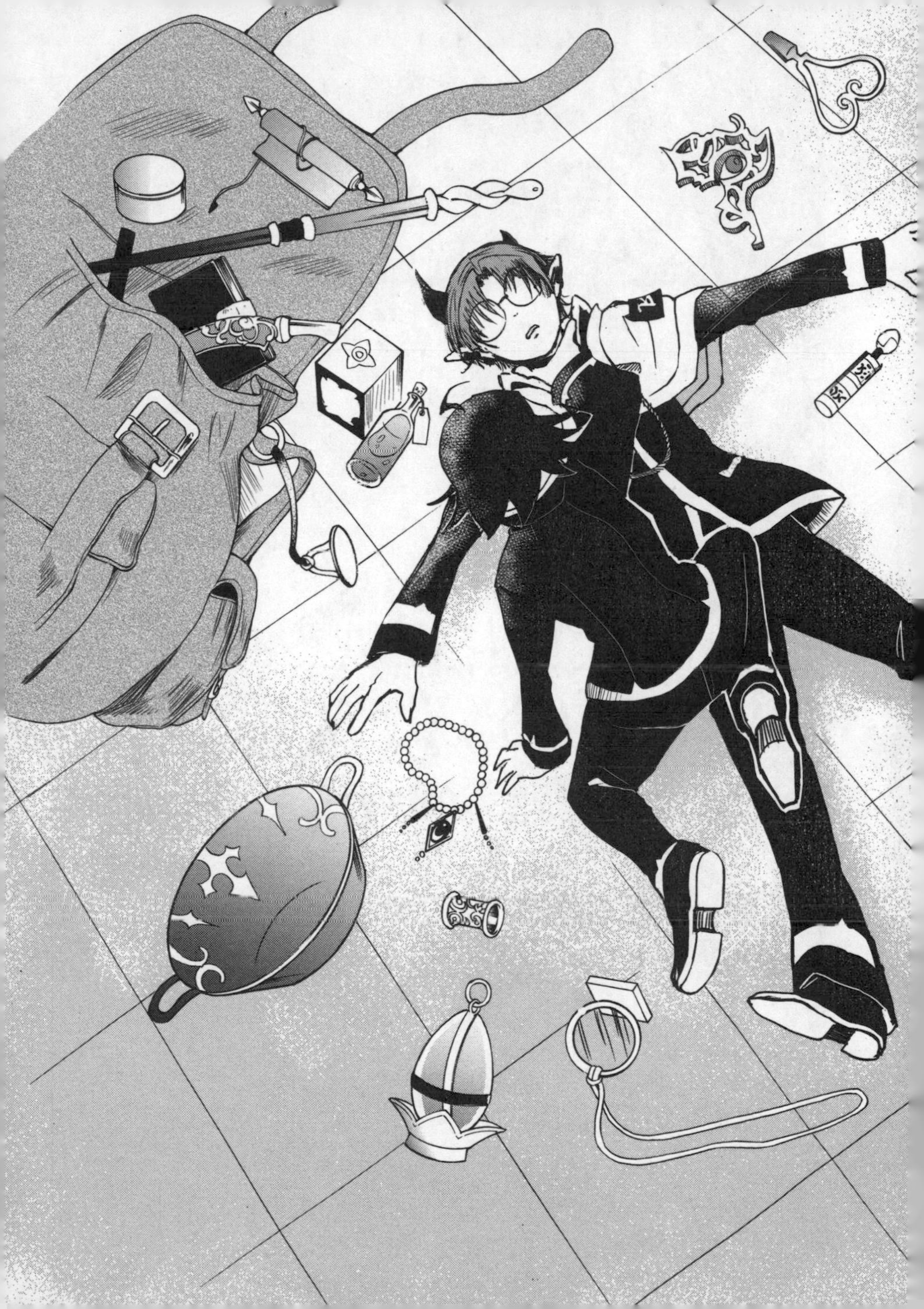

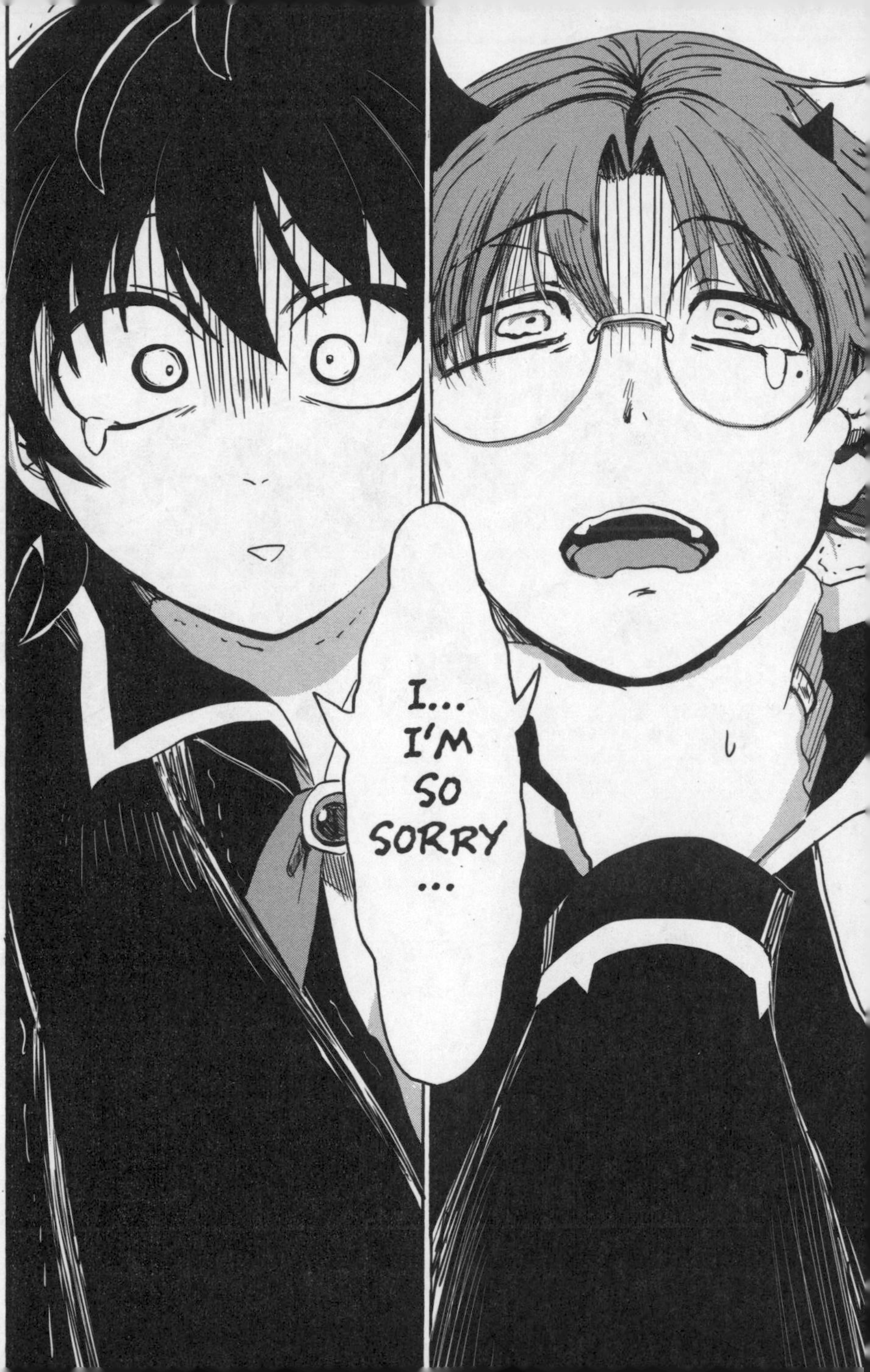
I... I'M SO SORRY ...

CHAPTER 20 THE DEMON WITH NO MAGIC

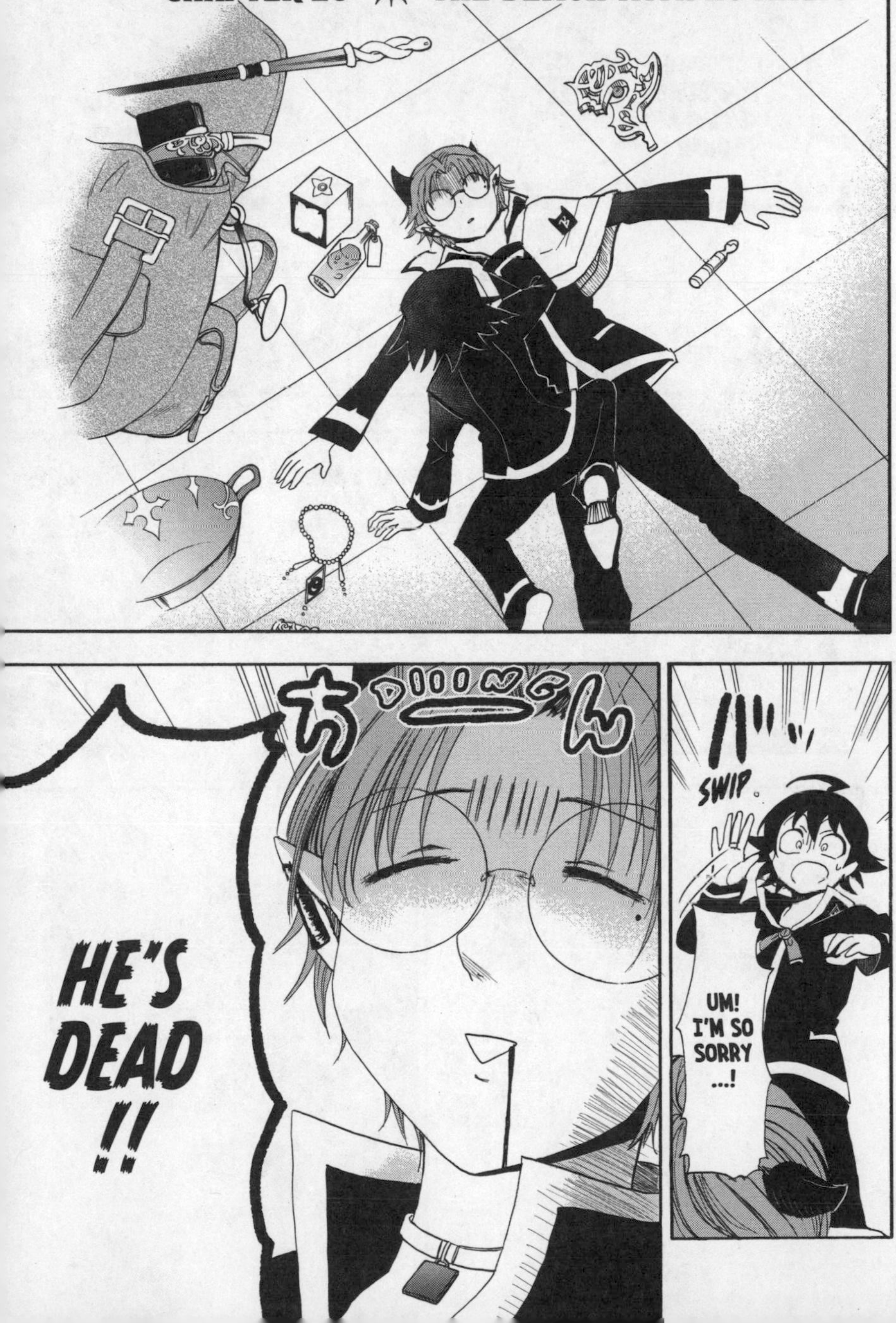
SWIP
UM! I'M SO SORRY ...!
DIIIING
HE'S DEAD !!

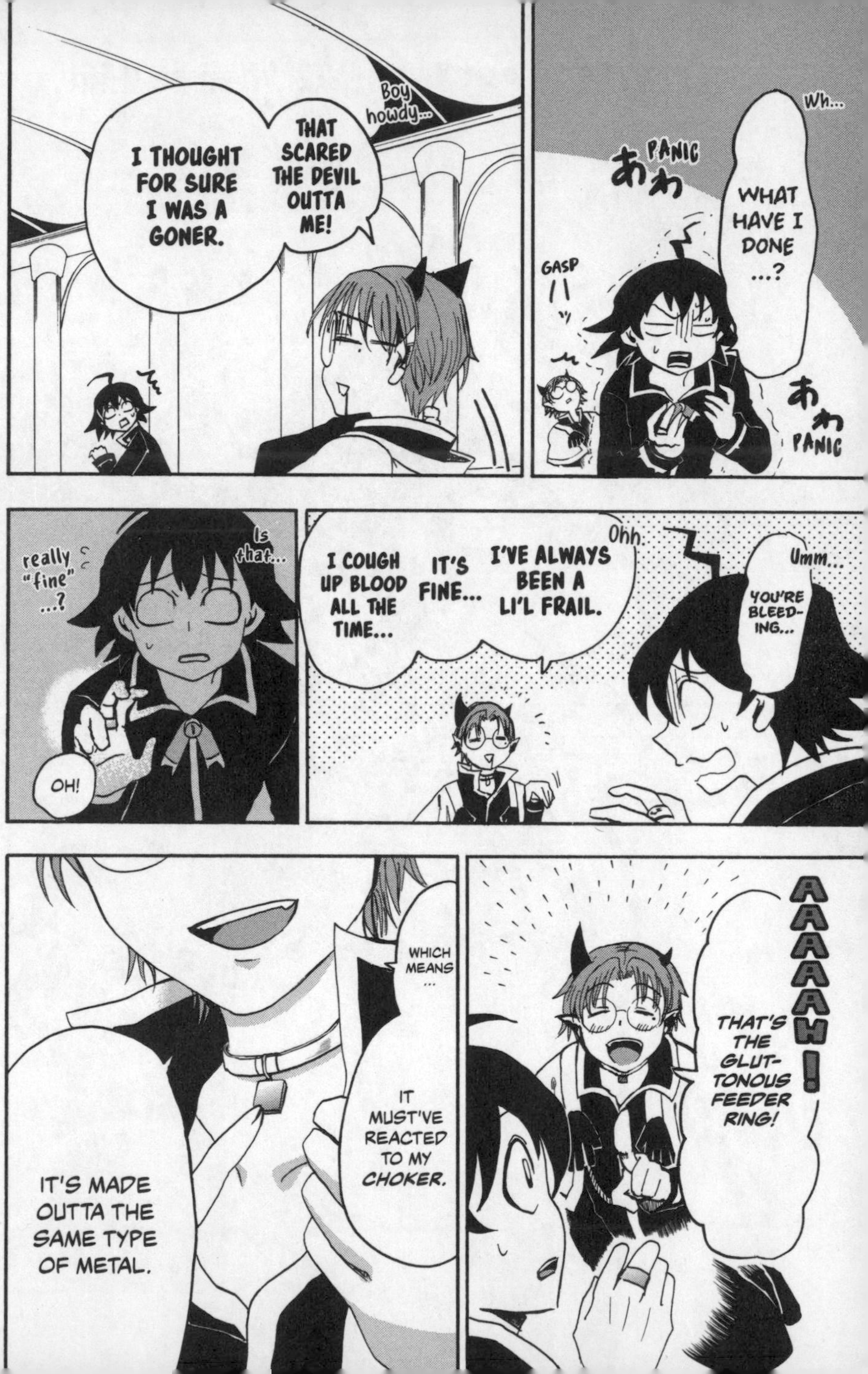
Wh...
WHAT HAVE I DONE ...?
あわ PANIC
GASP ハッ
あわ PANIC
Boy howdy...
THAT SCARED THE DEVIL OUTTA ME!
I THOUGHT FOR SURE I WAS A GONER.
Umm...
YOU'RE BLEED-ING...
Ohh.
I'VE ALWAYS BEEN A LI'L FRAIL.
IT'S FINE...
I COUGH UP BLOOD ALL THE TIME...
Is that...
really "fine" ...?
OH!
AAAAAAH!
THAT'S THE GLUT-TONOUS FEEDER RING!
WHICH MEANS ...
IT MUST'VE REACTED TO MY CHOKER.
IT'S MADE OUTTA THE SAME TYPE OF METAL.

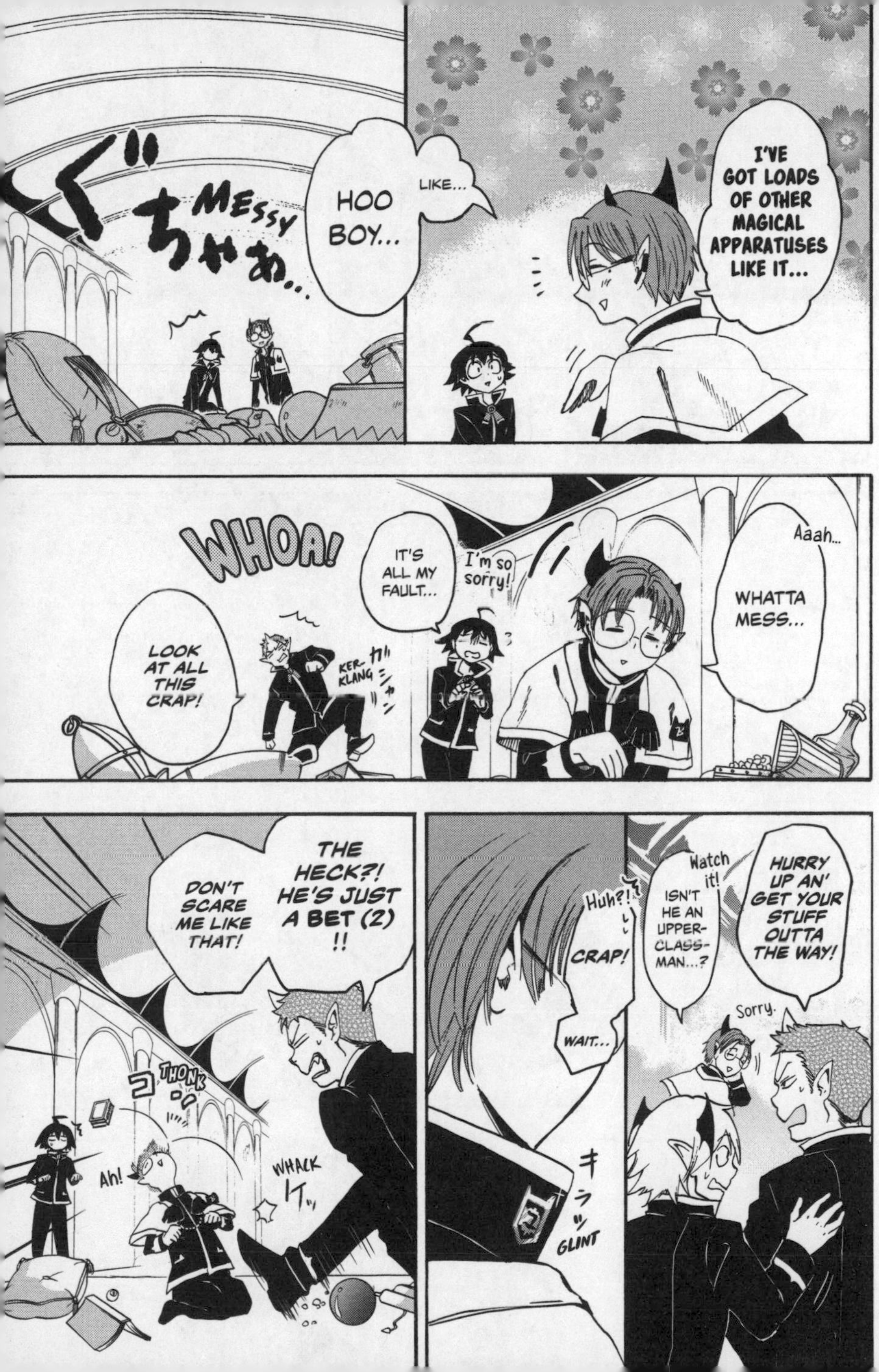

I'VE GOT LOADS OF OTHER MAGICAL APPARATUSES LIKE IT...
HOO BOY...
LIKE...
ぐちゃあ...
MESSY
Aaah...
WHATTA MESS...
I'm so sorry!
IT'S ALL MY FAULT...
KER-KLANG
LOOK AT ALL THIS CRAP!
WHOA!
HURRY UP AN' GET YOUR STUFF OUTTA THE WAY!
Watch it!
Sorry.
ISN'T HE AN UPPER-CLASSMAN...?
Huh?!
CRAP!
WAIT...
キラッ
GLINT
THE HECK?! HE'S JUST A BET (2) !!
DON'T SCARE ME LIKE THAT!
THONK
WHACK
Ah!

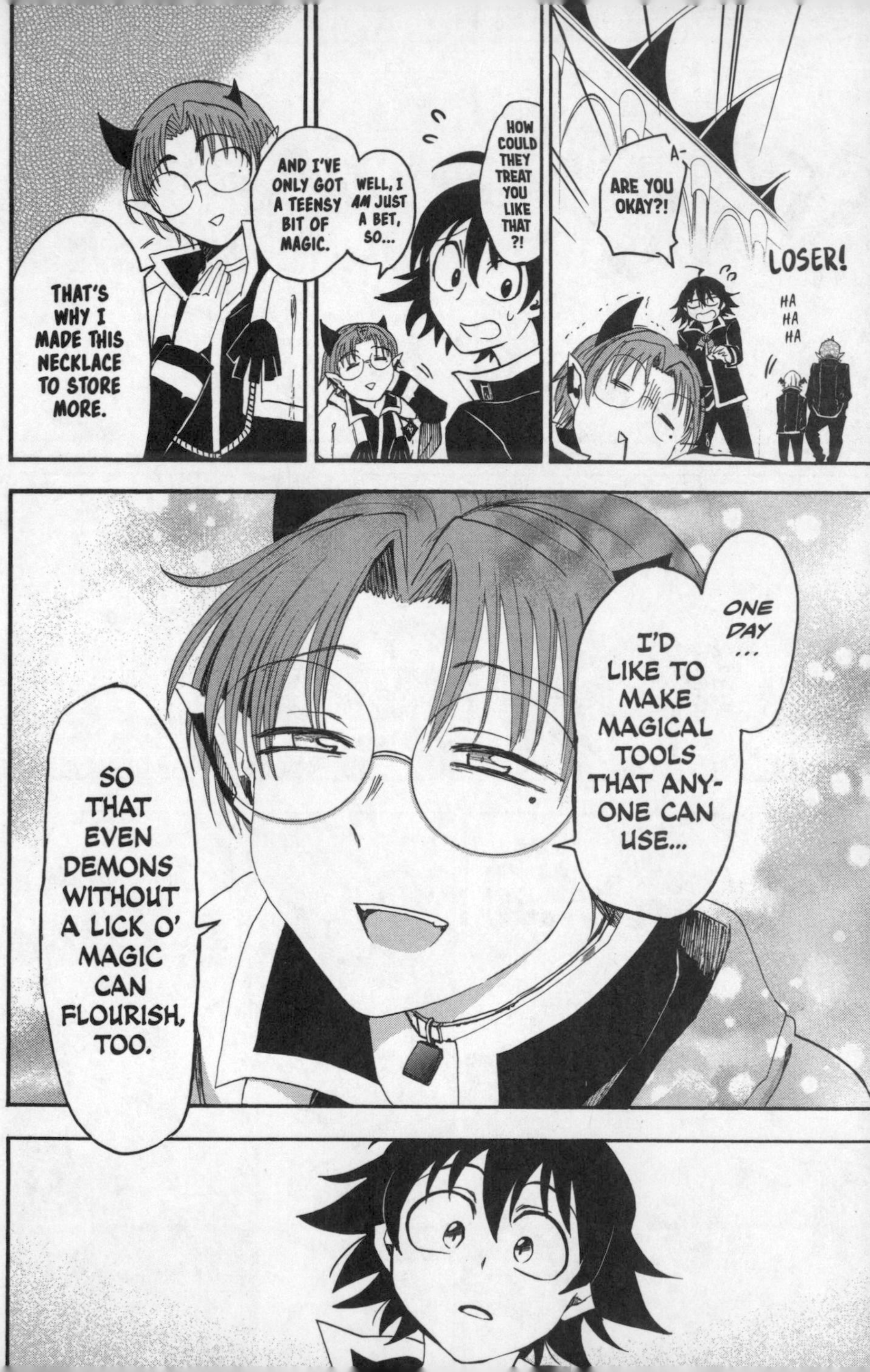
A-
ARE YOU OKAY?!
LOSER!
HA HA HA
HOW COULD THEY TREAT YOU LIKE THAT?!
WELL, I AM JUST A BET, SO...
AND I'VE ONLY GOT A TEENSY BIT OF MAGIC.
THAT'S WHY I MADE THIS NECKLACE TO STORE MORE.
ONE DAY...
I'D LIKE TO MAKE MAGICAL TOOLS THAT ANY-ONE CAN USE...
SO THAT EVEN DEMONS WITHOUT A LICK O' MAGIC CAN FLOURISH, TOO.

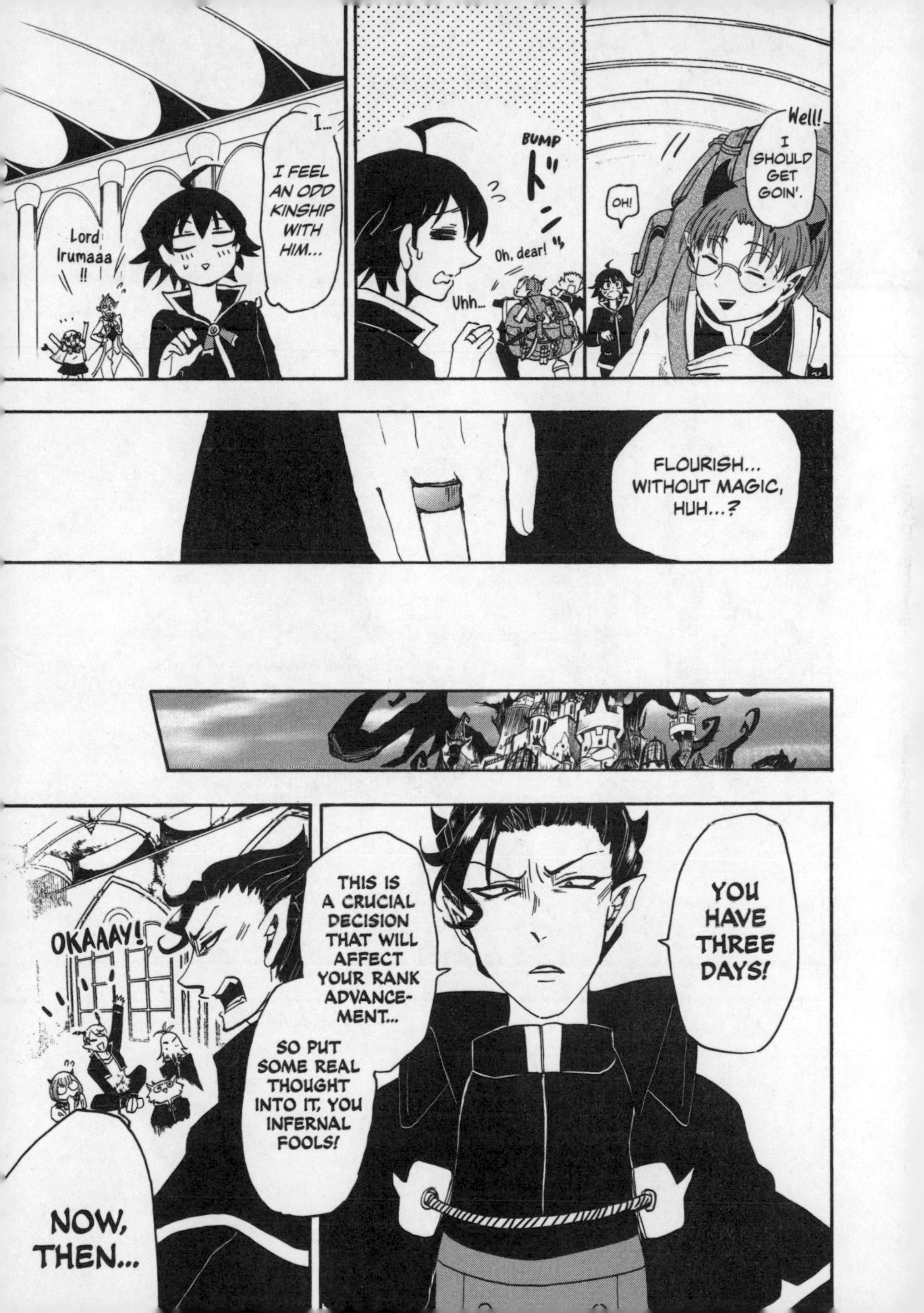
Well! I SHOULD GET GOIN'.
OH!
BUMP
ド
Oh, dear!
Uhh...
I...
I FEEL AN ODD KINSHIP WITH HIM...
Lord Irumaaa !!
FLOURISH... WITHOUT MAGIC, HUH...?
YOU HAVE THREE DAYS!
THIS IS A CRUCIAL DECISION THAT WILL AFFECT YOUR RANK ADVANCE-MENT...
SO PUT SOME REAL THOUGHT INTO IT, YOU INFERNAL FOOLS!
OKAAAY!
NOW, THEN...

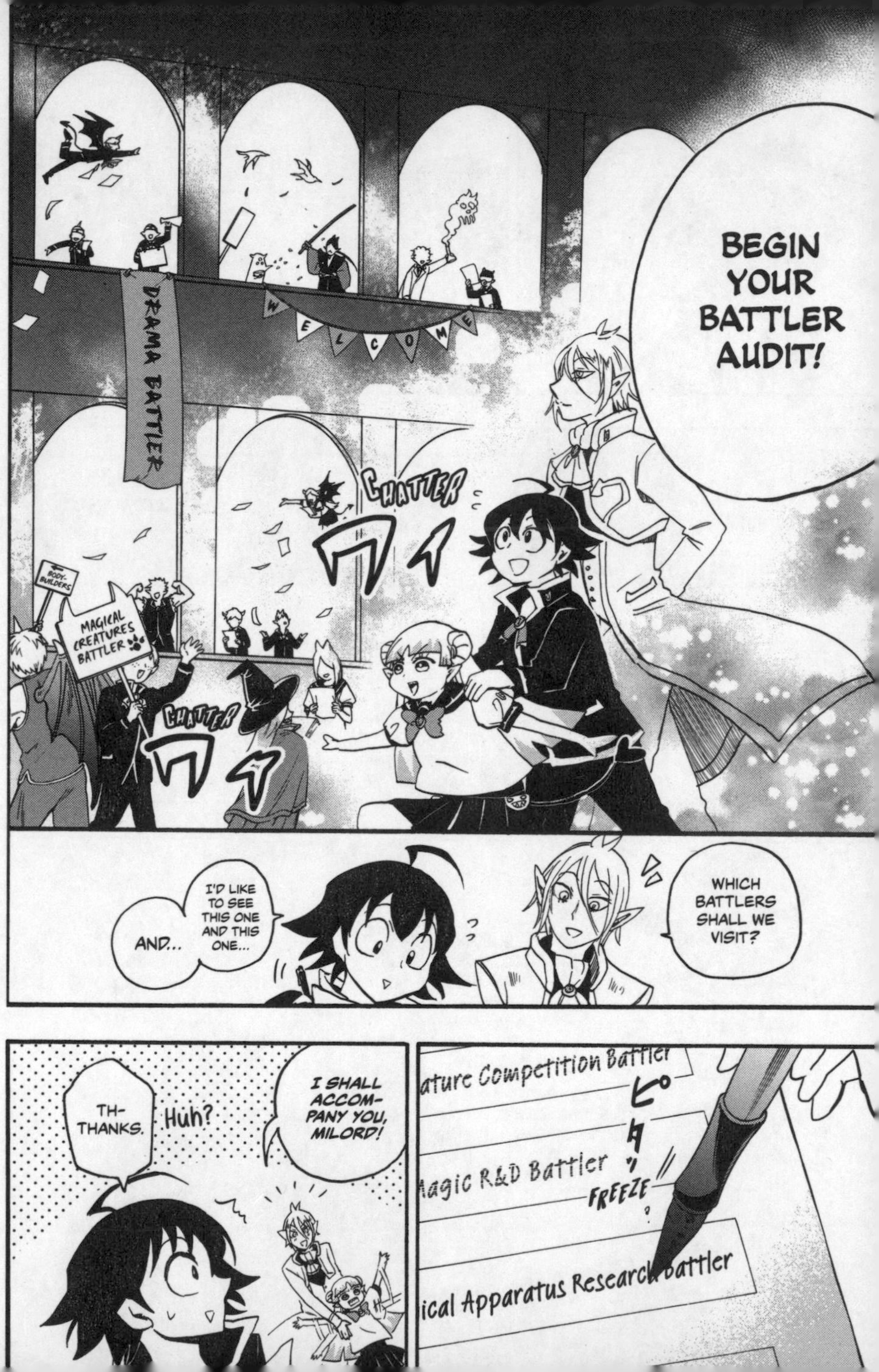
BEGIN YOUR BATTLER AUDIT!
WELCOME
DRAMA BATTLER
CHATTER
ワイ
BODY-BUILDERS
MAGICAL CREATURES BATTLER
CHATTER
ワイ
WHICH BATTLERS SHALL WE VISIT?
I'D LIKE TO SEE THIS ONE AND THIS ONE...
AND...
ature Competition Battler
Magic R&D Battler
ピタッ
FREEZE
ical Apparatus Research Battler
I SHALL ACCOMPANY YOU, MILORD!
Huh?
TH- THANKS.

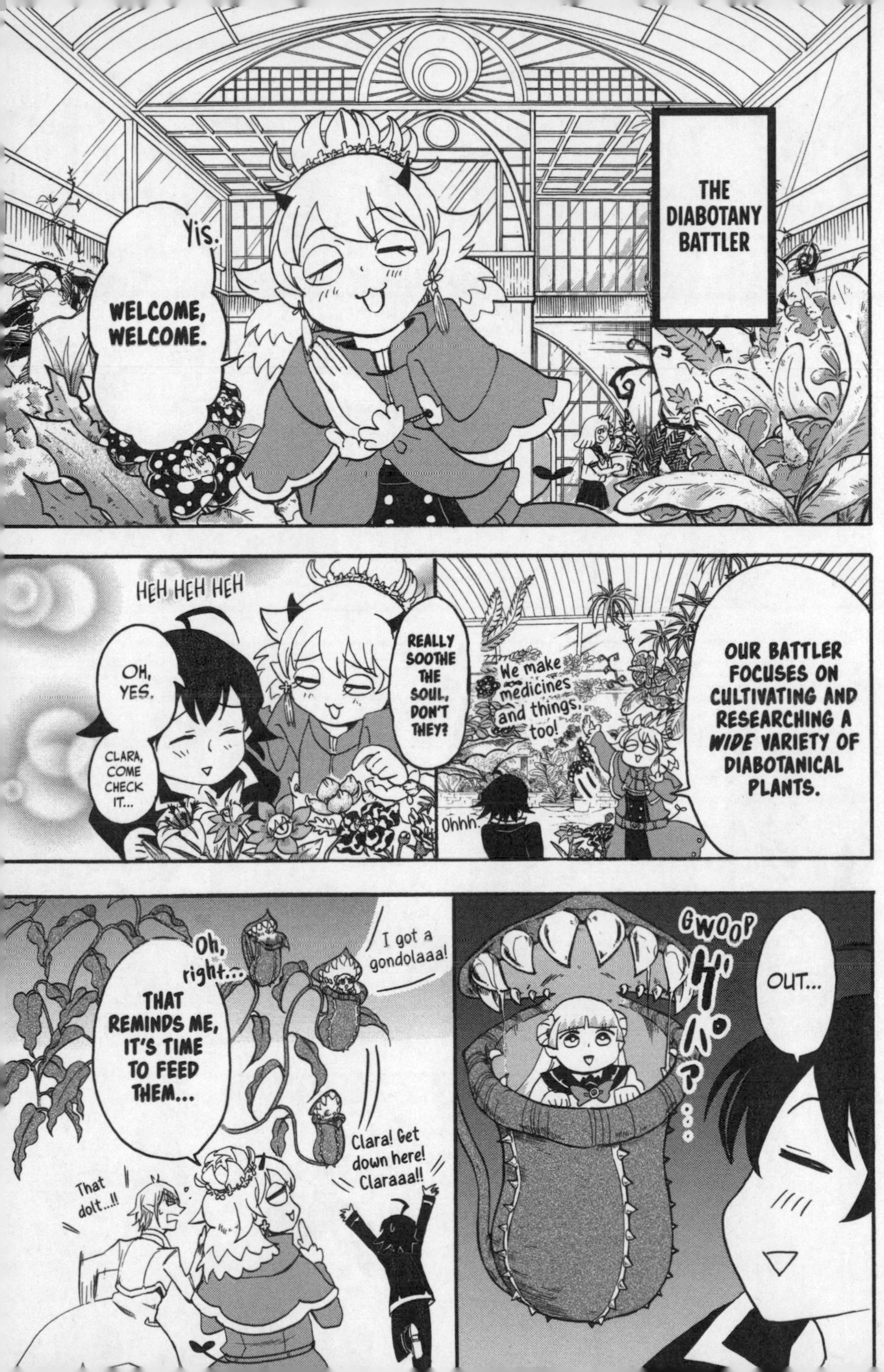
THE DIABOTANY BATTLER
Yis.
WELCOME, WELCOME.
OUR BATTLER FOCUSES ON CULTIVATING AND RESEARCHING A *WIDE* VARIETY OF DIABOTANICAL PLANTS.
We make medicines and things, too!
Ohhh.
HEH HEH HEH
REALLY SOOTHE THE SOUL, DON'T THEY?
OH, YES.
CLARA, COME CHECK IT...
GWOOP
ゴパァ...
OUT...
I got a gondolaaa!
Oh, right...
THAT REMINDS ME, IT'S TIME TO FEED THEM...
Clara! Get down here! Claraaa!!
That dolt...!!

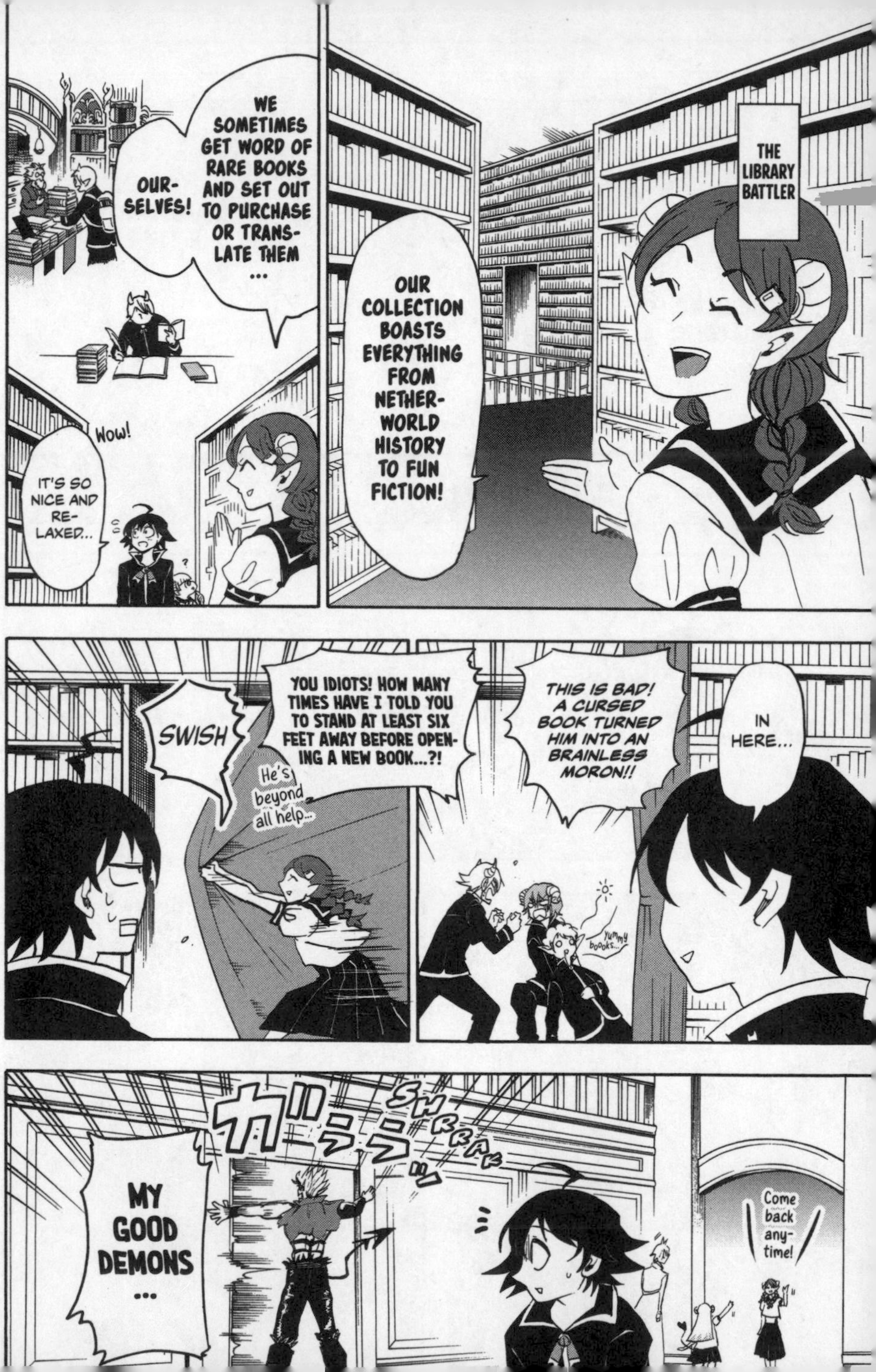
THE LIBRARY BATTLER
OUR COLLECTION BOASTS EVERYTHING FROM NETHER-WORLD HISTORY TO FUN FICTION!
WE SOMETIMES GET WORD OF RARE BOOKS AND SET OUT TO PURCHASE OR TRANS-LATE THEM ...
OUR-SELVES!
WOW!
IT'S SO NICE AND RE-LAXED...
IN HERE...
THIS IS BAD! A CURSED BOOK TURNED HIM INTO AN BRAINLESS MORON!!
yummy boooks...
YOU IDIOTS! HOW MANY TIMES HAVE I TOLD YOU TO STAND AT LEAST SIX FEET AWAY BEFORE OPEN-ING A NEW BOOK...?!
He's beyond all help...
SWISH
Come back any-time!
SHRRAK
MY GOOD DEMONS ...

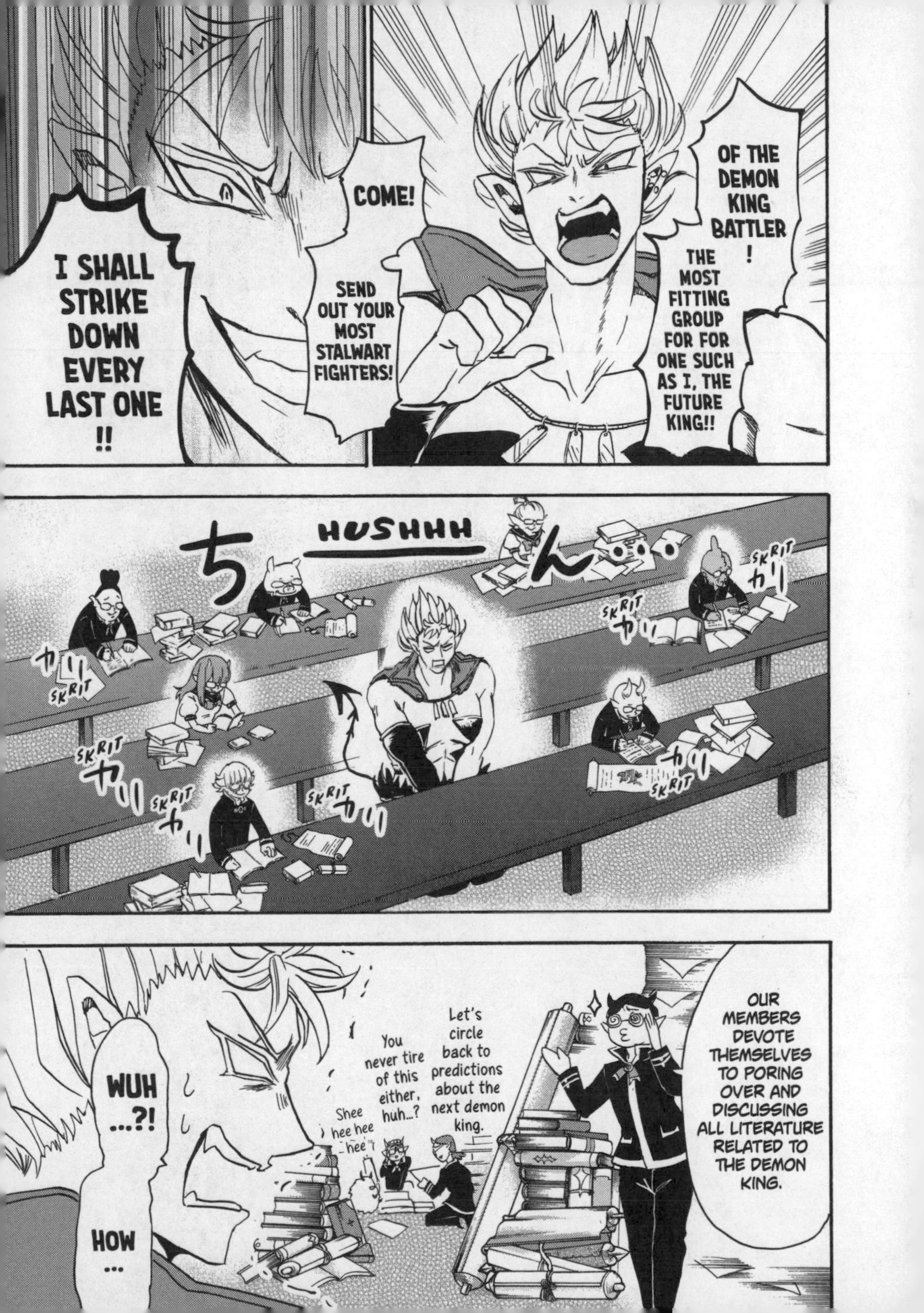
OF THE DEMON KING BATTLER!
THE MOST FITTING GROUP FOR FOR ONE SUCH AS I, THE FUTURE KING!!
COME!
SEND OUT YOUR MOST STALWART FIGHTERS!
I SHALL STRIKE DOWN EVERY LAST ONE!!
ち HUSHHH ん
SKRIT カリ
SKRIT カリ
SKRIT カリ
SKRIT カリ
SKRIT カリ
SKRIT カリ
SKRIT カリ
OUR MEMBERS DEVOTE THEMSELVES TO PORING OVER AND DISCUSSING ALL LITERATURE RELATED TO THE DEMON KING.
Let's circle back to predictions about the next demon king.
You never tire of this either, huh...?
Shee hee hee hee
WUH ...?!
HOW ...

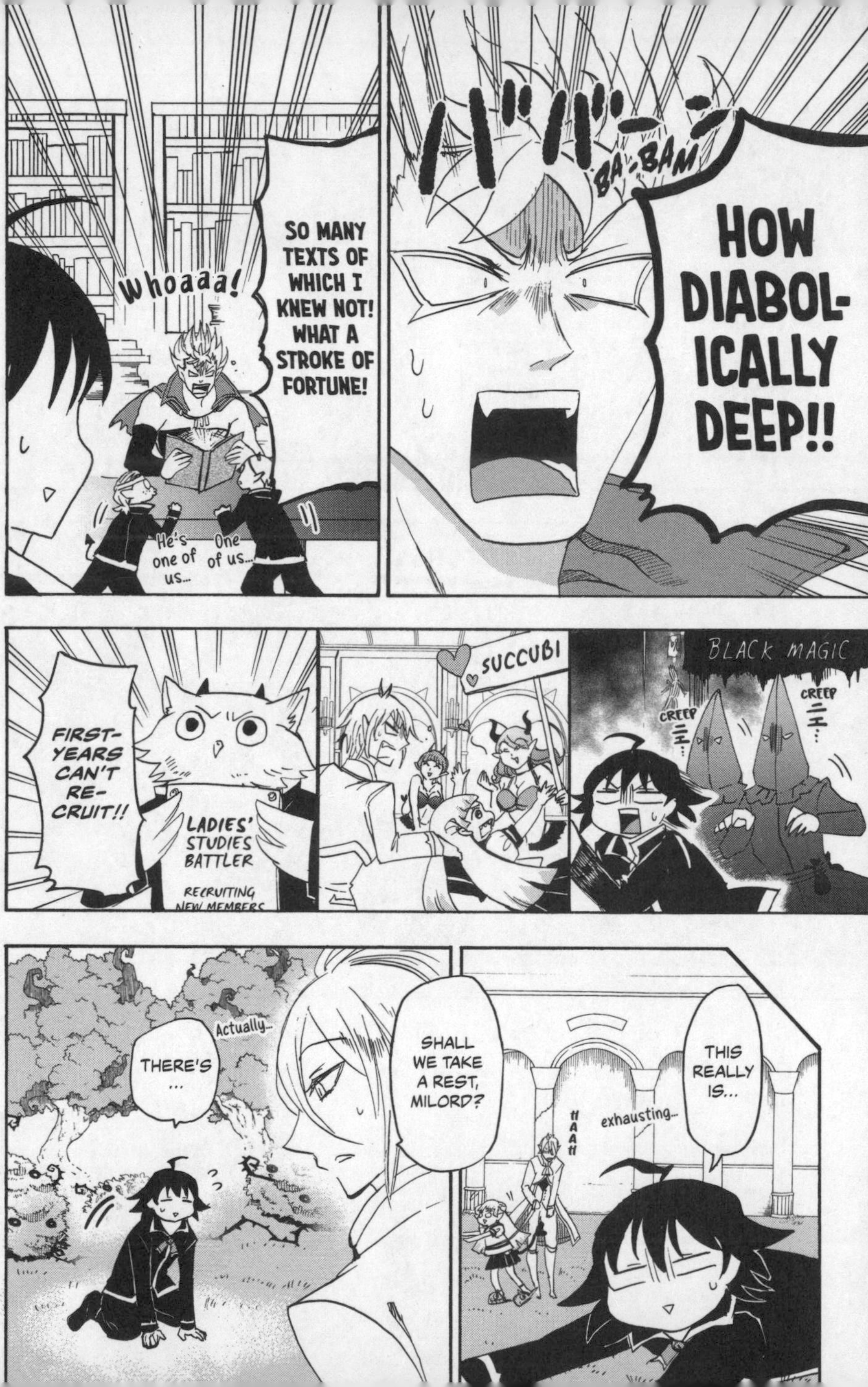
BA-BAM
HOW DIABOLICALLY DEEP!!
SO MANY TEXTS OF WHICH I KNEW NOT! WHAT A STROKE OF FORTUNE!
Whoaaa!
One of us...
He's one of us...
BLACK MAGIC
CREEP
CREEP
SUCCUBI
FIRST-YEARS CAN'T RE-CRUIT!!
LADIES' STUDIES BATTLER
RECRUITING NEW MEMBERS
THIS REALLY IS...
exhausting...
SHALL WE TAKE A REST, MILORD?
Actually...
THERE'S ...

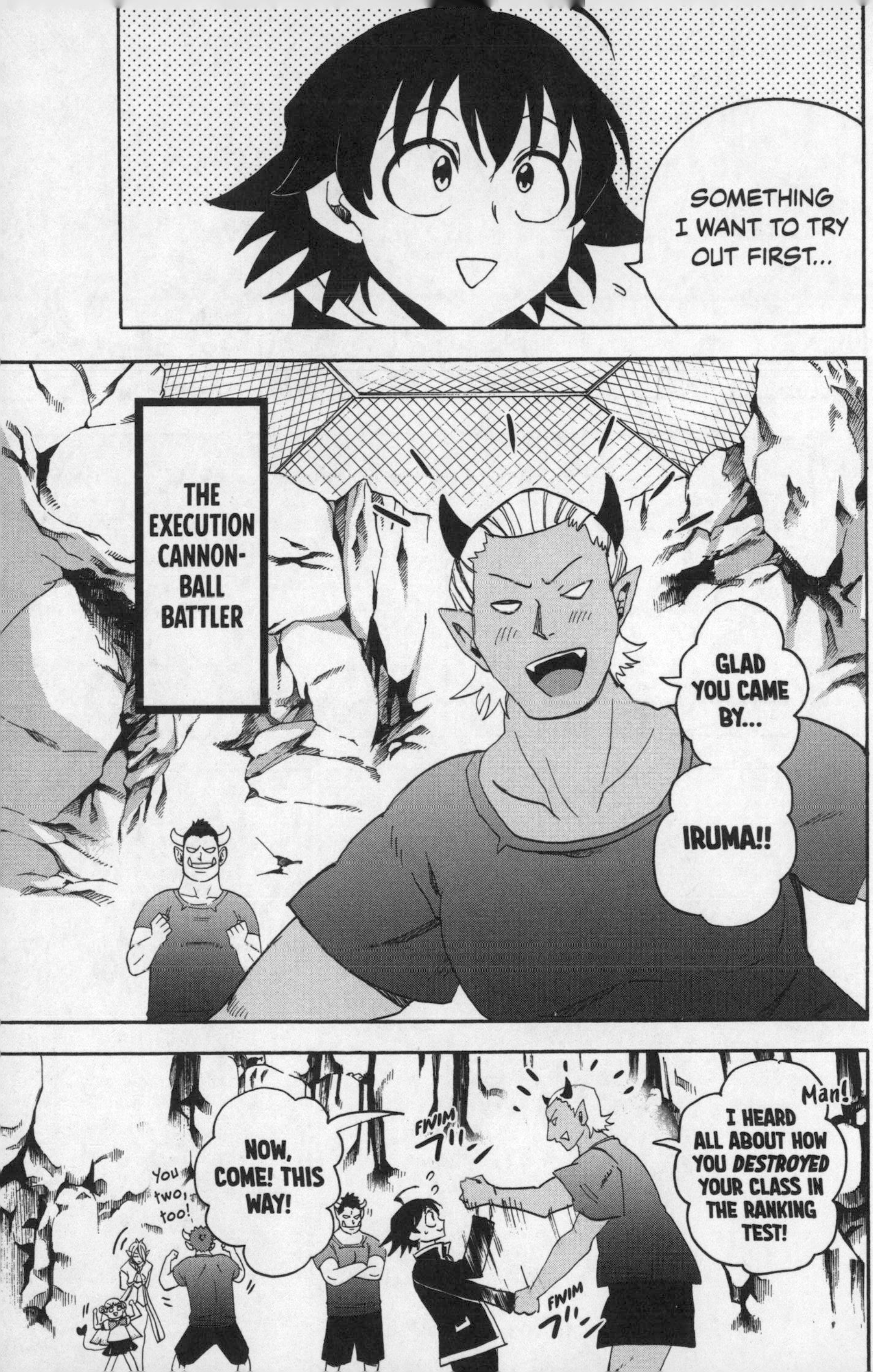
SOMETHING I WANT TO TRY OUT FIRST...
THE EXECUTION CANNON-BALL BATTLER
GLAD YOU CAME BY...
IRUMA!!
Man!
I HEARD ALL ABOUT HOW YOU *DESTROYED* YOUR CLASS IN THE RANKING TEST!
FWIM
NOW, COME! THIS WAY!
You two, too!
FWIM

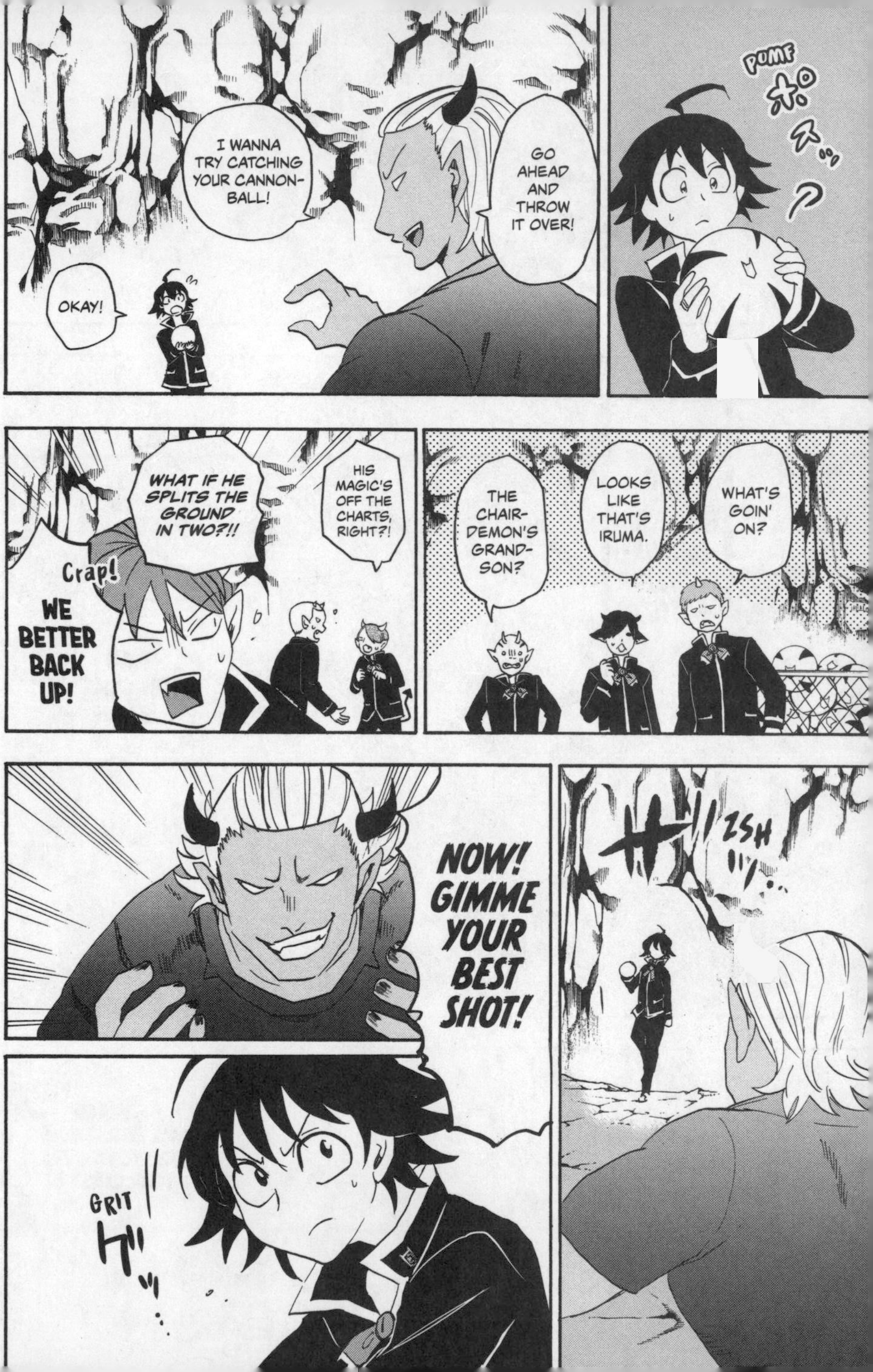
POMF
GO AHEAD AND THROW IT OVER!
I WANNA TRY CATCHING YOUR CANNON-BALL!
OKAY!
WHAT'S GOIN' ON?
LOOKS LIKE THAT'S IRUMA.
THE CHAIR-DEMON'S GRANDSON?
HIS MAGIC'S OFF THE CHARTS, RIGHT?!
WHAT IF HE SPLITS THE GROUND IN TWO?!!
Crap!
WE BETTER BACK UP!
ZSH
NOW! GIMME YOUR BEST SHOT!
GRIT

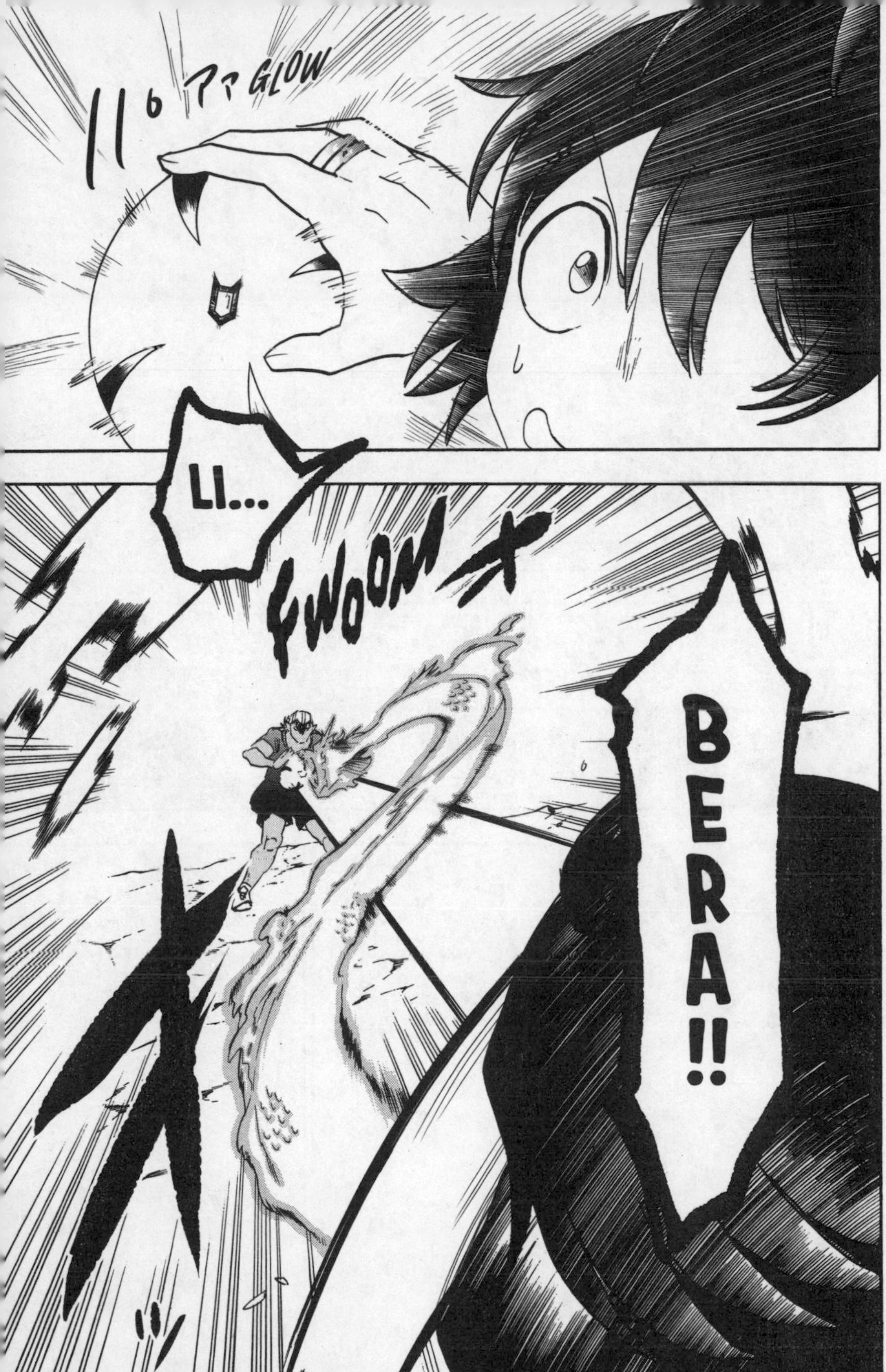
GLOW
LI...
BERA!!
FWOOM

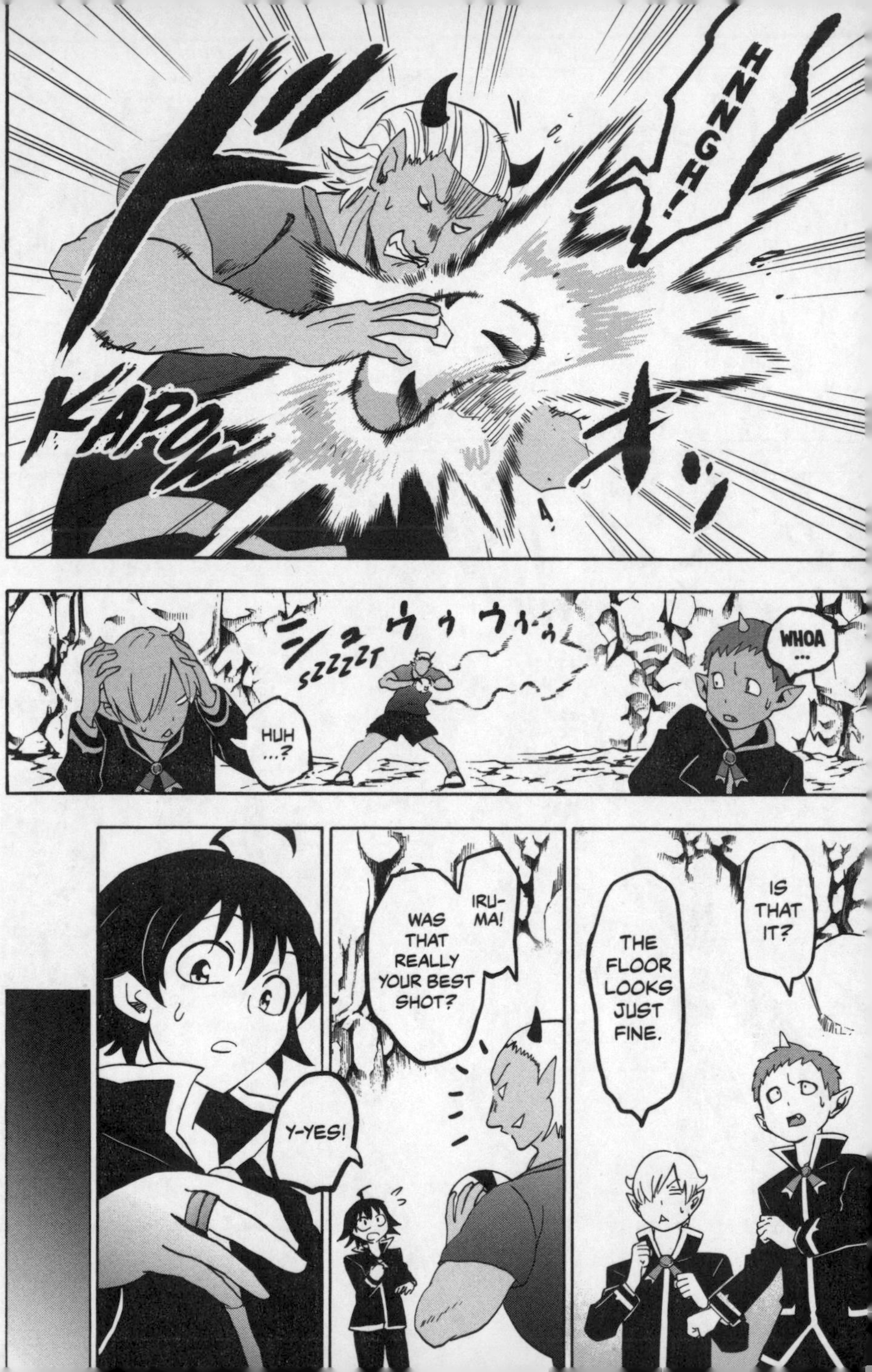
HNNGH!
KAPOW
WHOA ...
SZZZZT
HUH ...?
IS THAT IT?
THE FLOOR LOOKS JUST FINE.
IRUMA!
WAS THAT REALLY YOUR BEST SHOT?
Y-YES!

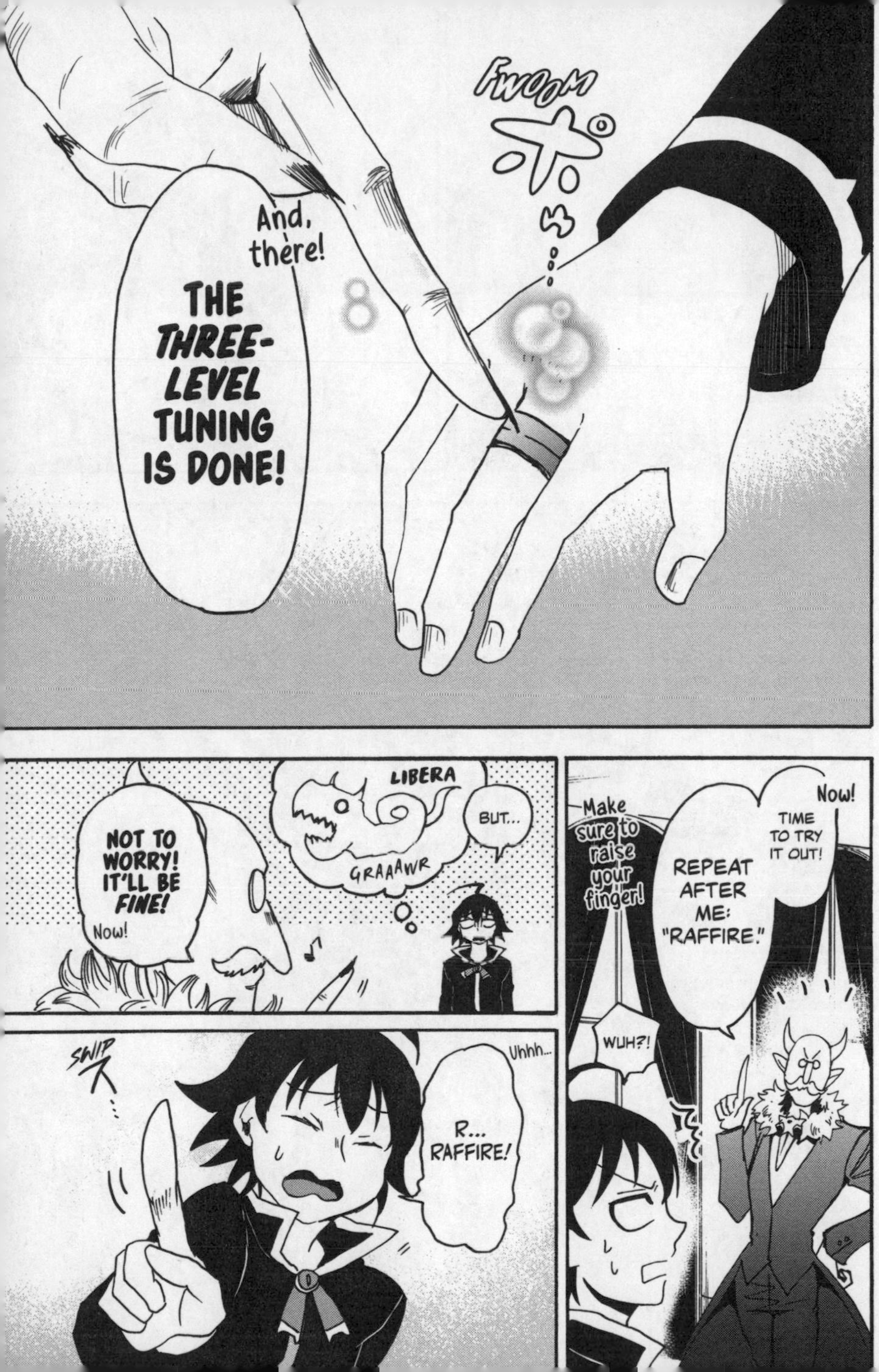
FWOOM
And, there!
THE THREE-LEVEL TUNING IS DONE!
Now!
TIME TO TRY IT OUT!
REPEAT AFTER ME: "RAFFIRE."
Make sure to raise your finger!
WUH?!
BUT...
LIBERA
GRAAAWR
NOT TO WORRY! IT'LL BE FINE!
Now!
Uhhh...
R... RAFFIRE!
SWIP

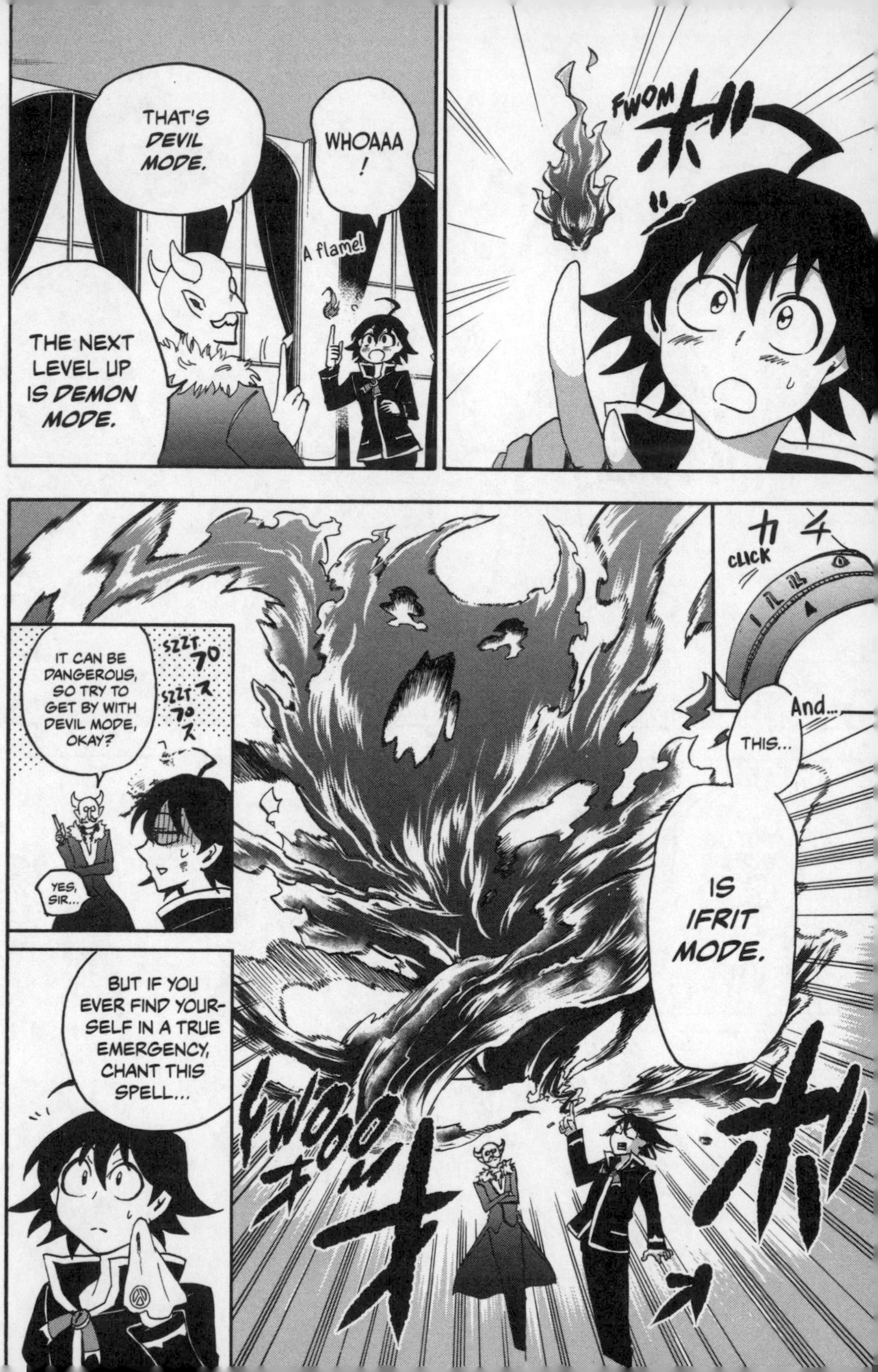
FWOM
WHOAAA !
A flame!
THAT'S DEVIL MODE.
THE NEXT LEVEL UP IS DEMON MODE.
CLICK
And...
THIS...
IS IFRIT MODE.
FWOOM
IT CAN BE DANGEROUS, SO TRY TO GET BY WITH DEVIL MODE, OKAY?
SZZT SZZT
YES, SIR...
BUT IF YOU EVER FIND YOURSELF IN A TRUE EMERGENCY, CHANT THIS SPELL...

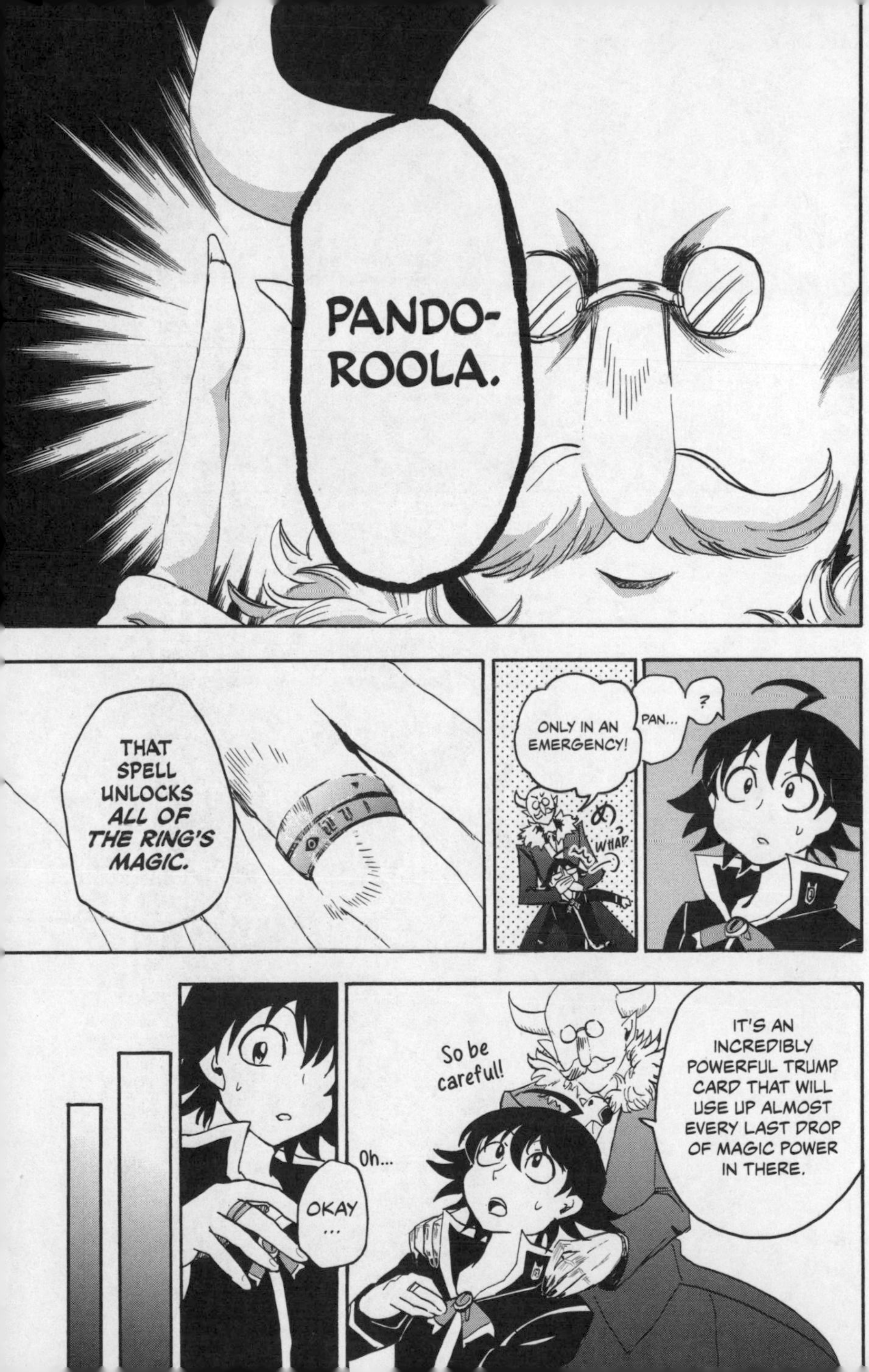
PANDO-ROOLA.
?
PAN...
ONLY IN AN EMERGENCY!
め
WHAP
THAT SPELL UNLOCKS ALL OF THE RING'S MAGIC.
IT'S AN INCREDIBLY POWERFUL TRUMP CARD THAT WILL USE UP ALMOST EVERY LAST DROP OF MAGIC POWER IN THERE.
So be careful!
Oh...
OKAY ...

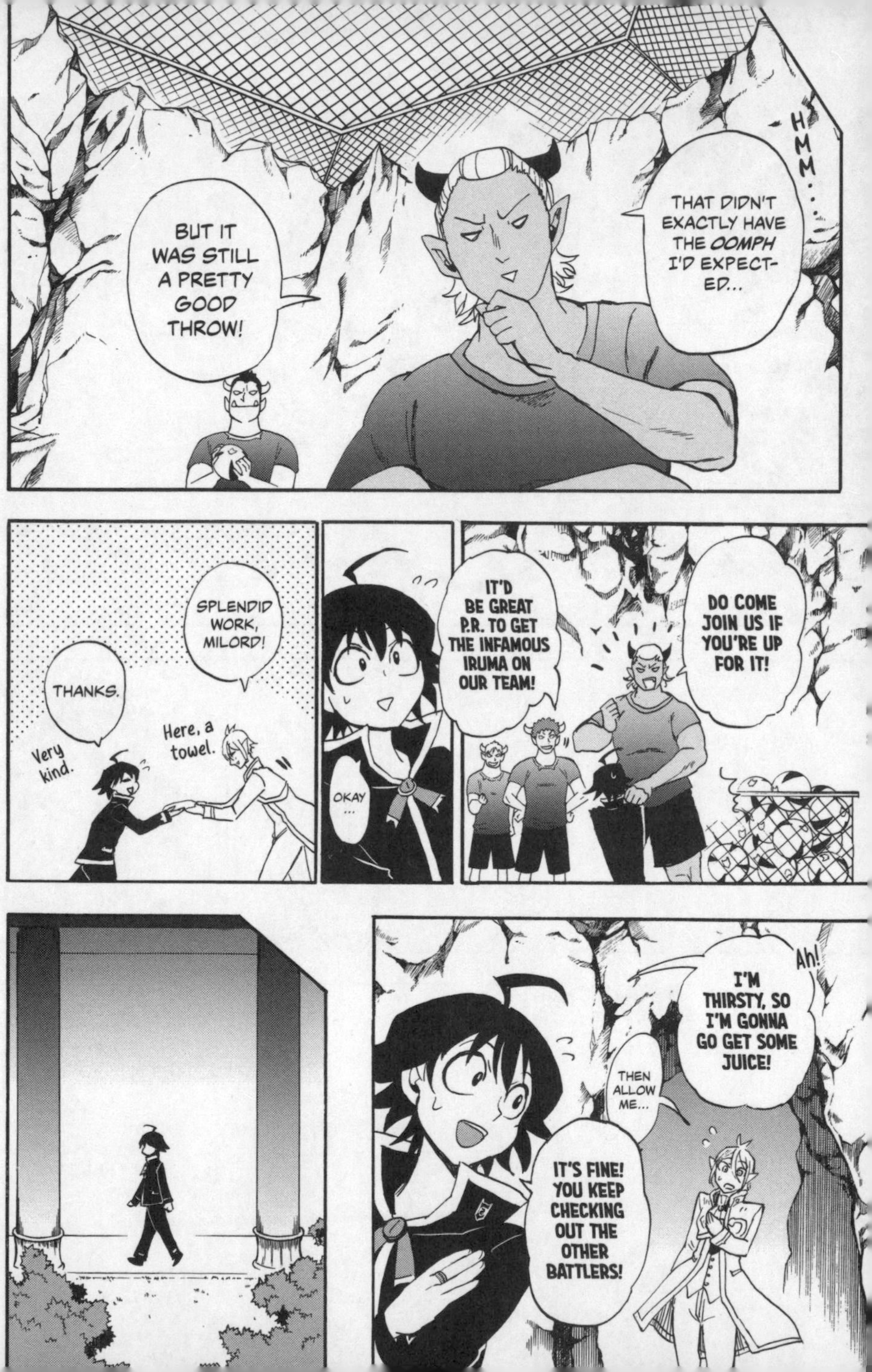
HMM...
THAT DIDN'T EXACTLY HAVE THE *OOMPH* I'D EXPECT-ED...
BUT IT WAS STILL A PRETTY GOOD THROW!
DO COME JOIN US IF YOU'RE UP FOR IT!
IT'D BE GREAT P.R. TO GET THE INFAMOUS IRUMA ON OUR TEAM!
OKAY...
SPLENDID WORK, MILORD!
THANKS.
Here, a towel.
Very kind.
Ah!
I'M THIRSTY, SO I'M GONNA GO GET SOME JUICE!
THEN ALLOW ME...
IT'S FINE! YOU KEEP CHECKING OUT THE OTHER BATTLERS!

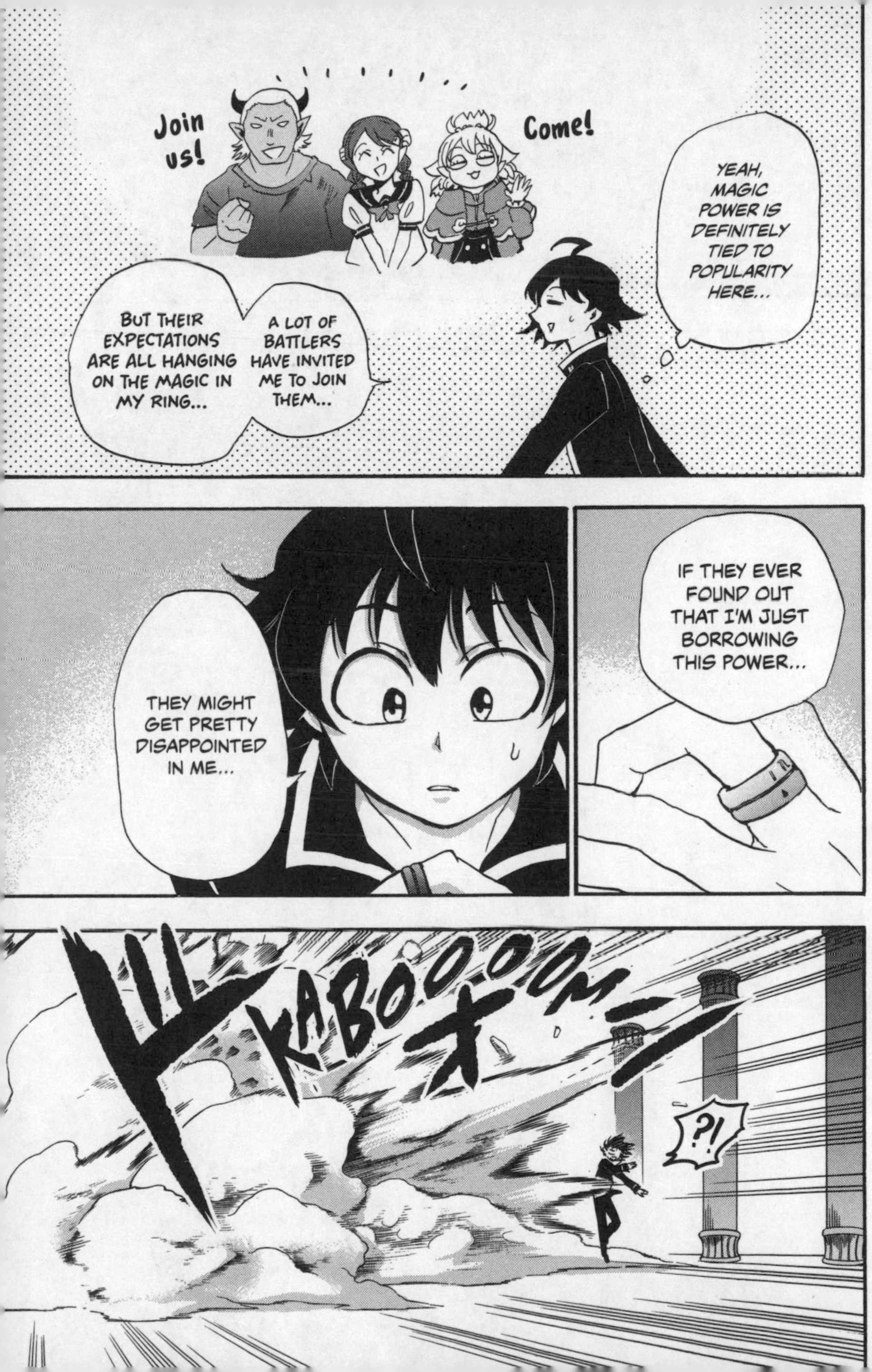
YEAH, MAGIC POWER IS DEFINITELY TIED TO POPULARITY HERE...
Come!
Join us!
A LOT OF BATTLERS HAVE INVITED ME TO JOIN THEM...
BUT THEIR EXPECTATIONS ARE ALL HANGING ON THE MAGIC IN MY RING...
IF THEY EVER FOUND OUT THAT I'M JUST BORROWING THIS POWER...
THEY MIGHT GET PRETTY DISAPPOINTED IN ME...
KABOOOOOM
?!

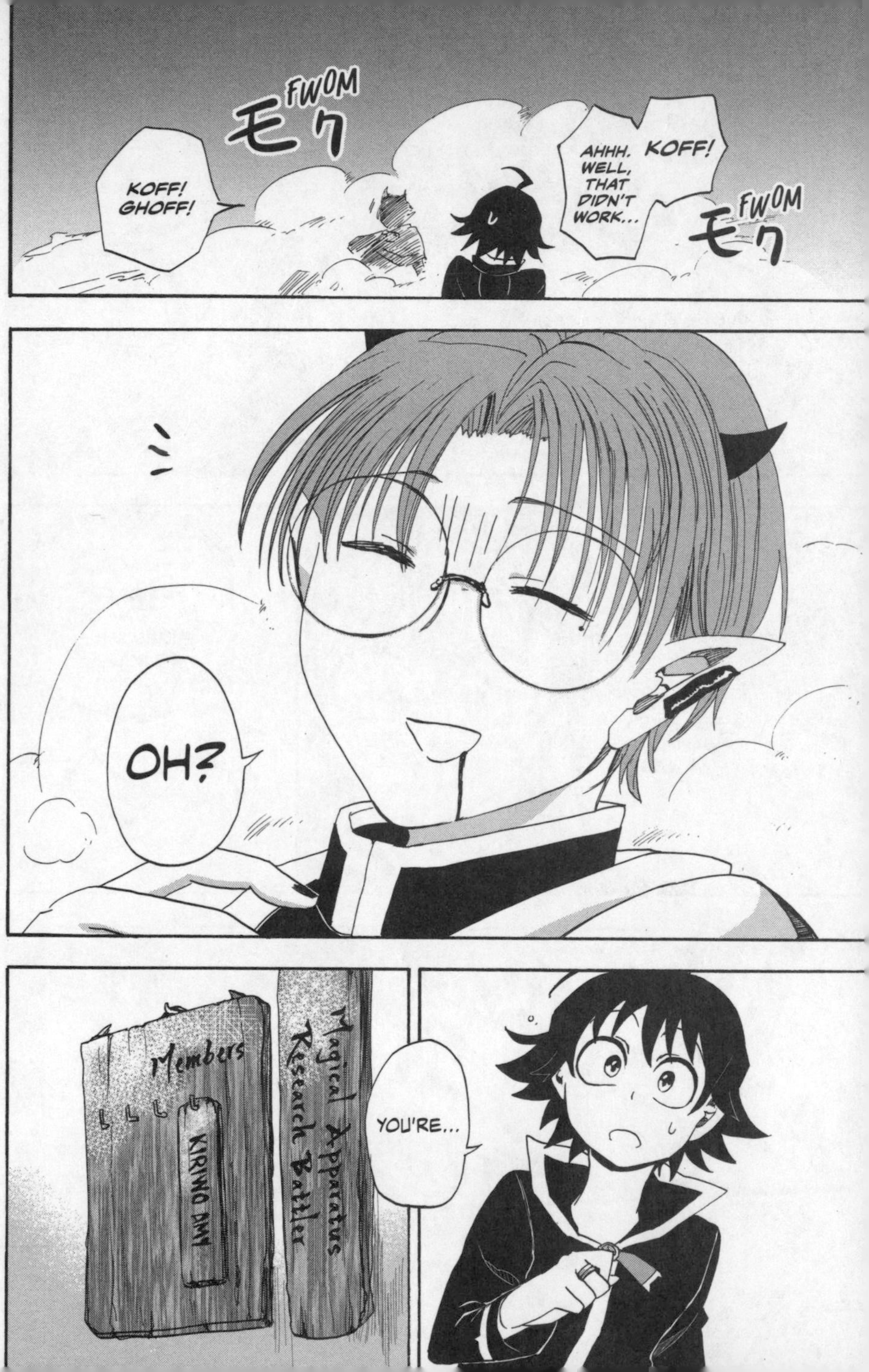
AHHH. KOFF! WELL, THAT DIDN'T WORK...
FWOM
FWOM
KOFF! GHOFF!
OH?
YOU'RE...
Magical Apparatus Research Battler
Members
KIRIWO AMY

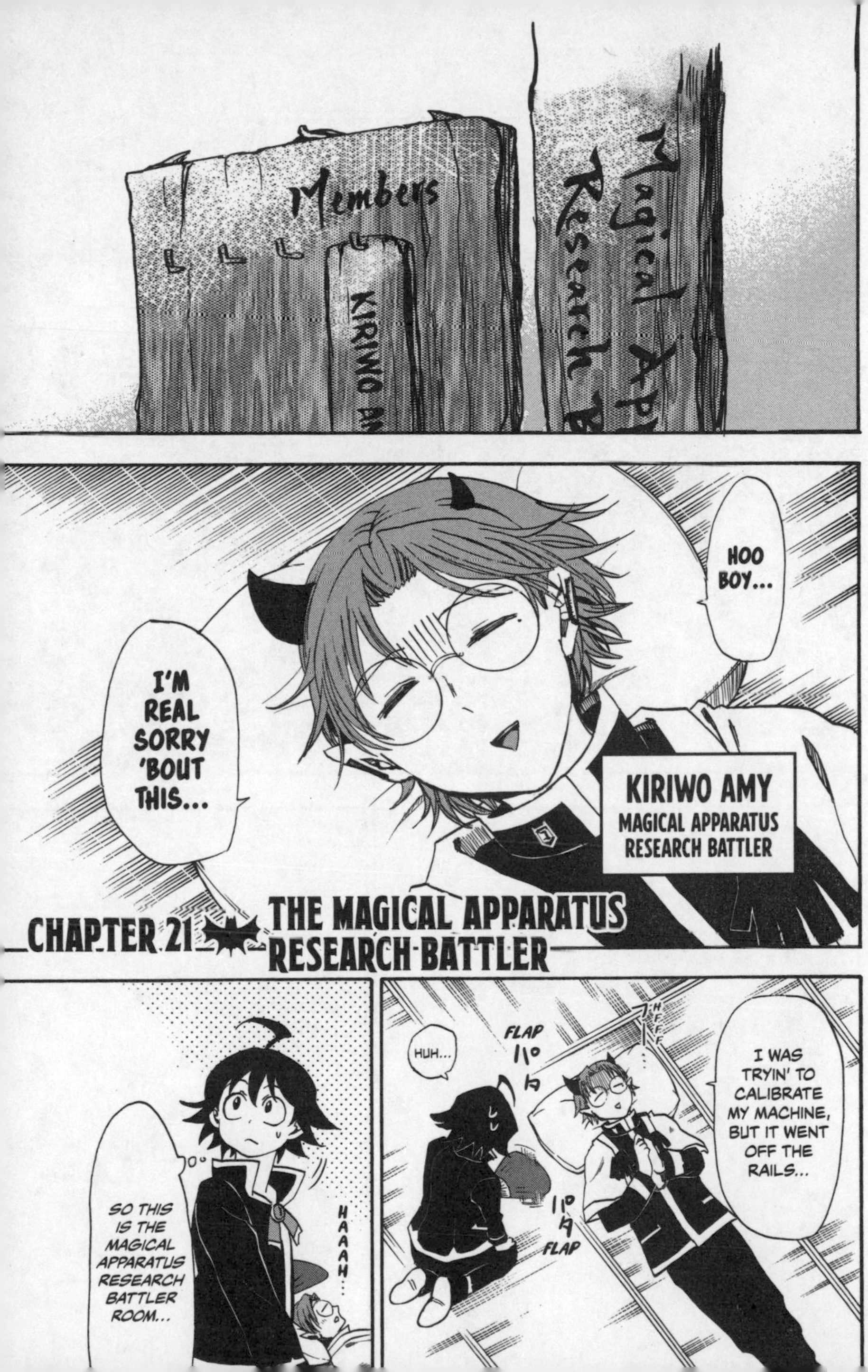
Magical
Research
Members
KIRIWO
HOO BOY...
I'M REAL SORRY 'BOUT THIS...
KIRIWO AMY
MAGICAL APPARATUS RESEARCH BATTLER
CHAPTER 21 THE MAGICAL APPARATUS RESEARCH BATTLER
I WAS TRYIN' TO CALIBRATE MY MACHINE, BUT IT WENT OFF THE RAILS...
HFFFF
FLAP
HUH...
FLAP
HAAAAH...
SO THIS IS THE MAGICAL APPARATUS RESEARCH BATTLER ROOM...

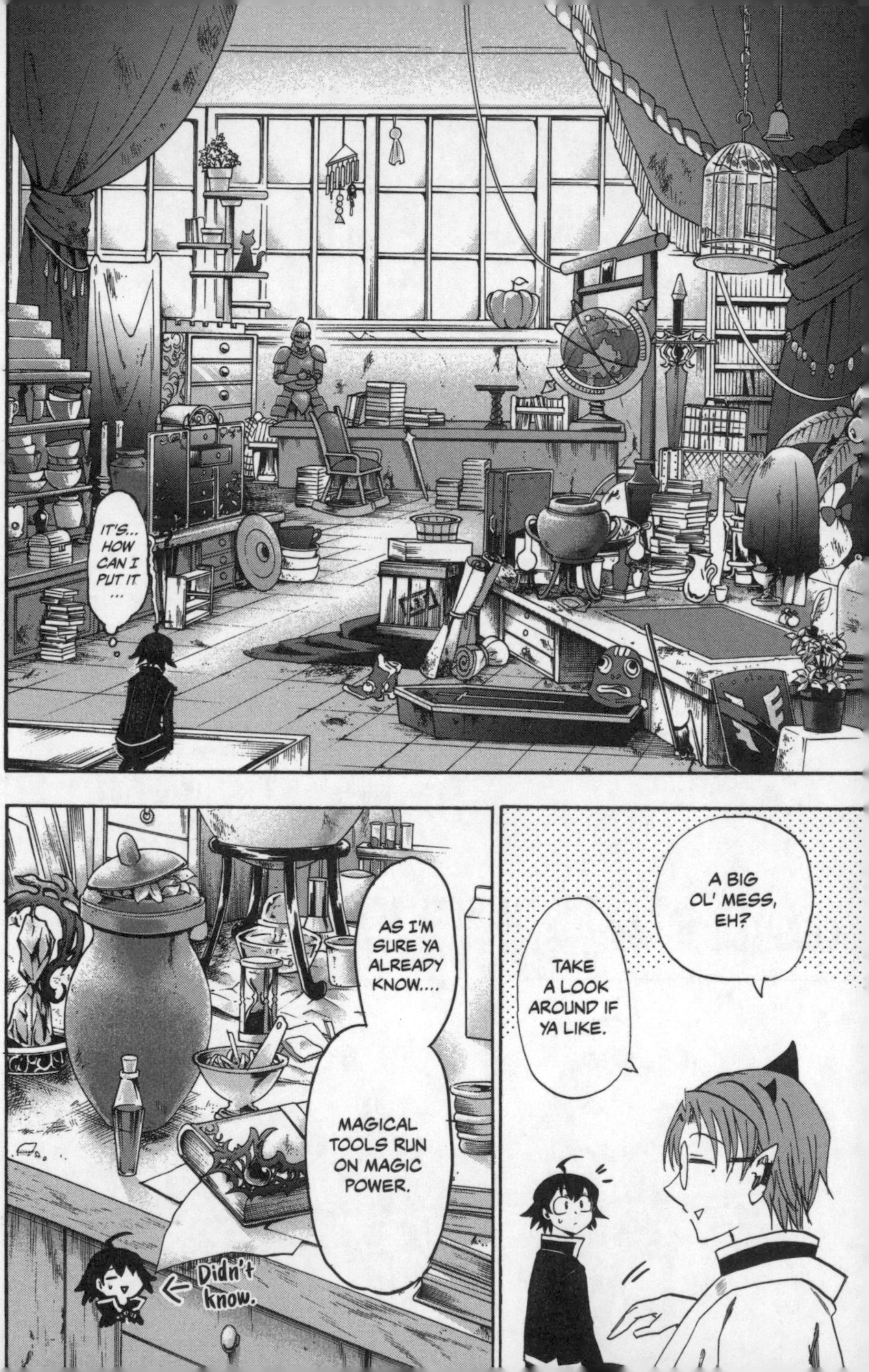
IT'S... HOW CAN I PUT IT ...
A BIG OL' MESS, EH?
TAKE A LOOK AROUND IF YA LIKE.
AS I'M SURE YA ALREADY KNOW....
MAGICAL TOOLS RUN ON MAGIC POWER.
Didn't know.

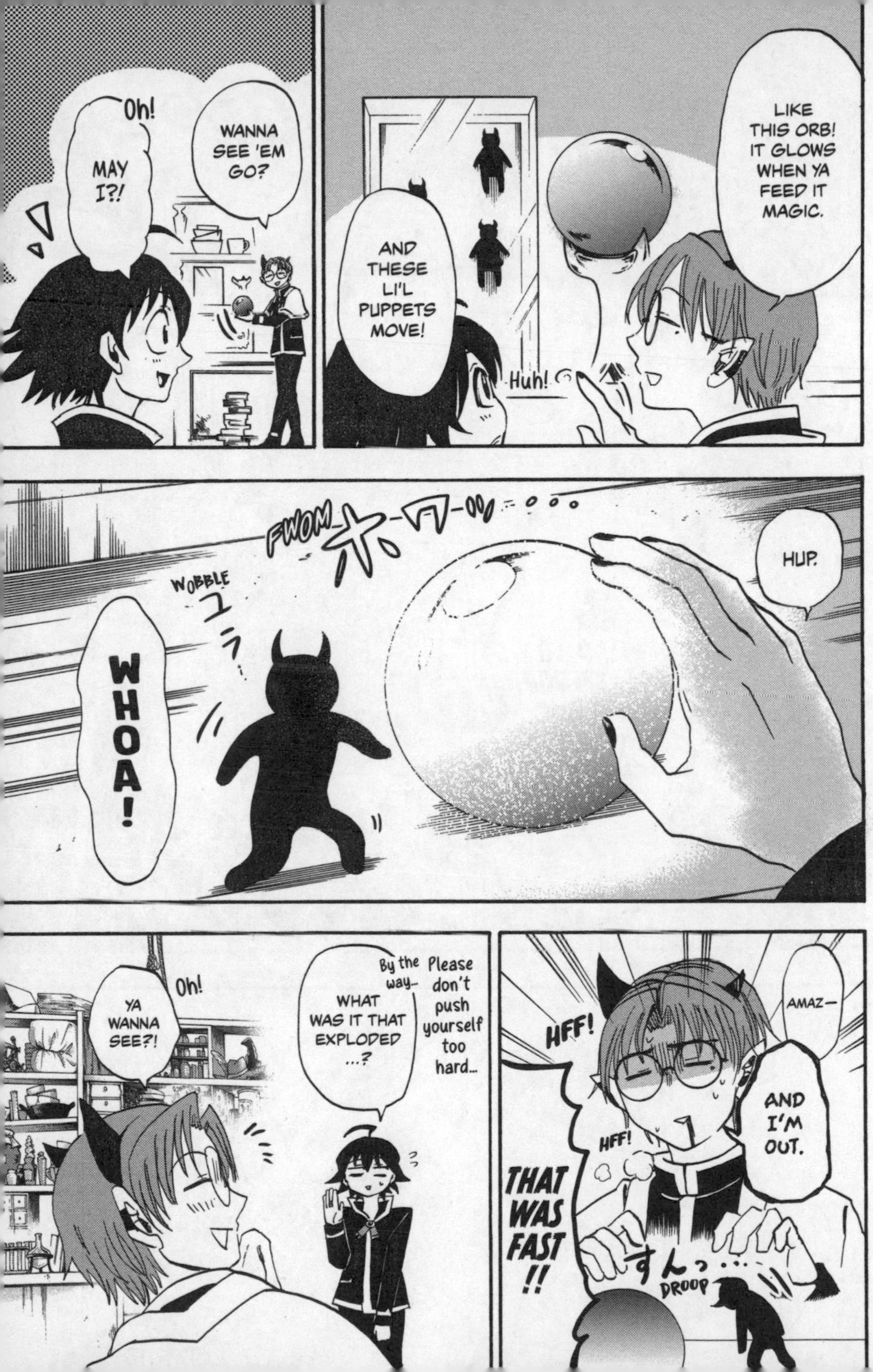
LIKE THIS ORB! IT GLOWS WHEN YA FEED IT MAGIC.
AND THESE LI'L PUPPETS MOVE!
Huh!
WANNA SEE 'EM GO?
Oh!
MAY I?!
HUP.
FWOM
WOBBLE
WHOA!
AMAZ—
AND I'M OUT.
HFF!
HFF!
THAT WAS FAST!!
DROOP
Please don't push yourself too hard...
By the way...
WHAT WAS IT THAT EXPLODED ...?
Oh!
YA WANNA SEE?!

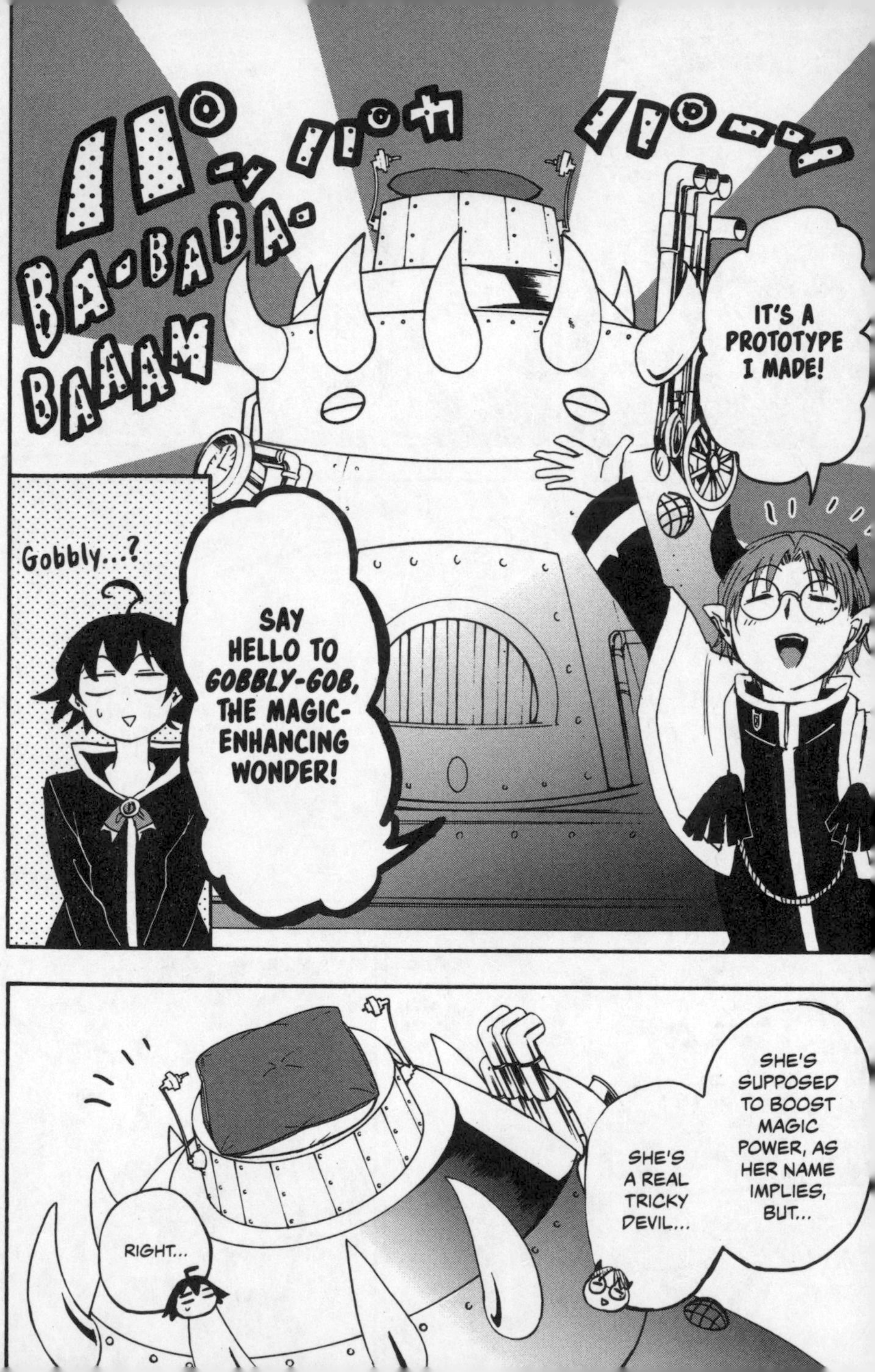
BA-BADA-BAAAM
IT'S A PROTOTYPE I MADE!
SAY HELLO TO GOBBLY-GOB, THE MAGIC-ENHANCING WONDER!
Gobbly...?
SHE'S SUPPOSED TO BOOST MAGIC POWER, AS HER NAME IMPLIES, BUT...
SHE'S A REAL TRICKY DEVIL...
RIGHT...

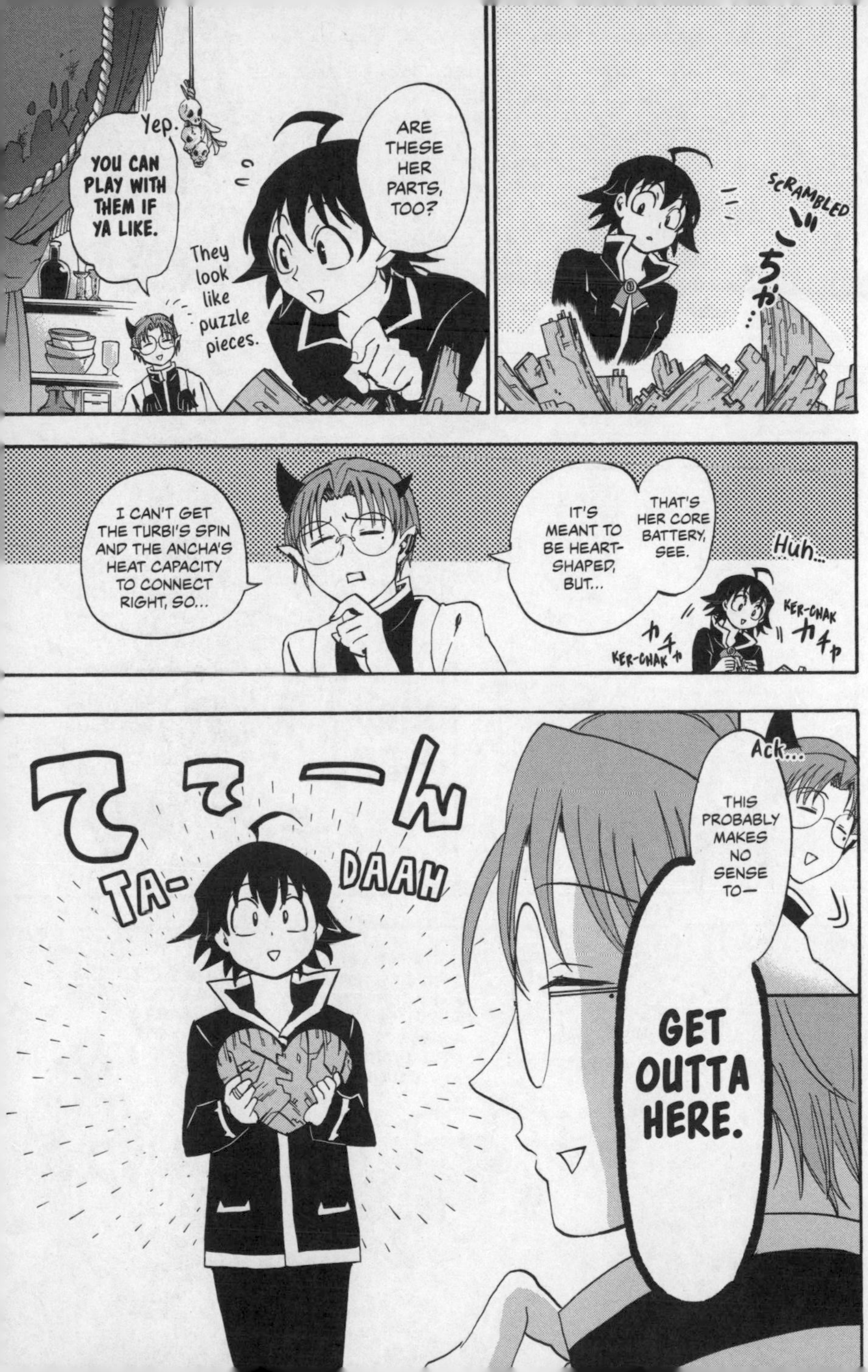
SCRAMBLED
ごちゃ…
ARE THESE HER PARTS, TOO?
They look like puzzle pieces.
Yep.
YOU CAN PLAY WITH THEM IF YA LIKE.
Huh...
KER-CHAK カチャ
KER-CHAK カチャ
THAT'S HER CORE BATTERY, SEE.
IT'S MEANT TO BE HEART-SHAPED, BUT...
I CAN'T GET THE TURBI'S SPIN AND THE ANCHA'S HEAT CAPACITY TO CONNECT RIGHT, SO...
Ack...
THIS PROBABLY MAKES NO SENSE TO—
GET OUTTA HERE.
てて一ん
TA-DAAH

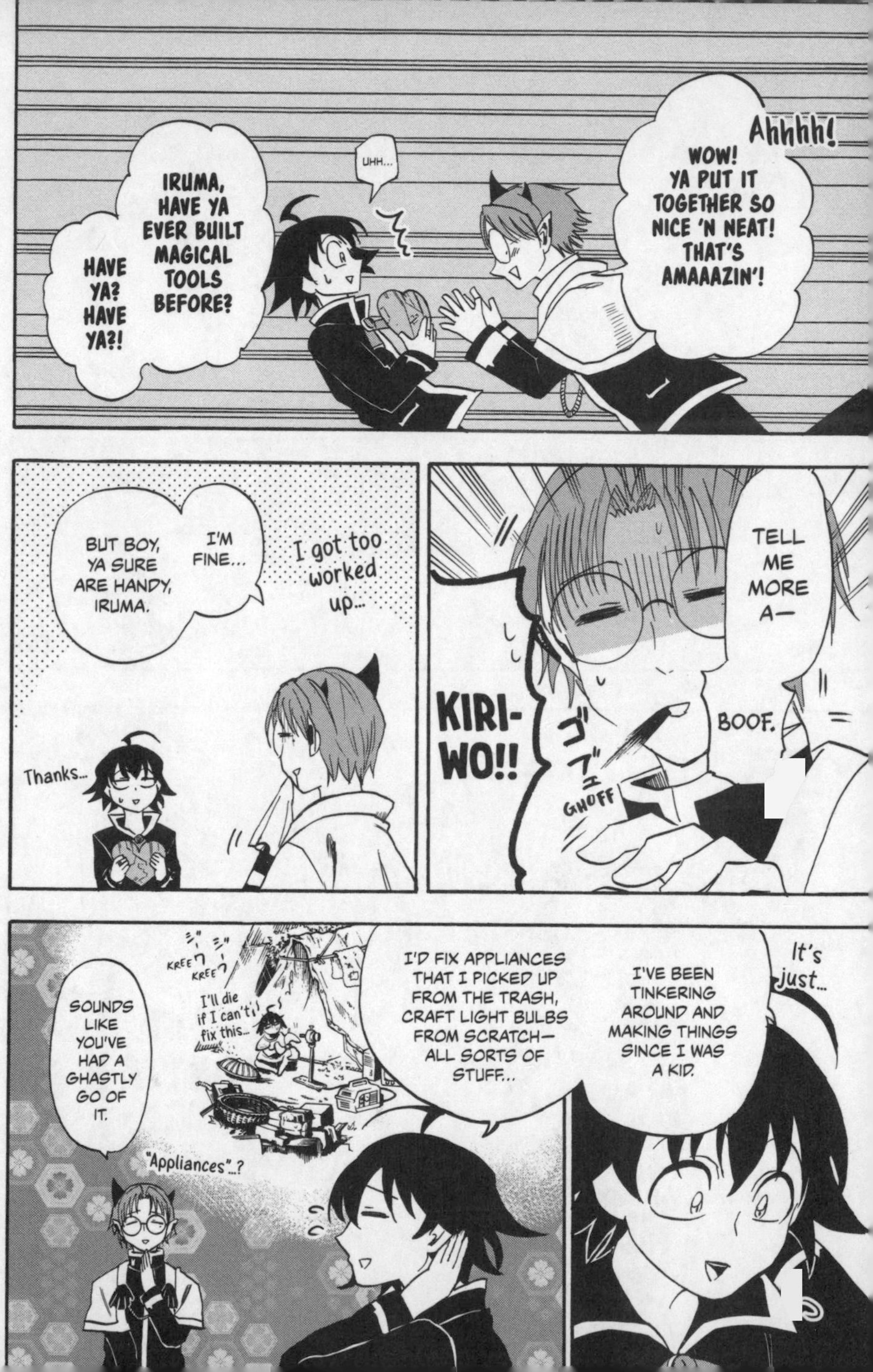

Ahhhh!
WOW! YA PUT IT TOGETHER SO NICE 'N NEAT! THAT'S AMAAAZIN'!
UHH...
IRUMA, HAVE YA EVER BUILT MAGICAL TOOLS BEFORE?
HAVE YA? HAVE YA?!
TELL ME MORE A—
BOOF.
ゴフェ GHOFF
KIRI-WO!!
I got too worked up...
I'M FINE...
BUT BOY, YA SURE ARE HANDY, IRUMA.
Thanks...
It's just...
I'VE BEEN TINKERING AROUND AND MAKING THINGS SINCE I WAS A KID.
I'D FIX APPLIANCES THAT I PICKED UP FROM THE TRASH, CRAFT LIGHT BULBS FROM SCRATCH— ALL SORTS OF STUFF...
ジ KREE ジ KREE
I'll die if I can't fix this...
SOUNDS LIKE YOU'VE HAD A GHASTLY GO OF IT.
"Appliances"...?

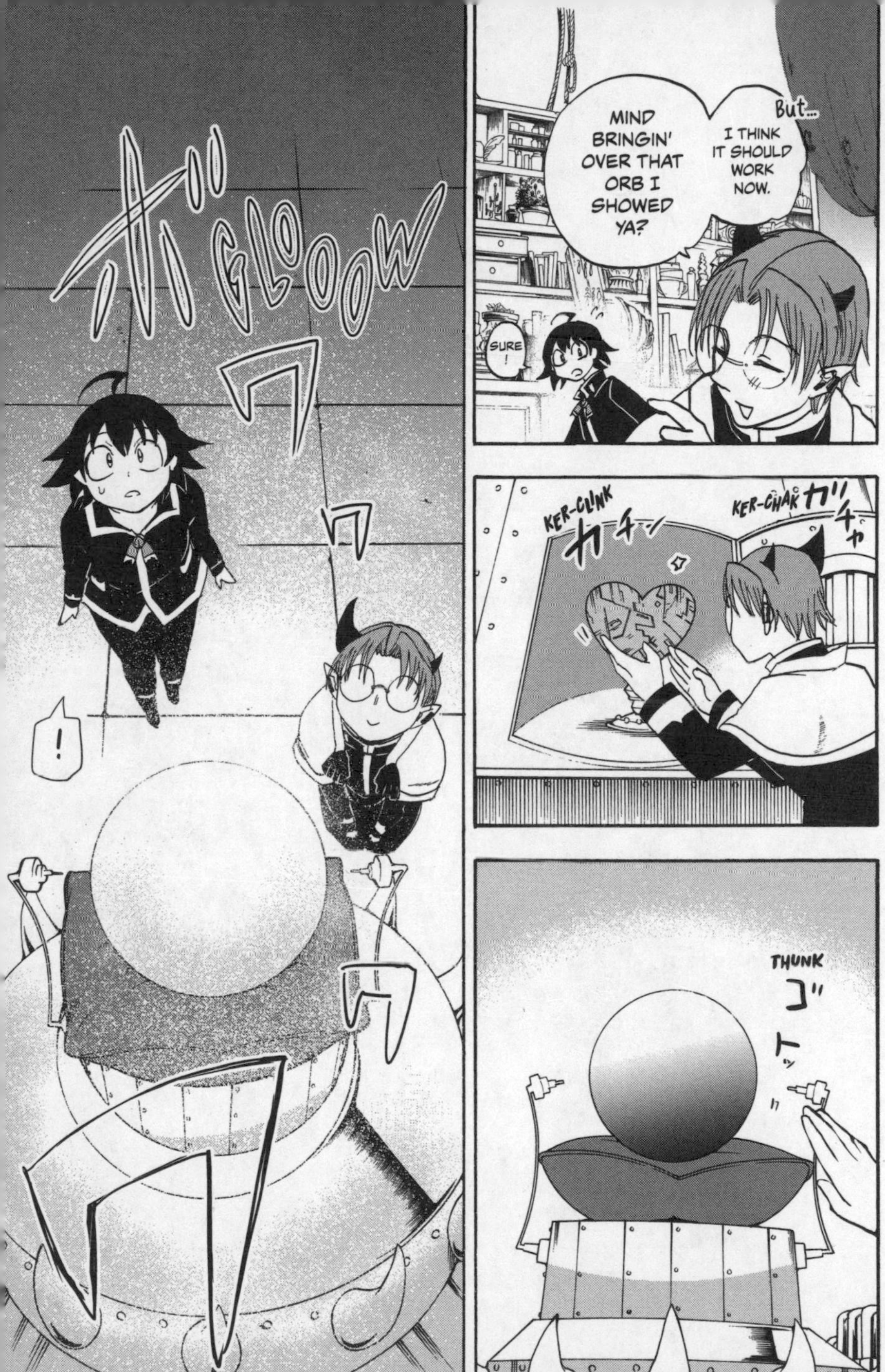
But...
I THINK IT SHOULD WORK NOW.
MIND BRINGIN' OVER THAT ORB I SHOWED YA?
SURE!
KER-CHAK カチャ
KER-CLINK カチッ
THUNK ゴトッ
GLOOOW
!

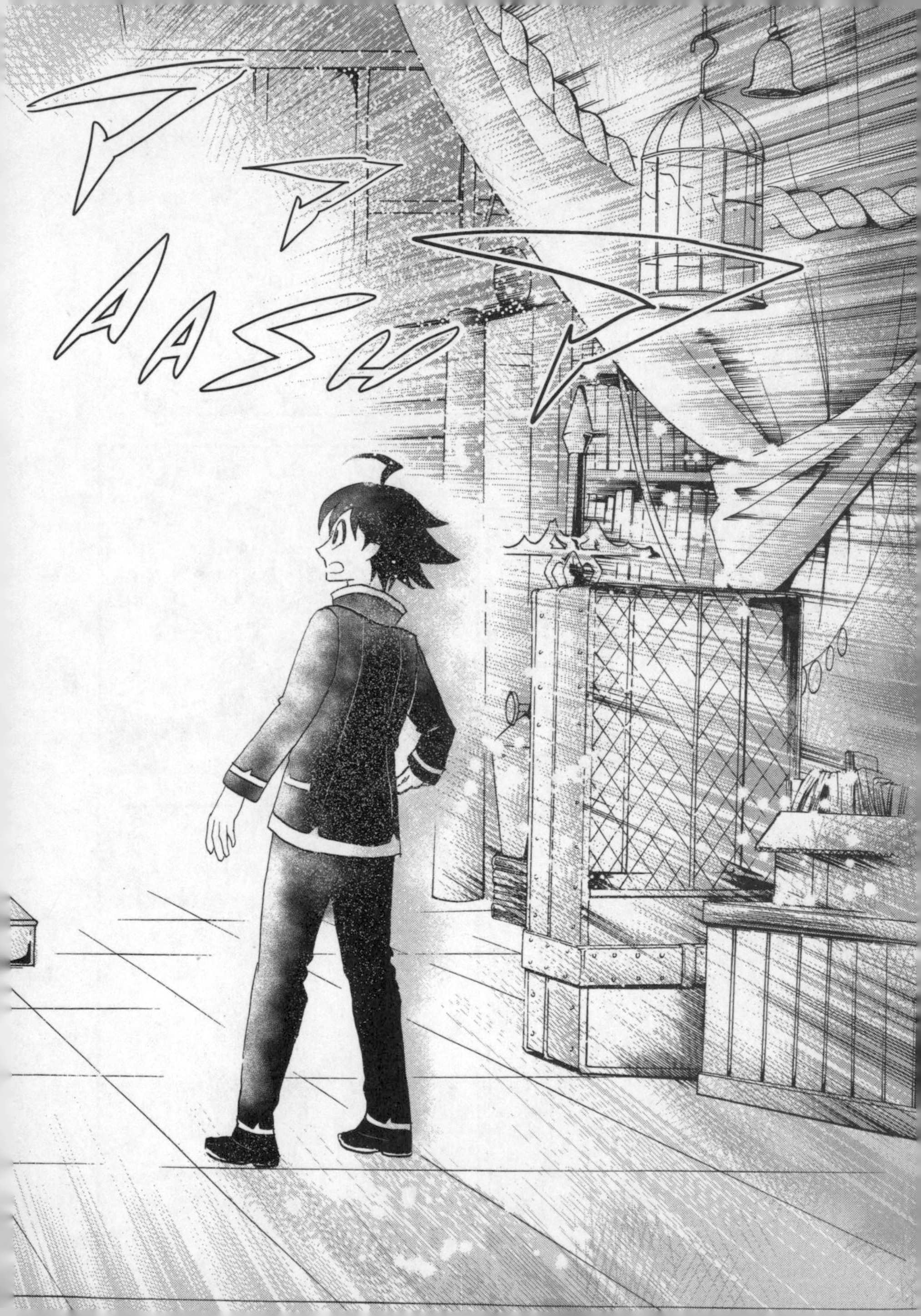
AASH

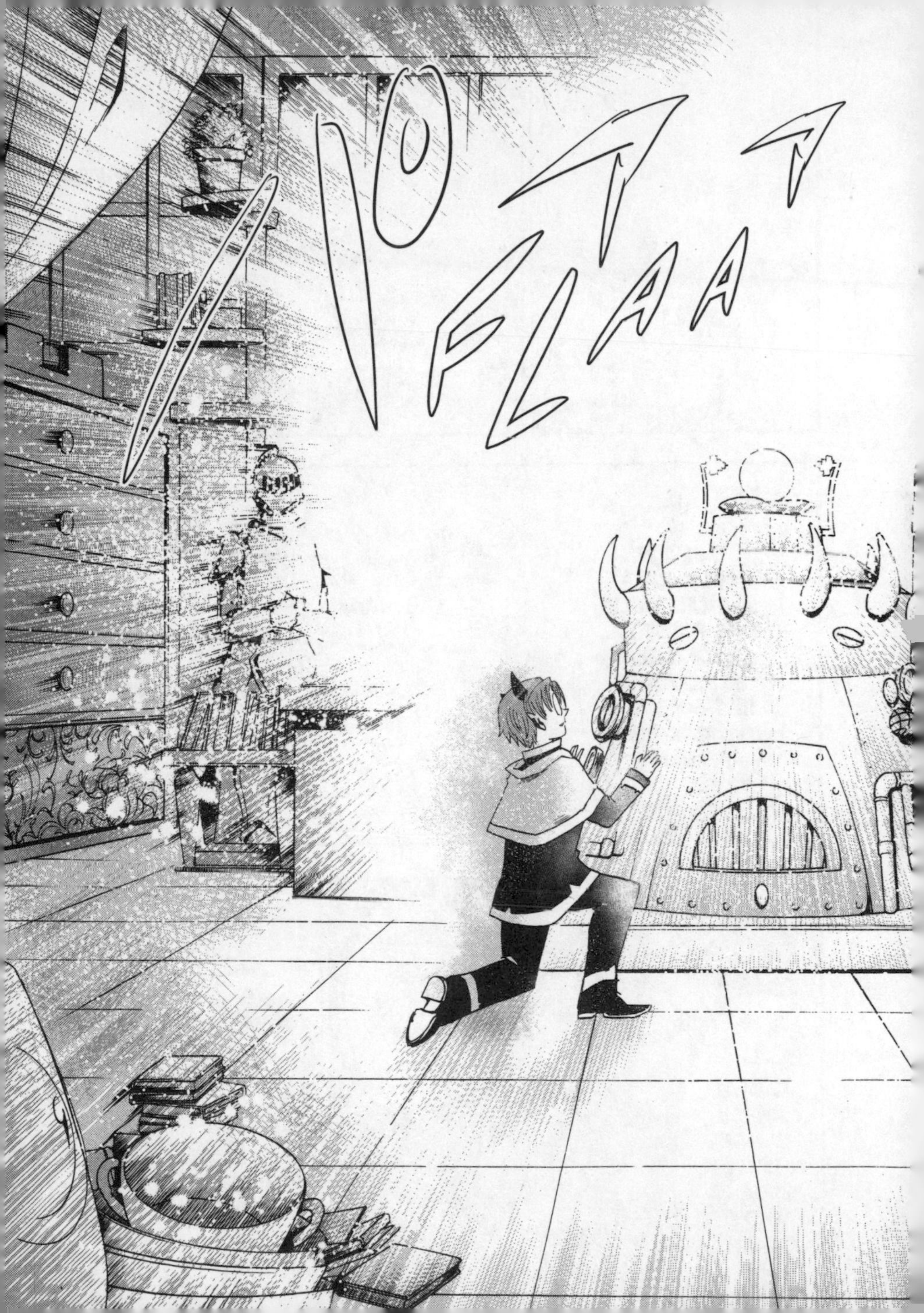
FLAAP

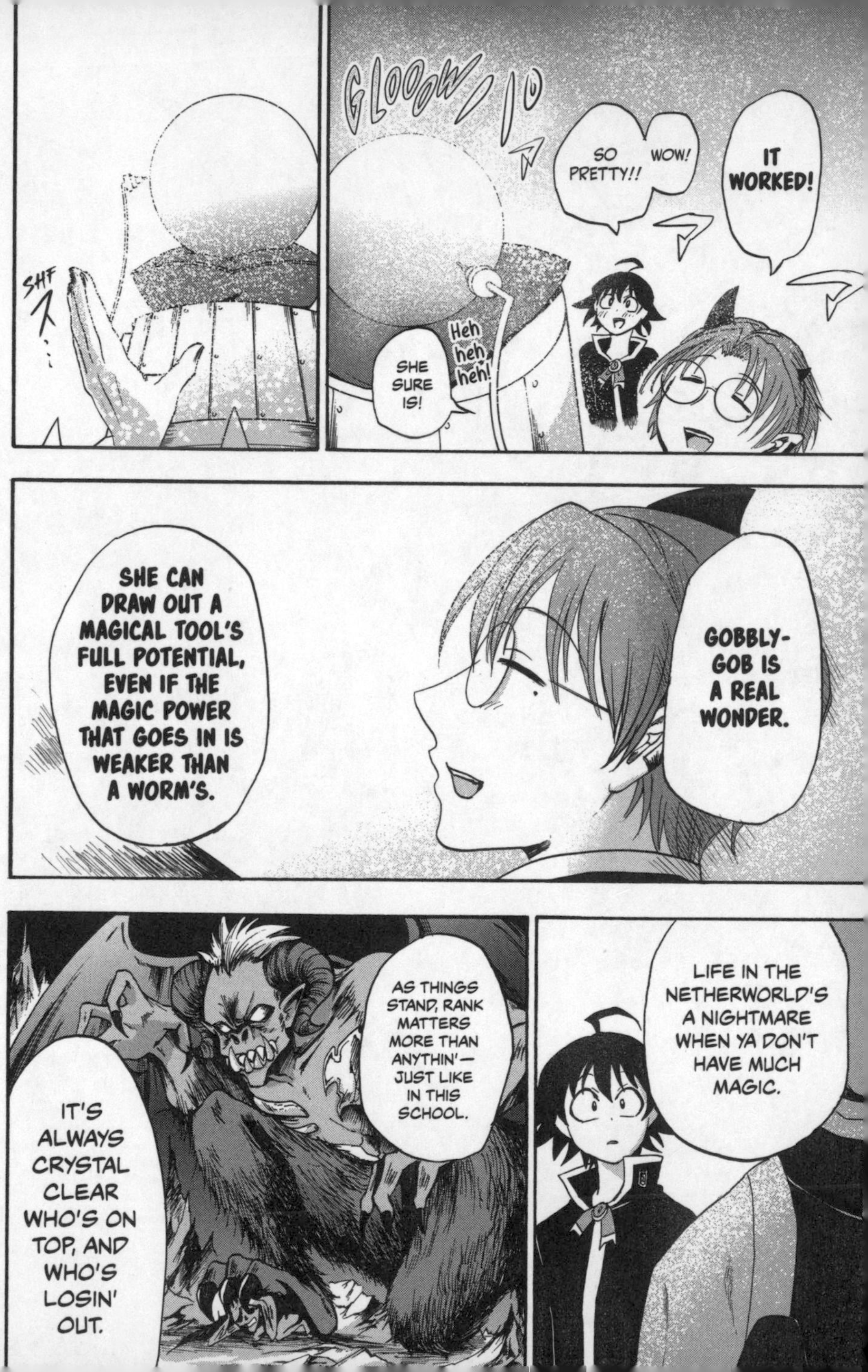
GLOOOW
IT WORKED!
WOW!
SO PRETTY!!
Heh heh heh!
SHE SURE IS!
SHF
GOBBLY-GOB IS A REAL WONDER.
SHE CAN DRAW OUT A MAGICAL TOOL'S FULL POTENTIAL, EVEN IF THE MAGIC POWER THAT GOES IN IS WEAKER THAN A WORM'S.
LIFE IN THE NETHERWORLD'S A NIGHTMARE WHEN YA DON'T HAVE MUCH MAGIC.
AS THINGS STAND, RANK MATTERS MORE THAN ANYTHIN'—JUST LIKE IN THIS SCHOOL.
IT'S ALWAYS CRYSTAL CLEAR WHO'S ON TOP, AND WHO'S LOSIN' OUT.

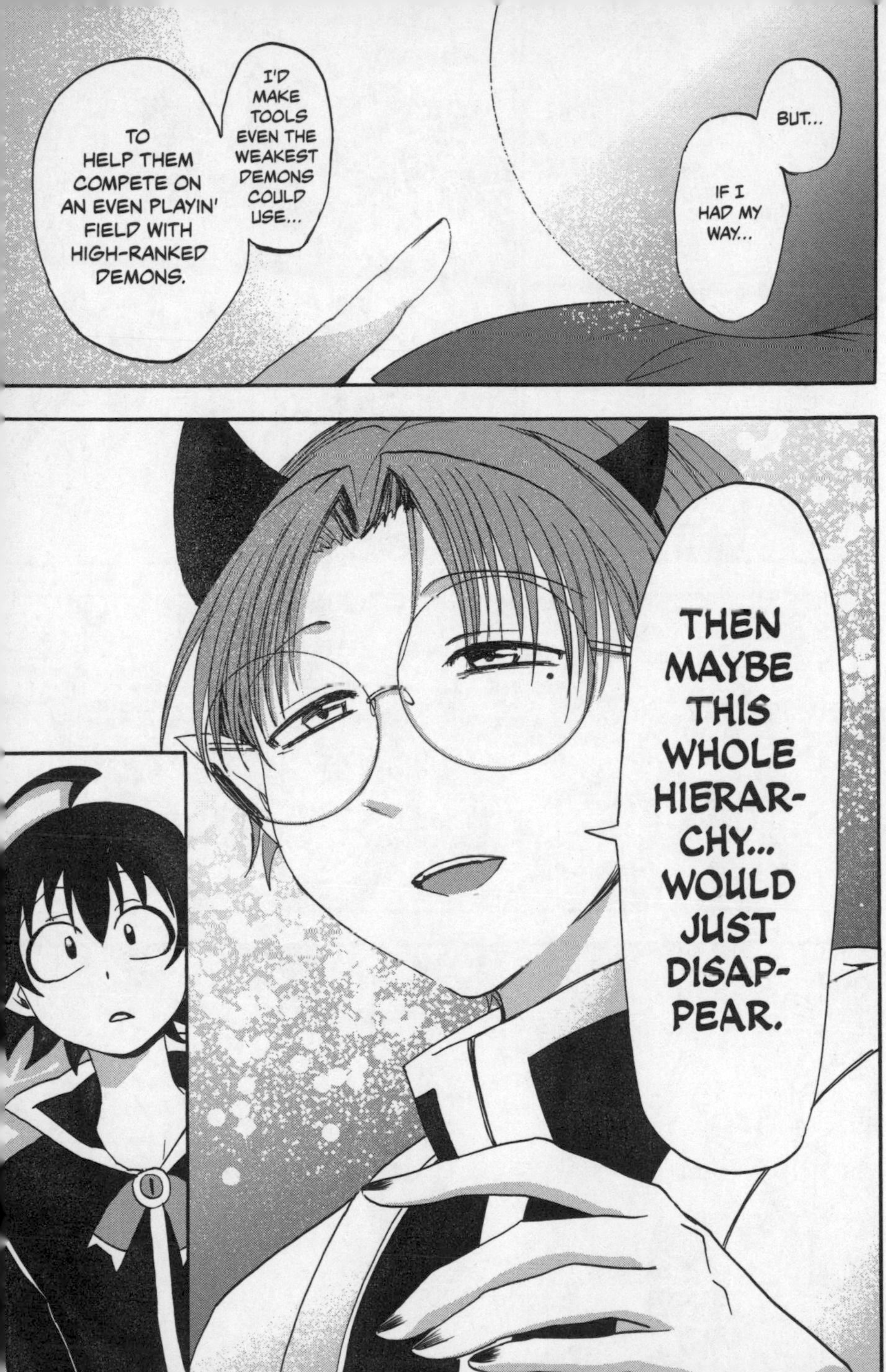
BUT... IF I HAD MY WAY...
I'D MAKE TOOLS EVEN THE WEAKEST DEMONS COULD USE...
TO HELP THEM COMPETE ON AN EVEN PLAYIN' FIELD WITH HIGH-RANKED DEMONS.
THEN MAYBE THIS WHOLE HIERARCHY... WOULD JUST DISAPPEAR.

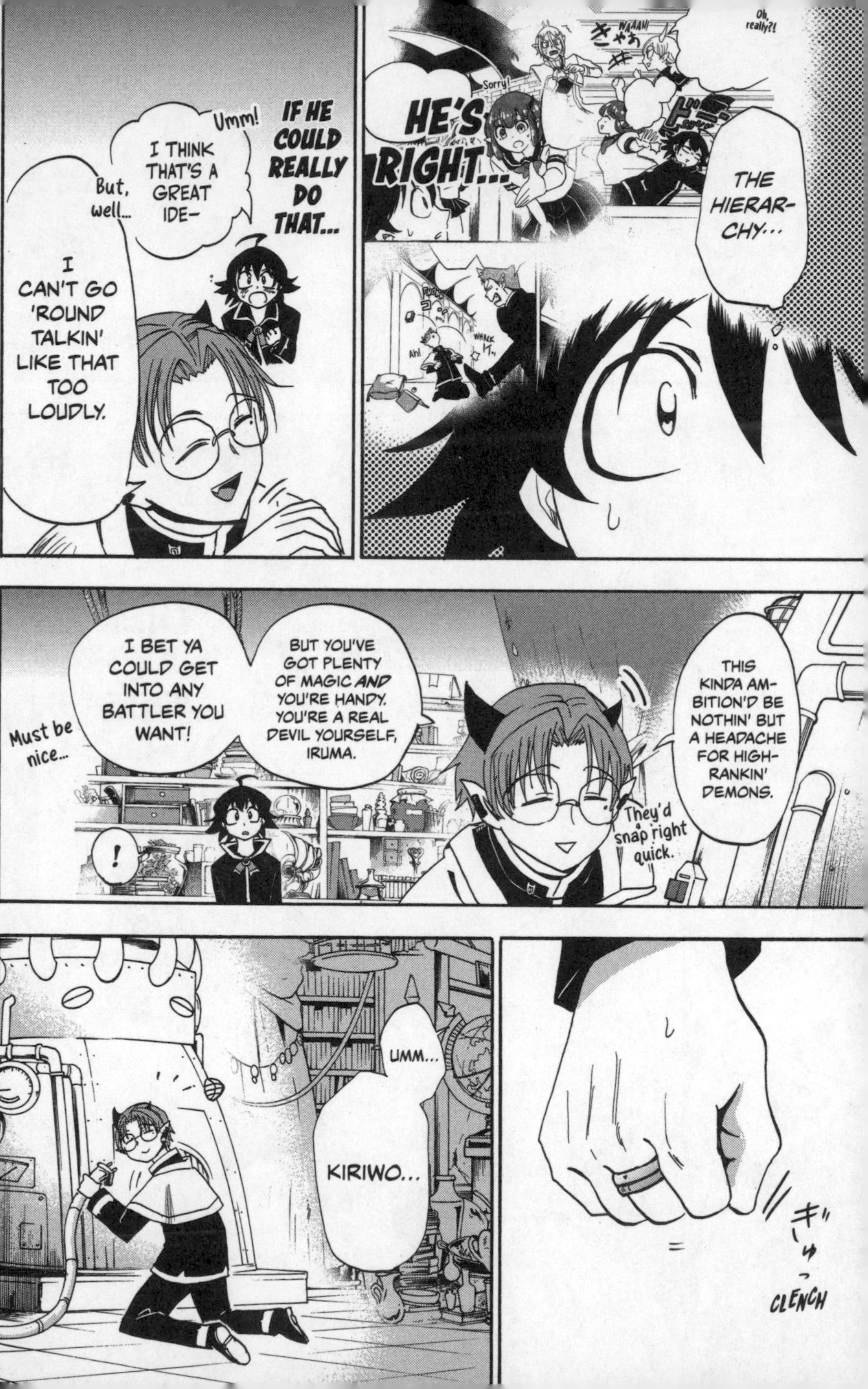
Oh, really?!
WAAAH!
Sorry!
HE'S RIGHT...
Ah!
WHAK
THE HIERAR-CHY...
IF HE COULD REALLY DO THAT...
Umm!
I THINK THAT'S A GREAT IDE-
But, well...
I CAN'T GO 'ROUND TALKIN' LIKE THAT TOO LOUDLY.
THIS KINDA AM-BITION'D BE NOTHIN' BUT A HEADACHE FOR HIGH-RANKIN' DEMONS.
They'd snap right quick.
BUT YOU'VE GOT PLENTY OF MAGIC AND YOU'RE HANDY. YOU'RE A REAL DEVIL YOURSELF, IRUMA.
I BET YA COULD GET INTO ANY BATTLER YOU WANT!
Must be nice...
!
CLENCH
UMM...
KIRIWO...

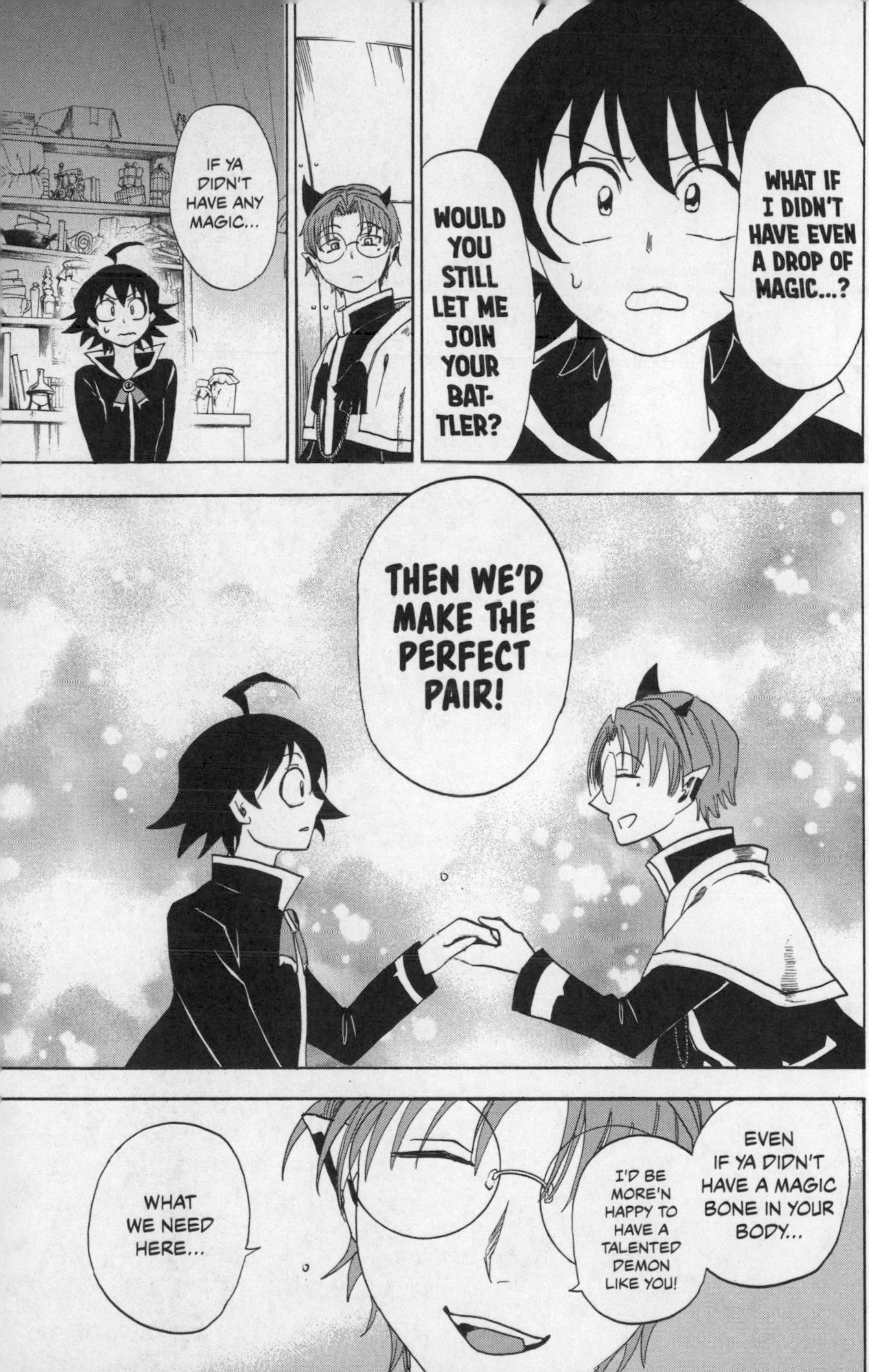
WHAT IF I DIDN'T HAVE EVEN A DROP OF MAGIC...?
WOULD YOU STILL LET ME JOIN YOUR BAT-TLER?
IF YA DIDN'T HAVE ANY MAGIC...
THEN WE'D MAKE THE PERFECT PAIR!
EVEN IF YA DIDN'T HAVE A MAGIC BONE IN YOUR BODY...
I'D BE MORE'N HAPPY TO HAVE A TALENTED DEMON LIKE YOU!
WHAT WE NEED HERE...

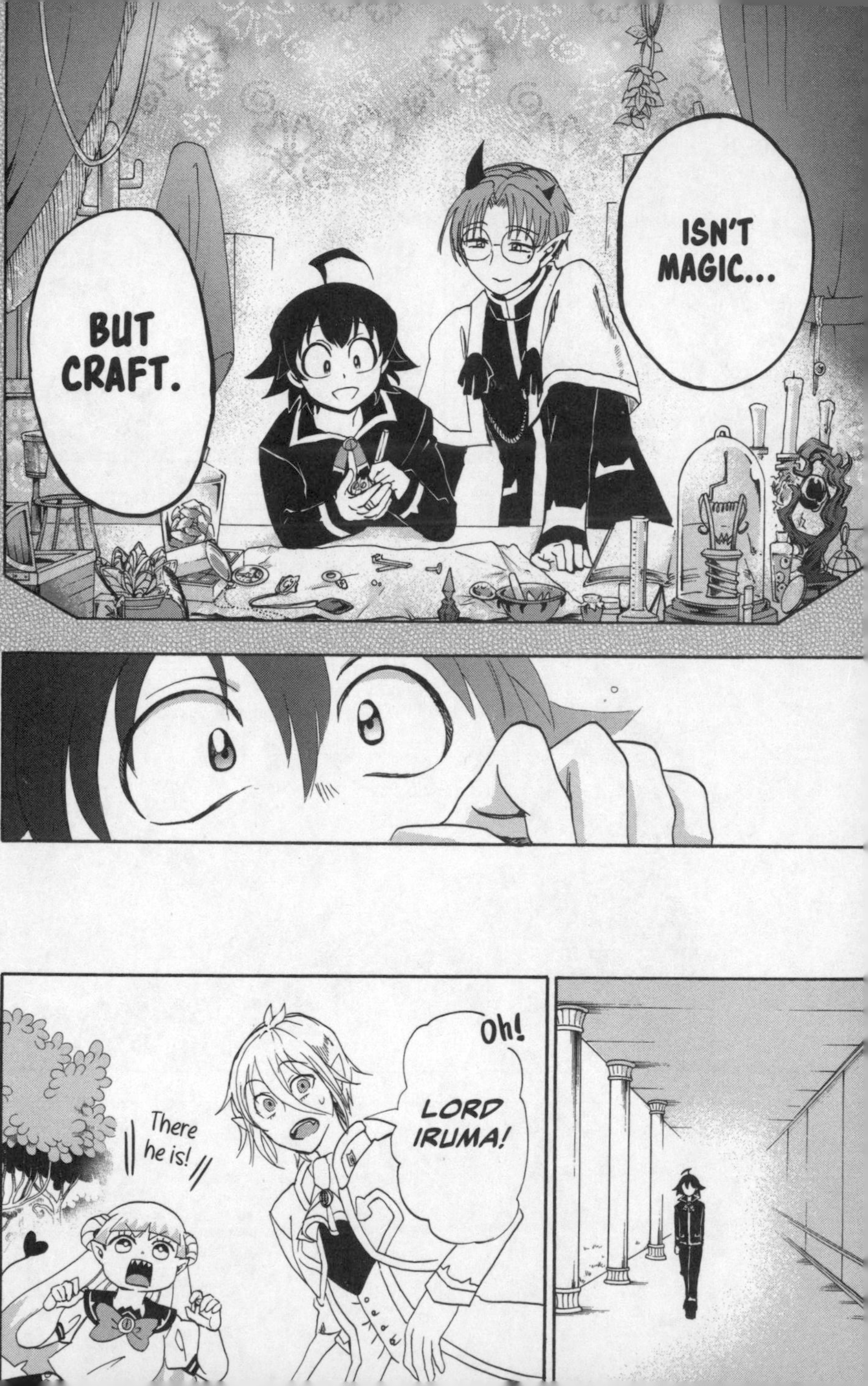
ISN'T MAGIC...
BUT CRAFT.
Oh!
LORD IRUMA!
There he is!

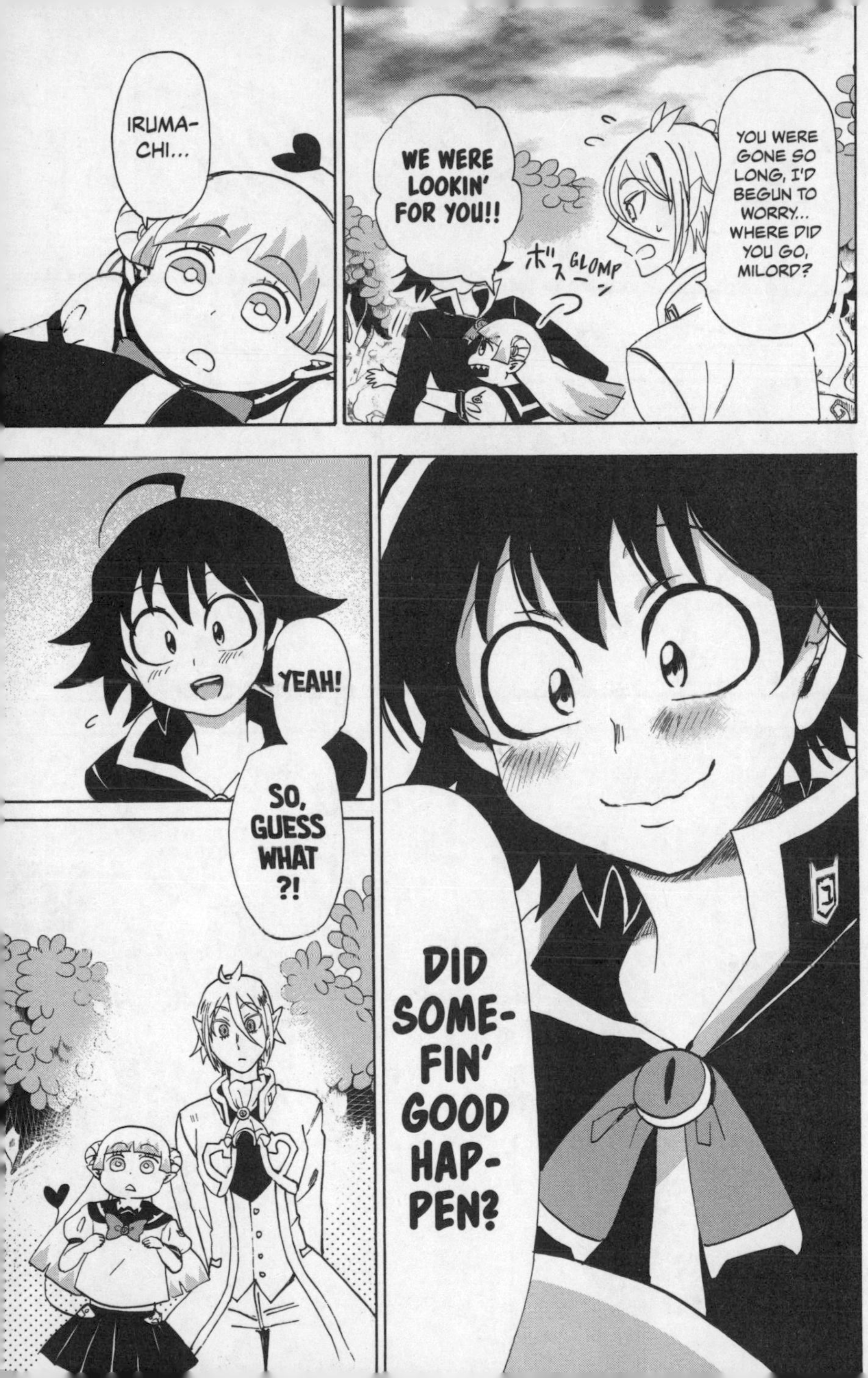
YOU WERE GONE SO LONG, I'D BEGUN TO WORRY... WHERE DID YOU GO, MILORD?
WE WERE LOOKIN' FOR YOU!!
ボスー
GLOMP
IRUMA-CHI...
DID SOME-FIN' GOOD HAP-PEN?
YEAH!
SO, GUESS WHAT?!

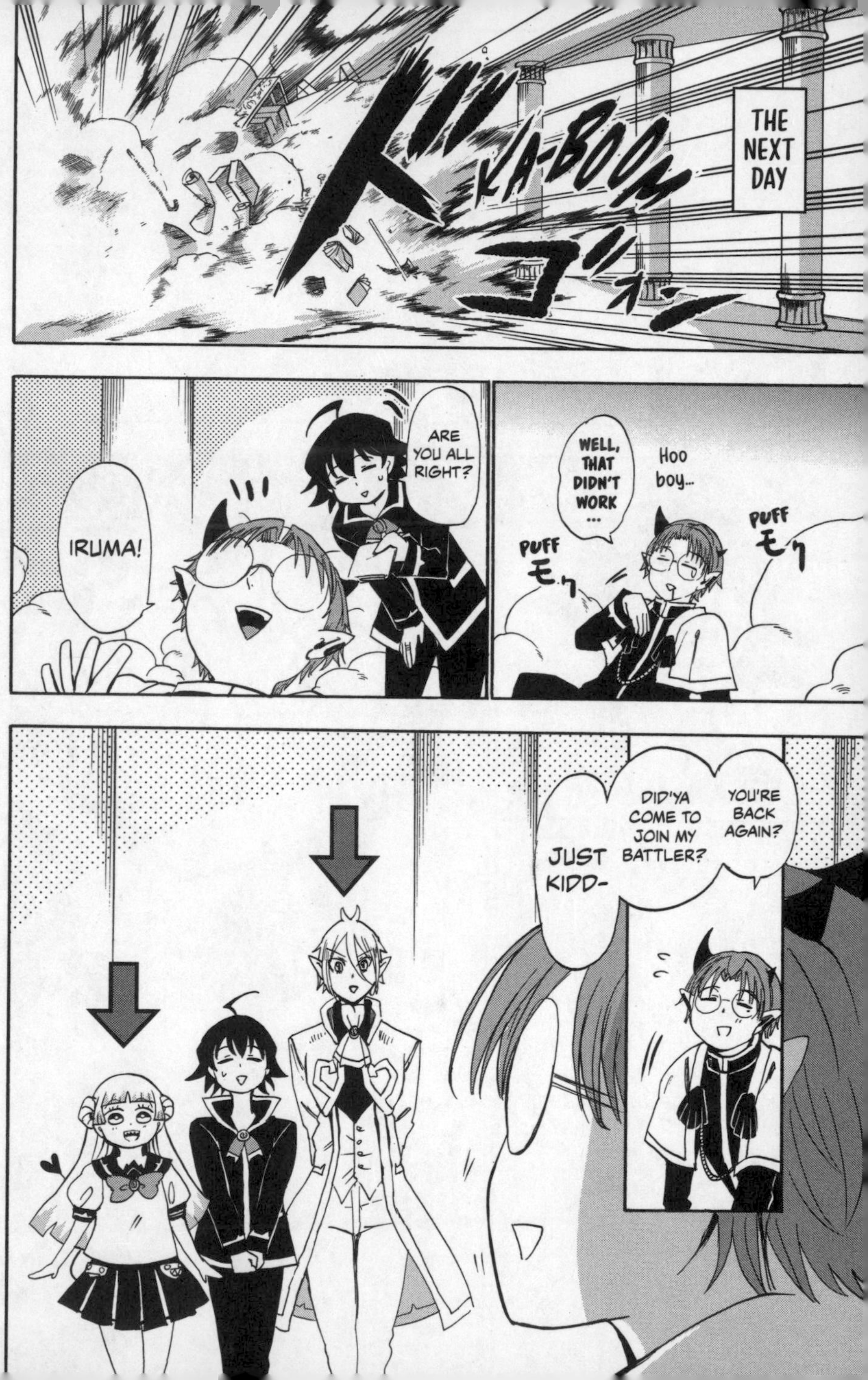
THE NEXT DAY
KA-BOOM
PUFF
PUFF
Hoo boy...
WELL, THAT DIDN'T WORK ...
ARE YOU ALL RIGHT?
IRUMA!
YOU'RE BACK AGAIN?
DID'YA COME TO JOIN MY BATTLER?
JUST KIDD-

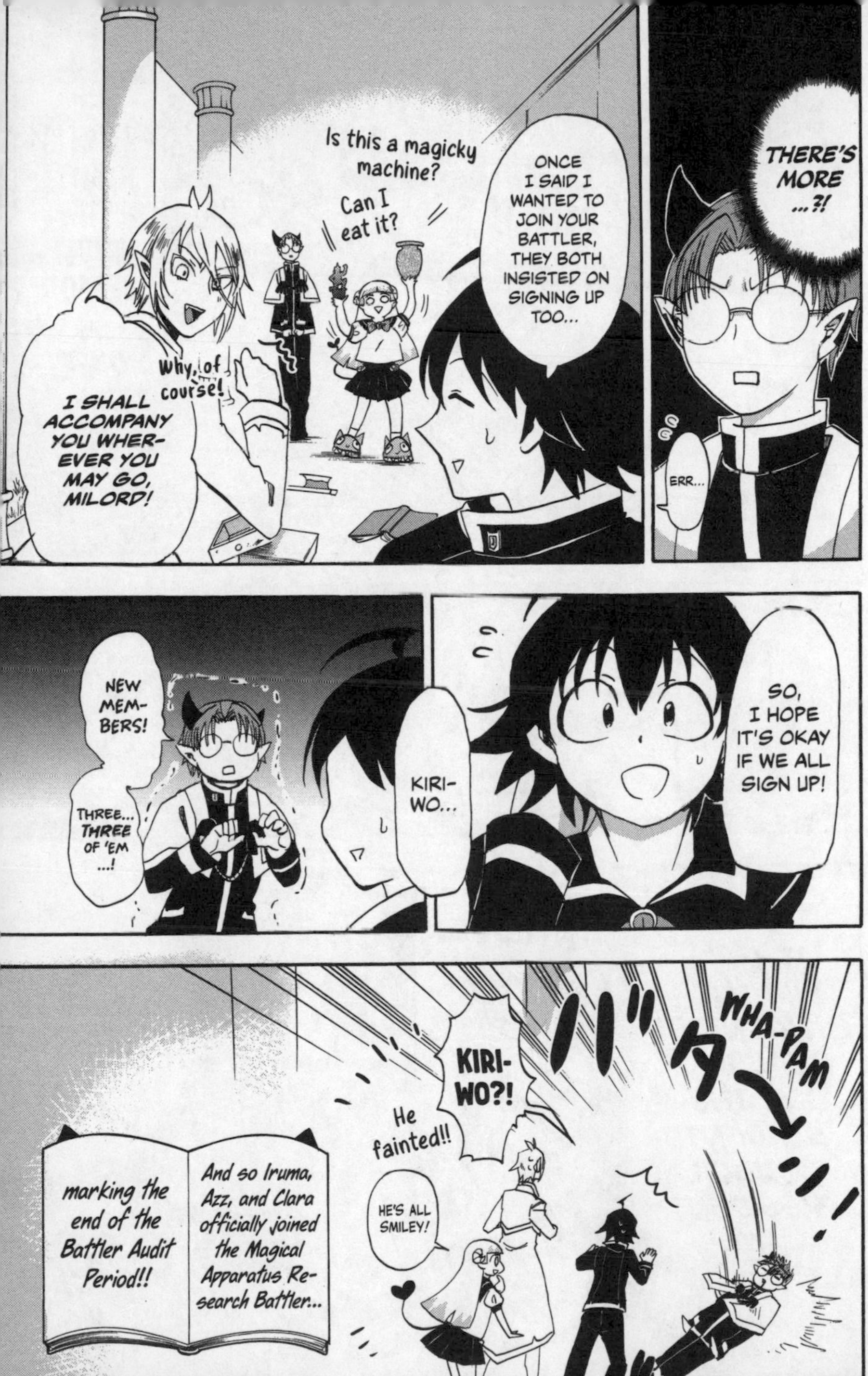
THERE'S MORE ...?!
ERR...
ONCE I SAID I WANTED TO JOIN YOUR BATTLER, THEY BOTH INSISTED ON SIGNING UP TOO...
Is this a magicky machine?
Can I eat it?
Why, of course!
I SHALL ACCOMPANY YOU WHEREVER YOU MAY GO, MILORD!
SO, I HOPE IT'S OKAY IF WE ALL SIGN UP!
KIRI-WO...
NEW MEMBERS!
THREE... THREE OF 'EM ...!
WHA-PAM
KIRI-WO?!
He fainted!!
HE'S ALL SMILEY!
And so Iruma, Azz, and Clara officially joined the Magical Apparatus Research Battler...
marking the end of the Battler Audit Period!!

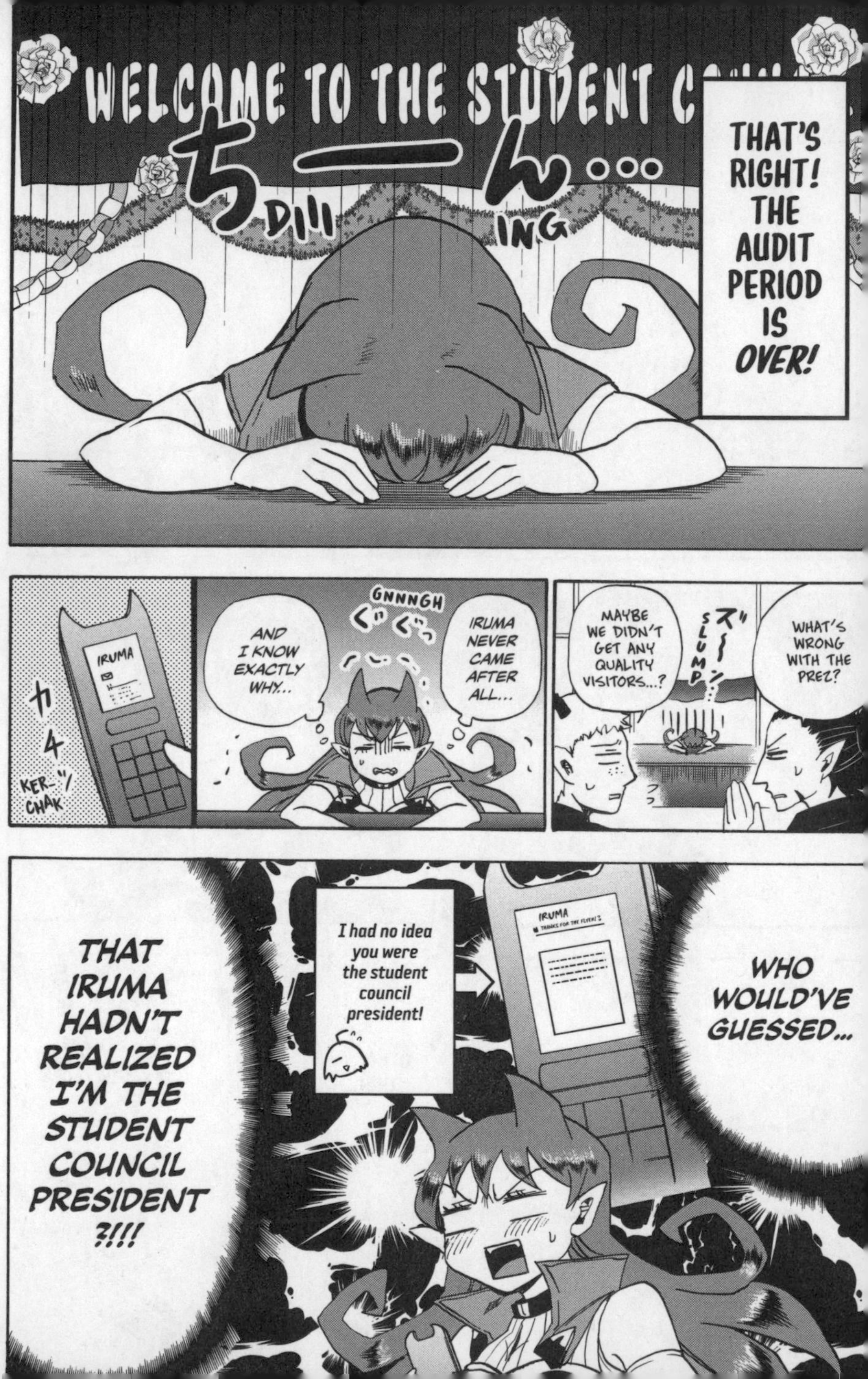
WELCOME TO THE STUDENT C
THAT'S RIGHT! THE AUDIT PERIOD IS OVER!
ちーん…
DIIIING
WHAT'S WRONG WITH THE PREZ?
ズーン
SLUMP
MAYBE WE DIDN'T GET ANY QUALITY VISITORS...?
IRUMA NEVER CAME AFTER ALL...
GNNNGH
AND I KNOW EXACTLY WHY...
IRUMA
KER-CHAK
WHO WOULD'VE GUESSED...
IRUMA
I had no idea you were the student council president!
THAT IRUMA HADN'T REALIZED I'M THE STUDENT COUNCIL PRESIDENT?!!!

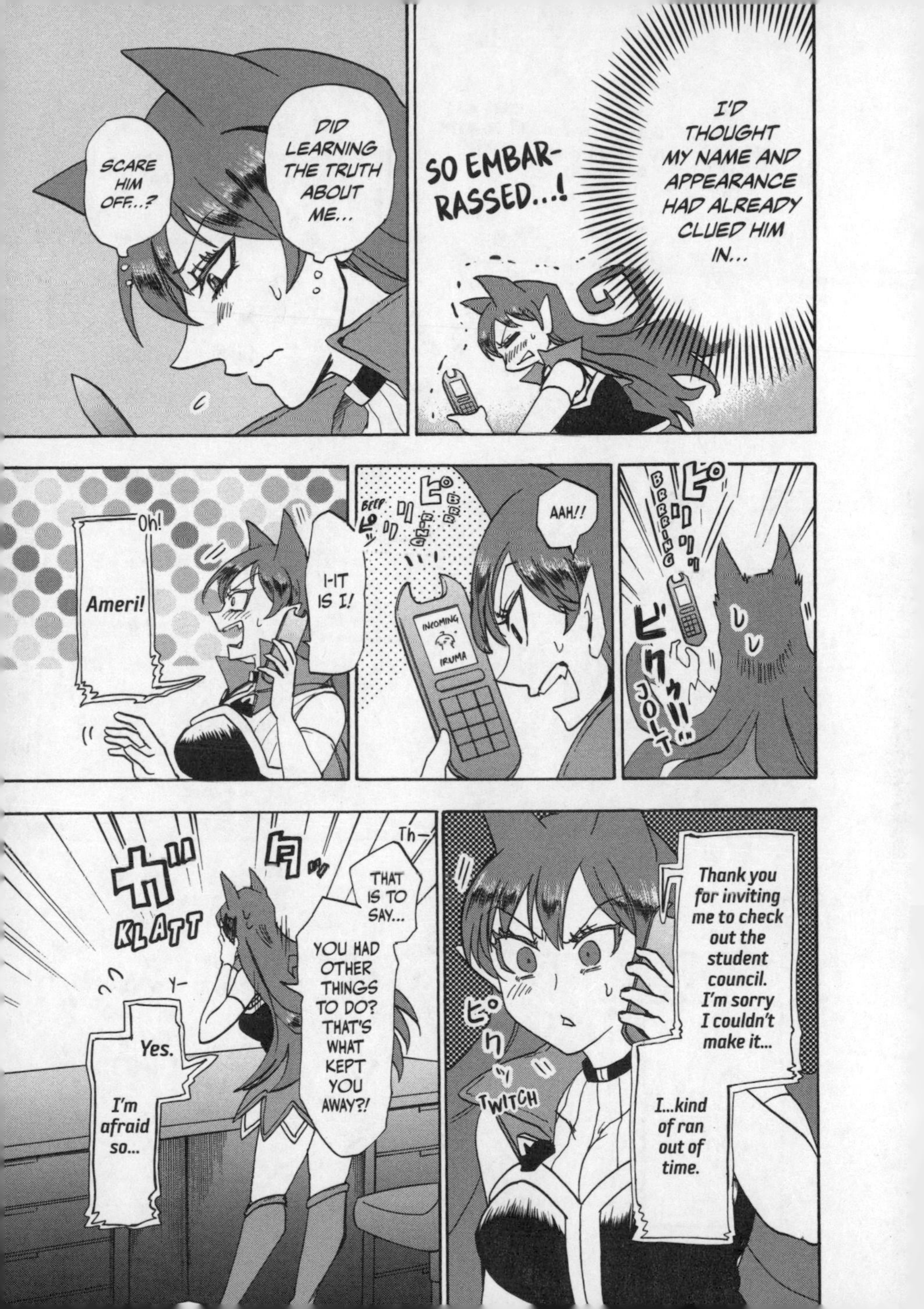
I'D THOUGHT MY NAME AND APPEARANCE HAD ALREADY CLUED HIM IN...
SO EMBAR-RASSED...!
DID LEARNING THE TRUTH ABOUT ME...
SCARE HIM OFF...?
BRRRING
JOLT
AAH!!
BEEP
BRRRING
INCOMING
IRUMA
I-IT IS I!
Oh!
Ameri!
Thank you for inviting me to check out the student council. I'm sorry I couldn't make it...
I...kind of ran out of time.
TWITCH
Th—
THAT IS TO SAY...
YOU HAD OTHER THINGS TO DO? THAT'S WHAT KEPT YOU AWAY?!
KLATT
Y—
Yes.
I'm afraid so...

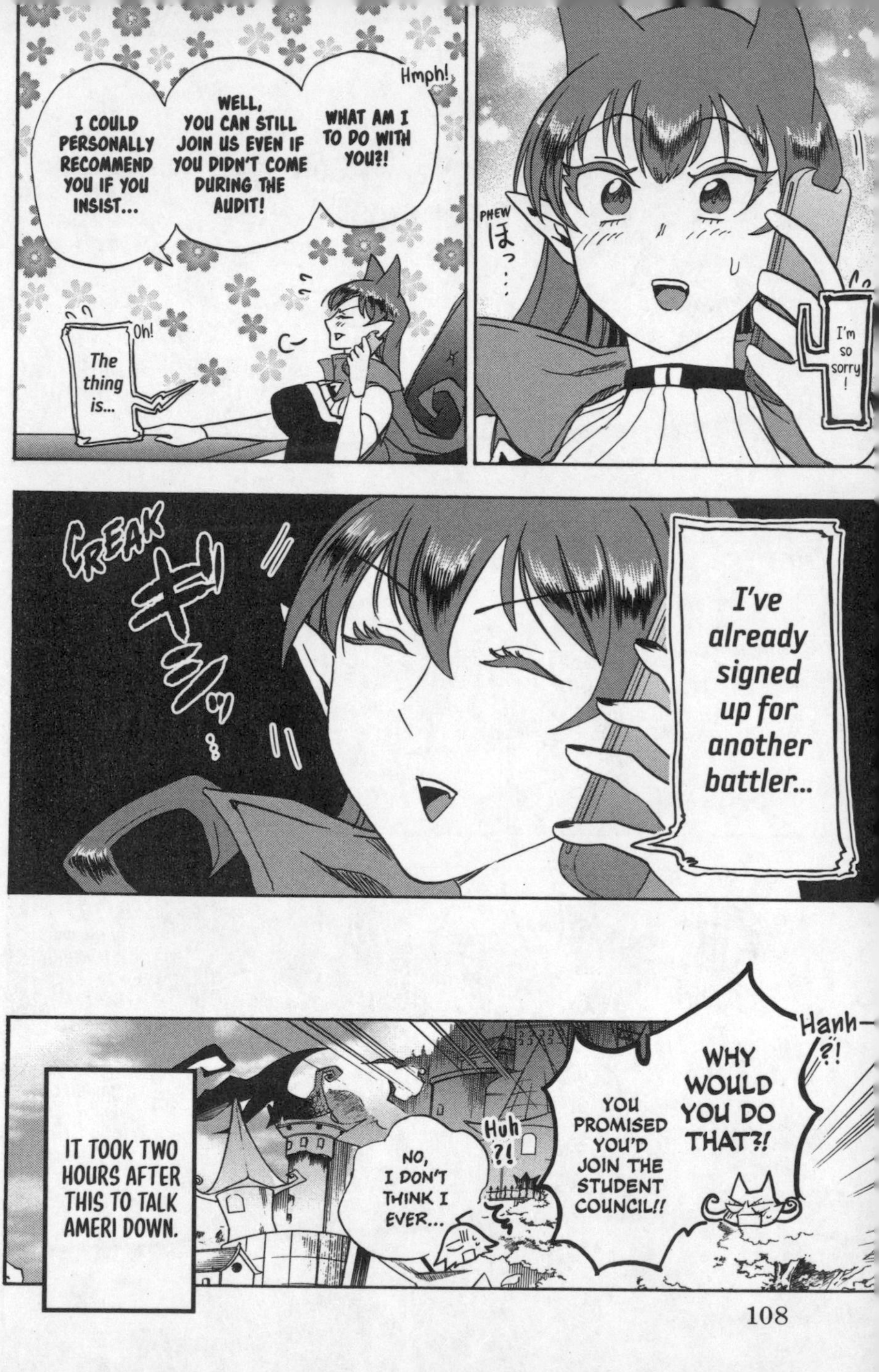
PHEW
ほっ…
I'm so sorry!
Hmph!
WHAT AM I TO DO WITH YOU?!
WELL, YOU CAN STILL JOIN US EVEN IF YOU DIDN'T COME DURING THE AUDIT!
I COULD PERSONALLY RECOMMEND YOU IF YOU INSIST...
Oh!
The thing is...
I've already signed up for another battler...
CREAK
ギシッ
Hanh-?!
WHY WOULD YOU DO THAT?!
YOU PROMISED YOU'D JOIN THE STUDENT COUNCIL!!
Huh?!
NO, I DON'T THINK I EVER...
IT TOOK TWO HOURS AFTER THIS TO TALK AMERI DOWN.

CHAPTER 22 MY FAMILIAR AND ME ♪

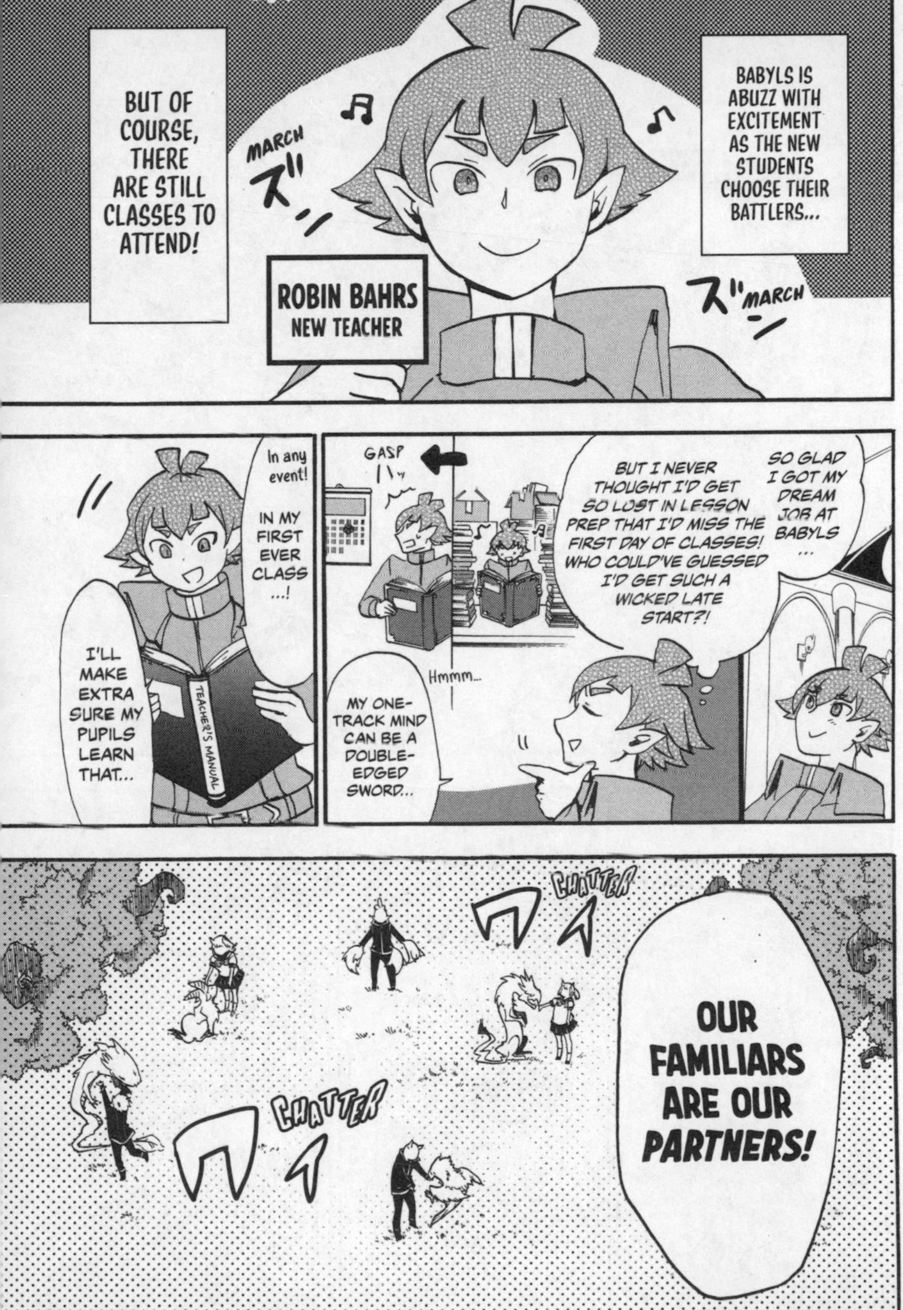
BABYLS IS ABUZZ WITH EXCITEMENT AS THE NEW STUDENTS CHOOSE THEIR BATTLERS...
MARCH
BUT OF COURSE, THERE ARE STILL CLASSES TO ATTEND!
MARCH
ROBIN BAHRS
NEW TEACHER
SO GLAD I GOT MY DREAM JOB AT BABYLS ...
BUT I NEVER THOUGHT I'D GET SO LOST IN LESSON PREP THAT I'D MISS THE FIRST DAY OF CLASSES! WHO COULD'VE GUESSED I'D GET SUCH A WICKED LATE START?!
GASP
Hmmm...
MY ONE-TRACK MIND CAN BE A DOUBLE-EDGED SWORD...
In any event!
IN MY FIRST EVER CLASS ...!
I'LL MAKE EXTRA SURE MY PUPILS LEARN THAT...
TEACHER'S MANUAL
OUR FAMILIARS ARE OUR PARTNERS!
CHATTER
CHATTER

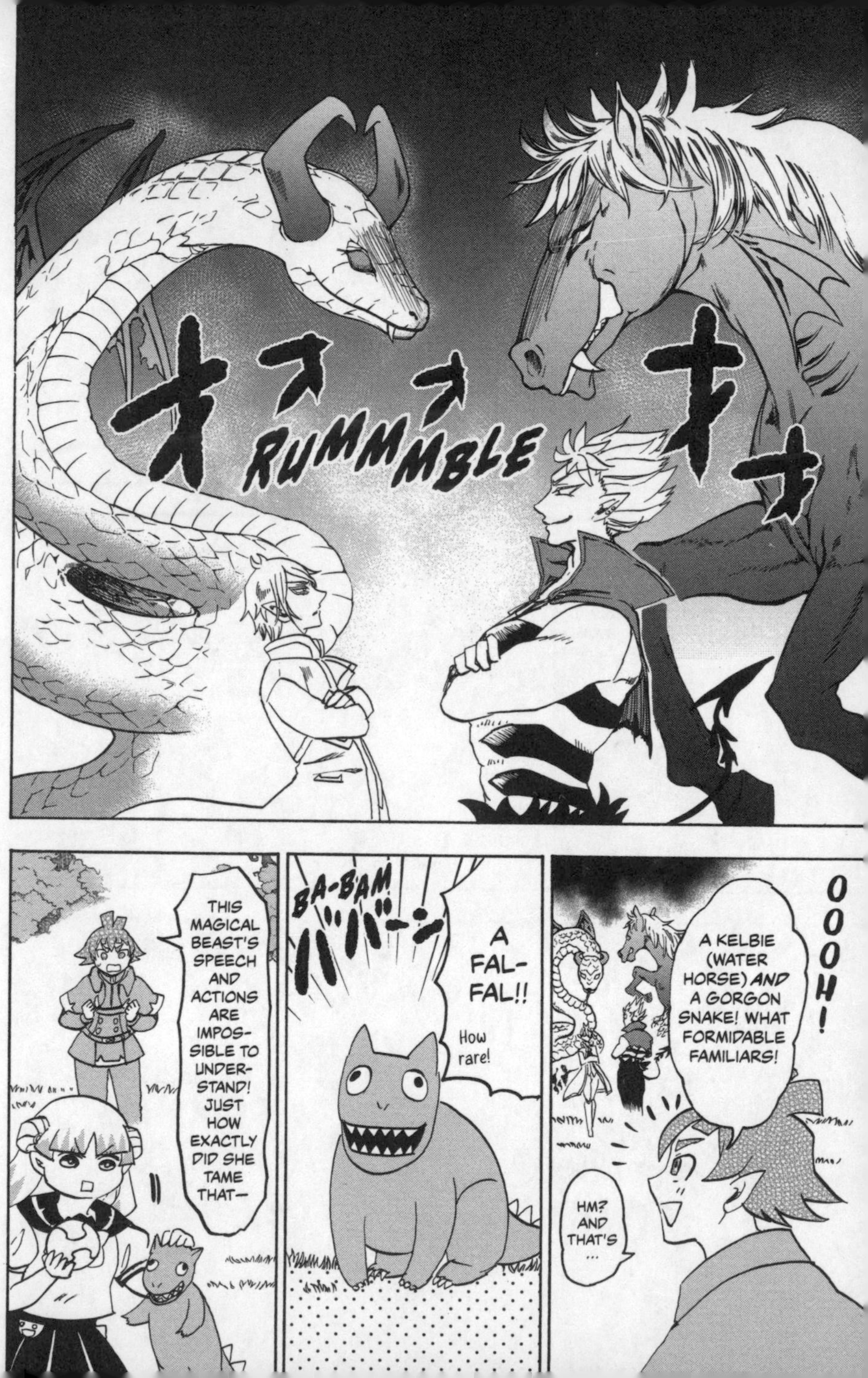
RUMMMBLE
OOOOH!
A KELBIE (WATER HORSE) AND A GORGON SNAKE! WHAT FORMIDABLE FAMILIARS!
HM? AND THAT'S ...
BA-BAM
A FAL-FAL!!
How rare!
THIS MAGICAL BEAST'S SPEECH AND ACTIONS ARE IMPOSSIBLE TO UNDERSTAND! JUST HOW EXACTLY DID SHE TAME THAT—

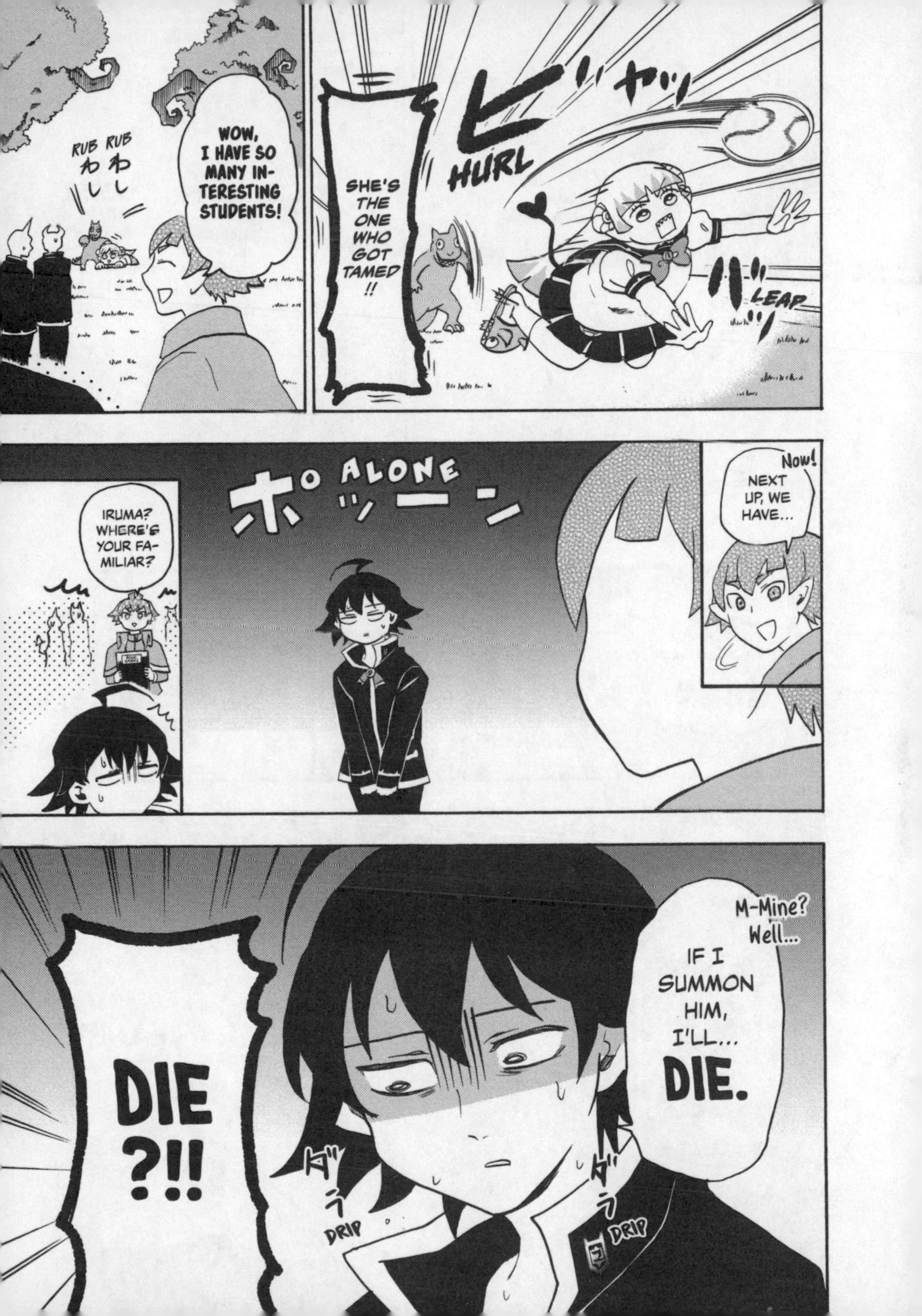
ビシャッ
HURL
パッ
LEAP
SHE'S THE ONE WHO GOT TAMED!!
WOW, I HAVE SO MANY INTERESTING STUDENTS!
RUB RUB
わしわし
Now! NEXT UP, WE HAVE...
ポツーン
ALONE
IRUMA? WHERE'S YOUR FAMILIAR?
M-Mine? Well...
IF I SUMMON HIM, I'LL... DIE.
ダラ
DRIP
DIE?!!
ダラ
DRIP

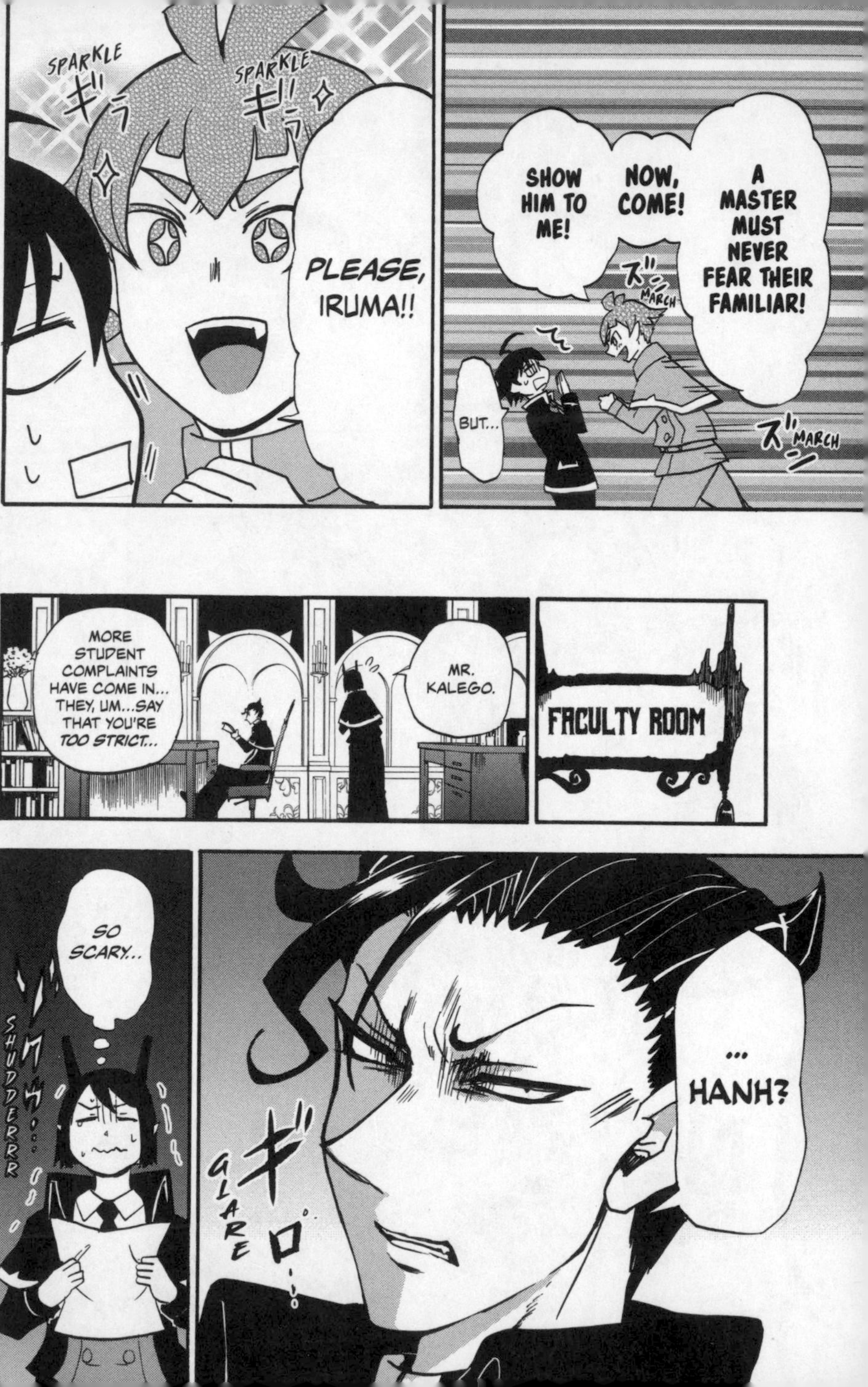
A MASTER MUST NEVER FEAR THEIR FAMILIAR!
NOW, COME!
SHOW HIM TO ME!
MARCH
BUT...
MARCH
SPARKLE
SPARKLE
PLEASE, IRUMA!!
FACULTY ROOM
MR. KALEGO.
MORE STUDENT COMPLAINTS HAVE COME IN... THEY, UM...SAY THAT YOU'RE *TOO STRICT*...
... HANH?
GLARE
SO SCARY...
SHUDDERRR

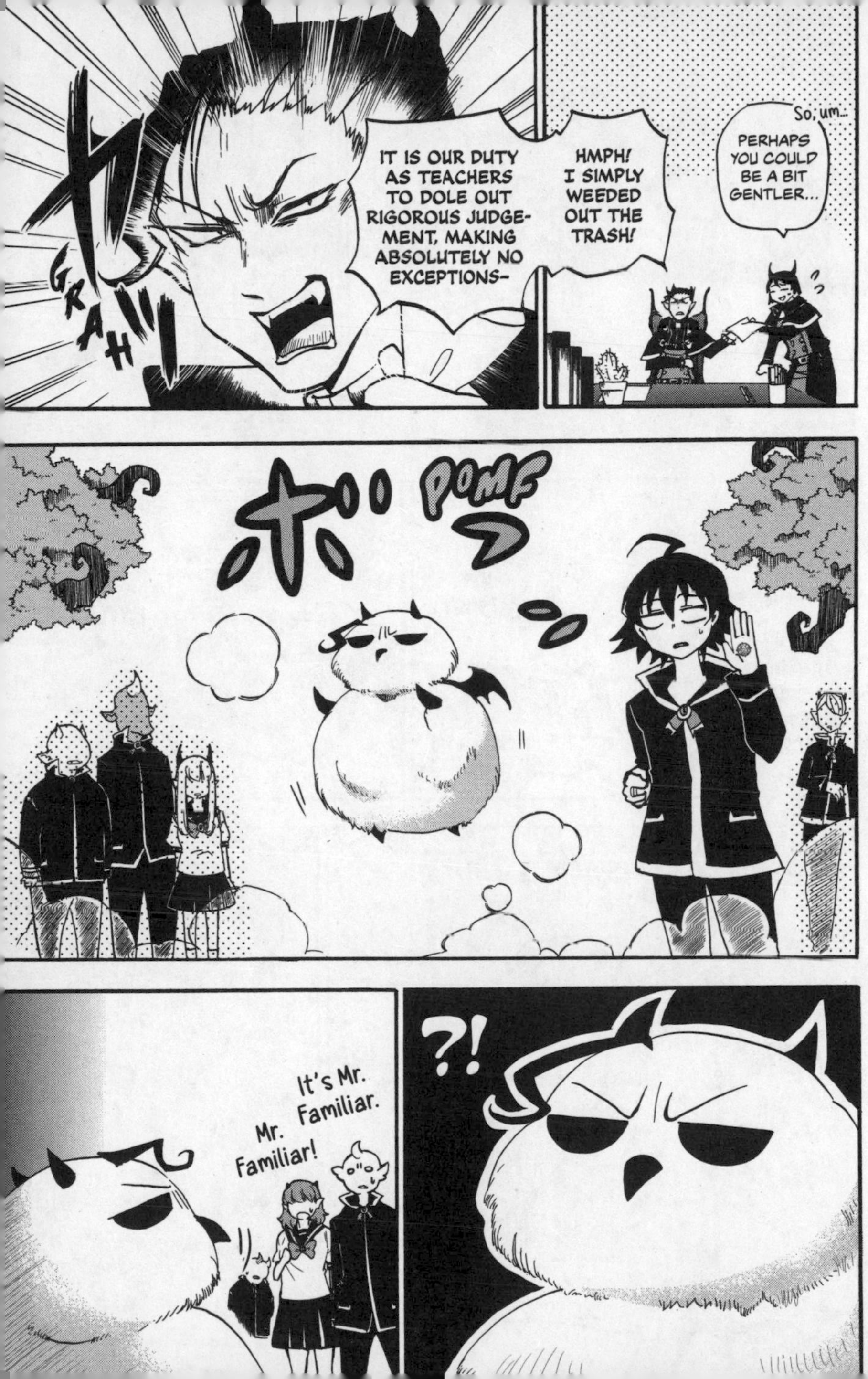
So, um...
PERHAPS YOU COULD BE A BIT GENTLER...
HMPH! I SIMPLY WEEDED OUT THE TRASH!
IT IS OUR DUTY AS TEACHERS TO DOLE OUT RIGOROUS JUDGEMENT, MAKING ABSOLUTELY NO EXCEPTIONS–
GRAHH
POMF
?!
It's Mr. Familiar.
Mr. Familiar!

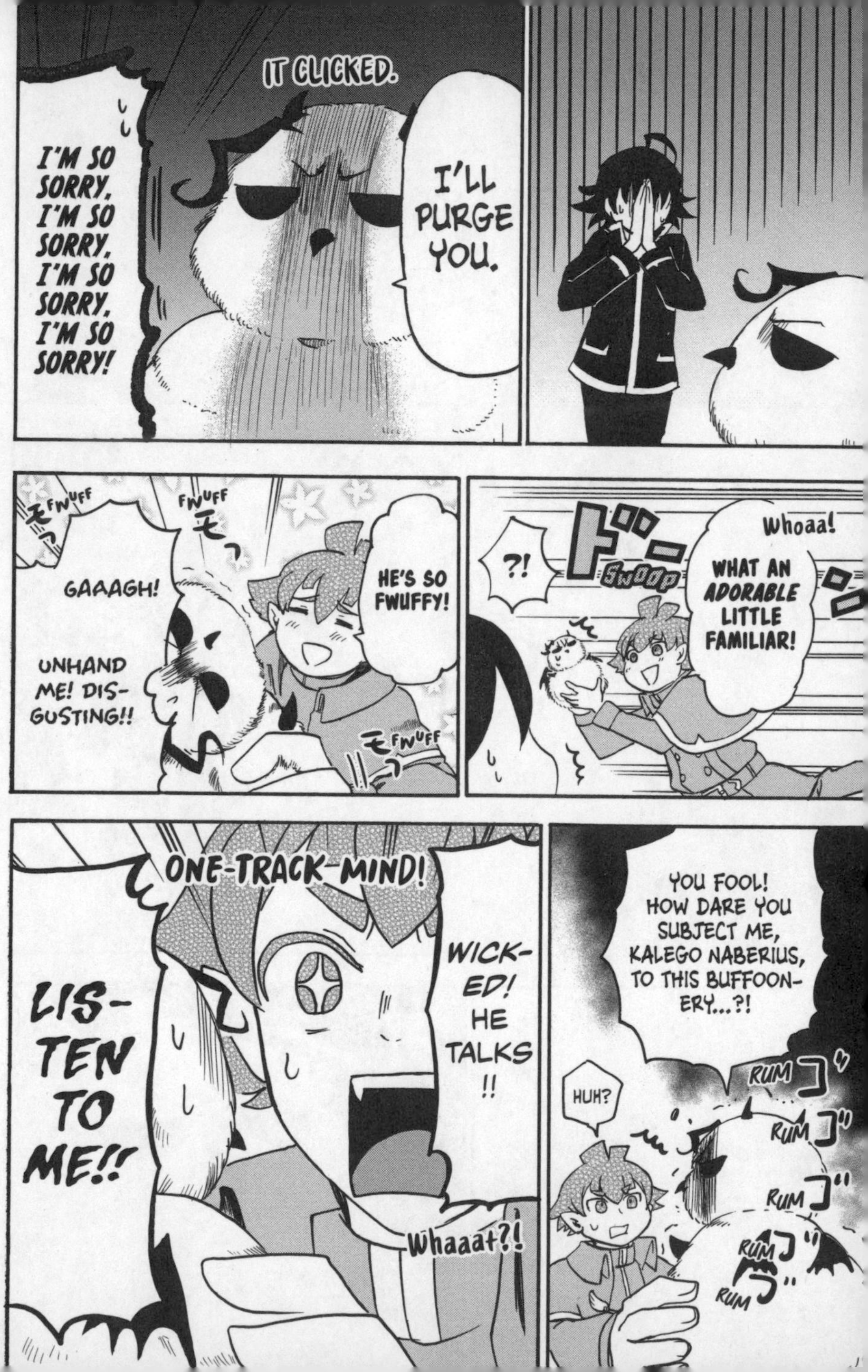
IT CLICKED.
I'LL PURGE YOU.
I'M SO SORRY, I'M SO SORRY, I'M SO SORRY, I'M SO SORRY!
Whoaa!
WHAT AN ADORABLE LITTLE FAMILIAR!
?!
SWOOP
FWUFF
HE'S SO FWUFFY!
FWUFF
GAAAGH!
UNHAND ME! DIS-GUSTING!!
FWUFF
YOU FOOL! HOW DARE YOU SUBJECT ME, KALEGO NABERIUS, TO THIS BUFFOONER-ERY...?!
HUH?
RUM
RUM
RUM
RUM
RUM
ONE-TRACK-MIND!
WICK-ED! HE TALKS!!
LIS-TEN TO ME!!
Whaaat?!

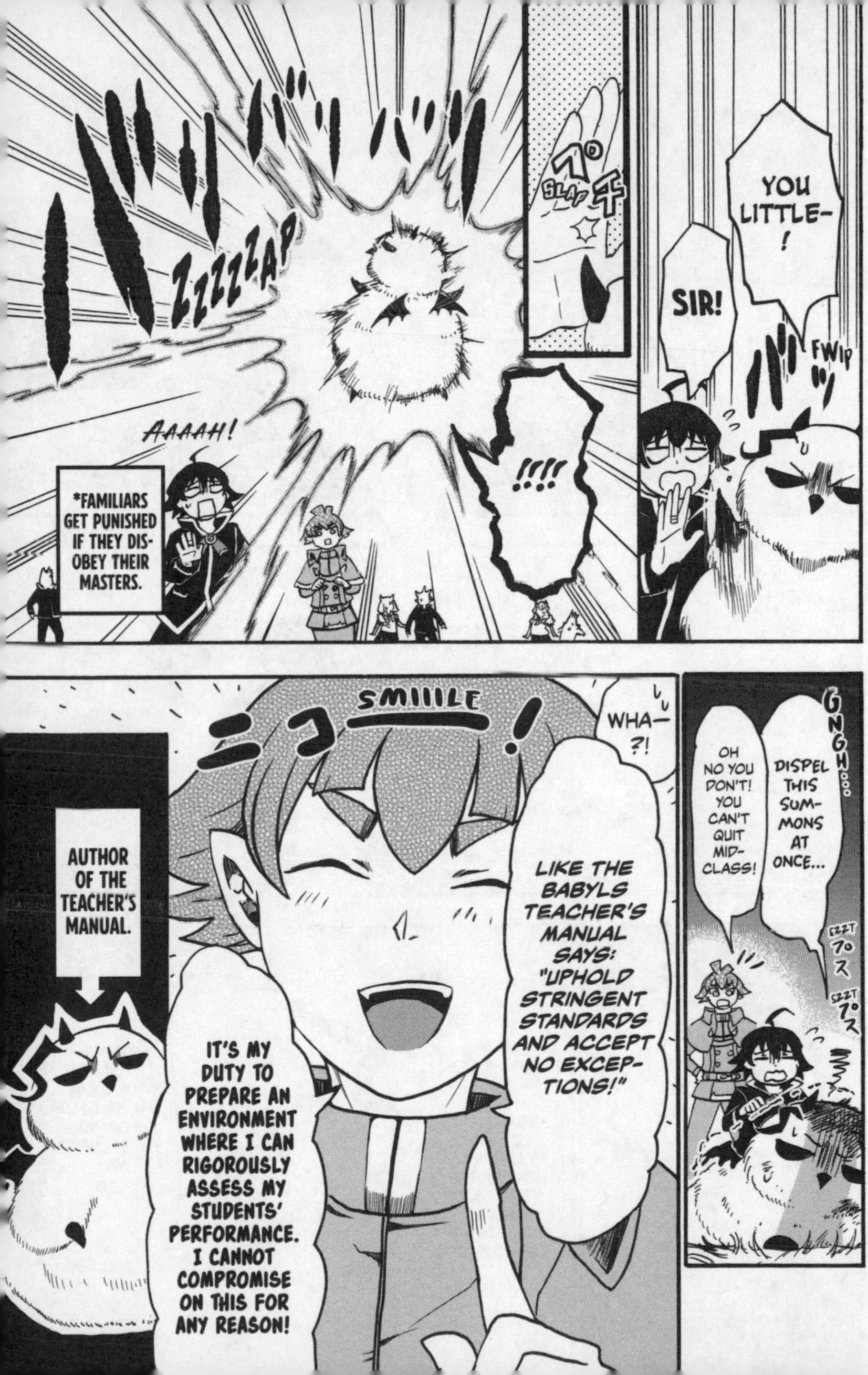
YOU LITTLE-!
SIR!
FWIP
SLAP
ZZZZZAP
!!!!
AAAAH!
*FAMILIARS GET PUNISHED IF THEY DISOBEY THEIR MASTERS.
GNGH...
DISPEL THIS SUMMONS AT ONCE...
OH NO YOU DON'T! YOU CAN'T QUIT MID-CLASS!
SZZT
SZZT
SMIIILE
WHA-?!
LIKE THE BABYLS TEACHER'S MANUAL SAYS: "UPHOLD STRINGENT STANDARDS AND ACCEPT NO EXCEPTIONS!"
IT'S MY DUTY TO PREPARE AN ENVIRONMENT WHERE I CAN RIGOROUSLY ASSESS MY STUDENTS' PERFORMANCE. I CANNOT COMPROMISE ON THIS FOR ANY REASON!
AUTHOR OF THE TEACHER'S MANUAL.

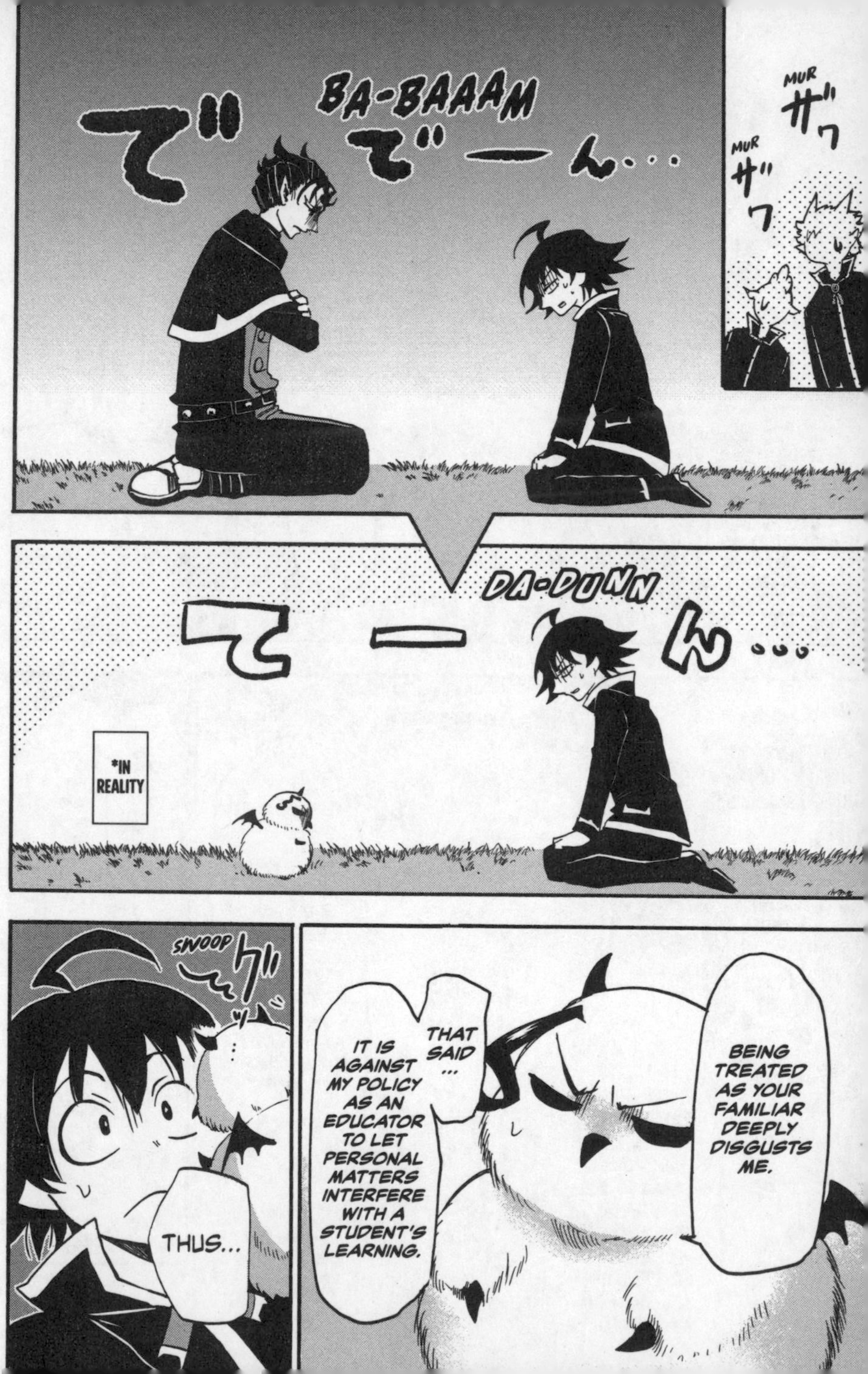
MUR
ザワ
MUR
ザワ
BA-BAAAM
ででーん…
DA-DUNN
てーん…
*IN REALITY
BEING TREATED AS YOUR FAMILIAR DEEPLY DISGUSTS ME.
THAT SAID...
IT IS AGAINST MY POLICY AS AN EDUCATOR TO LET PERSONAL MATTERS INTERFERE WITH A STUDENT'S LEARNING.
SWOOP
THUS...

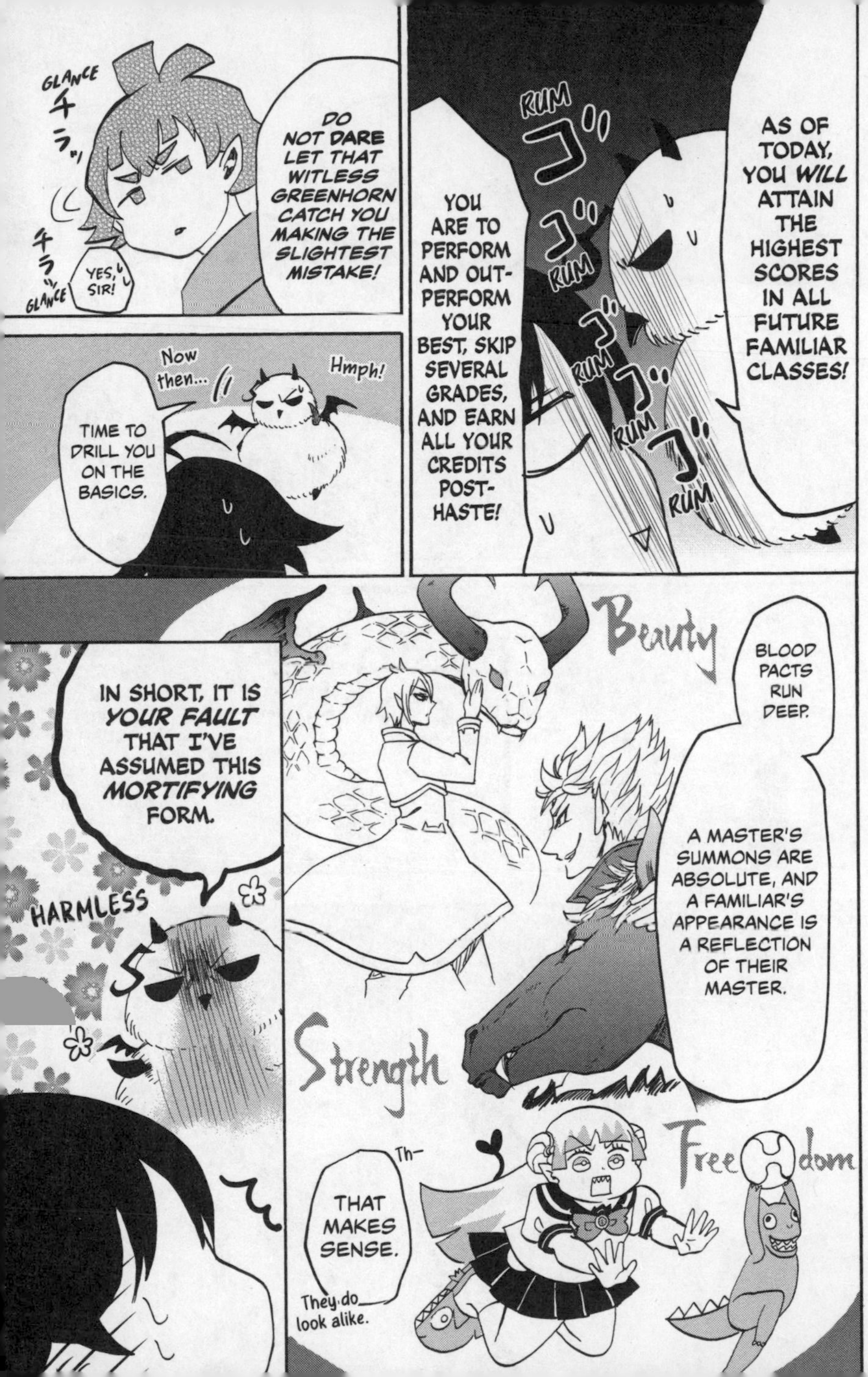

AS OF TODAY, YOU *WILL* ATTAIN THE HIGHEST SCORES IN ALL FUTURE FAMILIAR CLASSES!
YOU ARE TO PERFORM AND OUT-PERFORM YOUR BEST, SKIP SEVERAL GRADES, AND EARN ALL YOUR CREDITS POST-HASTE!
RUM
RUM
RUM
RUM
RUM
GLANCE
DO NOT DARE LET THAT WITLESS GREENHORN CATCH YOU MAKING THE SLIGHTEST MISTAKE!
YES, SIR!
GLANCE
Hmph!
Now then...
TIME TO DRILL YOU ON THE BASICS.
BLOOD PACTS RUN DEEP.
Beauty
A MASTER'S SUMMONS ARE ABSOLUTE, AND A FAMILIAR'S APPEARANCE IS A REFLECTION OF THEIR MASTER.
Strength
Freedom
Th-
THAT MAKES SENSE.
They do look alike.
IN SHORT, IT IS *YOUR FAULT* THAT I'VE ASSUMED THIS *MORTIFYING* FORM.
HARMLESS

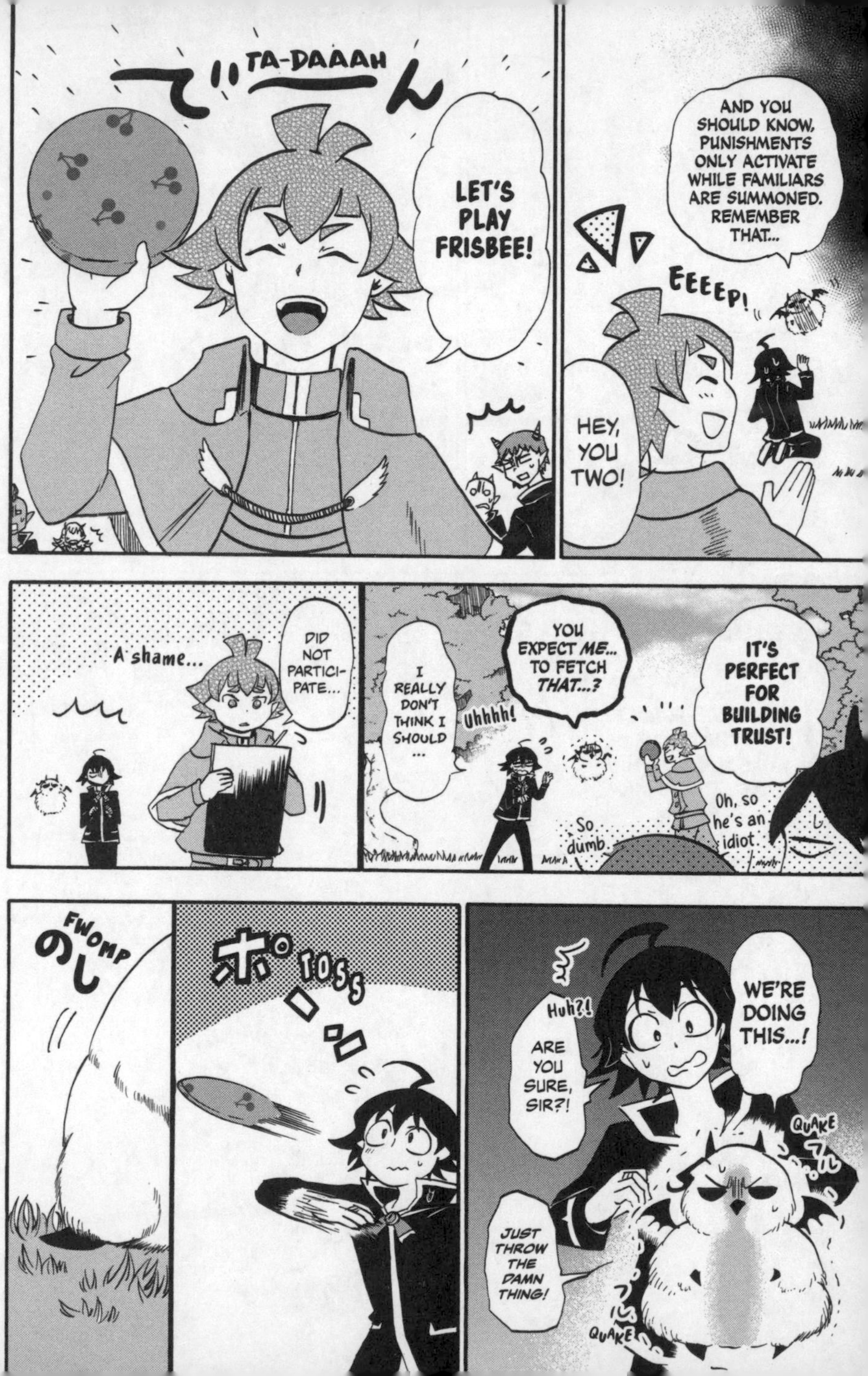
AND YOU SHOULD KNOW, PUNISHMENTS ONLY ACTIVATE WHILE FAMILIARS ARE SUMMONED. REMEMBER THAT...
EEEEP!
HEY, YOU TWO!
TA-DAAAH
LET'S PLAY FRISBEE!
IT'S PERFECT FOR BUILDING TRUST!
YOU EXPECT ME... TO FETCH THAT...?
Uhhhh!
I REALLY DON'T THINK I SHOULD ...
Oh, so he's an idiot.
So dumb.
DID NOT PARTICI-PATE...
A shame...
WE'RE DOING THIS...!
Huh?!
ARE YOU SURE, SIR?!
QUAKE
JUST THROW THE DAMN THING!
QUAKE
TOSS
FWOMP

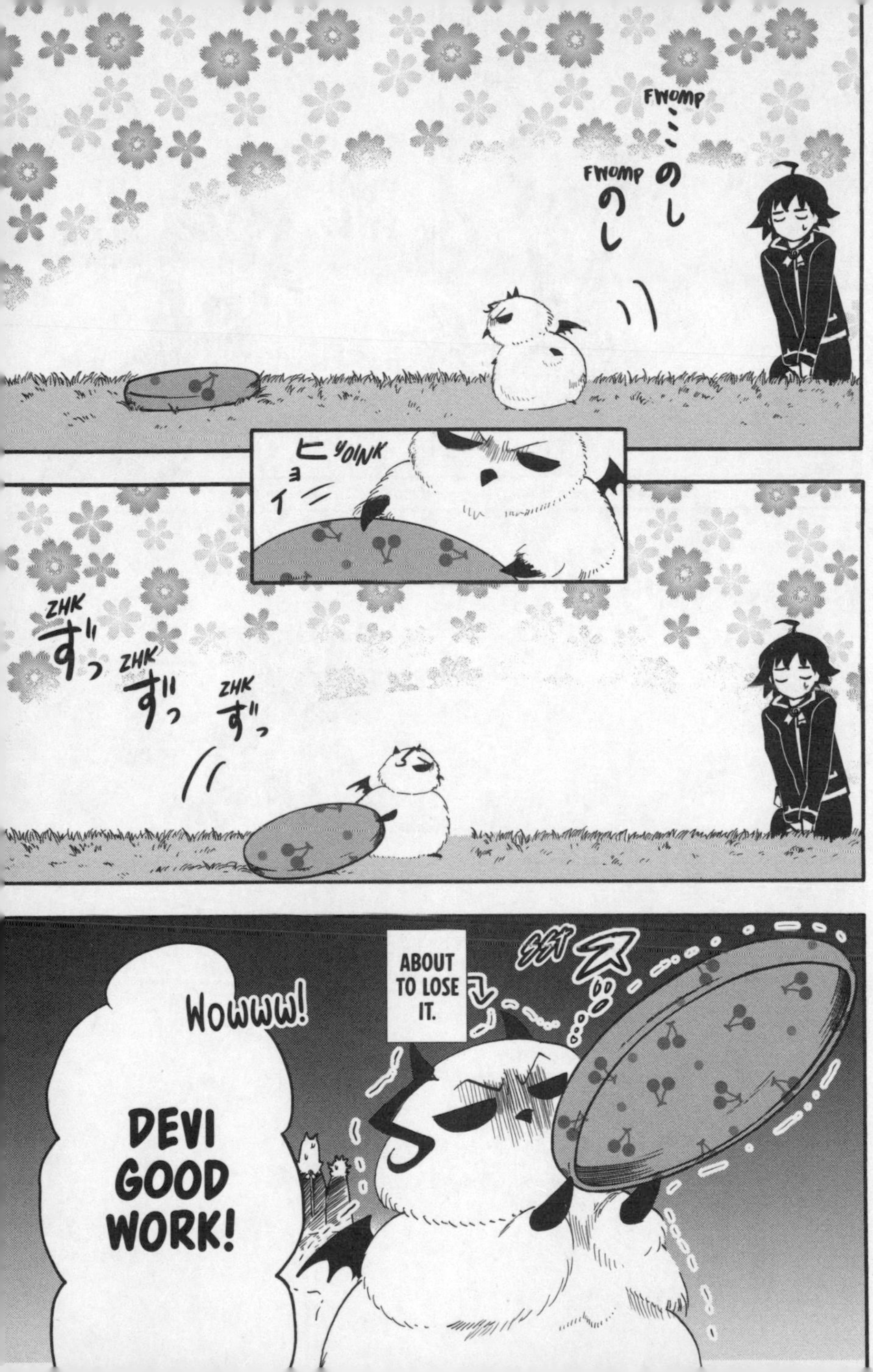
FWOMP
このし
FWOMP
のし
YOINK
ヒョイ
ZHK
ずっ
ZHK
ずっ
ZHK
ずっ
SST
ス
ABOUT TO LOSE IT.
Wowww!
DEVI GOOD WORK!

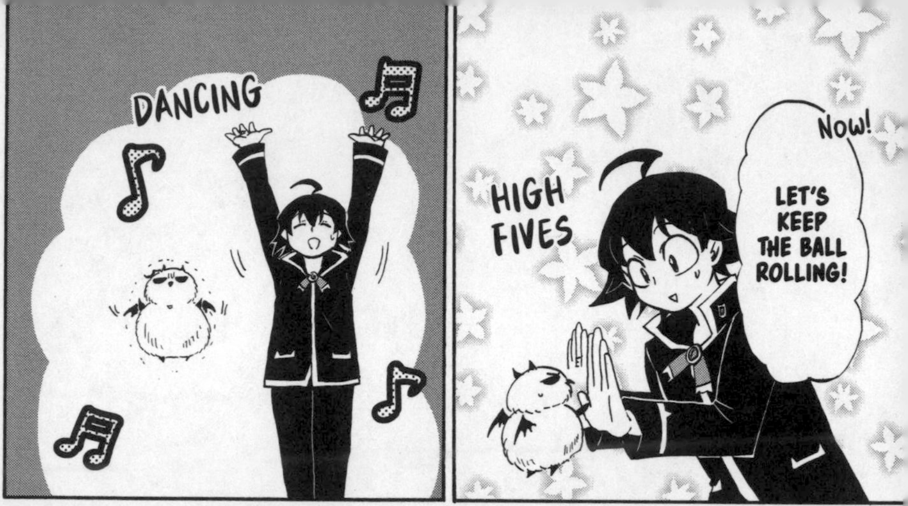
HIGH FIVES
Now!
LET'S KEEP THE BALL ROLLING!
DANCING

*Mentally replace these images with the adult demon Kalego and enjoy the ensuing hilarity.

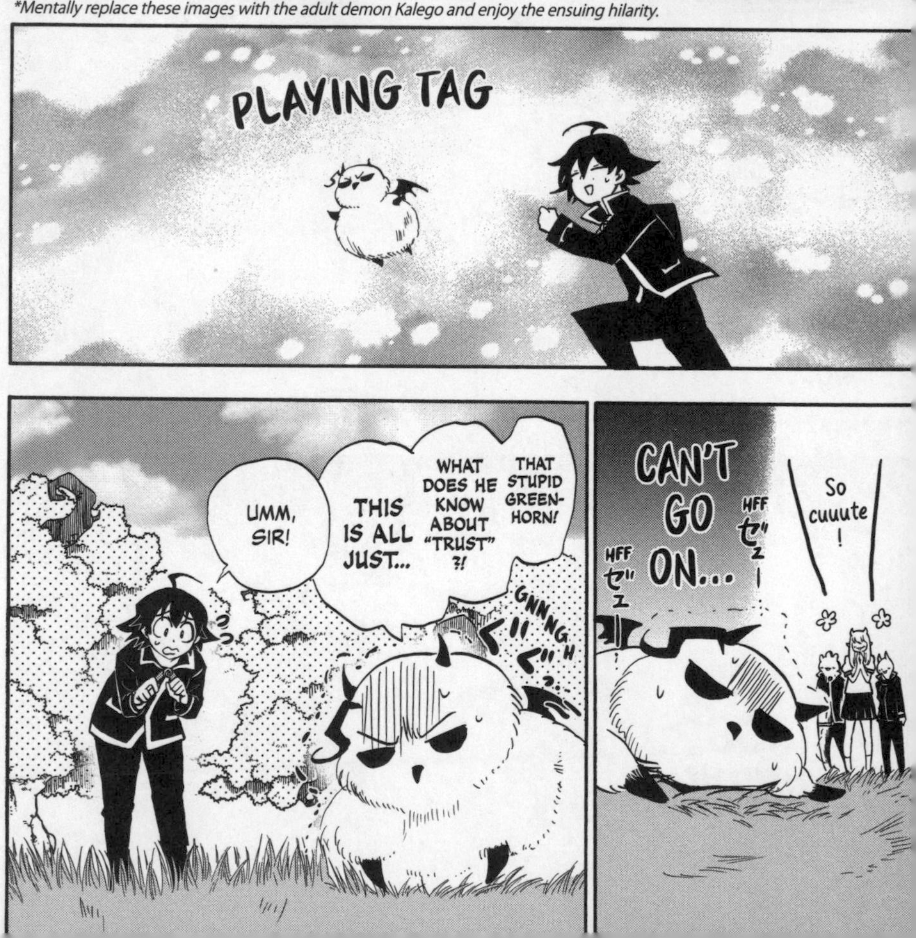
PLAYING TAG
CAN'T GO ON...
HFF ぜ
HFF ぜ
So cuuute!
THAT STUPID GREEN-HORN!
WHAT DOES HE KNOW ABOUT "TRUST" ?!
THIS IS ALL JUST...
UMM, SIR!
GNNNGH

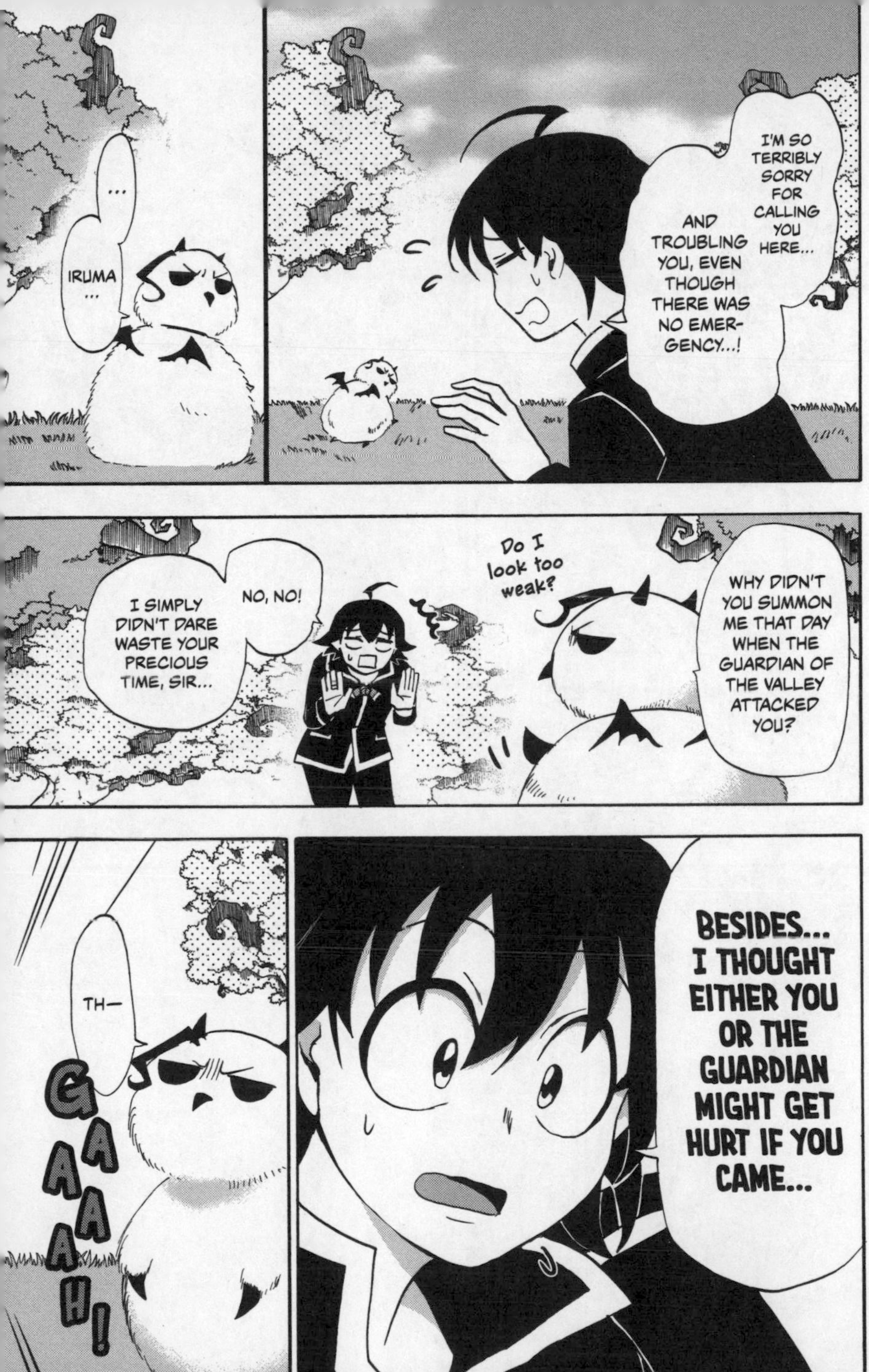
I'M SO TERRIBLY SORRY FOR CALLING YOU HERE...
AND TROUBLING YOU, EVEN THOUGH THERE WAS NO EMERGENCY...!
...
IRUMA ...
WHY DIDN'T YOU SUMMON ME THAT DAY WHEN THE GUARDIAN OF THE VALLEY ATTACKED YOU?
Do I look too weak?
NO, NO!
I SIMPLY DIDN'T DARE WASTE YOUR PRECIOUS TIME, SIR...
BESIDES... I THOUGHT EITHER YOU OR THE GUARDIAN MIGHT GET HURT IF YOU CAME...
TH—
GAAAAAH!

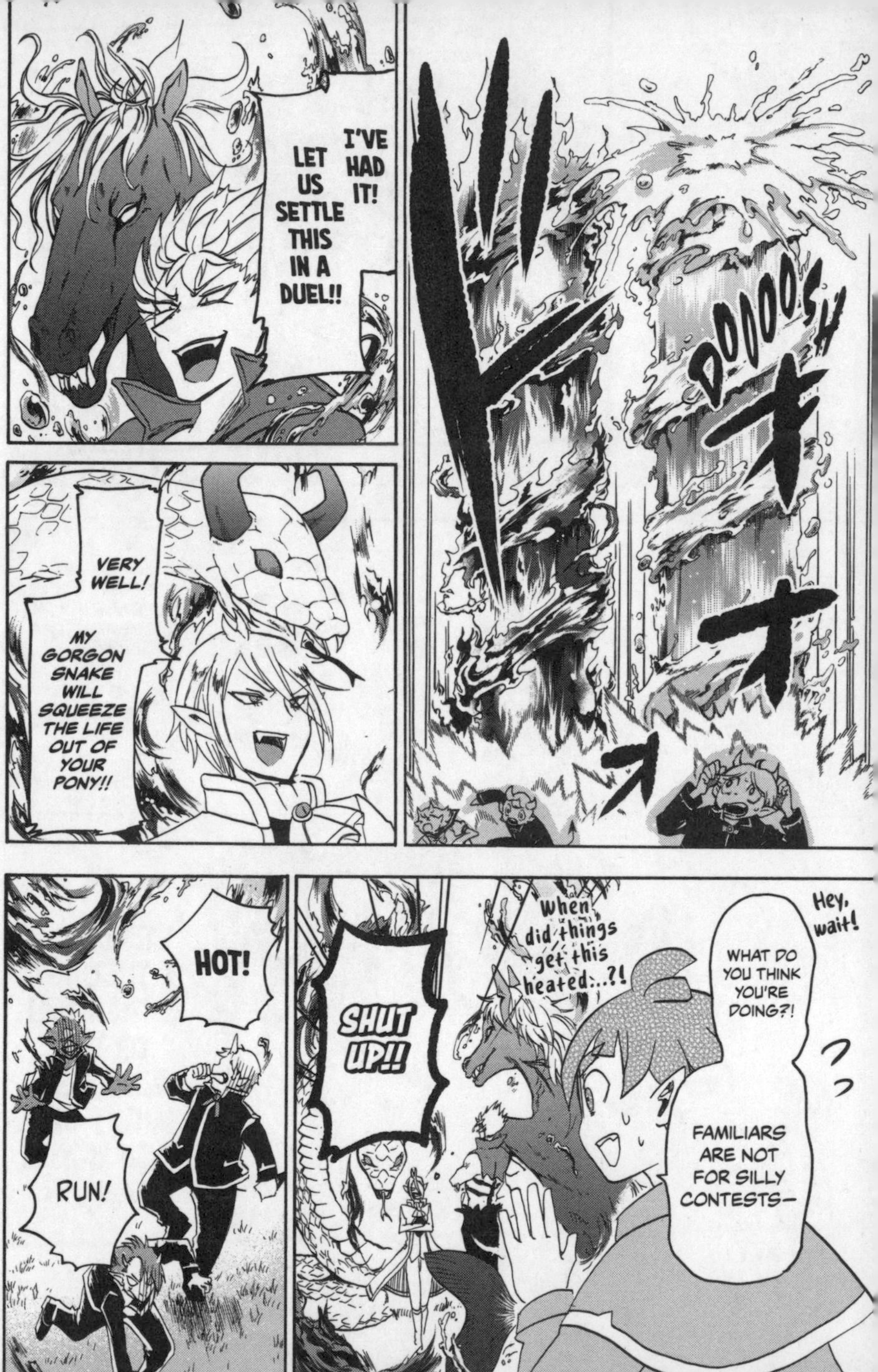
DOOOOSH
ドオオ
I'VE HAD IT!
LET US SETTLE THIS IN A DUEL!!
VERY WELL!
MY GORGON SNAKE WILL SQUEEZE THE LIFE OUT OF YOUR PONY!!
Hey, wait!
WHAT DO YOU THINK YOU'RE DOING?!
FAMILIARS ARE NOT FOR SILLY CONTESTS—
When did things get this heated...?!
SHUT UP!!
HOT!
RUN!

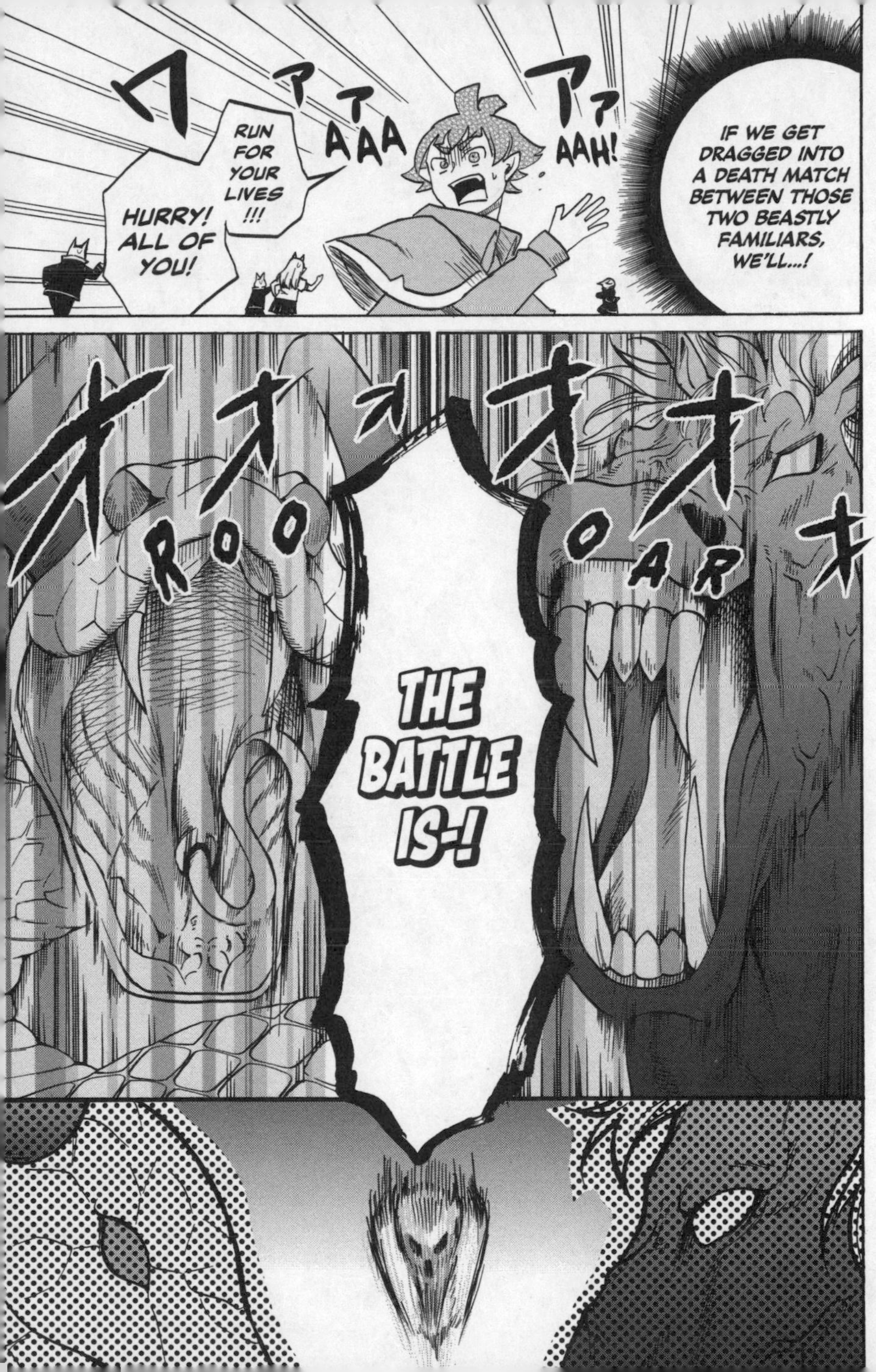
IF WE GET DRAGGED INTO A DEATH MATCH BETWEEN THOSE TWO BEASTLY FAMILIARS, WE'LL...!
ヘアアアァ
AAA AAH!
RUN FOR YOUR LIVES !!!
HURRY! ALL OF YOU!
オオォオオォ
ROOOAR
THE BATTLE IS-!

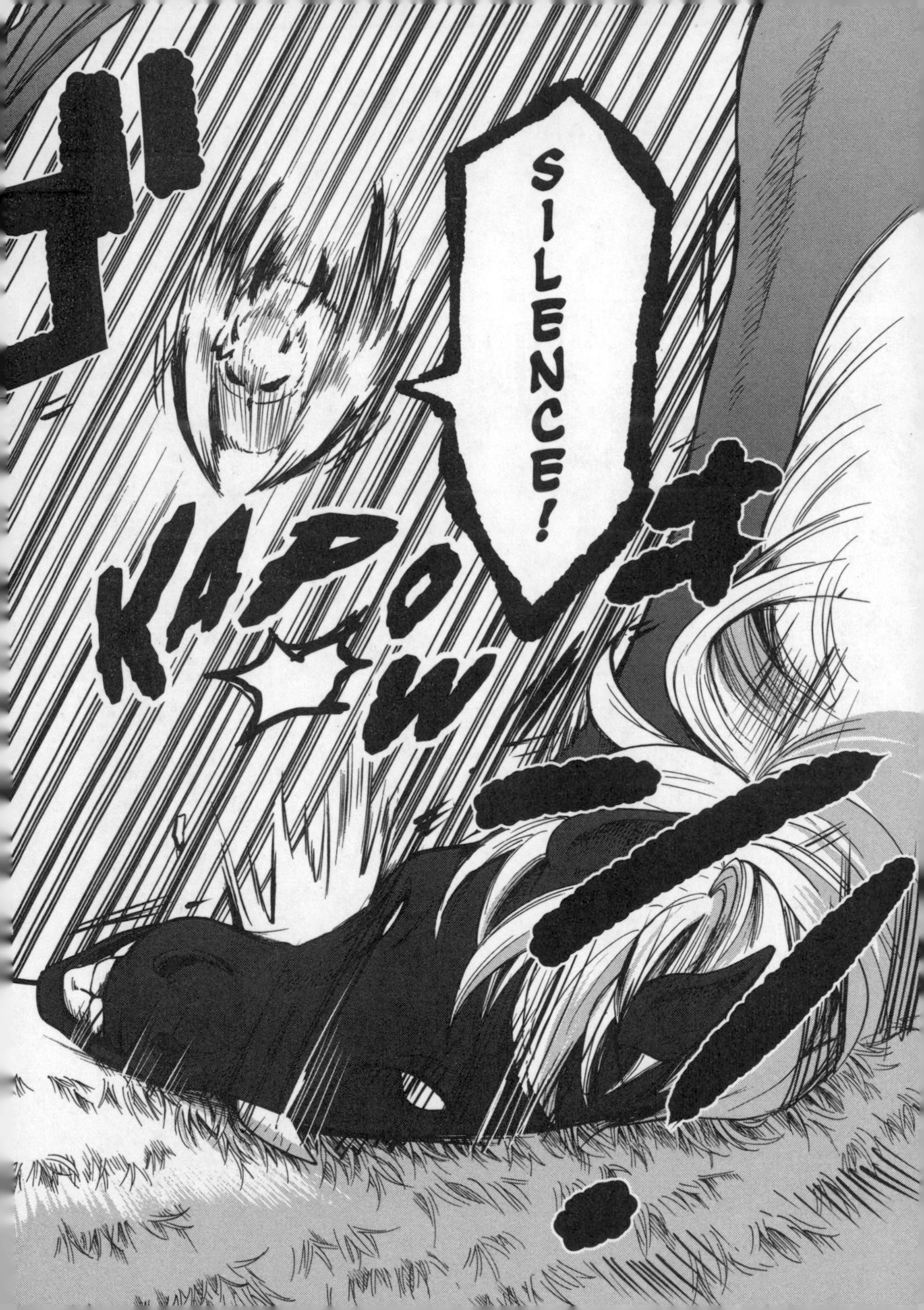
SILENCE!
KAPOW

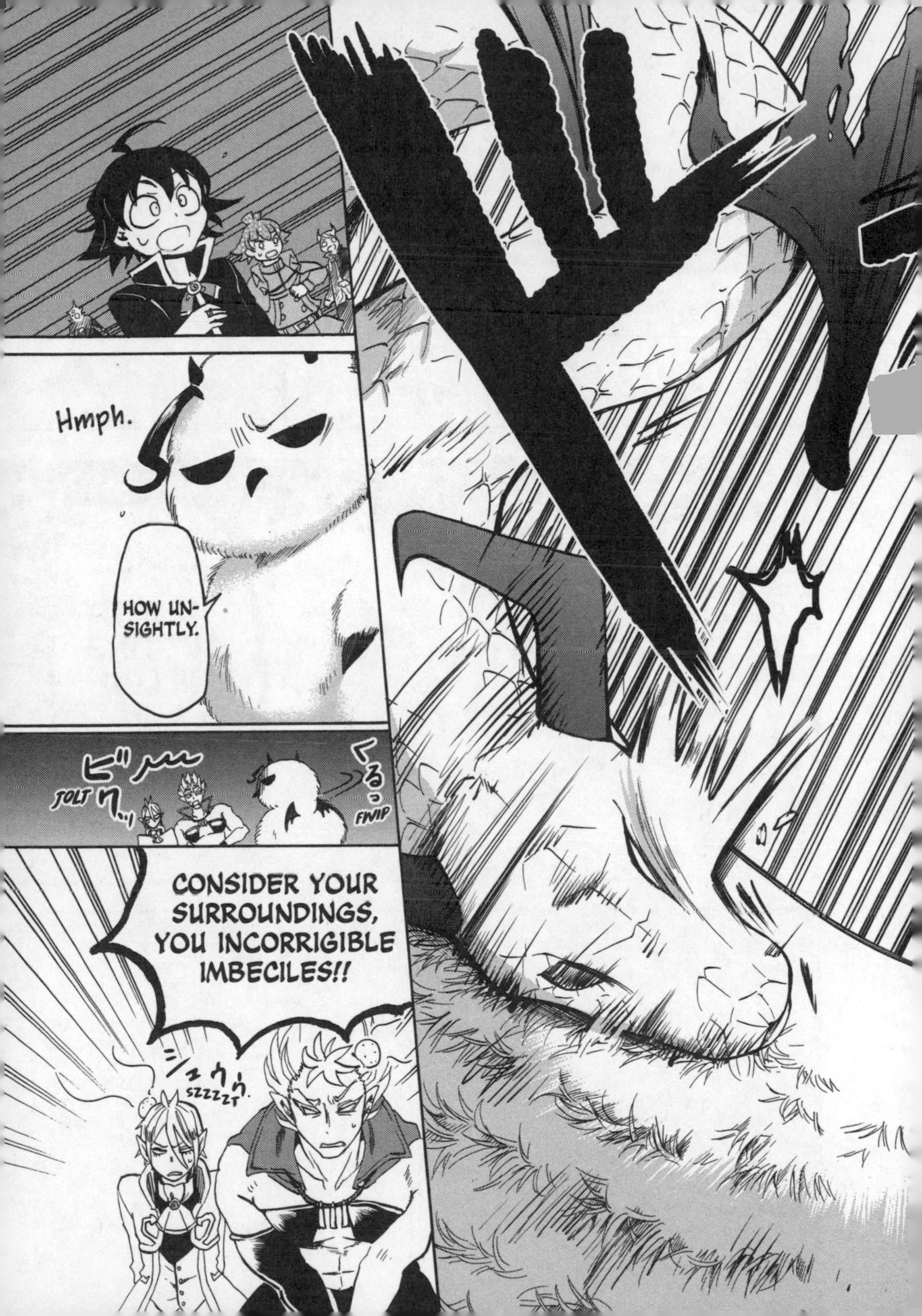
Hmph.
HOW UN-SIGHTLY.
くるっ
FWIP
JOLT
CONSIDER YOUR SURROUNDINGS, YOU INCORRIGIBLE IMBECILES!!
SZZZZT

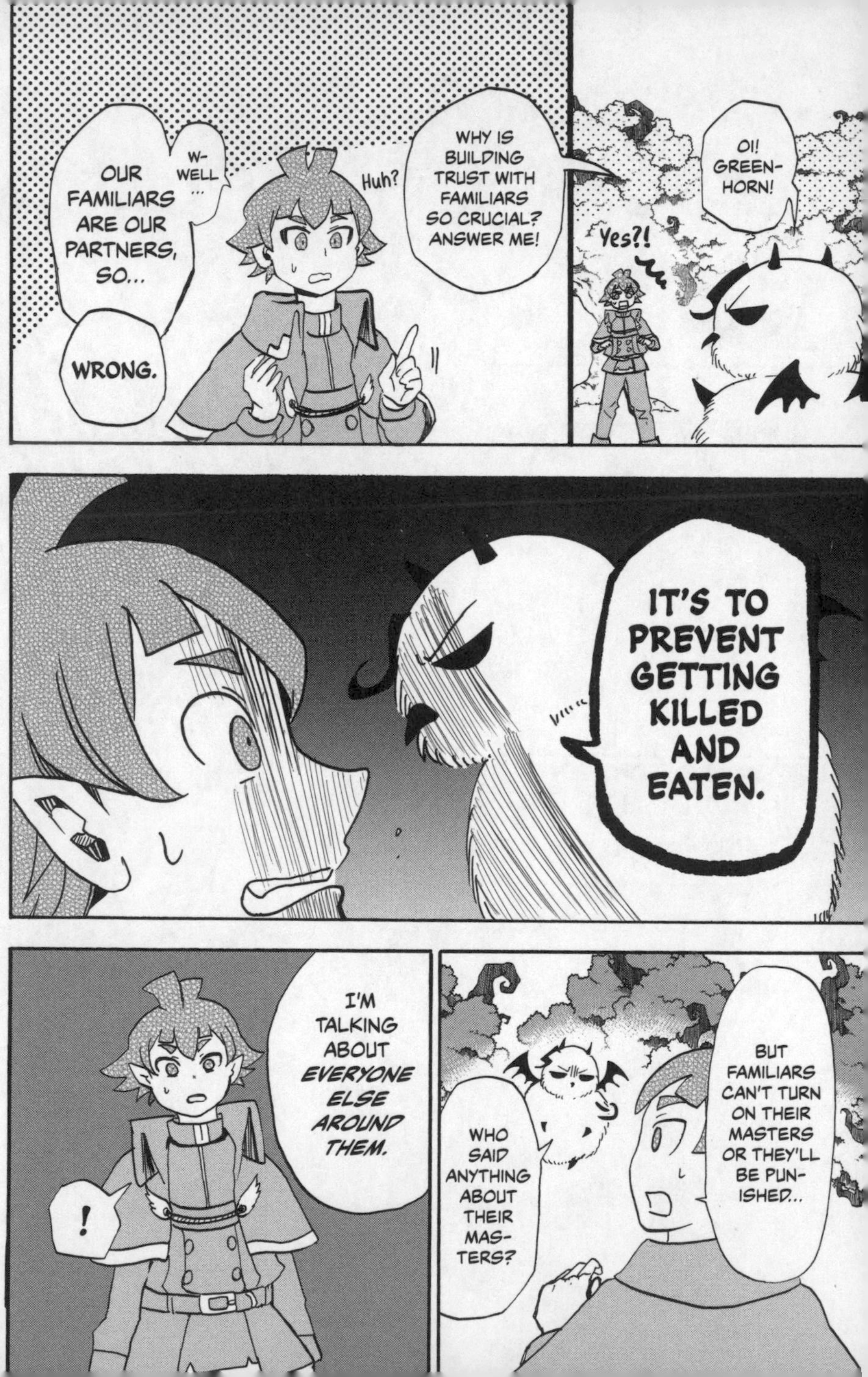
OI! GREEN-HORN!
Yes?!
WHY IS BUILDING TRUST WITH FAMILIARS SO CRUCIAL? ANSWER ME!
Huh?
W-WELL...
OUR FAMILIARS ARE OUR PARTNERS, SO...
WRONG.
IT'S TO PREVENT GETTING KILLED AND EATEN.
BUT FAMILIARS CAN'T TURN ON THEIR MASTERS OR THEY'LL BE PUN-ISHED...
WHO SAID ANYTHING ABOUT THEIR MAS-TERS?
I'M TALKING ABOUT *EVERYONE ELSE AROUND THEM.*
!

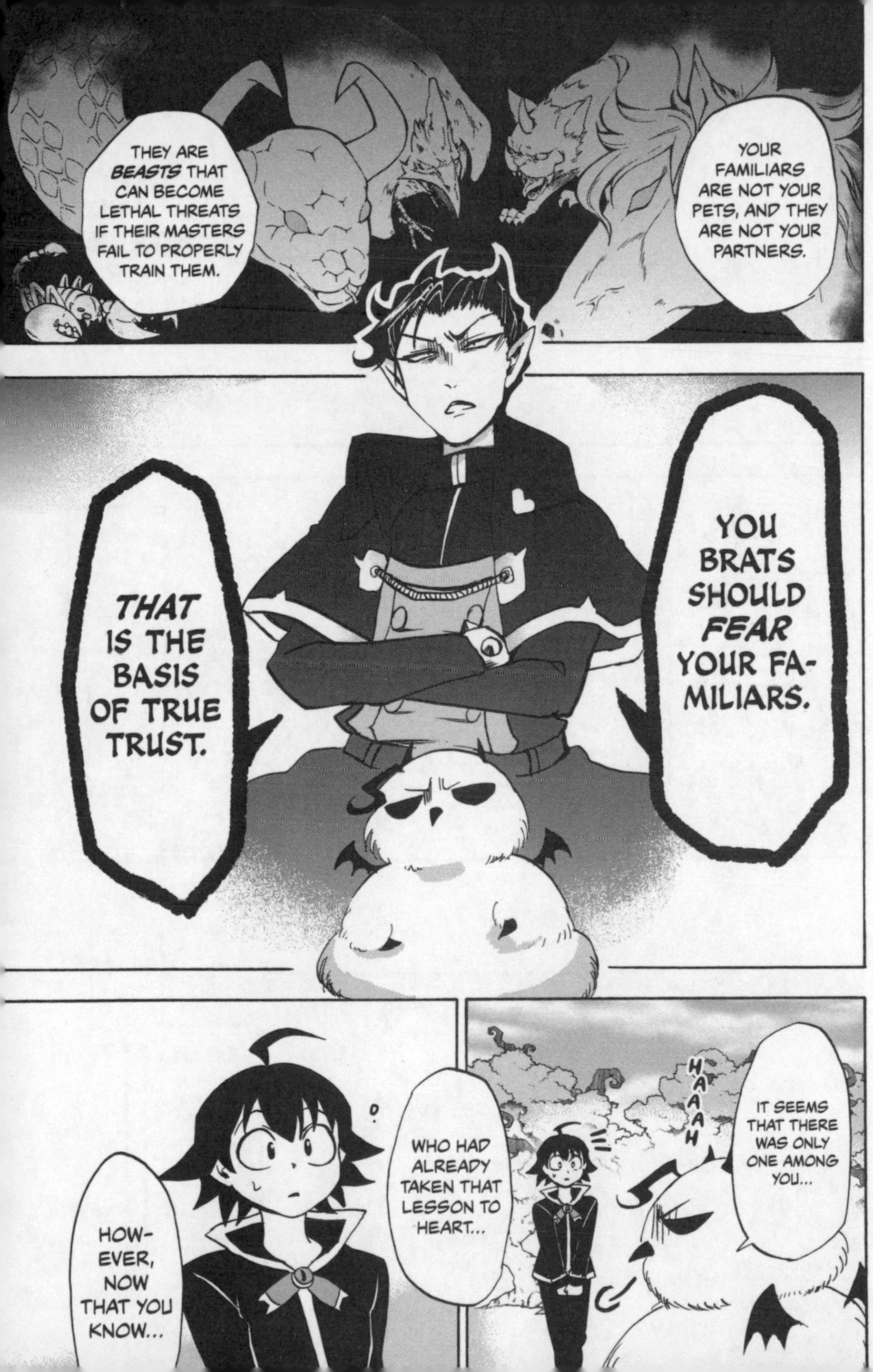
YOUR FAMILIARS ARE NOT YOUR PETS, AND THEY ARE NOT YOUR PARTNERS.
THEY ARE BEASTS THAT CAN BECOME LETHAL THREATS IF THEIR MASTERS FAIL TO PROPERLY TRAIN THEM.
YOU BRATS SHOULD FEAR YOUR FA-MILIARS.
THAT IS THE BASIS OF TRUE TRUST.
HAAAAH
IT SEEMS THAT THERE WAS ONLY ONE AMONG YOU...
WHO HAD ALREADY TAKEN THAT LESSON TO HEART...
HOW-EVER, NOW THAT YOU KNOW...

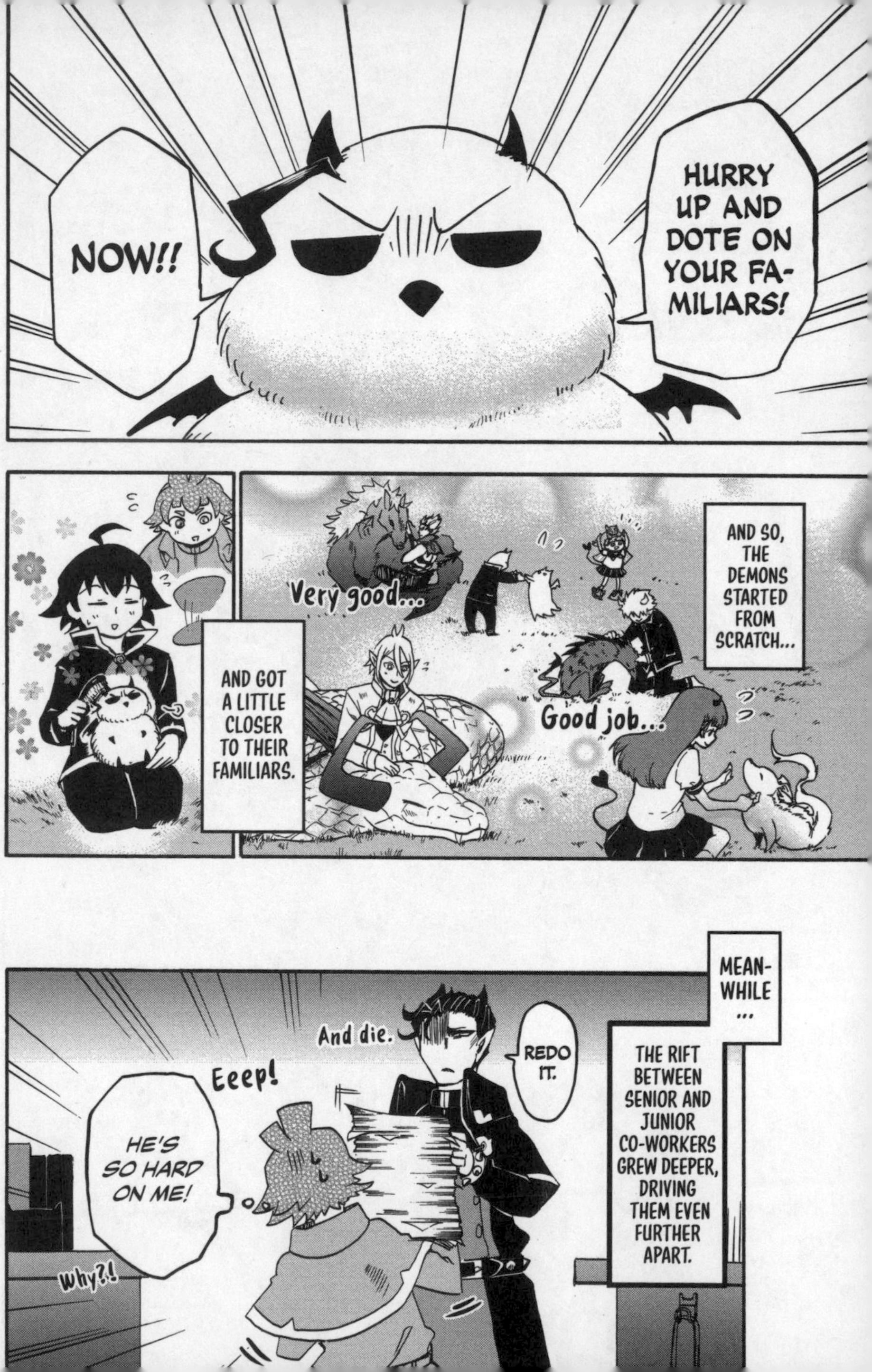
HURRY UP AND DOTE ON YOUR FA-MILIARS!
NOW!!
AND SO, THE DEMONS STARTED FROM SCRATCH...
Very good...
Good job...
AND GOT A LITTLE CLOSER TO THEIR FAMILIARS.
MEAN-WHILE ...
THE RIFT BETWEEN SENIOR AND JUNIOR CO-WORKERS GREW DEEPER, DRIVING THEM EVEN FURTHER APART.
REDO IT.
And die.
Eeep!
HE'S SO HARD ON ME!
Why?!

CHAPTER 23 THE DINNER OF THE THIRTEEN CROWNS

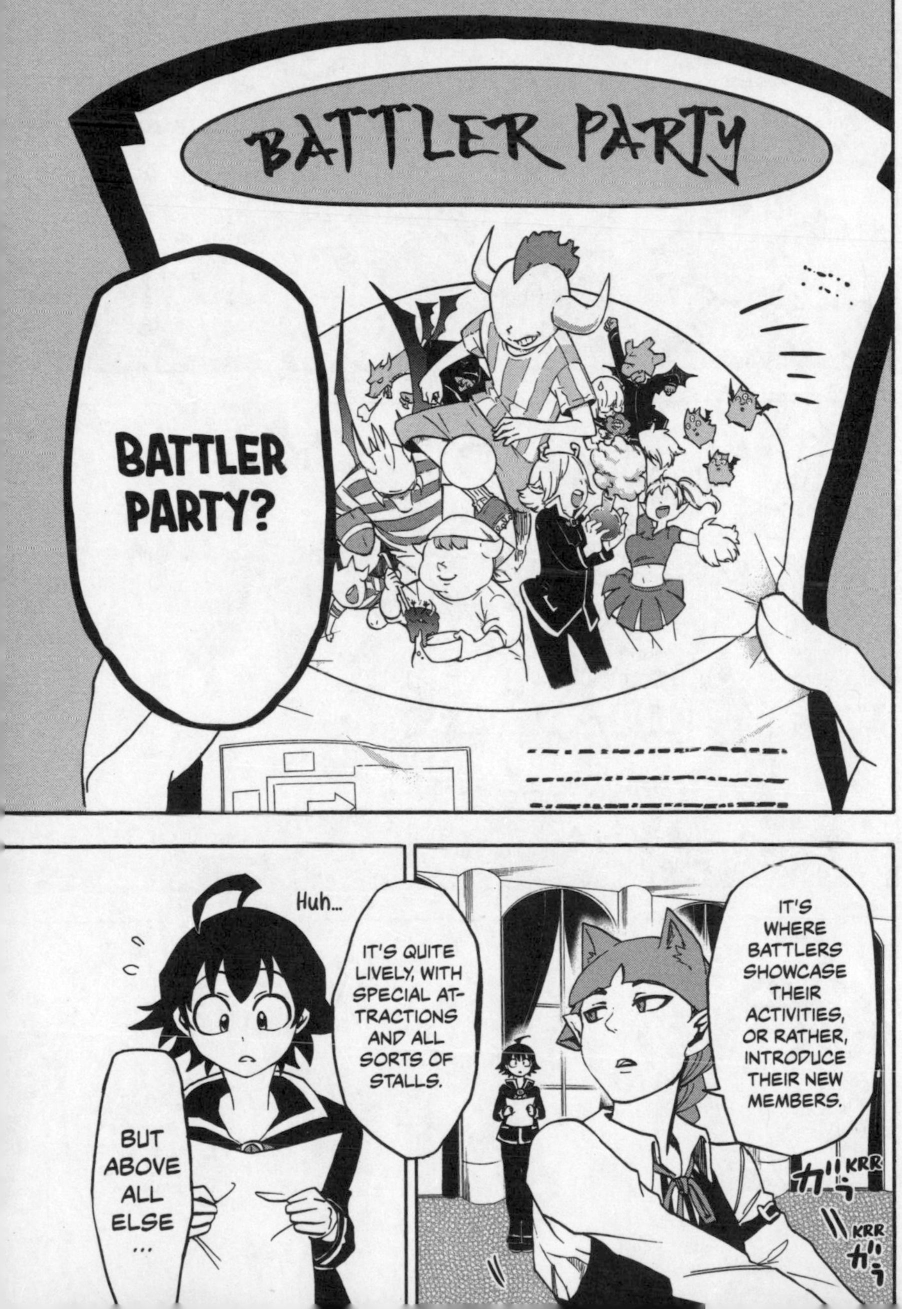
BATTLER PARTY
BATTLER PARTY?
IT'S WHERE BATTLERS SHOWCASE THEIR ACTIVITIES, OR RATHER, INTRODUCE THEIR NEW MEMBERS.
IT'S QUITE LIVELY, WITH SPECIAL ATTRACTIONS AND ALL SORTS OF STALLS.
KRR
KRR
Huh...
BUT ABOVE ALL ELSE ...

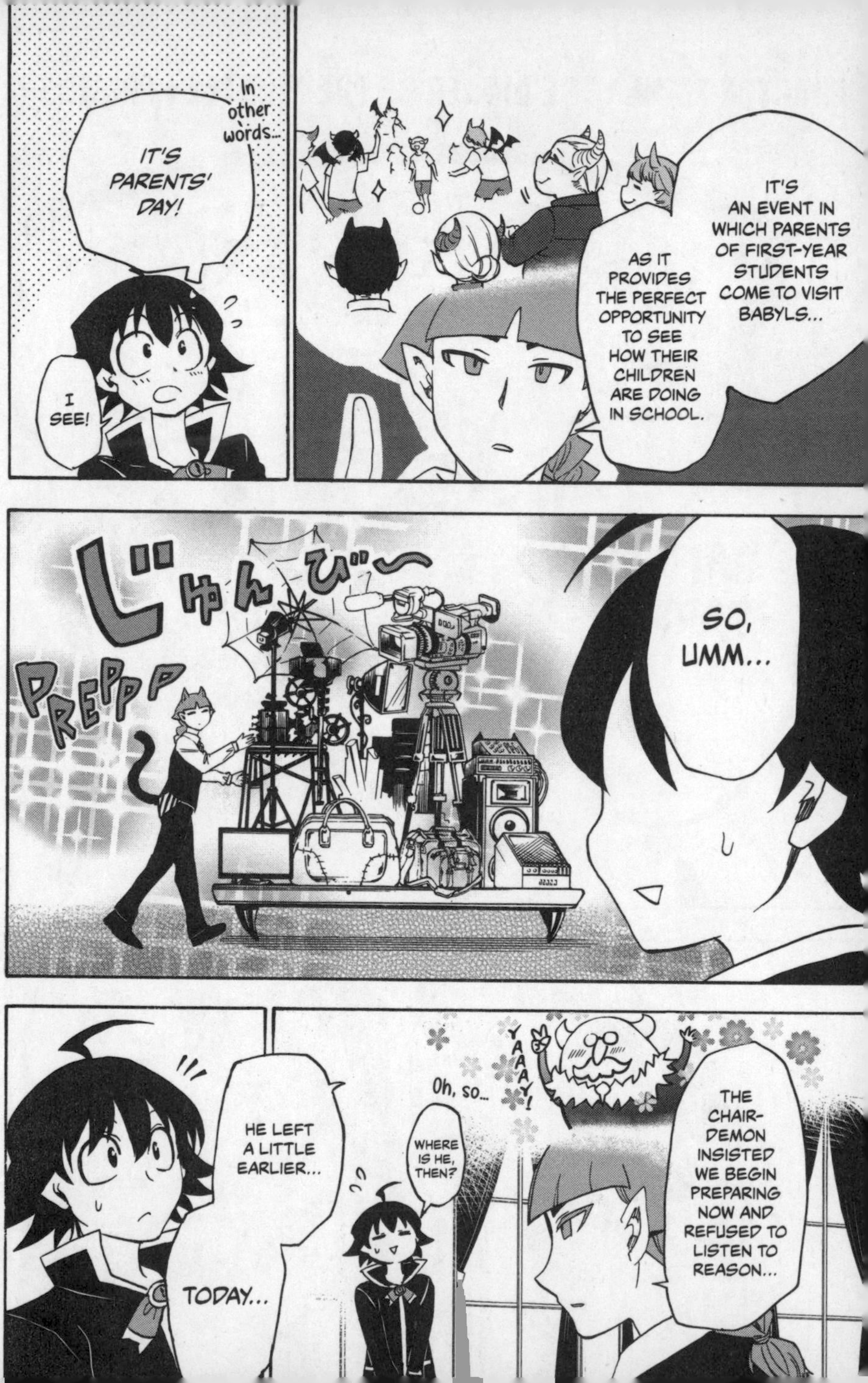
IT'S AN EVENT IN WHICH PARENTS OF FIRST-YEAR STUDENTS COME TO VISIT BABYLS...
AS IT PROVIDES THE PERFECT OPPORTUNITY TO SEE HOW THEIR CHILDREN ARE DOING IN SCHOOL.
In other words...
IT'S PARENTS' DAY!
I SEE!
SO, UMM...
じゅんび〜
PREPPP
THE CHAIR-DEMON INSISTED WE BEGIN PREPARING NOW AND REFUSED TO LISTEN TO REASON...
YAAAAY!
Oh, so...
WHERE IS HE, THEN?
HE LEFT A LITTLE EARLIER...
TODAY...

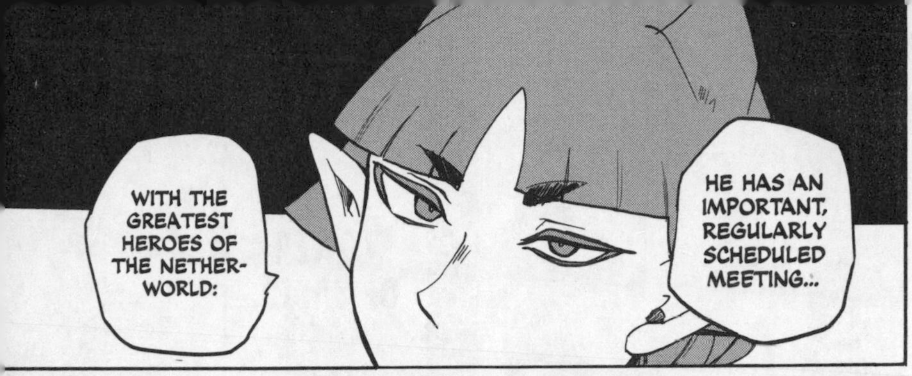
HE HAS AN IMPORTANT, REGULARLY SCHEDULED MEETING...
WITH THE GREATEST HEROES OF THE NETHER-WORLD:

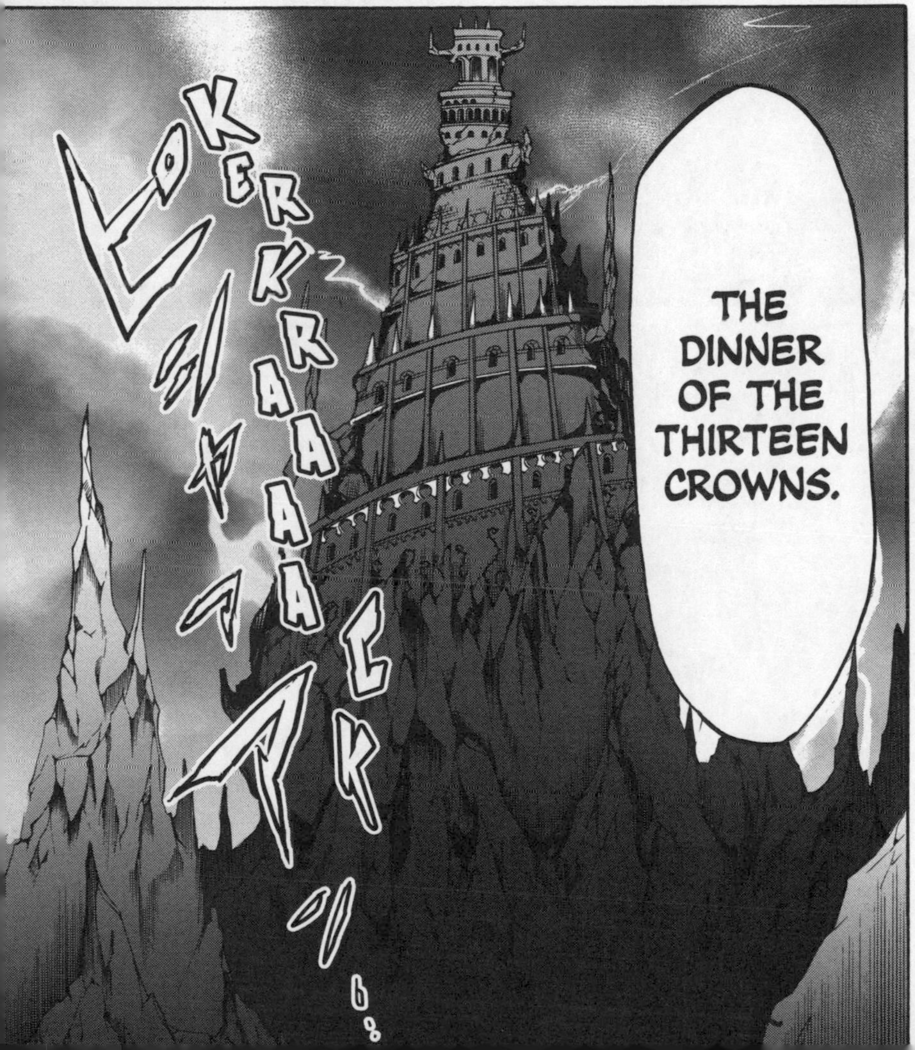
THE DINNER OF THE THIRTEEN CROWNS.
KERKRAAAACK

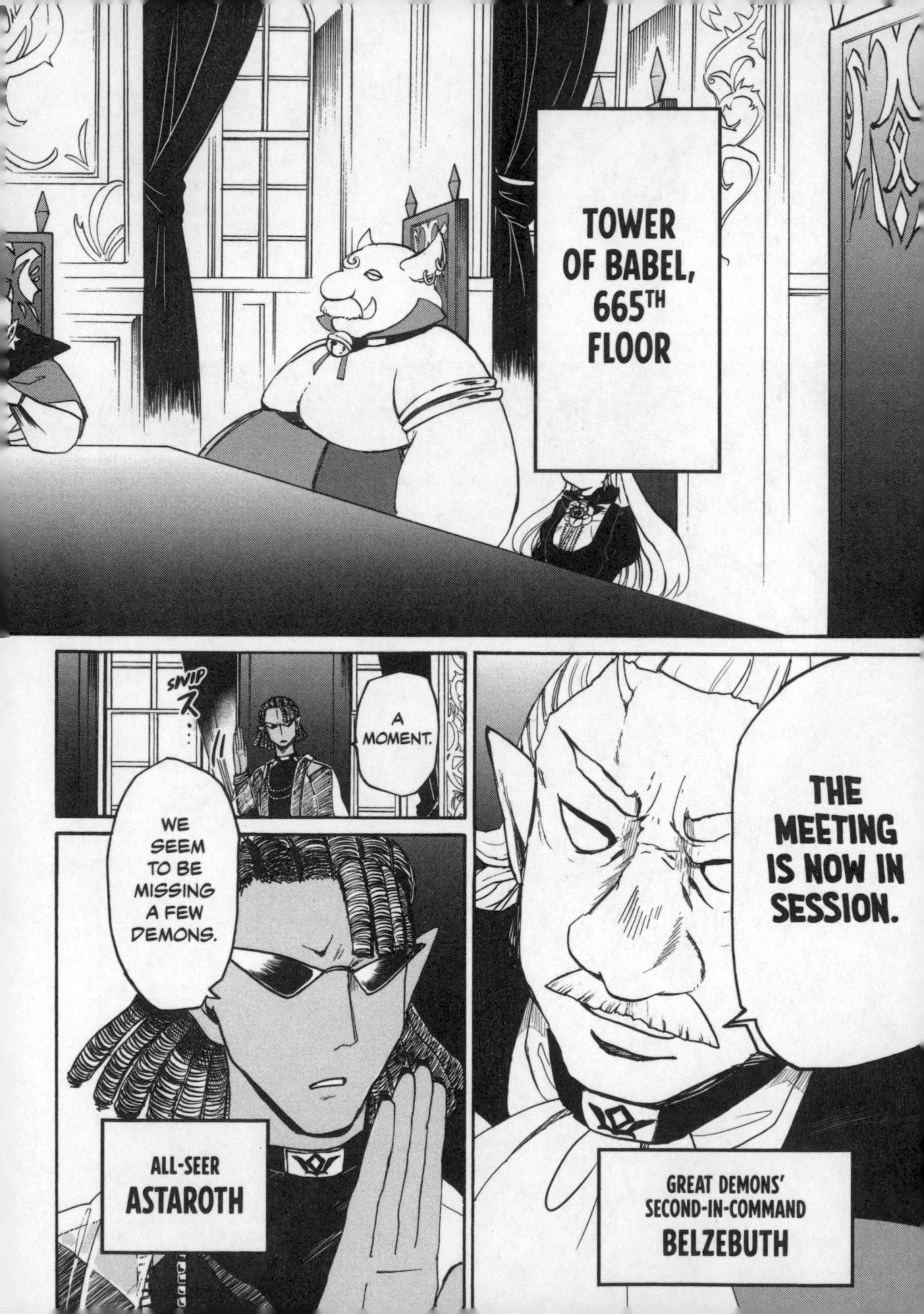
TOWER OF BABEL, 665TH FLOOR
THE MEETING IS NOW IN SESSION.
GREAT DEMONS' SECOND-IN-COMMAND BELZEBUTH
SWIP
A MOMENT.
WE SEEM TO BE MISSING A FEW DEMONS.
ALL-SEER ASTAROTH

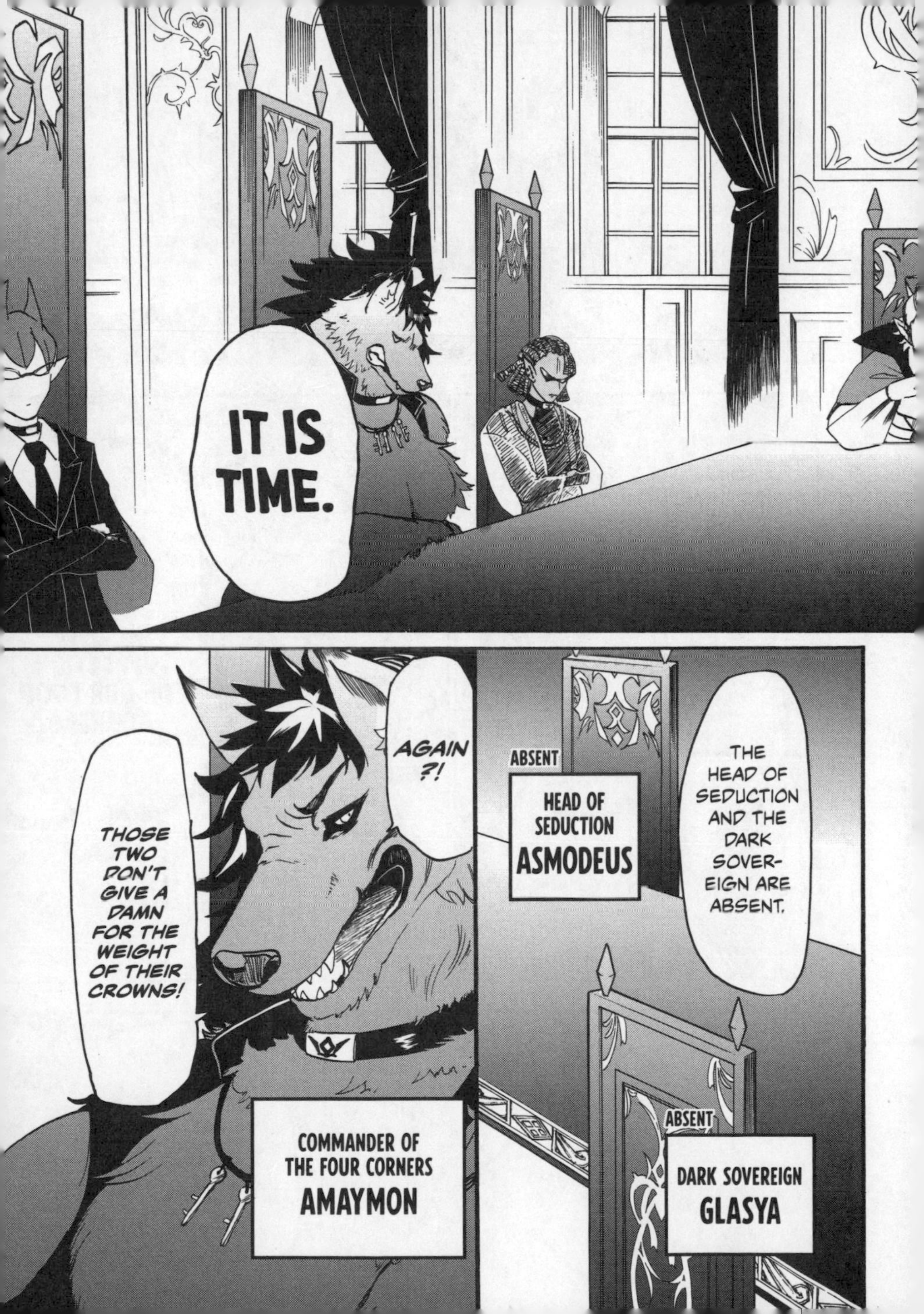
IT IS TIME.
THE HEAD OF SEDUCTION AND THE DARK SOVEREIGN ARE ABSENT.
ABSENT
HEAD OF SEDUCTION
ASMODEUS
ABSENT
DARK SOVEREIGN
GLASYA
AGAIN?!
THOSE TWO DON'T GIVE A DAMN FOR THE WEIGHT OF THEIR CROWNS!
COMMANDER OF THE FOUR CORNERS
AMAYMON

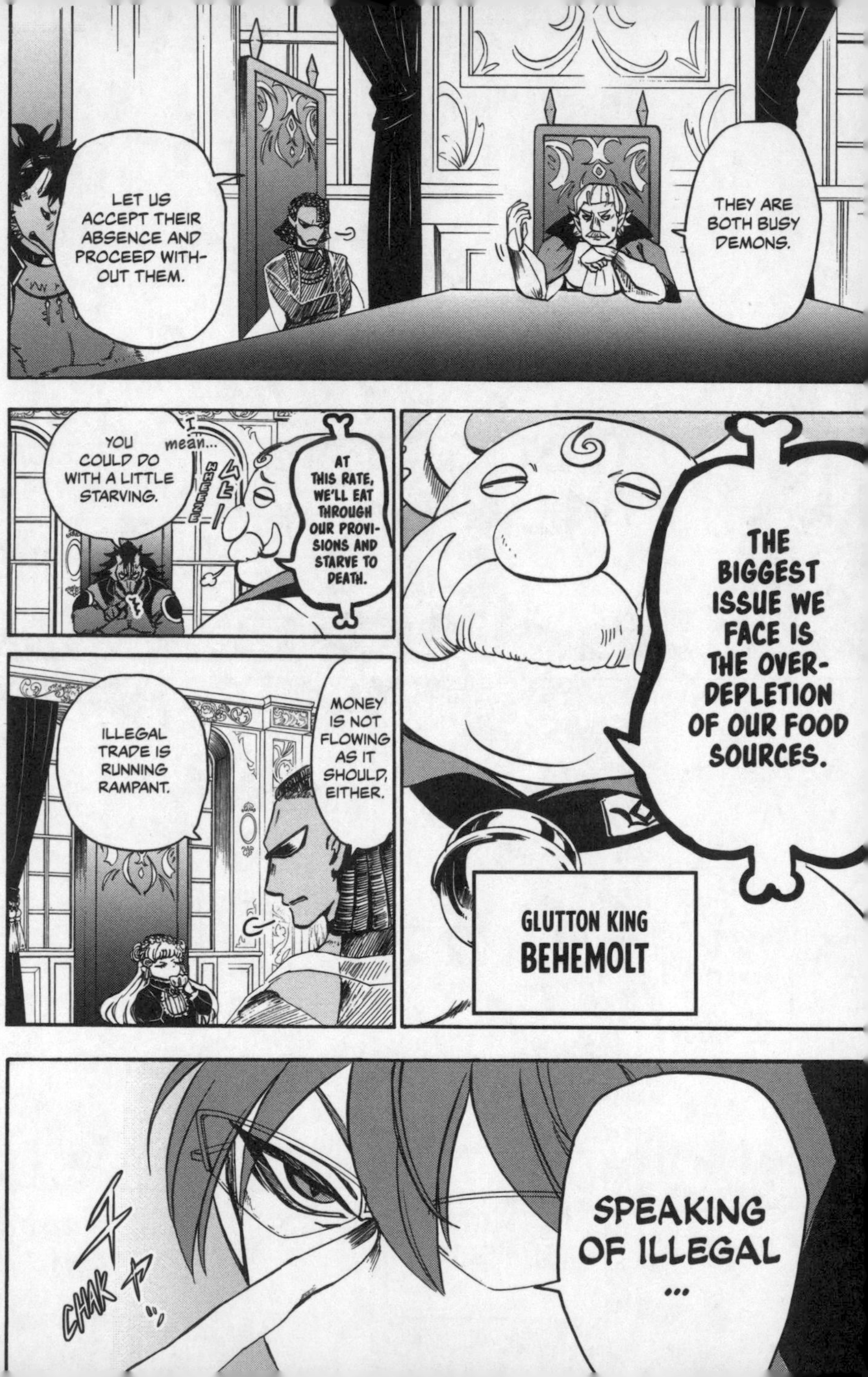
THEY ARE BOTH BUSY DEMONS.
LET US ACCEPT THEIR ABSENCE AND PROCEED WITH-OUT THEM.
THE BIGGEST ISSUE WE FACE IS THE OVER-DEPLETION OF OUR FOOD SOURCES.
GLUTTON KING BEHEMOLT
AT THIS RATE, WE'LL EAT THROUGH OUR PROVI-SIONS AND STARVE TO DEATH.
WHEEZE
I mean...
YOU COULD DO WITH A LITTLE STARVING.
MONEY IS NOT FLOWING AS IT SHOULD, EITHER.
ILLEGAL TRADE IS RUNNING RAMPANT.
SPEAKING OF ILLEGAL...
CHAK

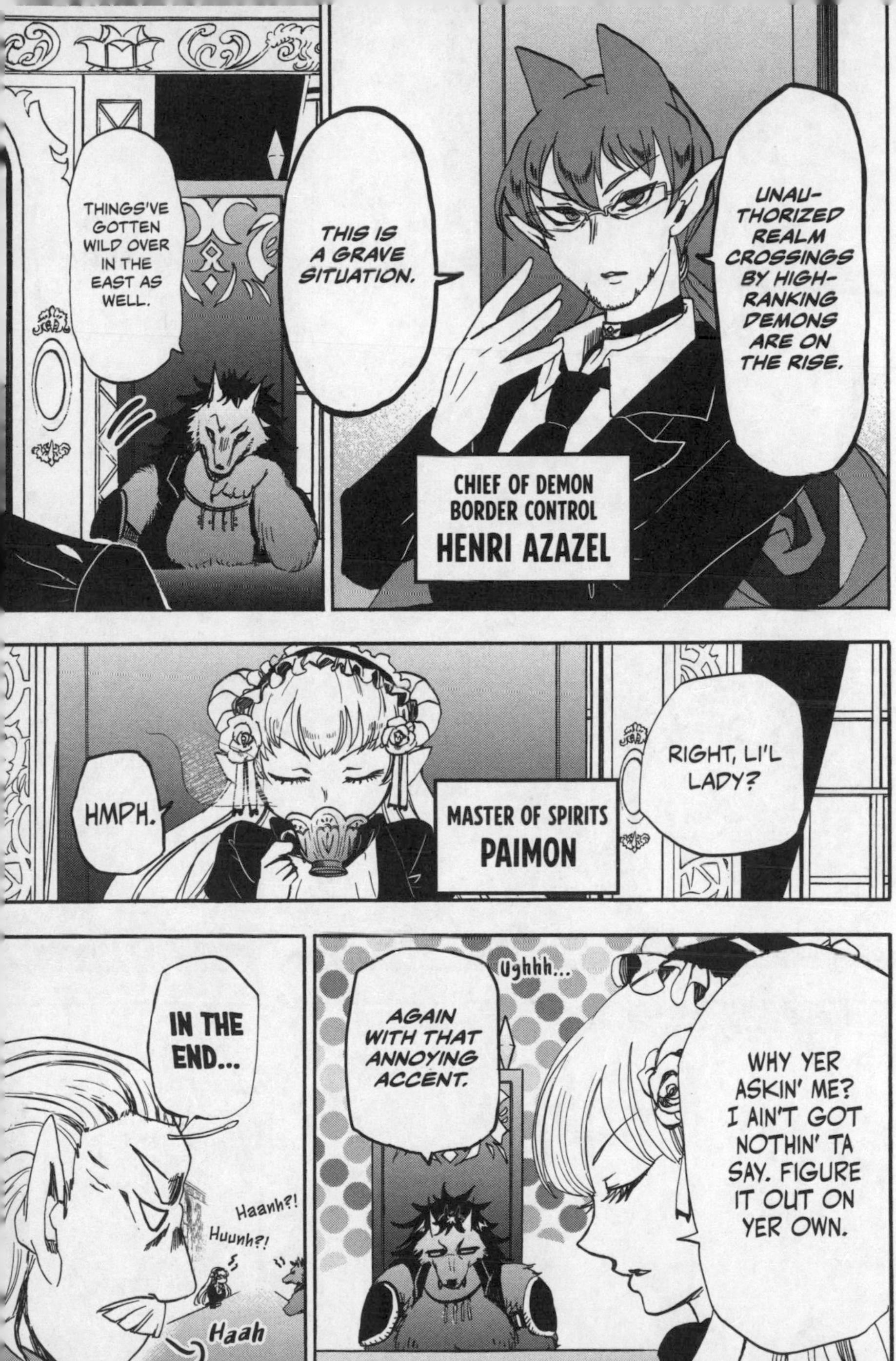
UNAU-
THORIZED
REALM
CROSSINGS
BY HIGH-
RANKING
DEMONS
ARE ON
THE RISE.
CHIEF OF DEMON BORDER CONTROL
HENRI AZAZEL
THIS IS A GRAVE SITUATION.
THINGS'VE GOTTEN WILD OVER IN THE EAST AS WELL.
RIGHT, LI'L LADY?
MASTER OF SPIRITS
PAIMON
HMPH.
WHY YER ASKIN' ME? I AIN'T GOT NOTHIN' TA SAY. FIGURE IT OUT ON YER OWN.
Ughhh...
AGAIN WITH THAT ANNOYING ACCENT.
IN THE END...
Haanh?!
Huunh?!
Haah

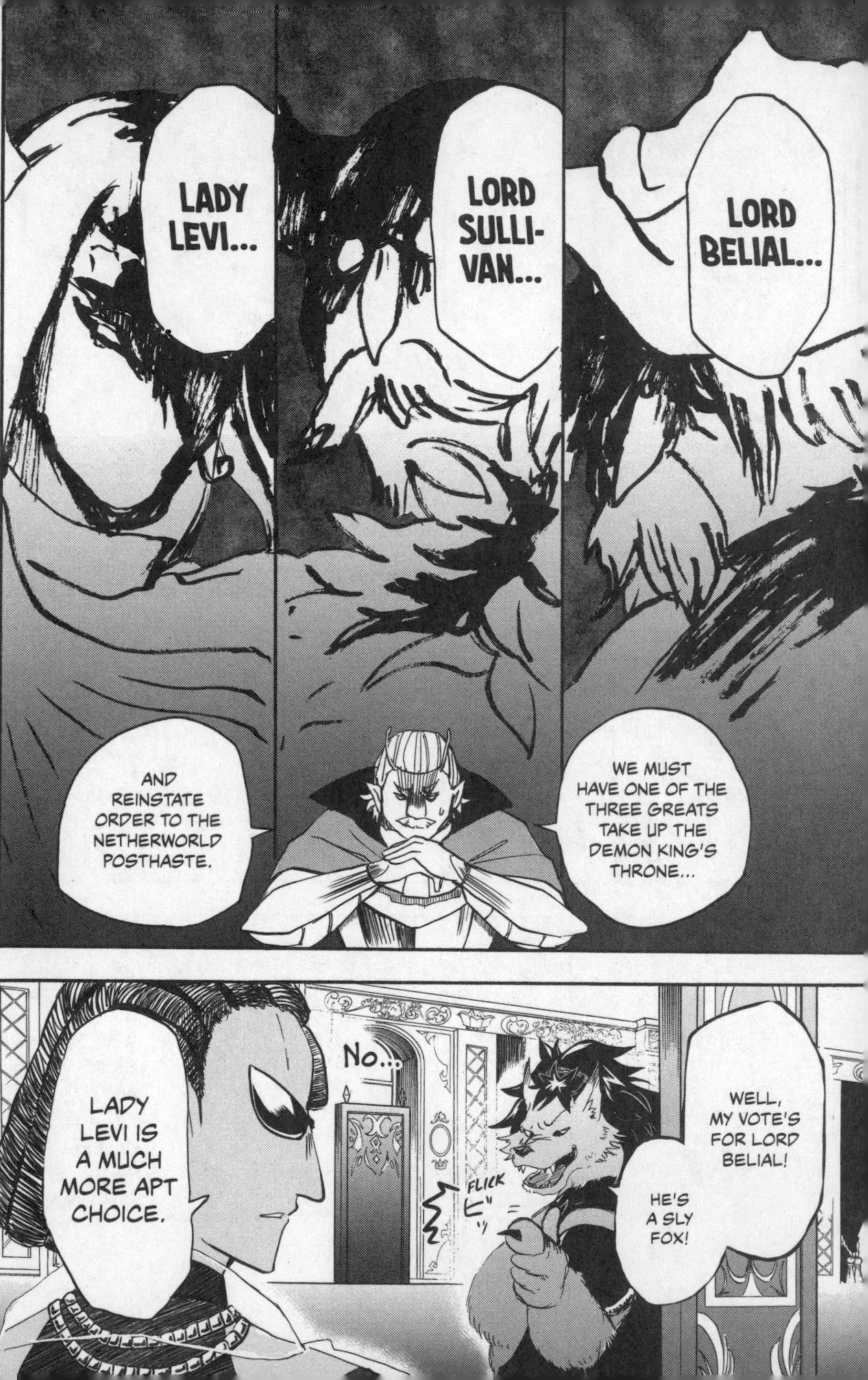
LORD BELIAL...
LORD SULLIVAN...
LADY LEVI...
WE MUST HAVE ONE OF THE THREE GREATS TAKE UP THE DEMON KING'S THRONE...
AND REINSTATE ORDER TO THE NETHERWORLD POSTHASTE.
WELL, MY VOTE'S FOR LORD BELIAL!
HE'S A SLY FOX!
FLICK
No...
LADY LEVI IS A MUCH MORE APT CHOICE.

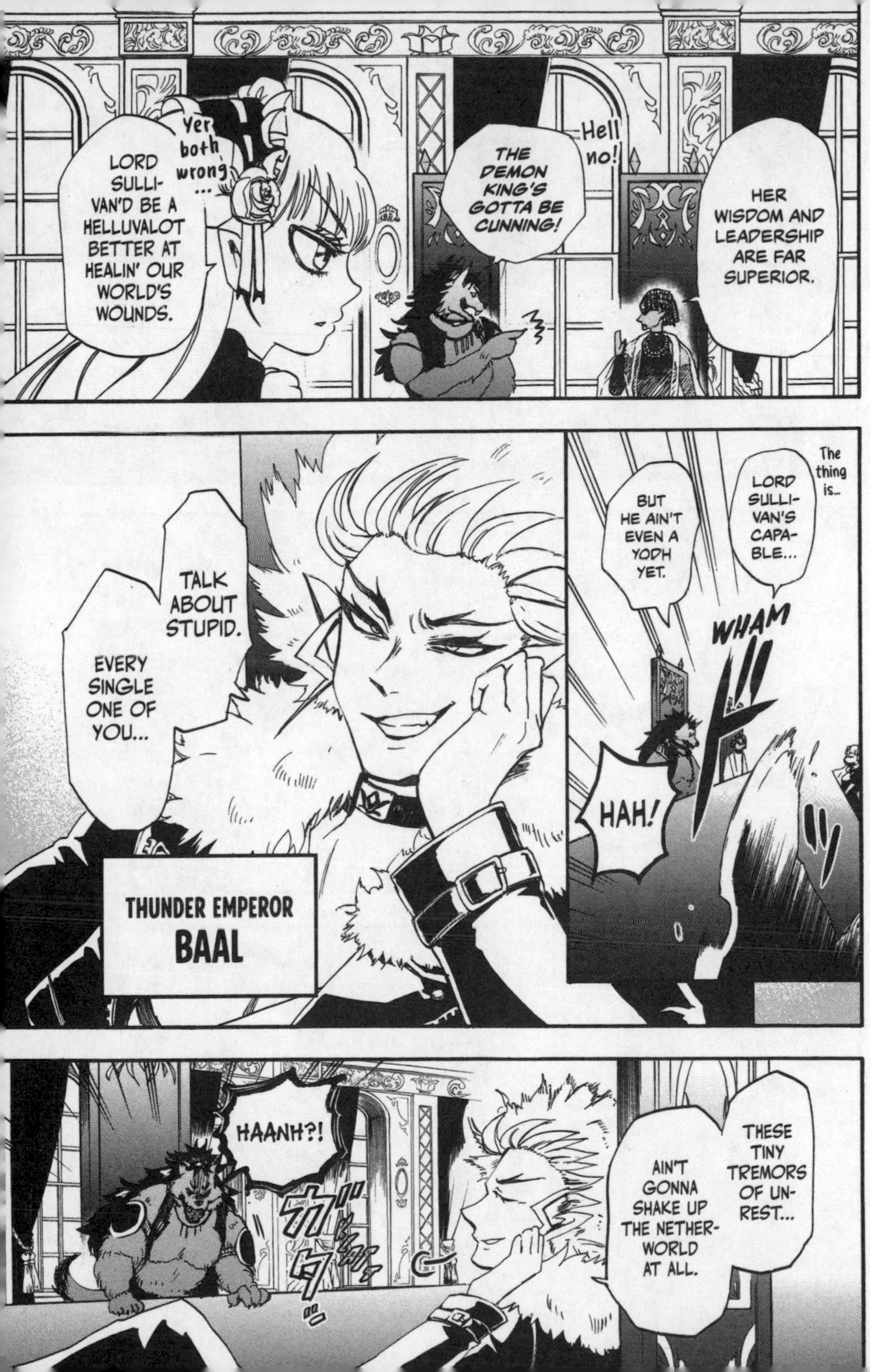

HER WISDOM AND LEADERSHIP ARE FAR SUPERIOR.
Hell no!
THE DEMON KING'S GOTTA BE CUNNING!
Yer both wrong...
LORD SULLIVAN'D BE A HELLUVALOT BETTER AT HEALIN' OUR WORLD'S WOUNDS.
The thing is..
LORD SULLIVAN'S CAPABLE...
BUT HE AIN'T EVEN A YODH YET.
WHAM
HAH!
TALK ABOUT STUPID.
EVERY SINGLE ONE OF YOU...
THUNDER EMPEROR BAAL
THESE TINY TREMORS OF UNREST...
AIN'T GONNA SHAKE UP THE NETHERWORLD AT ALL.
HAANH?!

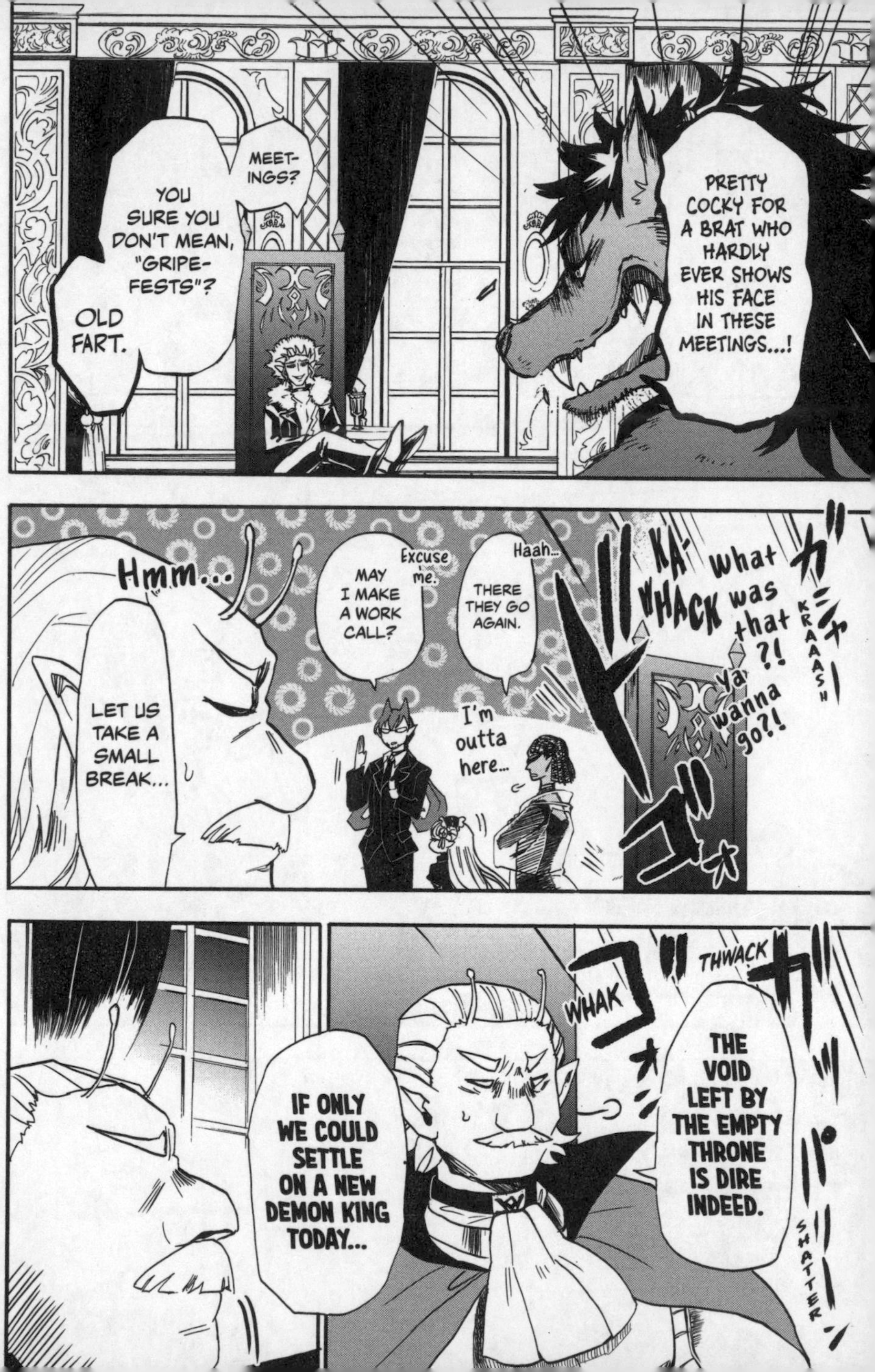
PRETTY COCKY FOR A BRAT WHO HARDLY EVER SHOWS HIS FACE IN THESE MEETINGS...!
MEET-INGS?
YOU SURE YOU DON'T MEAN, "GRIPE-FESTS"?
OLD FART.
KA-WHACK
what was that?!
KRAAASH
ya wanna go?!
Haah...
THERE THEY GO AGAIN.
Excuse me.
MAY I MAKE A WORK CALL?
I'm outta here...
Hmm...
LET US TAKE A SMALL BREAK...
THWACK
WHAK
THE VOID LEFT BY THE EMPTY THRONE IS DIRE INDEED.
SHATTER
IF ONLY WE COULD SETTLE ON A NEW DEMON KING TODAY...

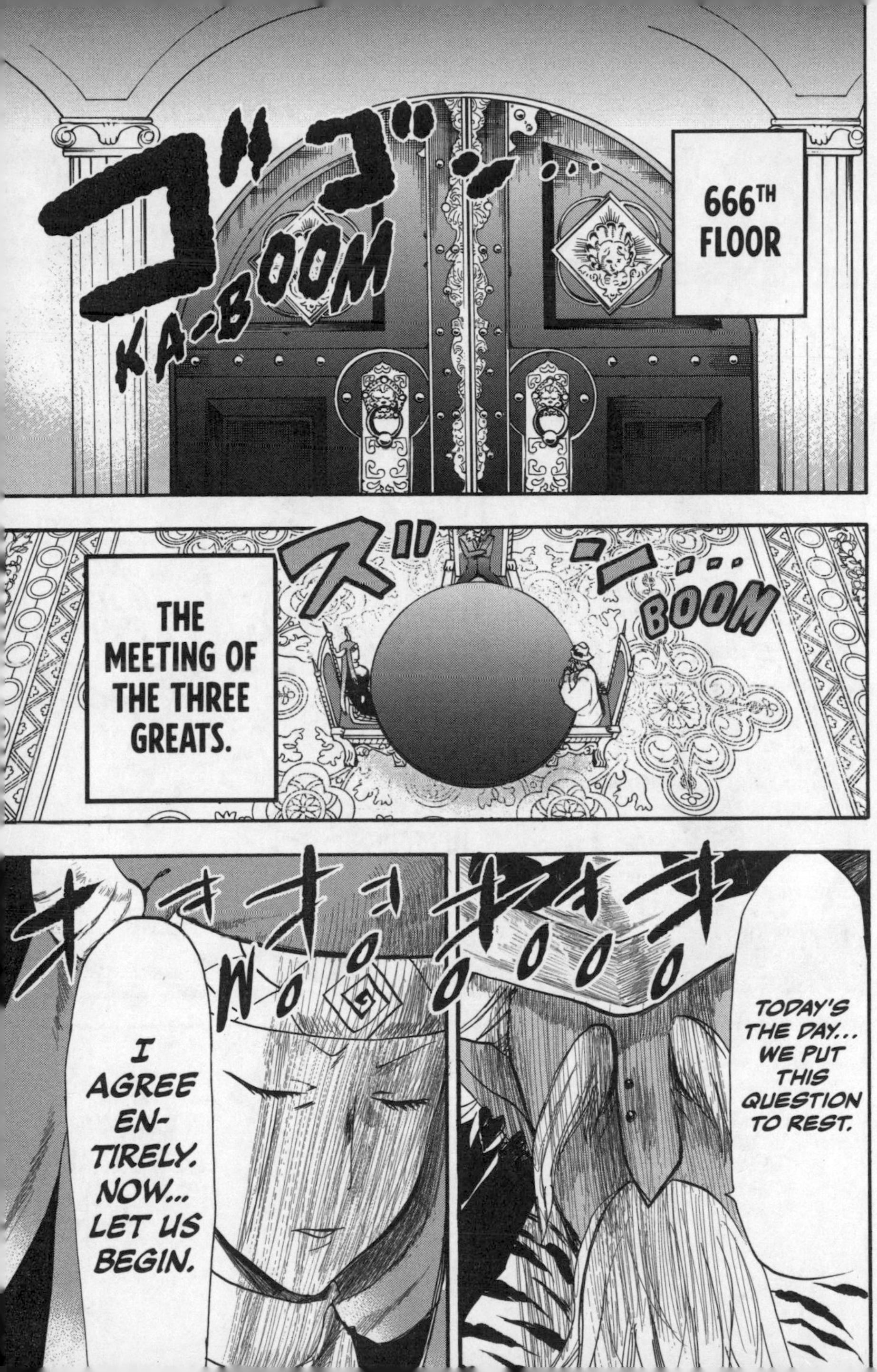
666TH FLOOR
ゴゴ…
KA-BOOM
ズー…
BOOM
THE MEETING OF THE THREE GREATS.
WOOOOOOO
TODAY'S THE DAY... WE PUT THIS QUESTION TO REST.
I AGREE EN-TIRELY. NOW... LET US BEGIN.

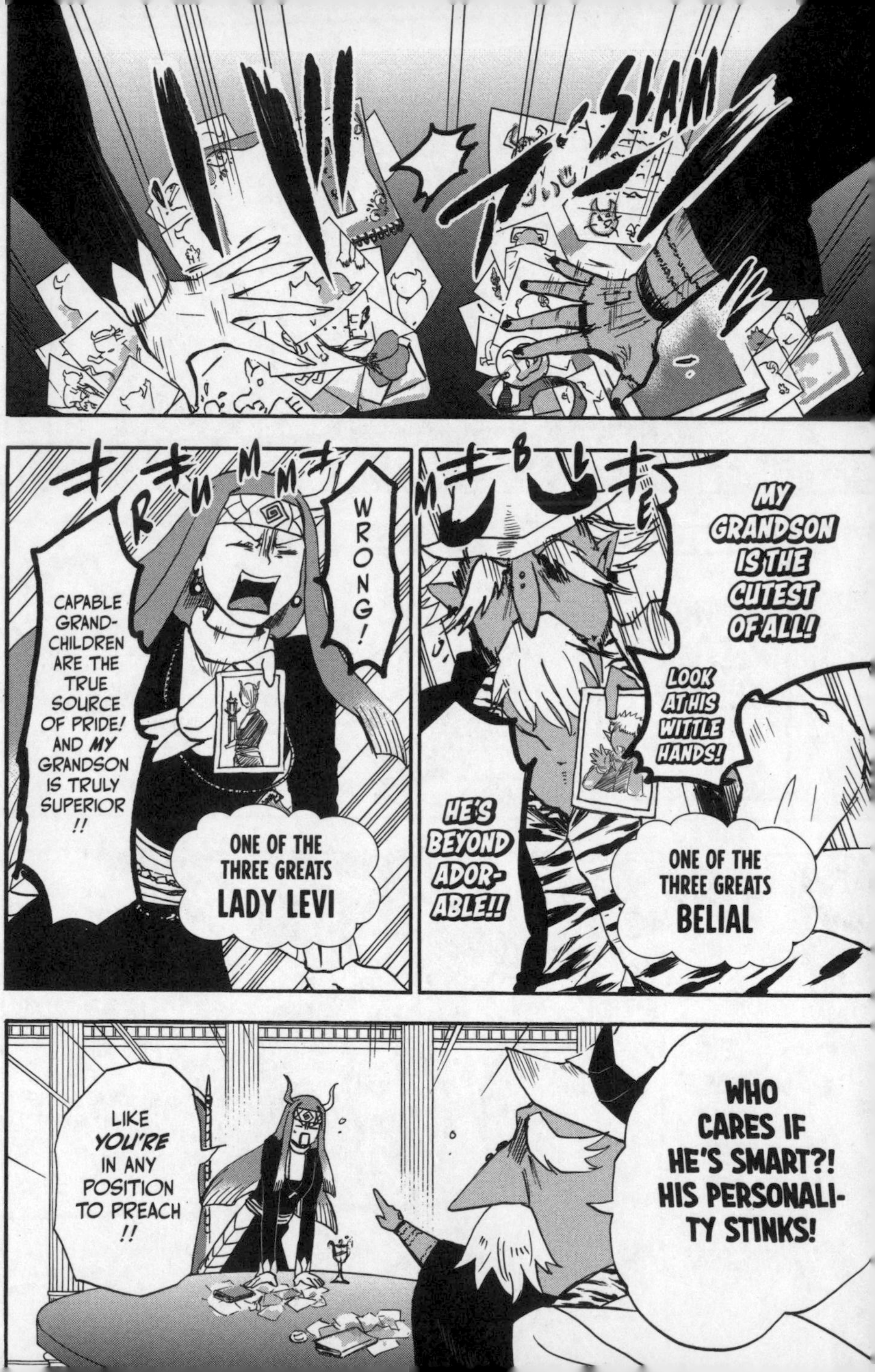
SLAM
RUMMMBLE
MY GRANDSON IS THE CUTEST OF ALL!
LOOK AT HIS WITTLE HANDS!
HE'S BEYOND ADOR-ABLE!!
ONE OF THE THREE GREATS BELIAL
WRONG!
CAPABLE GRAND-CHILDREN ARE THE TRUE SOURCE OF PRIDE! AND MY GRANDSON IS TRULY SUPERIOR!!
ONE OF THE THREE GREATS LADY LEVI
WHO CARES IF HE'S SMART?! HIS PERSONALI-TY STINKS!
LIKE YOU'RE IN ANY POSITION TO PREACH!!

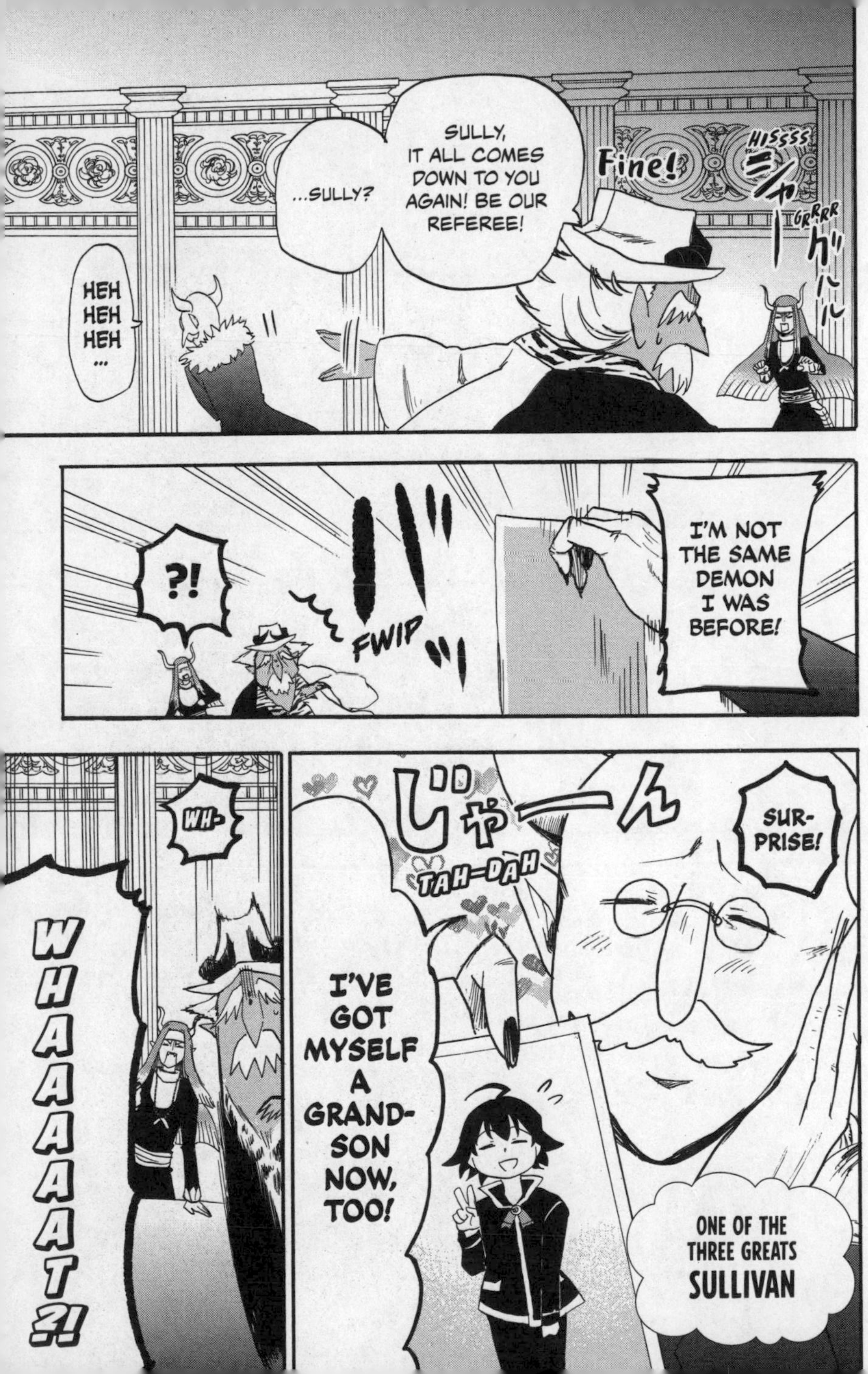
HISSSS
Fine!
GRRRR
SULLY, IT ALL COMES DOWN TO YOU AGAIN! BE OUR REFEREE!
...SULLY?
HEH HEH HEH ...
I'M NOT THE SAME DEMON I WAS BEFORE!
FWIP
?!
SUR-PRISE!
TAH-DAH
I'VE GOT MYSELF A GRAND-SON NOW, TOO!
ONE OF THE THREE GREATS SULLIVAN
WH-
WHAAAAAAAT?!

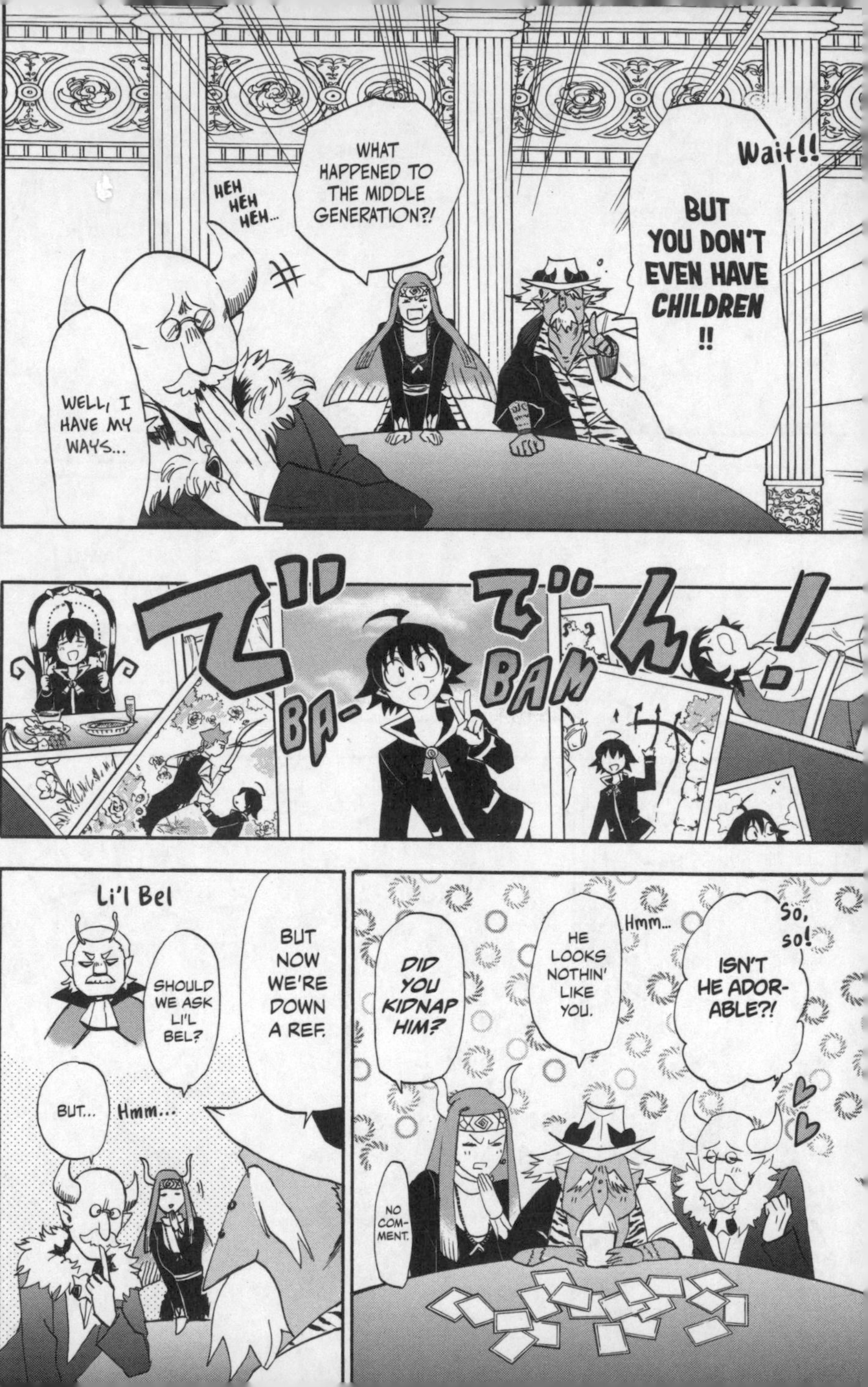
Wait!!
BUT YOU DON'T EVEN HAVE CHILDREN !!
WHAT HAPPENED TO THE MIDDLE GENERATION?!
HEH HEH HEH...
WELL, I HAVE MY WAYS...
でででん!
BA-BAM
So, so!
ISN'T HE ADOR-ABLE?!
Hmm...
HE LOOKS NOTHIN' LIKE YOU.
DID YOU KIDNAP HIM?
NO COM-MENT.
BUT NOW WE'RE DOWN A REF.
SHOULD WE ASK LI'L BEL?
Li'l Bel
Hmm...
BUT...

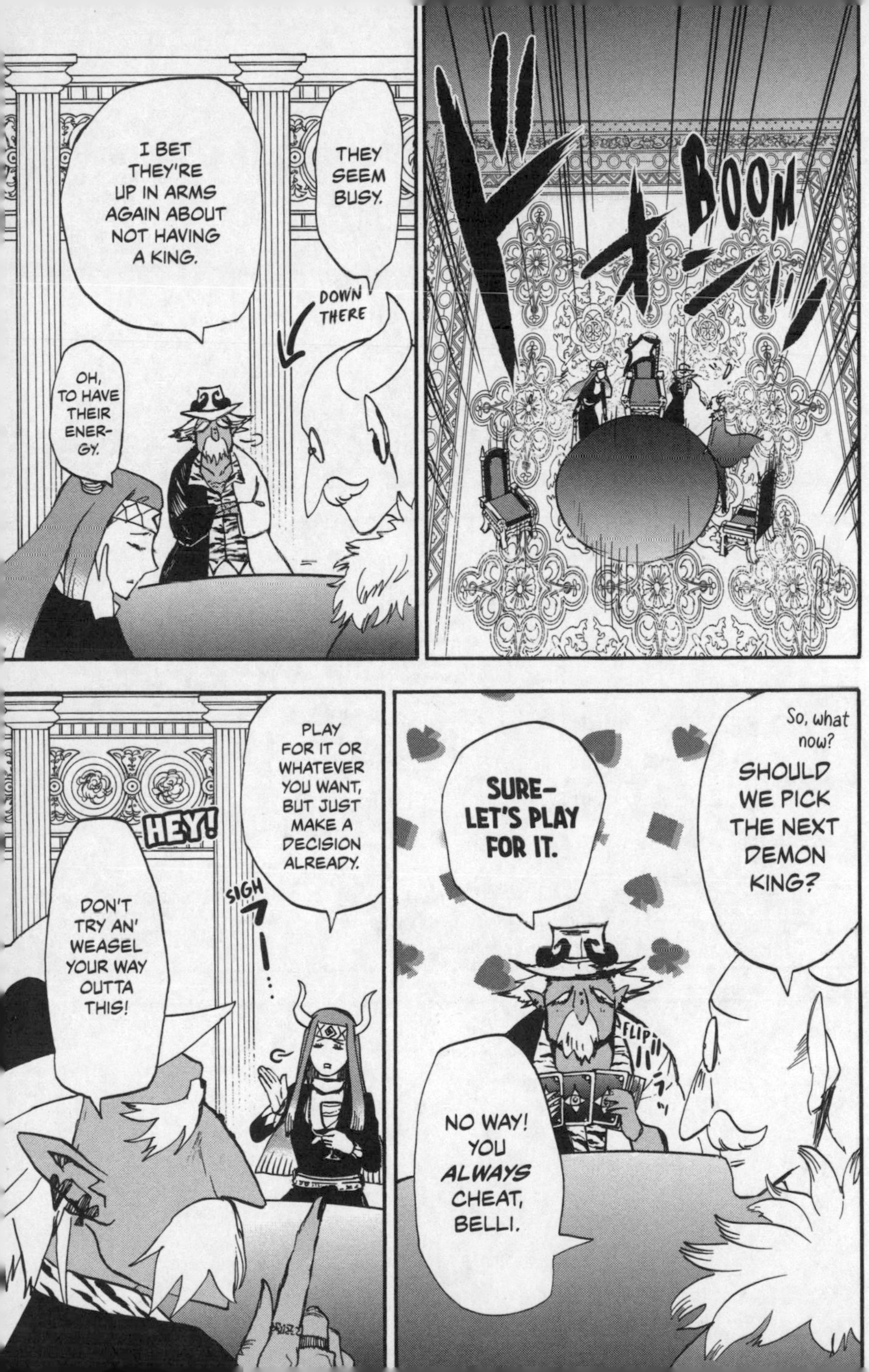
BOOM
THEY SEEM BUSY.
I BET THEY'RE UP IN ARMS AGAIN ABOUT NOT HAVING A KING.
DOWN THERE
OH, TO HAVE THEIR ENERGY.
So, what now?
SHOULD WE PICK THE NEXT DEMON KING?
SURE— LET'S PLAY FOR IT.
FLIP
NO WAY! YOU *ALWAYS* CHEAT, BELLI.
PLAY FOR IT OR WHATEVER YOU WANT, BUT JUST MAKE A DECISION ALREADY.
HEY!
SIGH
...
DON'T TRY AN' WEASEL YOUR WAY OUTTA THIS!

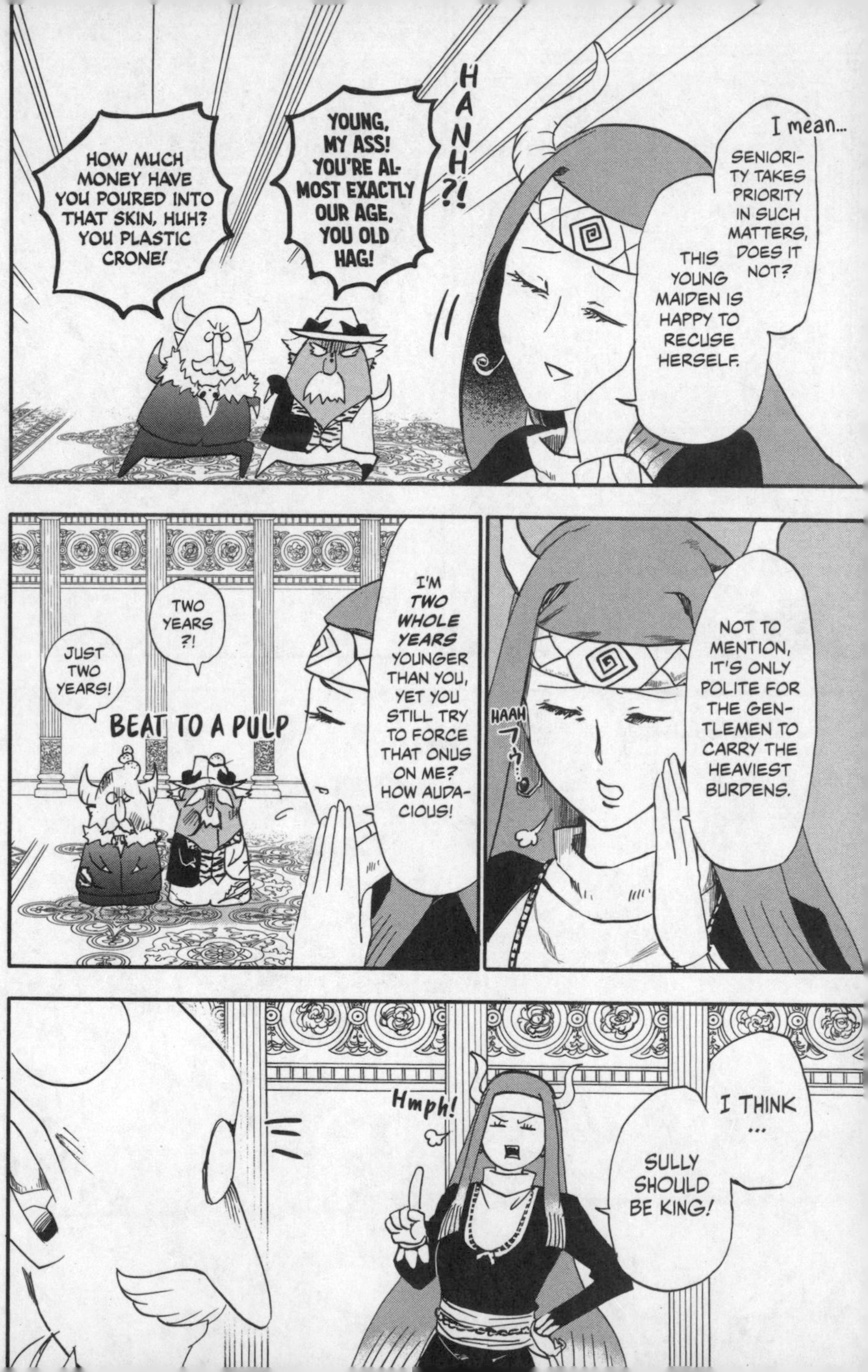
I mean...
SENIORITY TAKES PRIORITY IN SUCH MATTERS, DOES IT NOT?
THIS YOUNG MAIDEN IS HAPPY TO RECUSE HERSELF.
HANH?!
YOUNG, MY ASS! YOU'RE ALMOST EXACTLY OUR AGE, YOU OLD HAG!
HOW MUCH MONEY HAVE YOU POURED INTO THAT SKIN, HUH? YOU PLASTIC CRONE!
NOT TO MENTION, IT'S ONLY POLITE FOR THE GENTLEMEN TO CARRY THE HEAVIEST BURDENS.
HAAH
I'M *TWO WHOLE YEARS* YOUNGER THAN YOU, YET YOU STILL TRY TO FORCE THAT ONUS ON ME? HOW AUDACIOUS!
TWO YEARS?!
JUST TWO YEARS!
BEAT TO A PULP
I THINK ...
SULLY SHOULD BE KING!
Hmph!

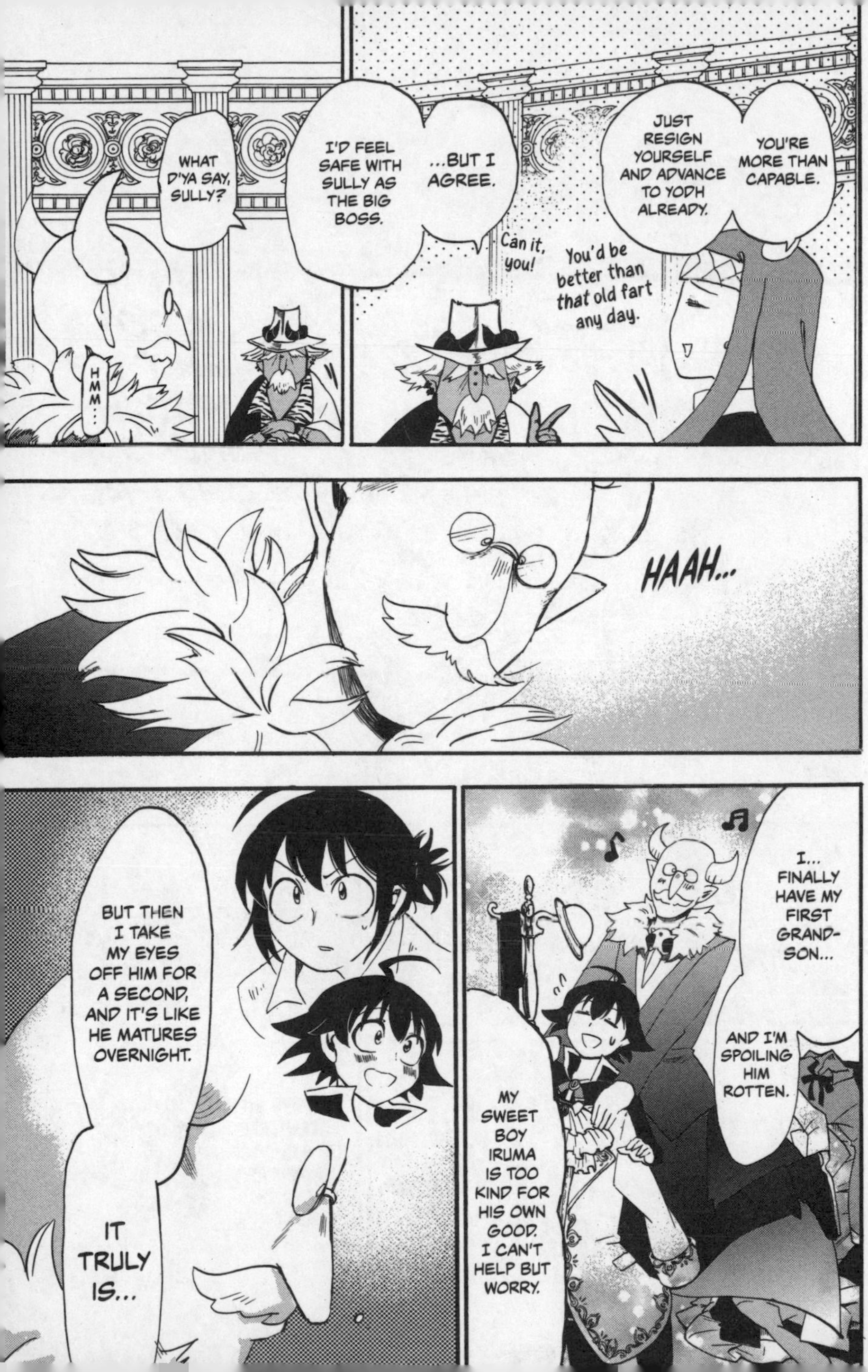
YOU'RE MORE THAN CAPABLE.
JUST RESIGN YOURSELF AND ADVANCE TO YODH ALREADY.
You'd be better than that old fart any day.
Can it, you!
...BUT I AGREE.
I'D FEEL SAFE WITH SULLY AS THE BIG BOSS.
WHAT D'YA SAY, SULLY?
HMM...
HAAH...
I... FINALLY HAVE MY FIRST GRANDSON...
AND I'M SPOILING HIM ROTTEN.
MY SWEET BOY IRUMA IS TOO KIND FOR HIS OWN GOOD. I CAN'T HELP BUT WORRY.
BUT THEN I TAKE MY EYES OFF HIM FOR A SECOND, AND IT'S LIKE HE MATURES OVERNIGHT.
IT TRULY IS...

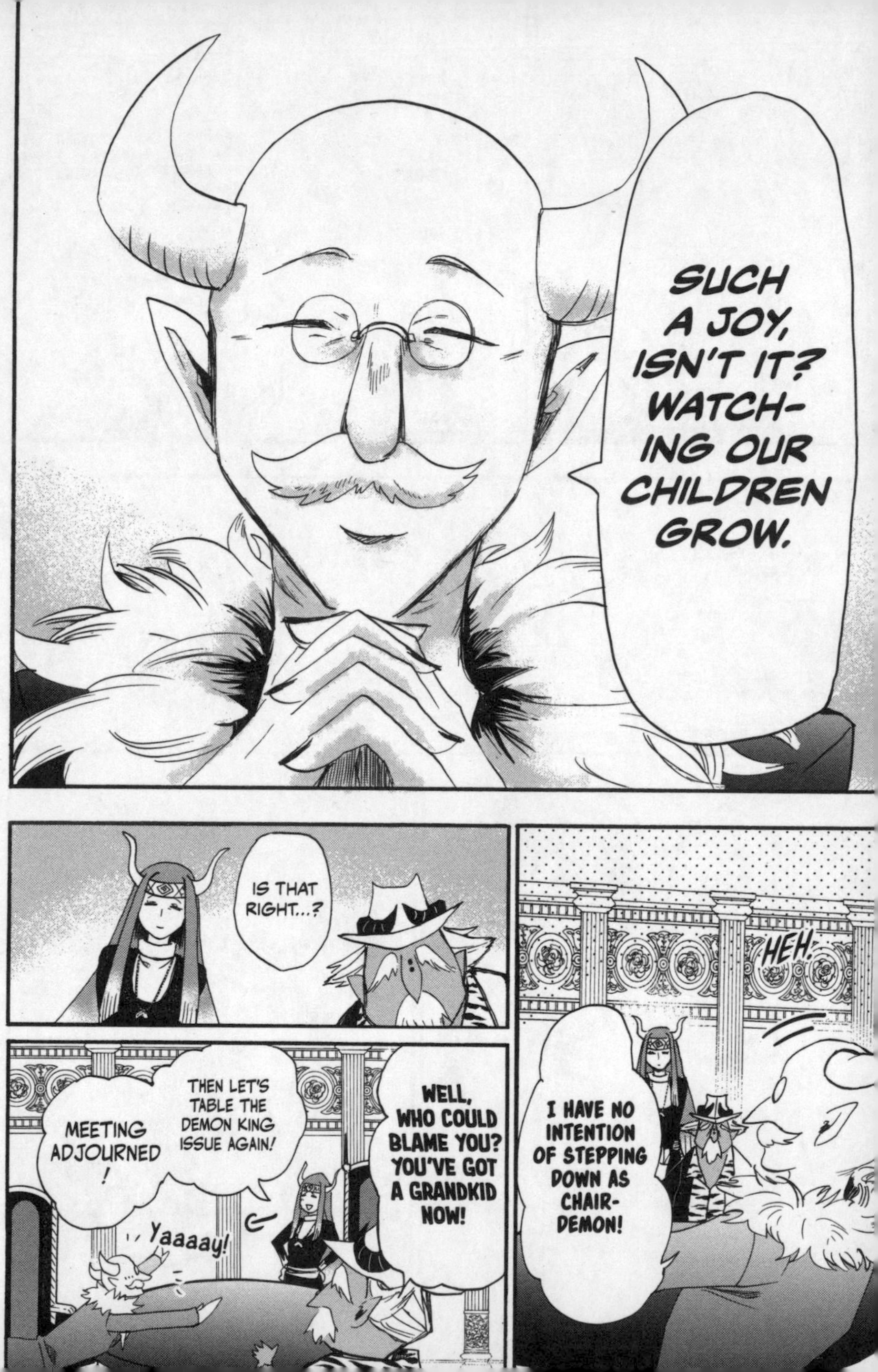
SUCH A JOY, ISN'T IT? WATCHING OUR CHILDREN GROW.
HEH.
I HAVE NO INTENTION OF STEPPING DOWN AS CHAIR-DEMON!
IS THAT RIGHT...?
WELL, WHO COULD BLAME YOU? YOU'VE GOT A GRANDKID NOW!
THEN LET'S TABLE THE DEMON KING ISSUE AGAIN!
MEETING ADJOURNED!
Yaaaay!

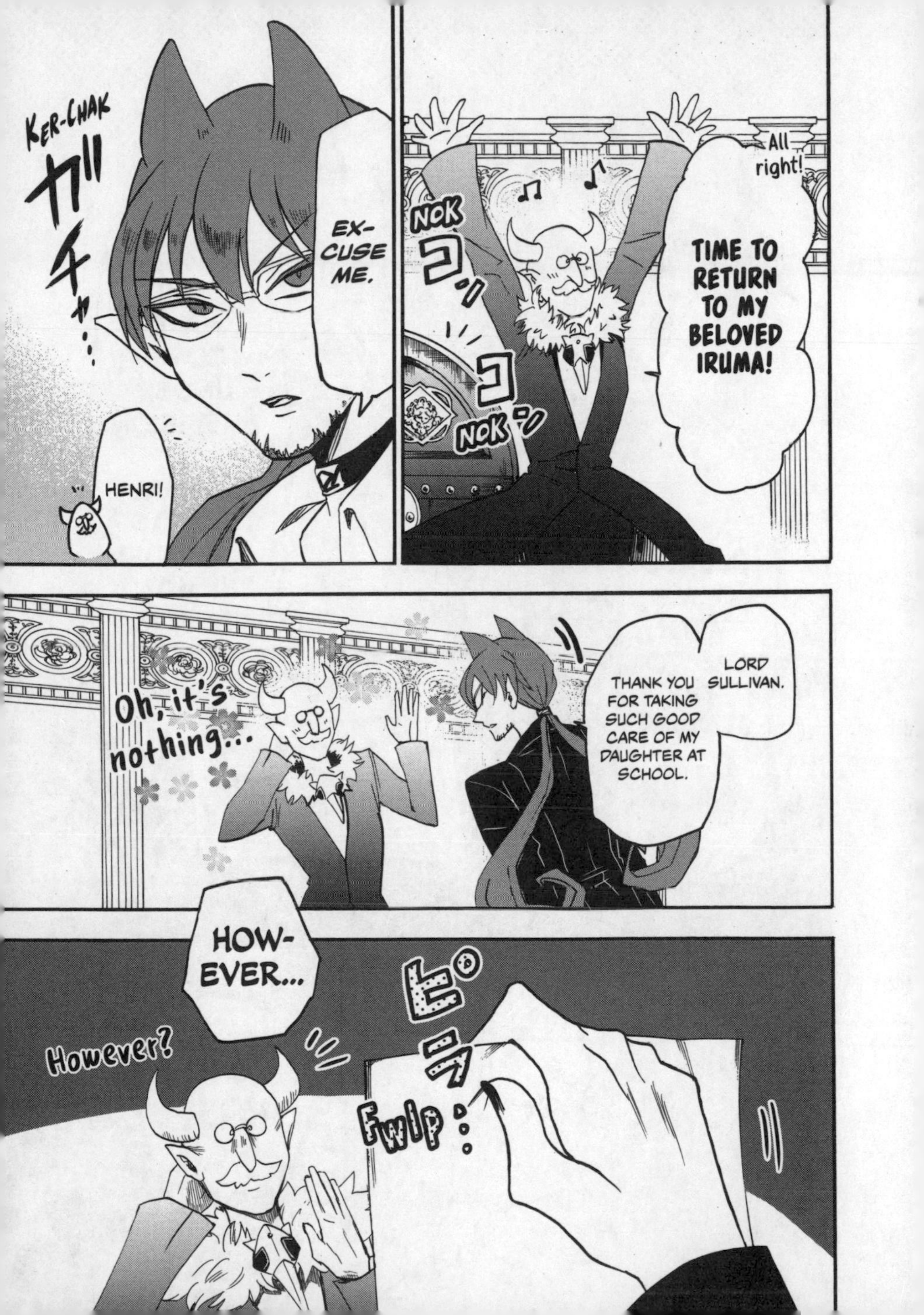
All right!
TIME TO RETURN TO MY BELOVED IRUMA!
NOK
NOK
EX-CUSE ME.
KER-CHAK
HENRI!
LORD SULLIVAN. THANK YOU FOR TAKING SUCH GOOD CARE OF MY DAUGHTER AT SCHOOL.
Oh, it's nothing...
HOW-EVER...
Fwip...
However?

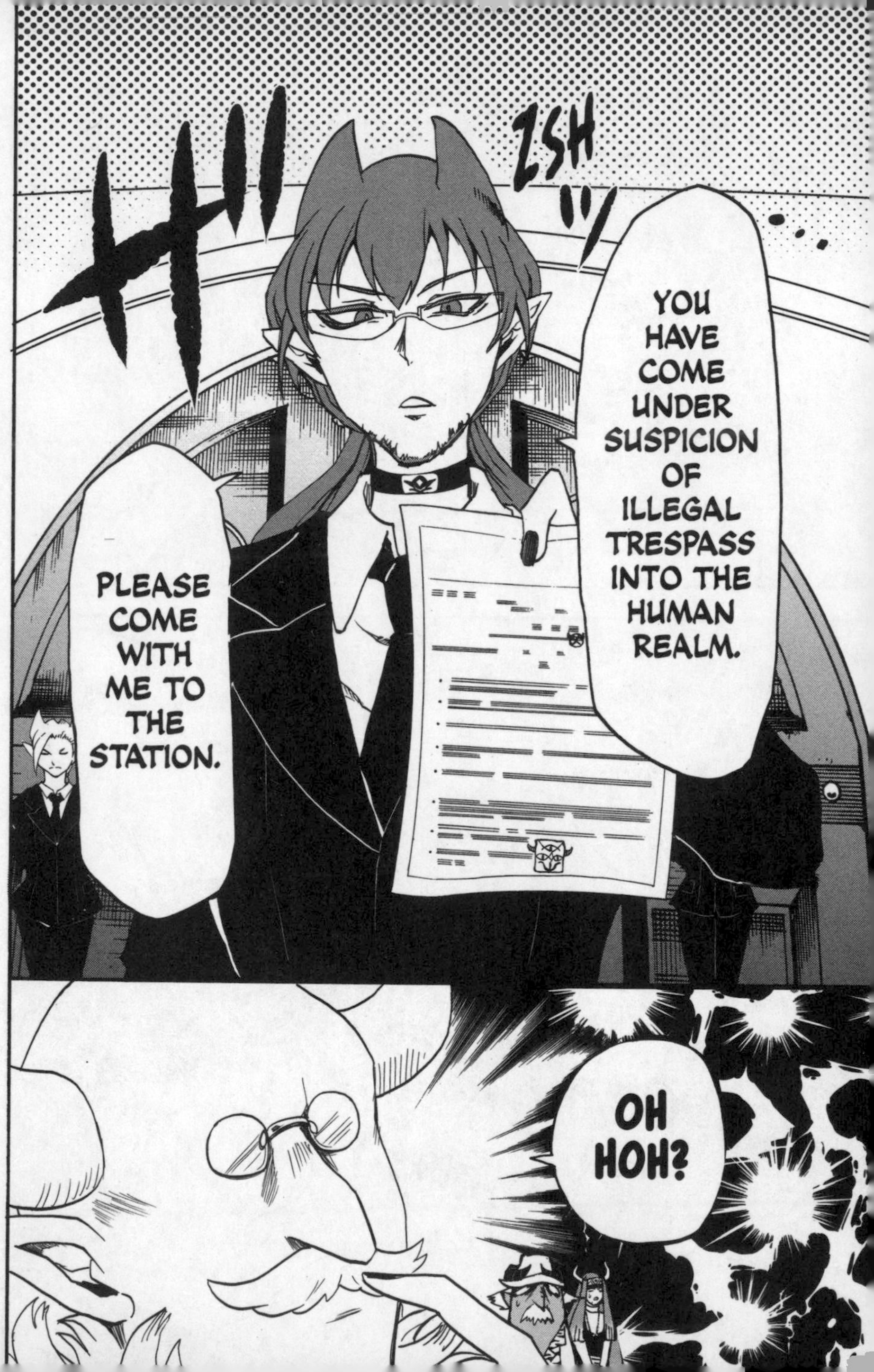
ZSH
...
YOU HAVE COME UNDER SUSPICION OF ILLEGAL TRESPASS INTO THE HUMAN REALM.
PLEASE COME WITH ME TO THE STATION.
OH HOH?

CHAPTER 24 THE BATTLER SHOWCASE

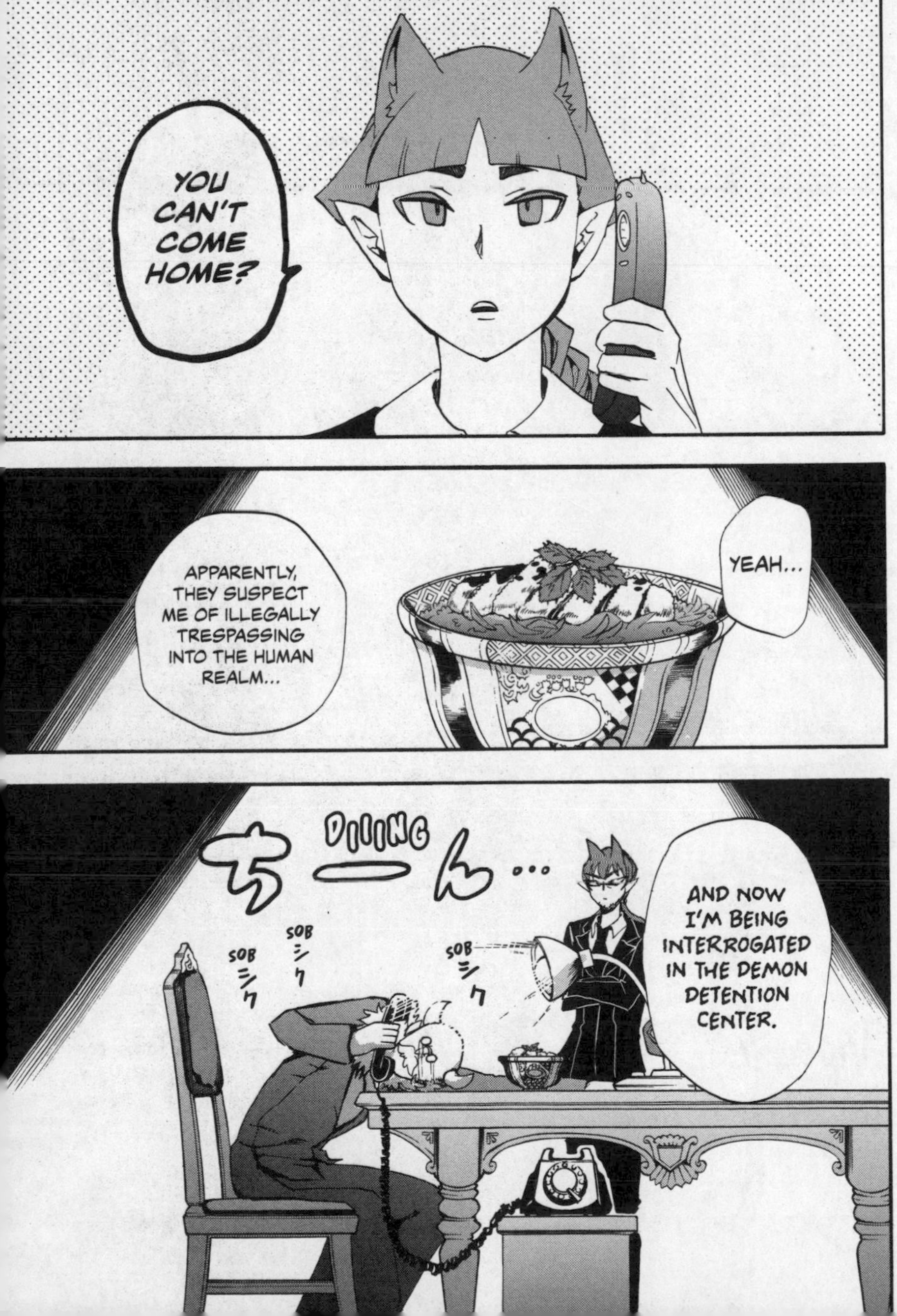
YOU CAN'T COME HOME?
YEAH...
APPARENTLY, THEY SUSPECT ME OF ILLEGALLY TRESPASSING INTO THE HUMAN REALM...
AND NOW I'M BEING INTERROGATED IN THE DEMON DETENTION CENTER.
DIIING
ちーん...
SOB シク
SOB シク
SOB シク

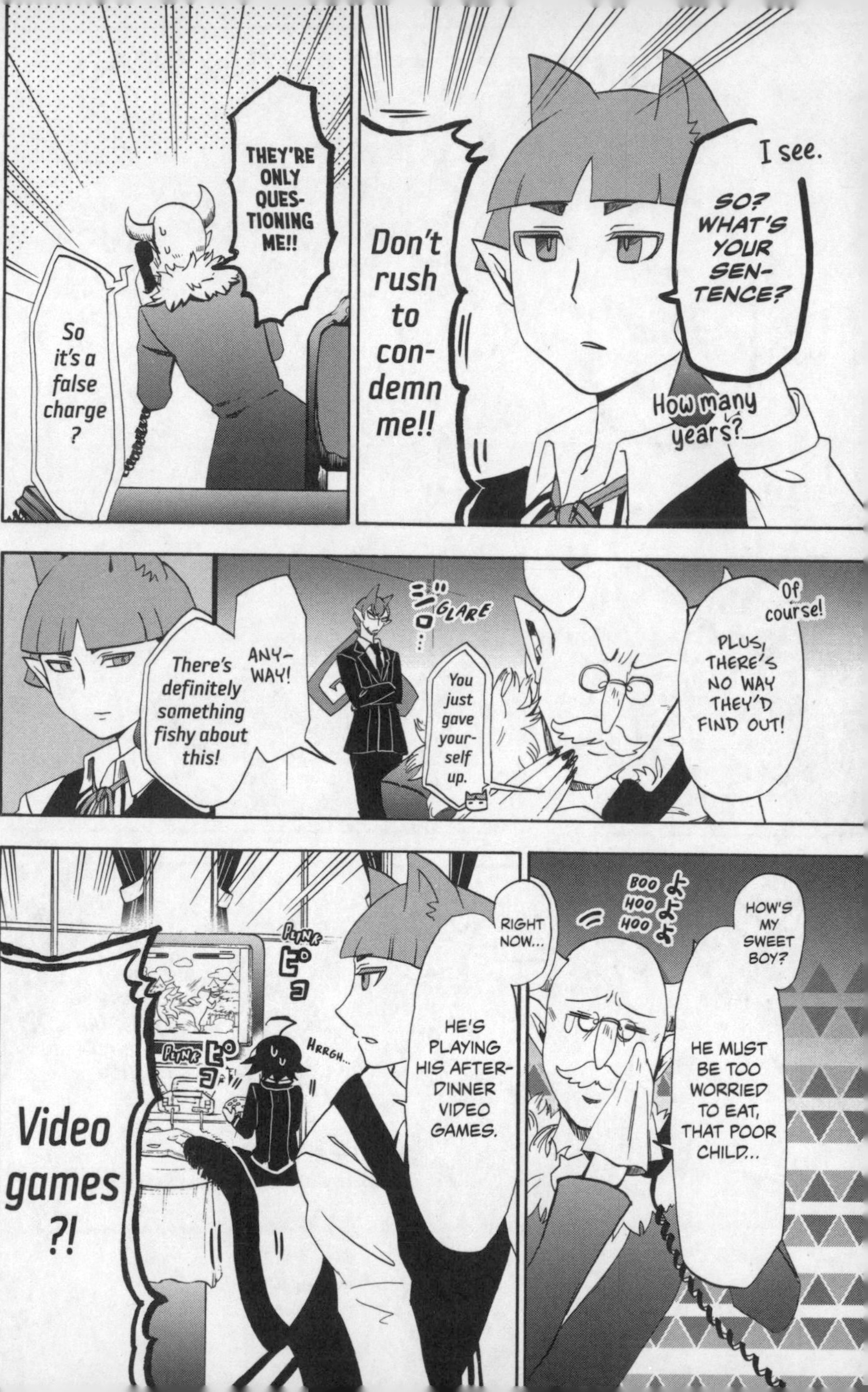
I see.
SO? WHAT'S YOUR SENTENCE?
How many years?
Don't rush to condemn me!!
THEY'RE ONLY QUESTIONING ME!!
So it's a false charge?
Of course!
PLUS, THERE'S NO WAY THEY'D FIND OUT!
You just gave yourself up.
ジロ… GLARE
ANYWAY!
There's definitely something fishy about this!
HOW'S MY SWEET BOY?
BOO HOO HOO よよよ
HE MUST BE TOO WORRIED TO EAT, THAT POOR CHILD...
RIGHT NOW...
HE'S PLAYING HIS AFTER-DINNER VIDEO GAMES.
PLINK ピコ
HRRGH...
PLINK ピコ
Video games?!

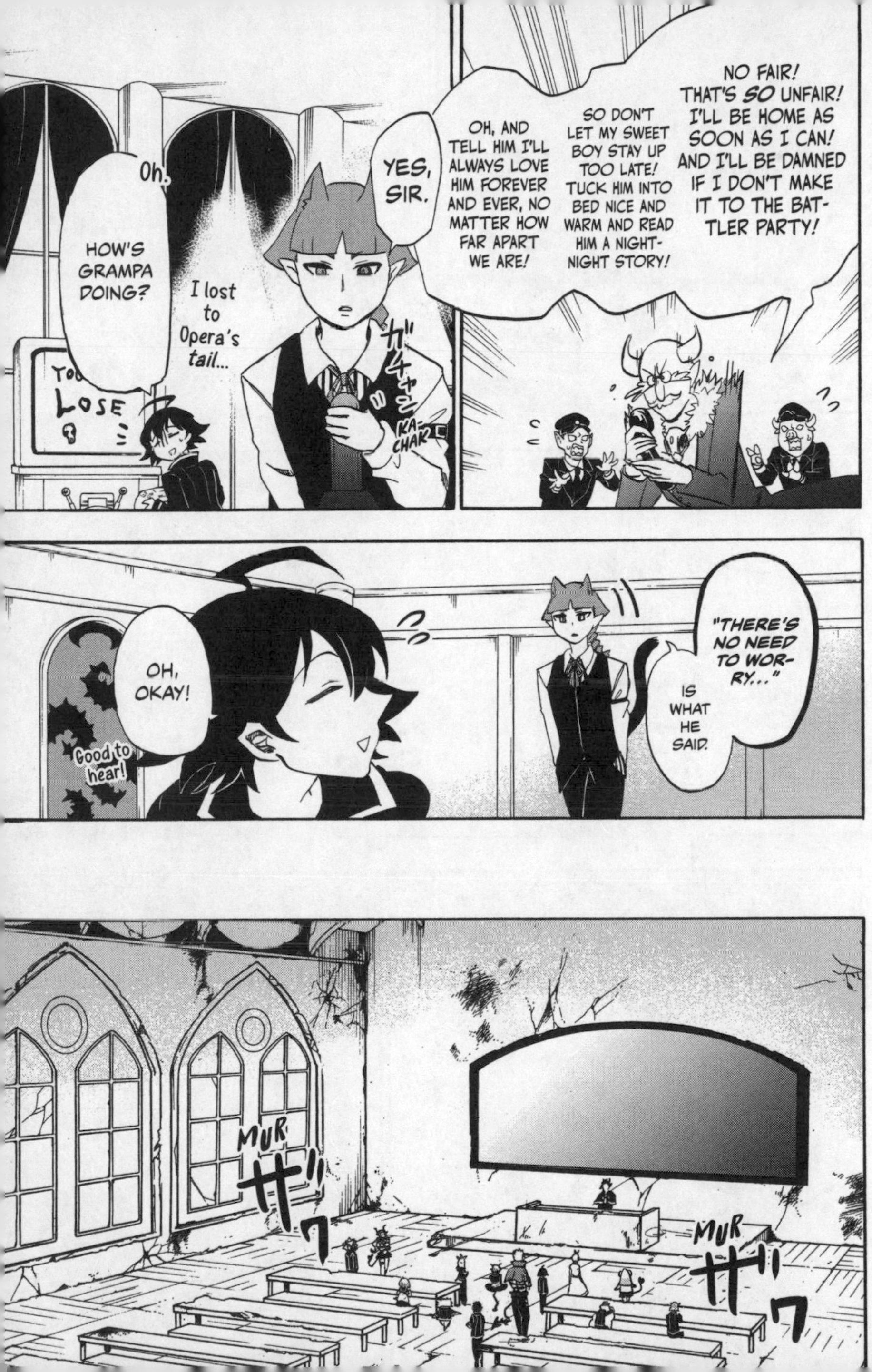
NO FAIR! THAT'S SO UNFAIR! I'LL BE HOME AS SOON AS I CAN! AND I'LL BE DAMNED IF I DON'T MAKE IT TO THE BAT-TLER PARTY!
SO DON'T LET MY SWEET BOY STAY UP TOO LATE! TUCK HIM INTO BED NICE AND WARM AND READ HIM A NIGHT-NIGHT STORY!
OH, AND TELL HIM I'LL ALWAYS LOVE HIM FOREVER AND EVER, NO MATTER HOW FAR APART WE ARE!
YES, SIR.
KA-CHAK
Oh.
HOW'S GRAMPA DOING?
I lost to Opera's tail...
YOU LOSE
"THERE'S NO NEED TO WOR-RY..."
IS WHAT HE SAID.
OH, OKAY!
Good to hear!
MUR
MUR

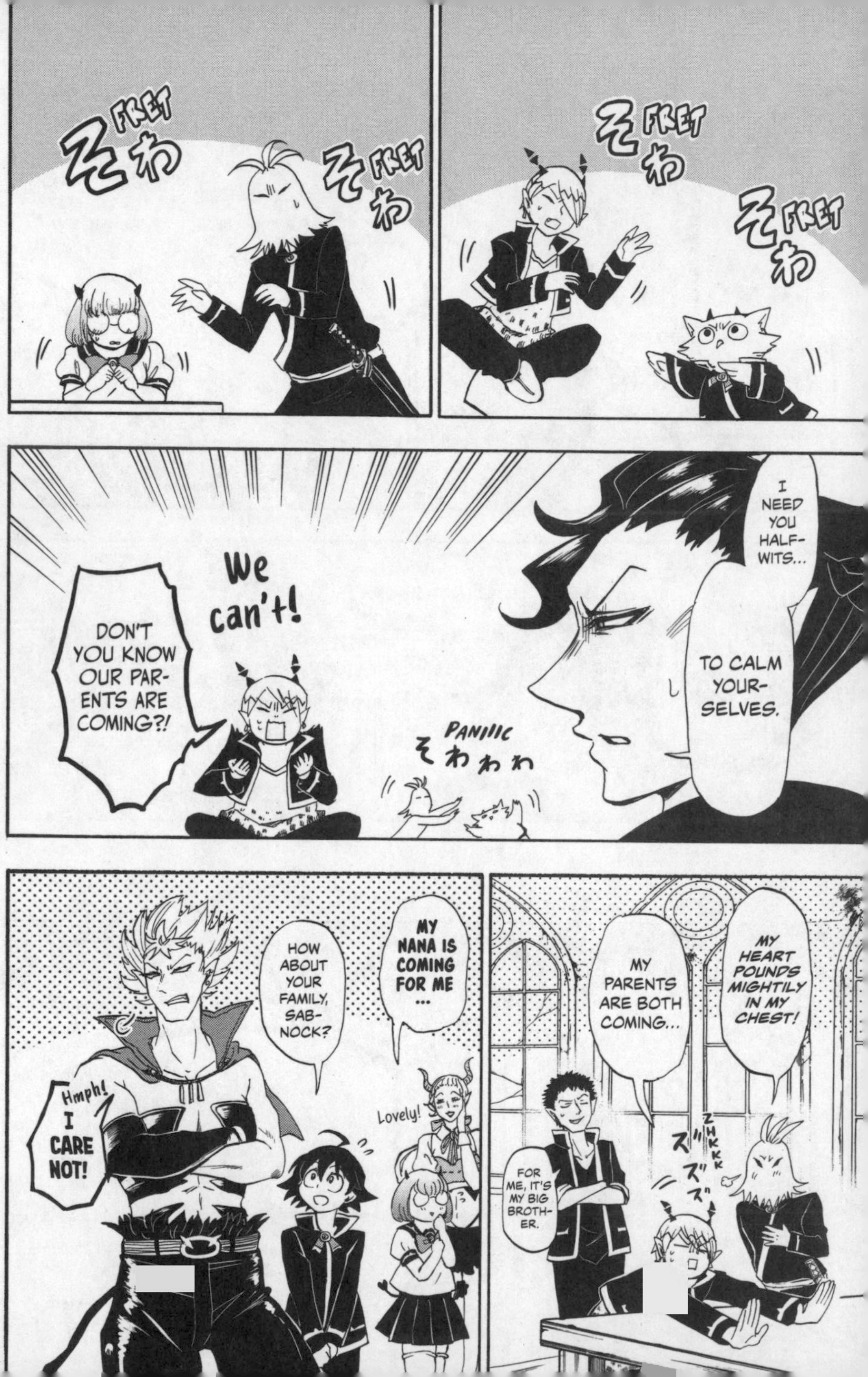
そわ FRET
そわ FRET
そわ FRET
そわ FRET
I NEED YOU HALF-WITS...
TO CALM YOURSELVES.
PANIIIC そわわわ
We can't!
DON'T YOU KNOW OUR PARENTS ARE COMING?!
MY HEART POUNDS MIGHTILY IN MY CHEST!
MY PARENTS ARE BOTH COMING...
ZHKKK ズズズ
FOR ME, IT'S MY BIG BROTHER.
MY NANA IS COMING FOR ME...
HOW ABOUT YOUR FAMILY, SABNOCK?
Lovely!
Hmph! I CARE NOT!

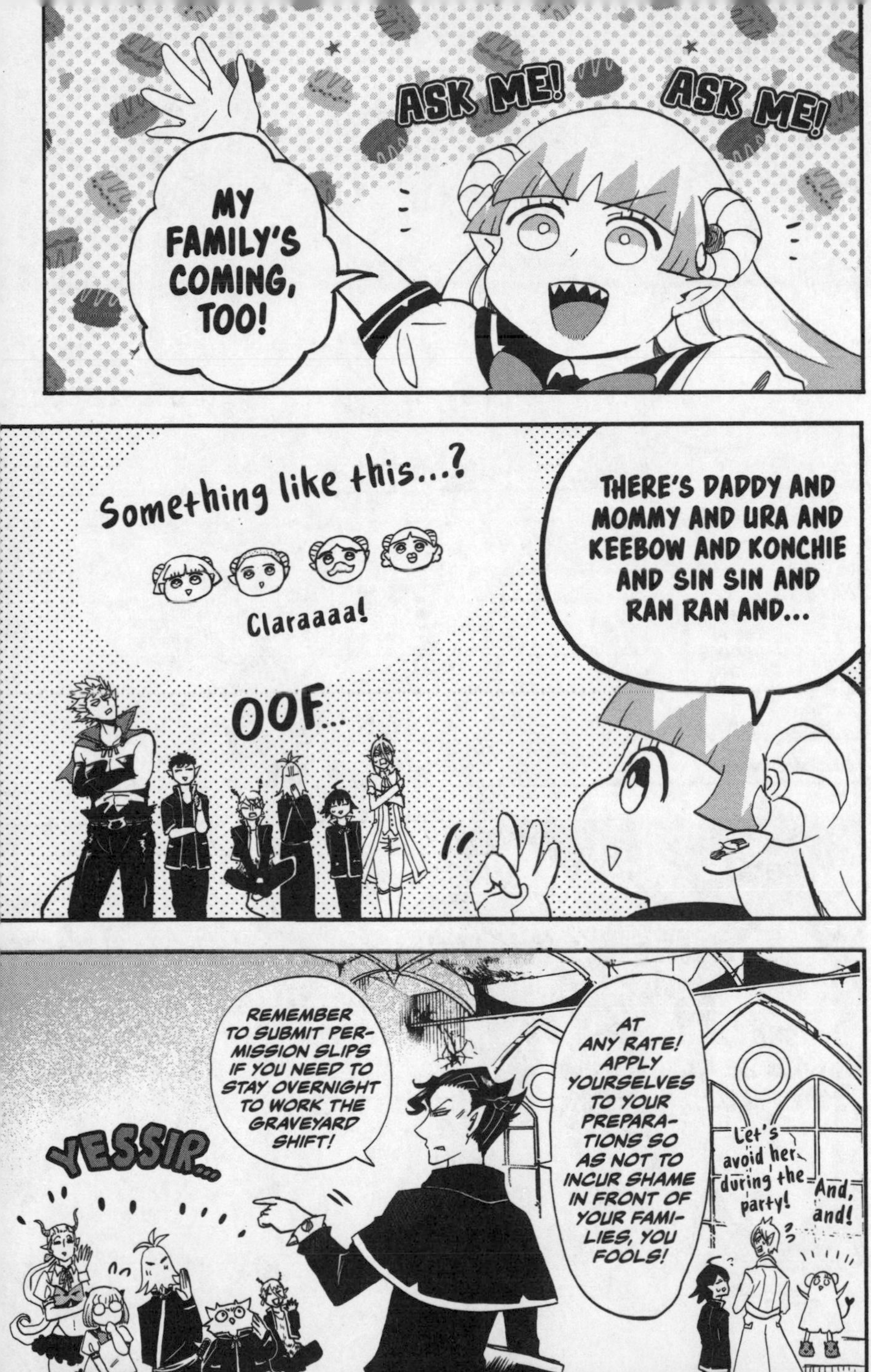
ASK ME!
ASK ME!
MY FAMILY'S COMING, TOO!
THERE'S DADDY AND MOMMY AND URA AND KEEBOW AND KONCHIE AND SIN SIN AND RAN RAN AND...
Something like this...?
Claraaaa!
OOF...
AT ANY RATE! APPLY YOURSELVES TO YOUR PREPARATIONS SO AS NOT TO INCUR SHAME IN FRONT OF YOUR FAMILIES, YOU FOOLS!
REMEMBER TO SUBMIT PERMISSION SLIPS IF YOU NEED TO STAY OVERNIGHT TO WORK THE GRAVEYARD SHIFT!
Let's avoid her during the party!
And, and!
YESSIR...

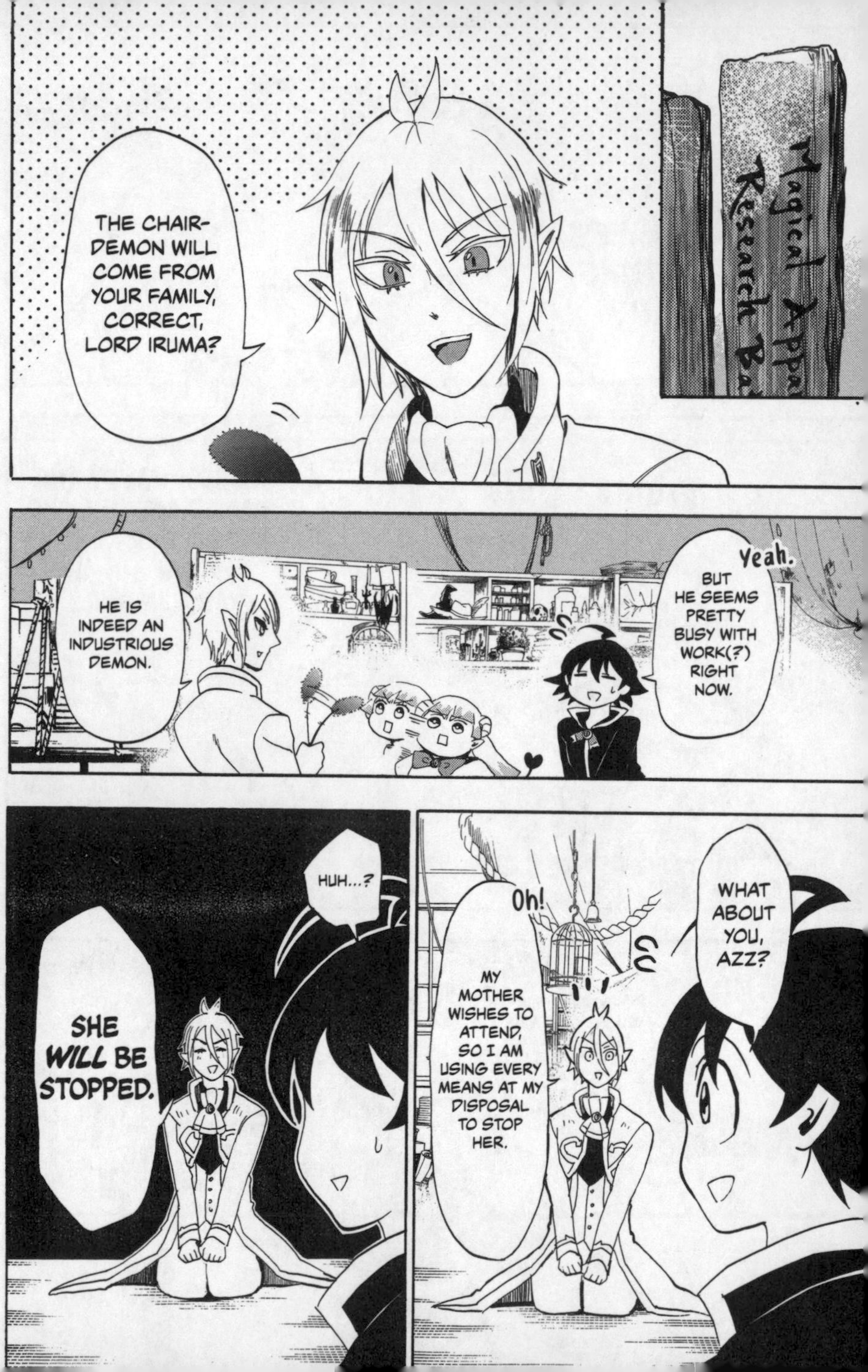
THE CHAIR-DEMON WILL COME FROM YOUR FAMILY, CORRECT, LORD IRUMA?
Yeah.
BUT HE SEEMS PRETTY BUSY WITH WORK(?) RIGHT NOW.
HE IS INDEED AN INDUSTRIOUS DEMON.
WHAT ABOUT YOU, AZZ?
Oh!
MY MOTHER WISHES TO ATTEND, SO I AM USING EVERY MEANS AT MY DISPOSAL TO STOP HER.
HUH...?
SHE **WILL** BE STOPPED.

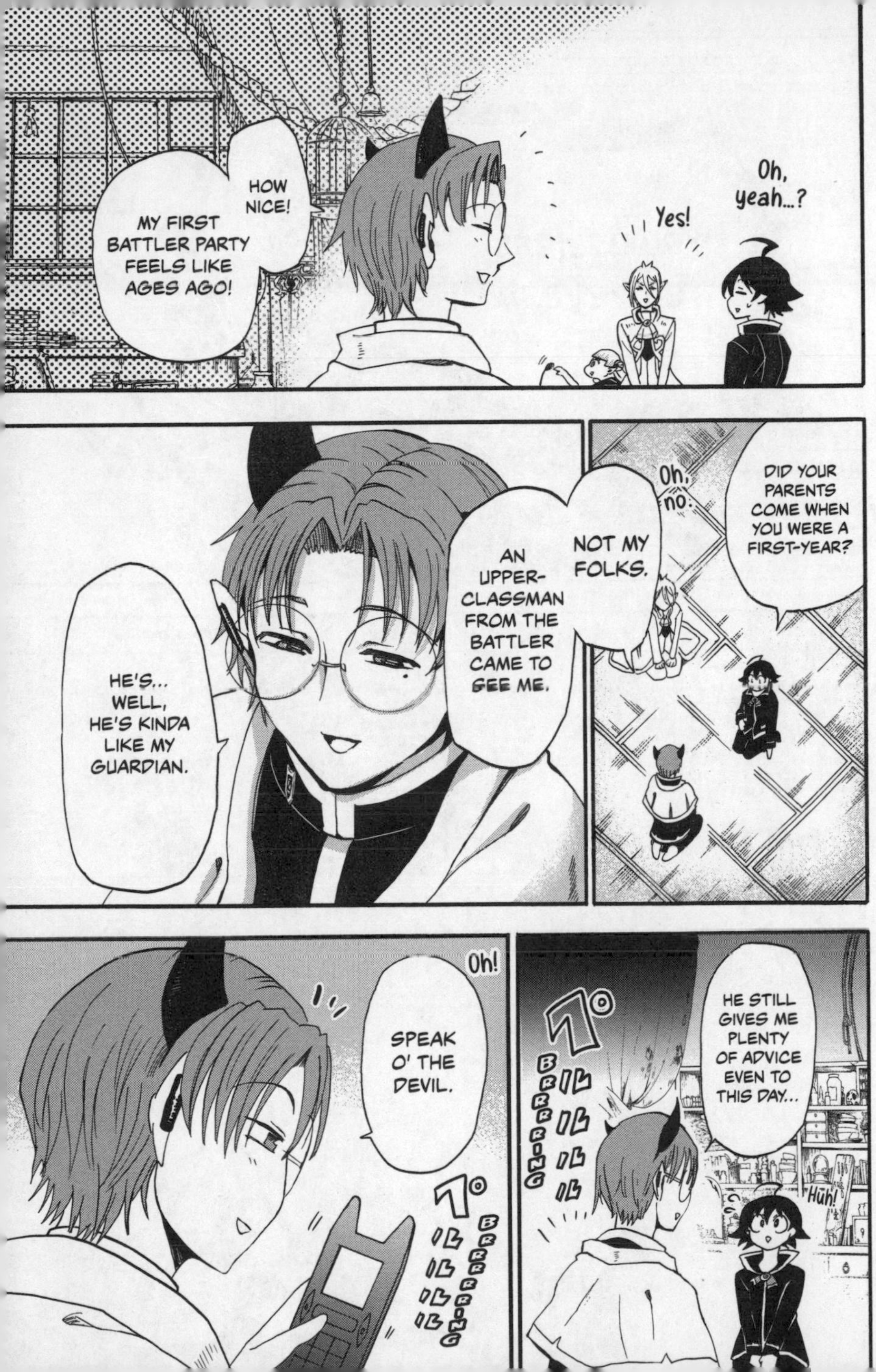
Oh, yeah...?
Yes!
HOW NICE!
MY FIRST BATTLER PARTY FEELS LIKE AGES AGO!
DID YOUR PARENTS COME WHEN YOU WERE A FIRST-YEAR?
Oh, no.
NOT MY FOLKS.
AN UPPER-CLASSMAN FROM THE BATTLER CAME TO SEE ME.
HE'S... WELL, HE'S KINDA LIKE MY GUARDIAN.
HE STILL GIVES ME PLENTY OF ADVICE EVEN TO THIS DAY...
BRRRRING
Huh!
Oh!
SPEAK O' THE DEVIL.
BRRRRRING

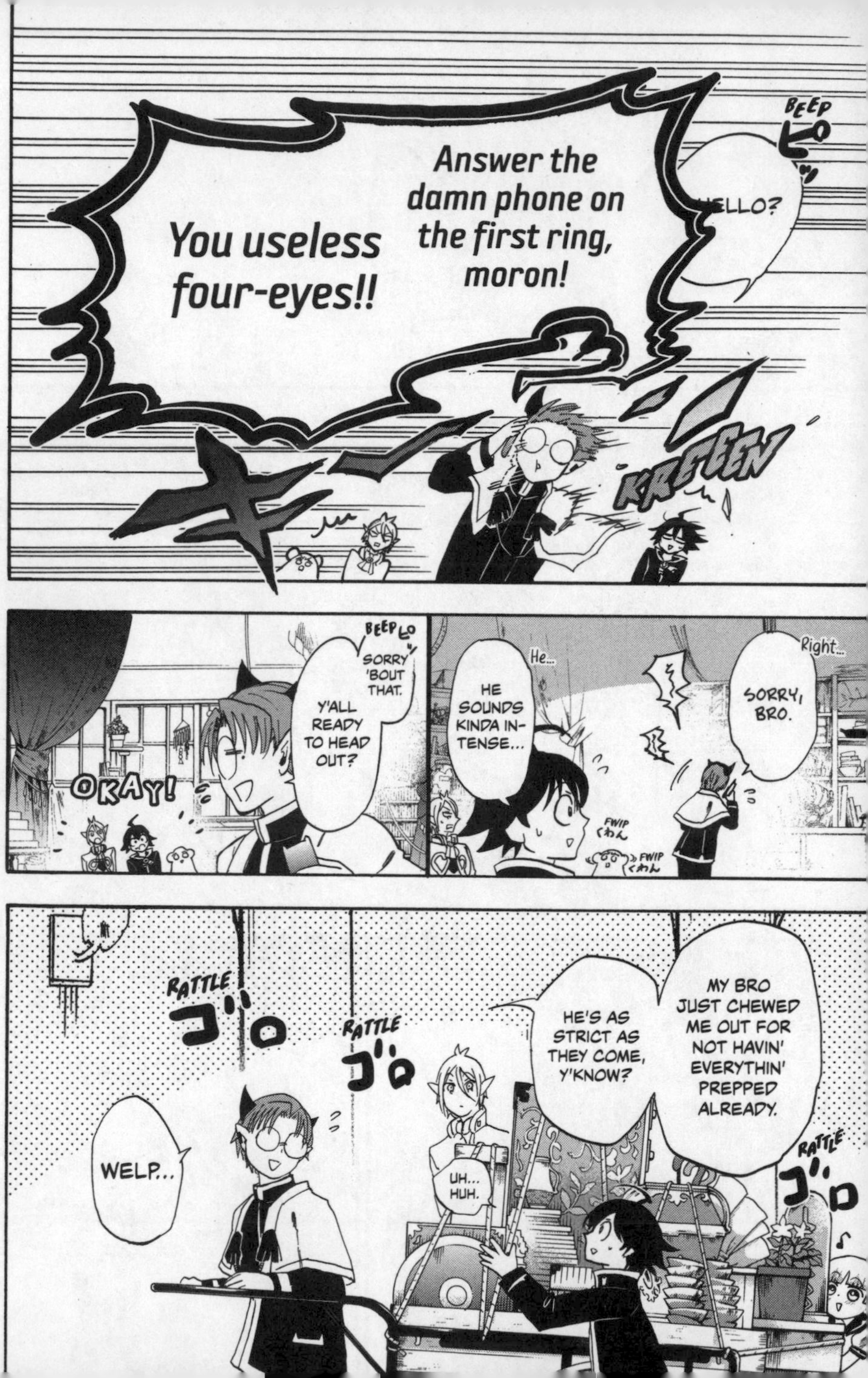
BEEP
ピロ
HELLO?
Answer the damn phone on the first ring, moron!
You useless four-eyes!!
KREEEN
Right...
SORRY, BRO.
He...
HE SOUNDS KINDA IN-TENSE...
FWIP
くわん
FWIP
くわん
BEEP
ピロ
SORRY 'BOUT THAT.
Y'ALL READY TO HEAD OUT?
OKAY!
MY BRO JUST CHEWED ME OUT FOR NOT HAVIN' EVERYTHIN' PREPPED ALREADY.
HE'S AS STRICT AS THEY COME, Y'KNOW?
RATTLE
ゴロ
UH... HUH.
RATTLE
ゴロ
RATTLE
ゴロ
WELP...

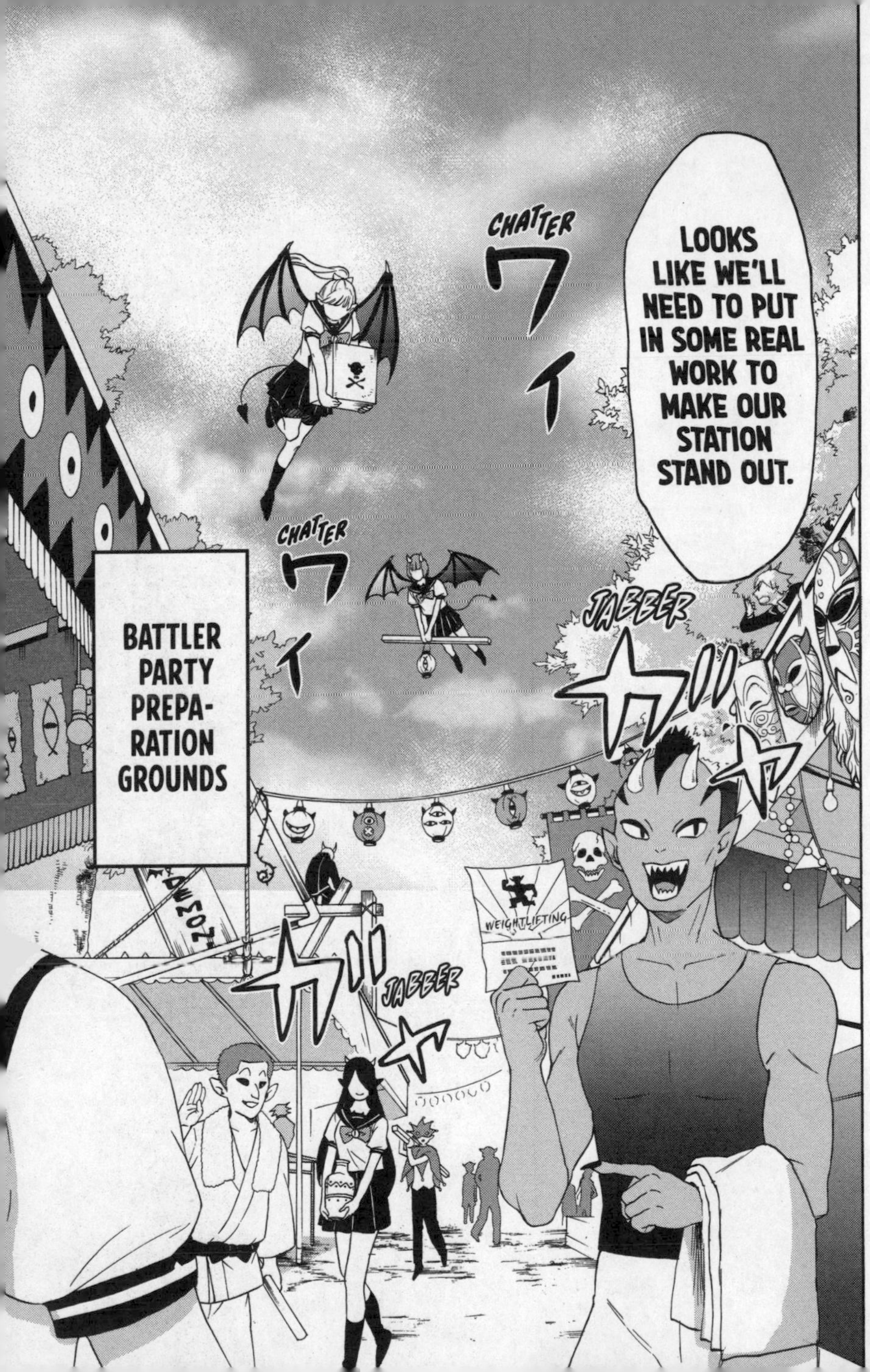
LOOKS LIKE WE'LL NEED TO PUT IN SOME REAL WORK TO MAKE OUR STATION STAND OUT.
CHATTER
JABBER
CHATTER
BATTLER PARTY PREPA-RATION GROUNDS
WEIGHTLIFTING
JABBER
DEMON

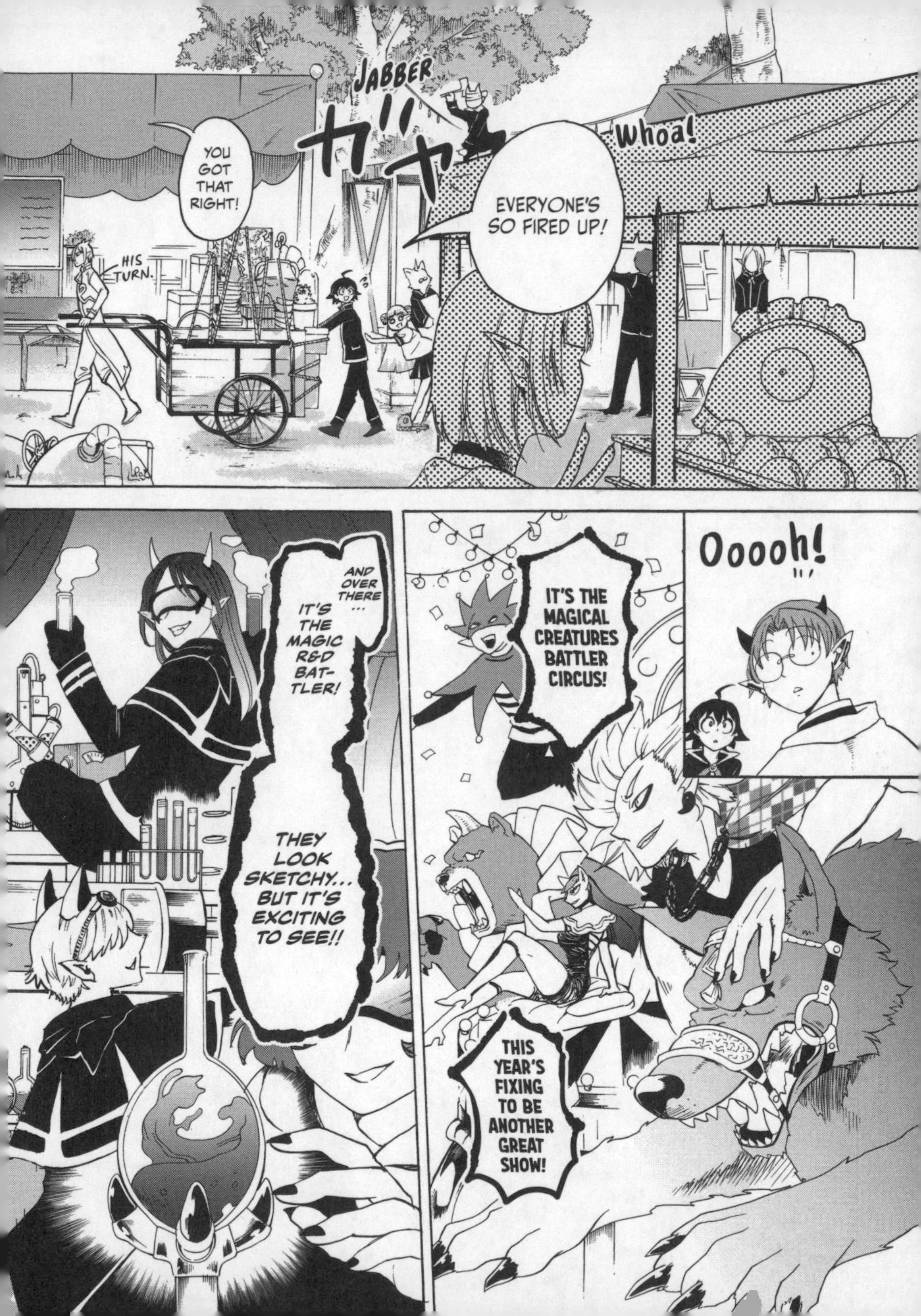
Whoa!
EVERYONE'S SO FIRED UP!
JABBER
YOU GOT THAT RIGHT!
HIS TURN.
Ooooh!
IT'S THE MAGICAL CREATURES BATTLER CIRCUS!
THIS YEAR'S FIXING TO BE ANOTHER GREAT SHOW!
AND OVER THERE...
IT'S THE MAGIC R&D BATTLER!
THEY LOOK SKETCHY... BUT IT'S EXCITING TO SEE!!

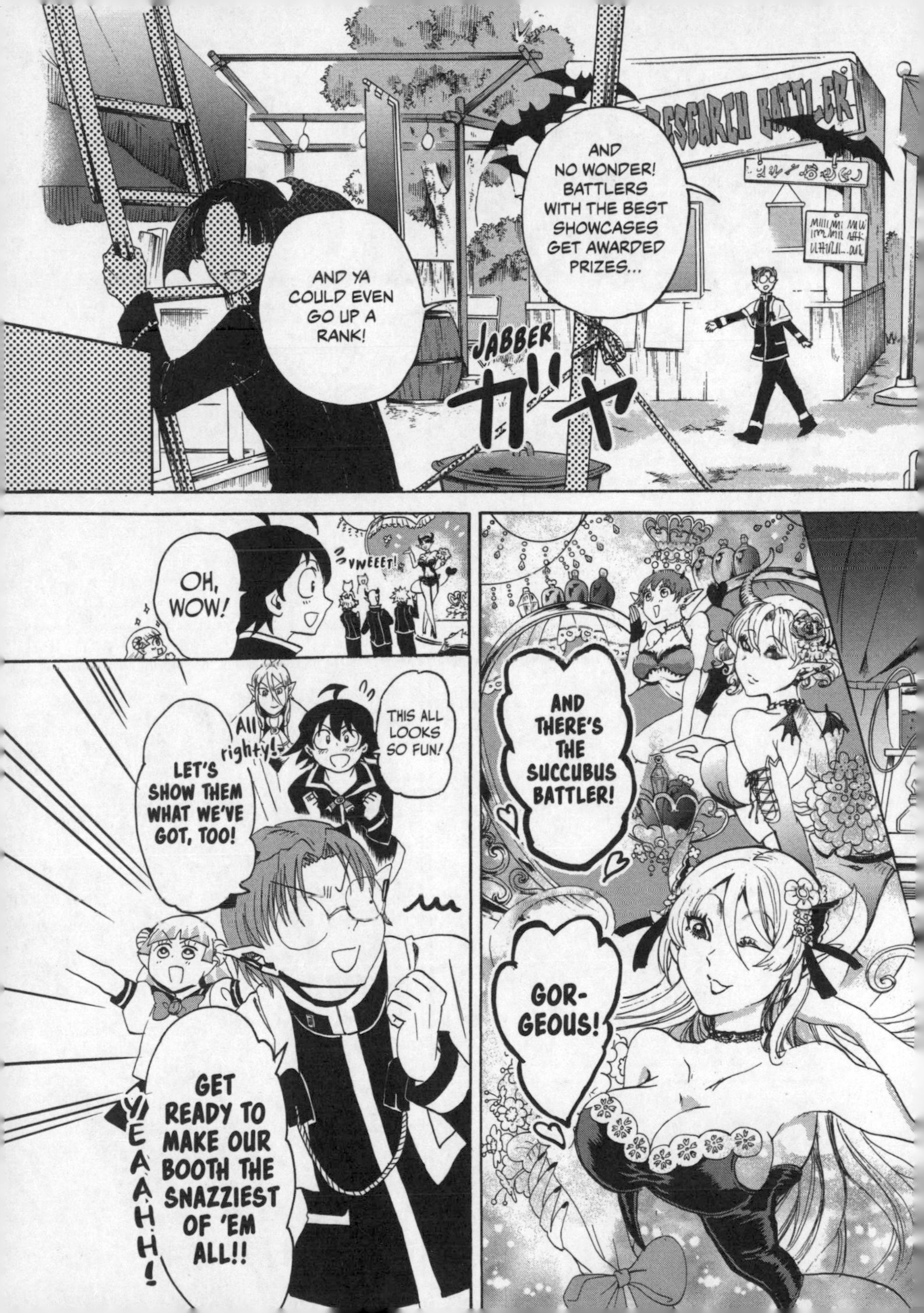
AND NO WONDER! BATTLERS WITH THE BEST SHOWCASES GET AWARDED PRIZES...
AND YA COULD EVEN GO UP A RANK!
JABBER
ガヤ
AND THERE'S THE SUCCUBUS BATTLER!
GOR-GEOUS!
VWEEET!
OH, WOW!
THIS ALL LOOKS SO FUN!
All righty!
LET'S SHOW THEM WHAT WE'VE GOT, TOO!
GET READY TO MAKE OUR BOOTH THE SNAZZIEST OF 'EM ALL!!
YEAAHH!

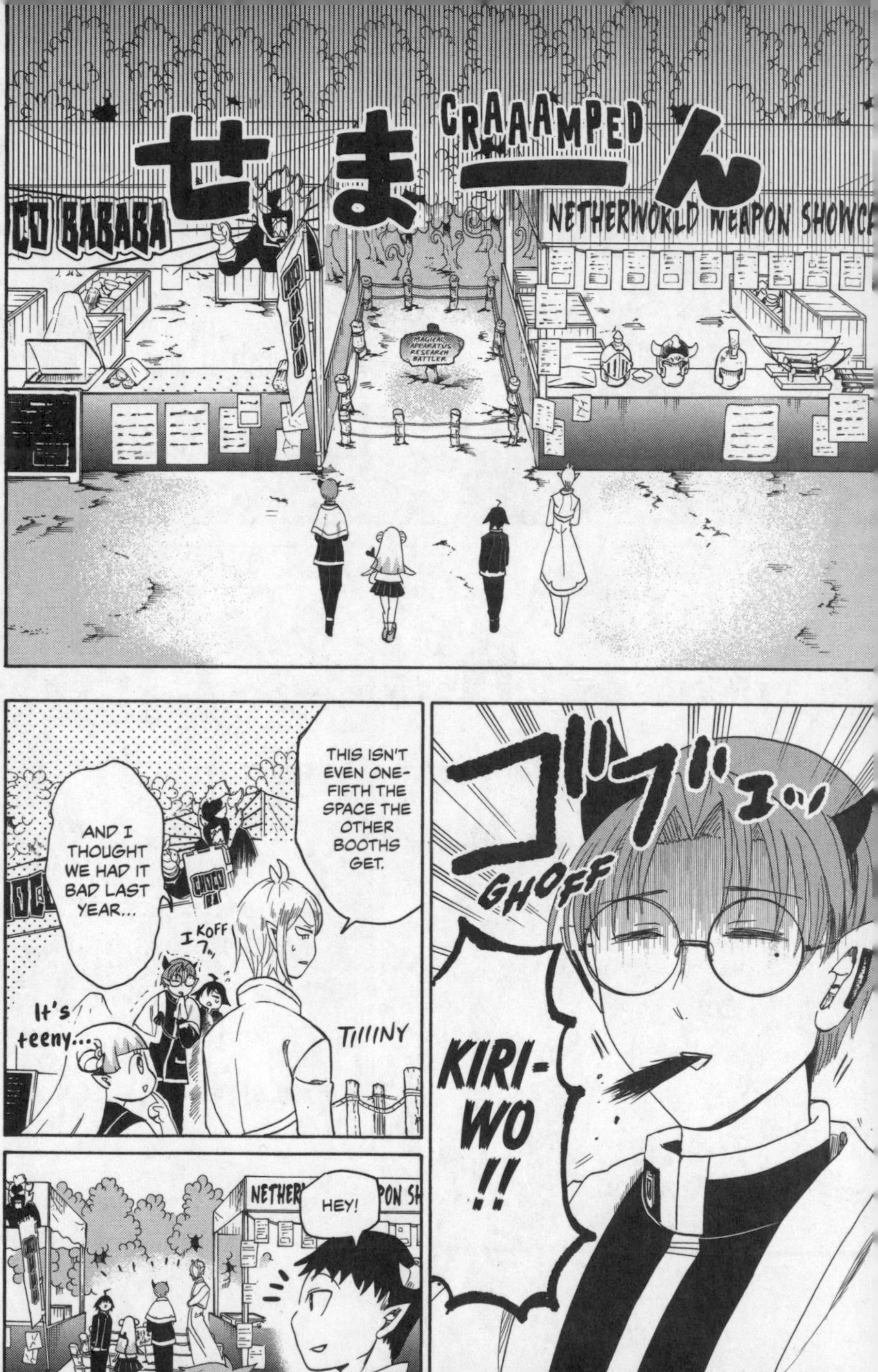

せまーん
CRAAAMPED
CO BABABA
NETHERWORLD WEAPON SHOWC
MAGICAL APPARATUS RESEARCH BATTLER
GHOFF
KIRI-WO!!
THIS ISN'T EVEN ONE-FIFTH THE SPACE THE OTHER BOOTHS GET.
AND I THOUGHT WE HAD IT BAD LAST YEAR...
I KOFF
TIIIINY
It's teeny...
NETHER PON SH
HEY!

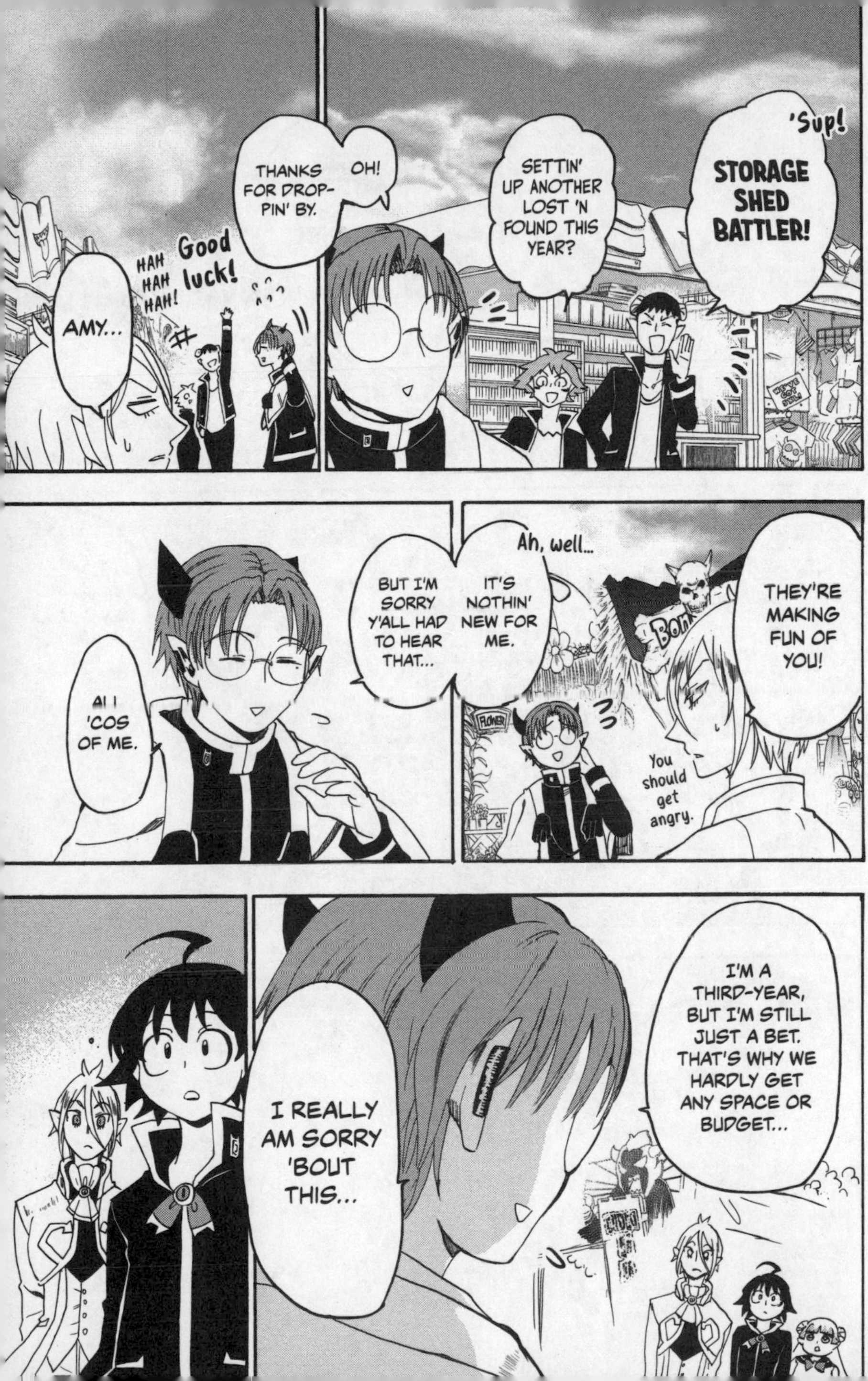
'Sup!
STORAGE SHED BATTLER!
SETTIN' UP ANOTHER LOST 'N FOUND THIS YEAR?
OH! THANKS FOR DROP-PIN' BY.
HAH HAH HAH!
Good luck!
AMY...
Ah, well...
THEY'RE MAKING FUN OF YOU!
You should get angry.
IT'S NOTHIN' NEW FOR ME.
BUT I'M SORRY Y'ALL HAD TO HEAR THAT...
FLOWER
ALL 'COS OF ME.
I'M A THIRD-YEAR, BUT I'M STILL JUST A BET. THAT'S WHY WE HARDLY GET ANY SPACE OR BUDGET...
I REALLY AM SORRY 'BOUT THIS...

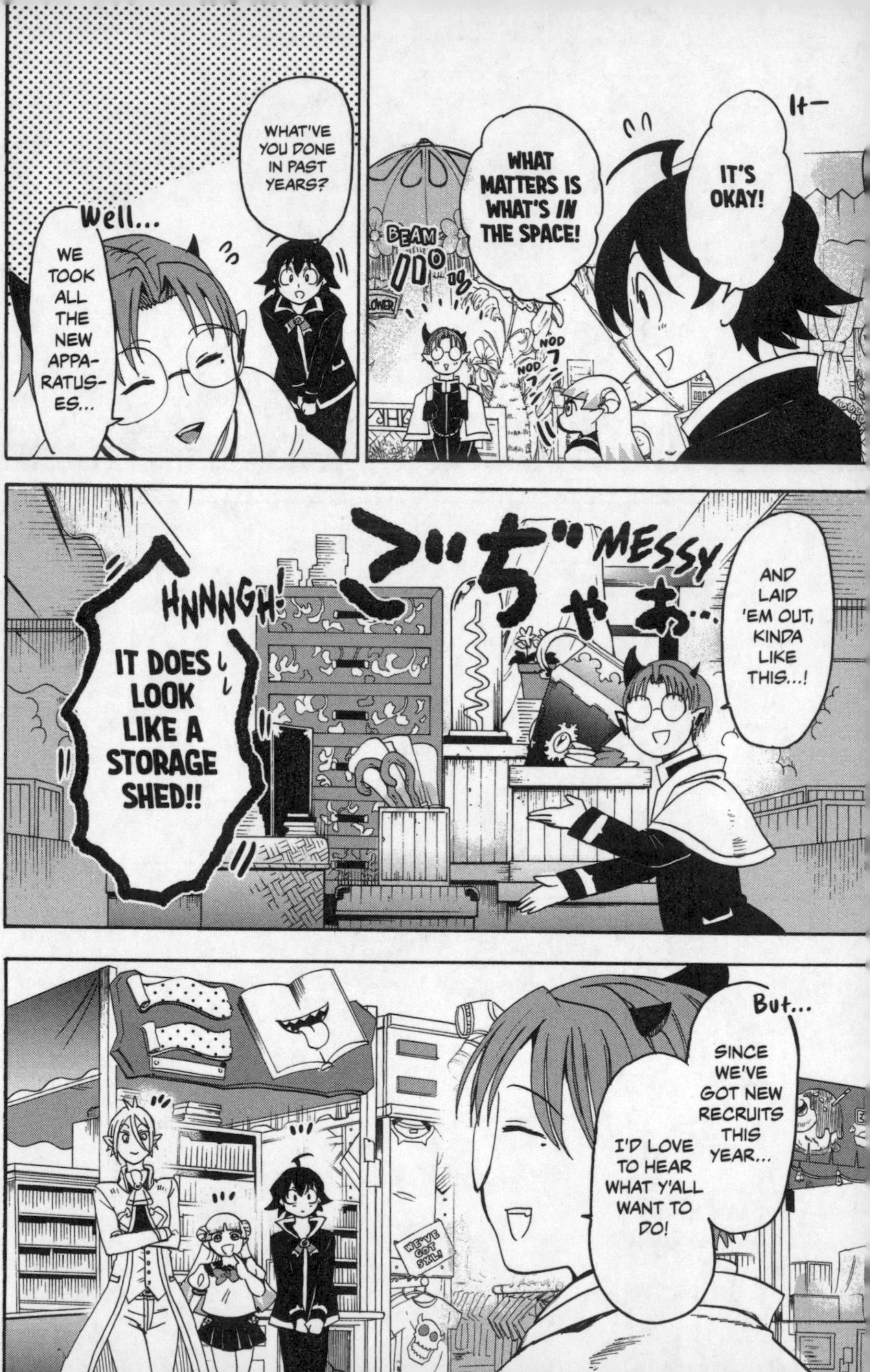
IT'S OKAY!
WHAT MATTERS IS WHAT'S IN THE SPACE!
BEAM
NOD NOD
WHAT'VE YOU DONE IN PAST YEARS?
Well...
WE TOOK ALL THE NEW APPARATUSES...
AND LAID 'EM OUT, KINDA LIKE THIS...!
MESSY
HNNNGH!
IT DOES LOOK LIKE A STORAGE SHED!!
But...
SINCE WE'VE GOT NEW RECRUITS THIS YEAR...
I'D LOVE TO HEAR WHAT Y'ALL WANT TO DO!
WE'VE GOT SKL!

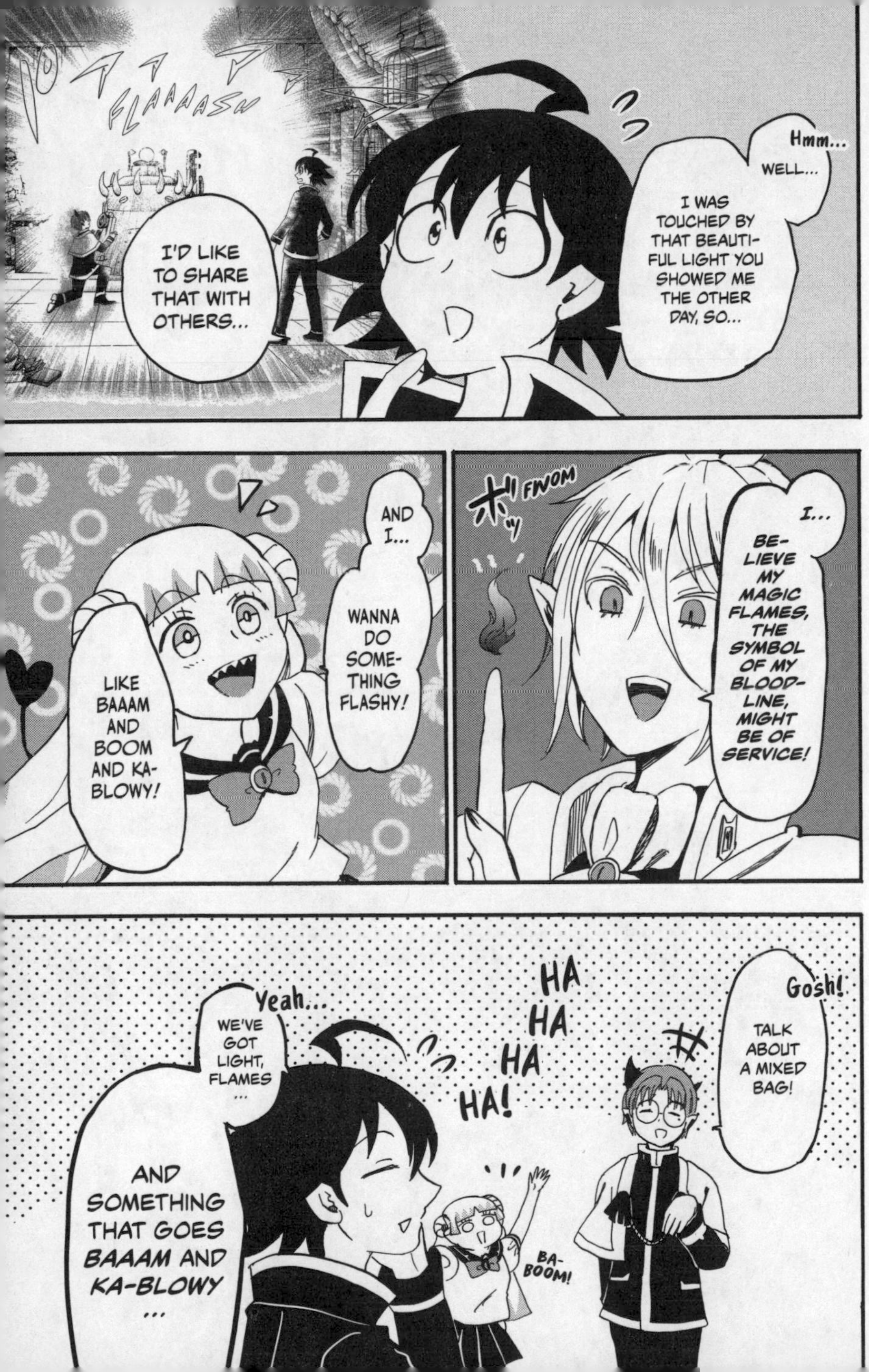
Hmm...
WELL...
I WAS TOUCHED BY THAT BEAUTIFUL LIGHT YOU SHOWED ME THE OTHER DAY, SO...
FLAAAASH
I'D LIKE TO SHARE THAT WITH OTHERS...
FWOM
I... BELIEVE MY MAGIC FLAMES, THE SYMBOL OF MY BLOODLINE, MIGHT BE OF SERVICE!
AND I...
WANNA DO SOMETHING FLASHY!
LIKE BAAAM AND BOOM AND KA-BLOWY!
Gosh!
TALK ABOUT A MIXED BAG!
HA HA HA HA!
Yeah...
WE'VE GOT LIGHT, FLAMES...
AND SOMETHING THAT GOES BAAAM AND KA-BLOWY...
BA-BOOM!

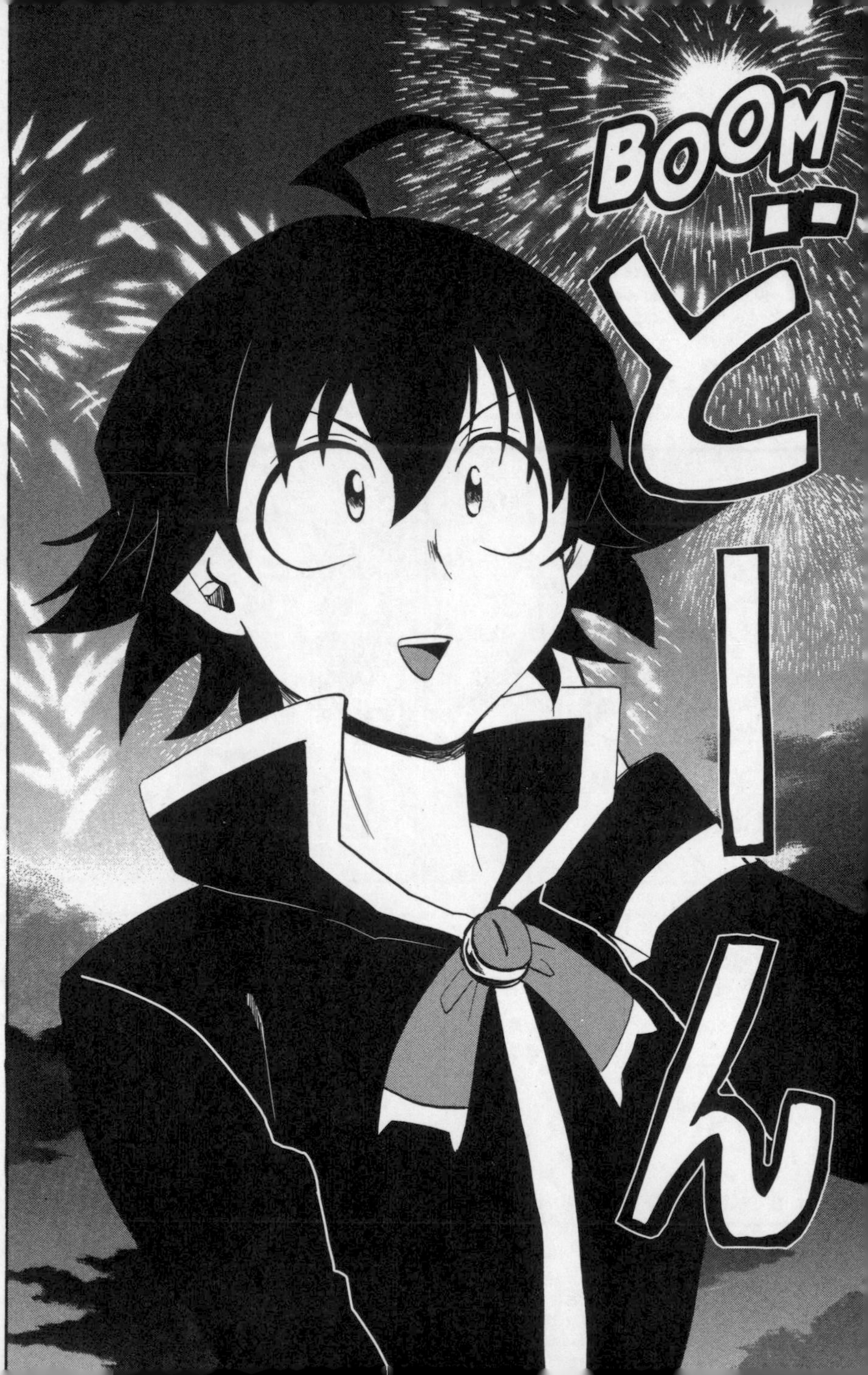
BOOM
どーん

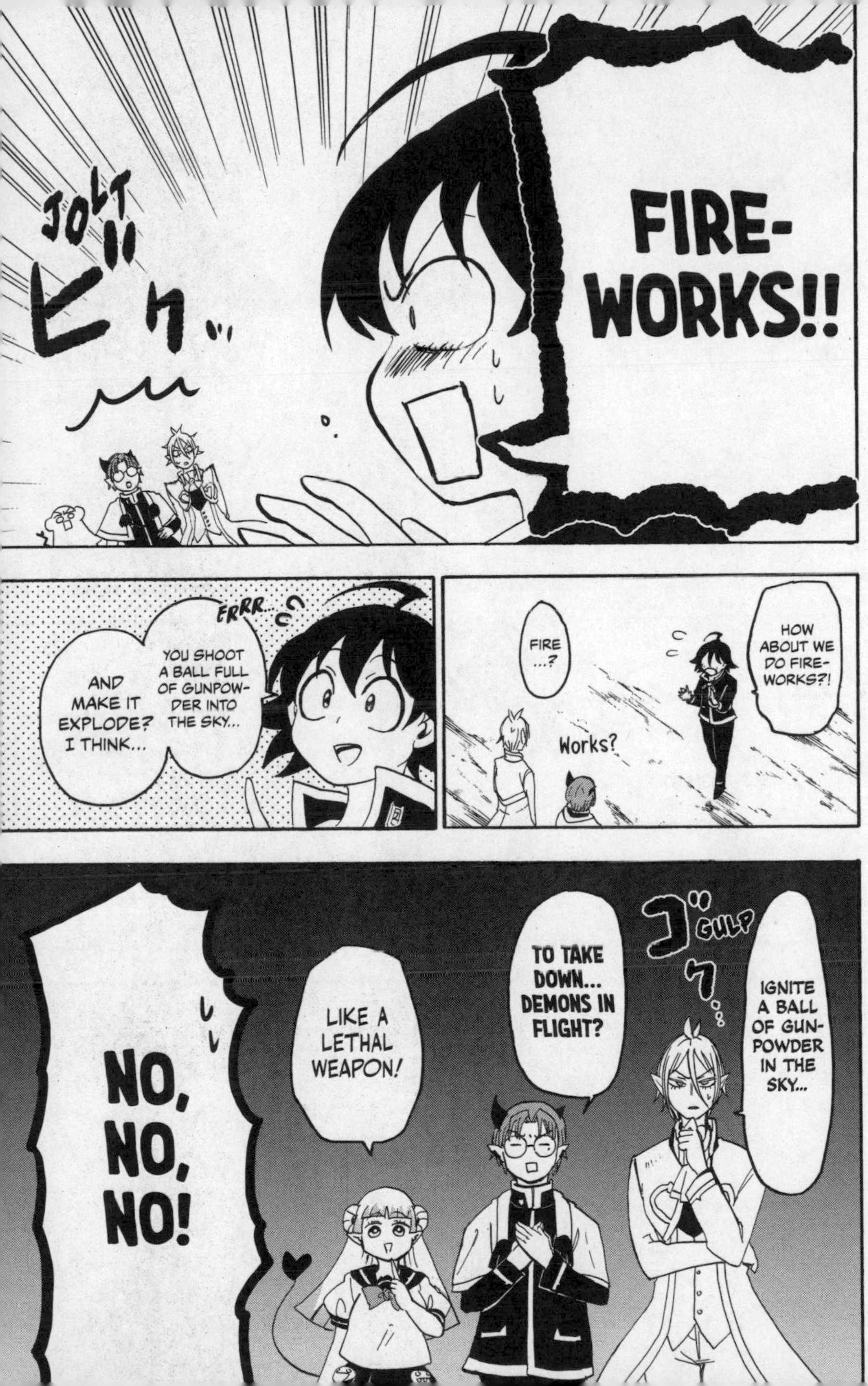
FIRE-WORKS!!
JOLT
HOW ABOUT WE DO FIRE-WORKS?!
FIRE ...?
Works?
ERRR...
YOU SHOOT A BALL FULL OF GUNPOW-DER INTO THE SKY...
AND MAKE IT EXPLODE? I THINK...
GULP
IGNITE A BALL OF GUN-POWDER IN THE SKY...
TO TAKE DOWN... DEMONS IN FLIGHT?
LIKE A LETHAL WEAPON!
NO, NO, NO, NO!

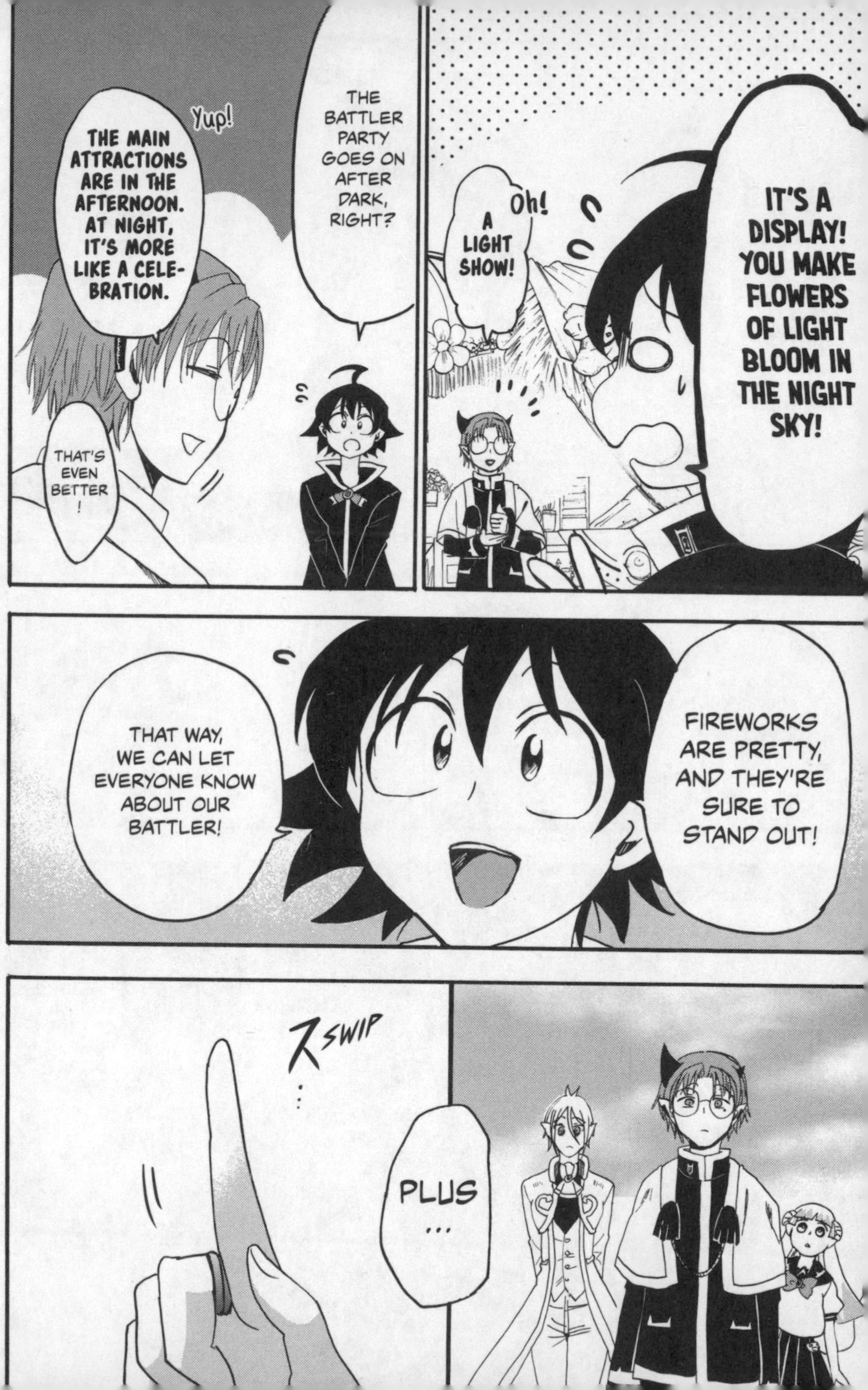
IT'S A DISPLAY! YOU MAKE FLOWERS OF LIGHT BLOOM IN THE NIGHT SKY!
Oh!
A LIGHT SHOW!
THE BATTLER PARTY GOES ON AFTER DARK, RIGHT?
Yup!
THE MAIN ATTRACTIONS ARE IN THE AFTERNOON. AT NIGHT, IT'S MORE LIKE A CELE-BRATION.
THAT'S EVEN BETTER!
FIREWORKS ARE PRETTY, AND THEY'RE SURE TO STAND OUT!
THAT WAY, WE CAN LET EVERYONE KNOW ABOUT OUR BATTLER!
PLUS ...
SWIP
...

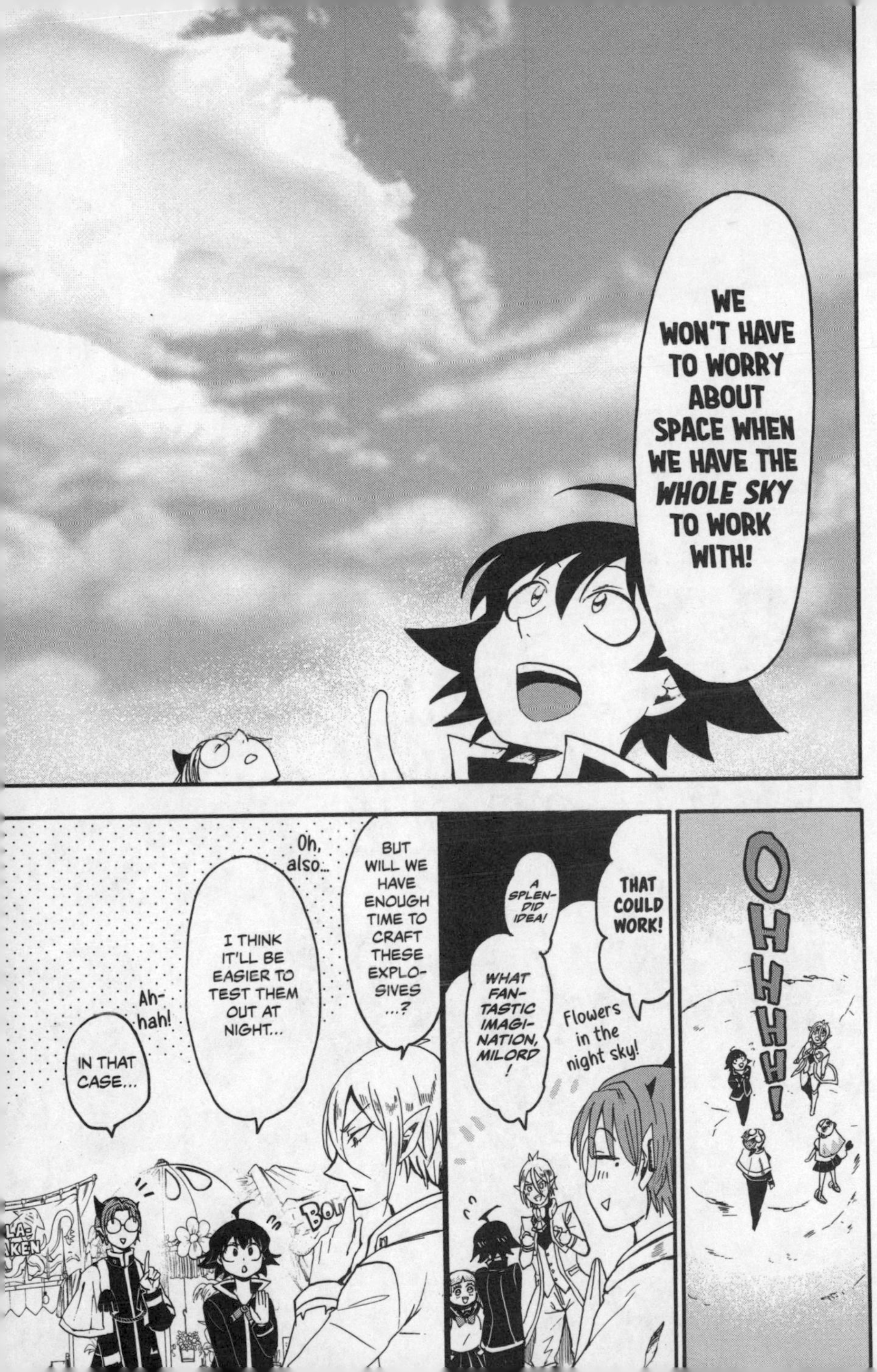
WE WON'T HAVE TO WORRY ABOUT SPACE WHEN WE HAVE THE *WHOLE SKY* TO WORK WITH!
OHHHHH!
THAT COULD WORK!
A SPLEN-DID IDEA!
Flowers in the night sky!
WHAT FAN-TASTIC IMAGI-NATION, MILORD!
BUT WILL WE HAVE ENOUGH TIME TO CRAFT THESE EXPLO-SIVES ...?
Oh, also...
I THINK IT'LL BE EASIER TO TEST THEM OUT AT NIGHT...
Ah-hah!
IN THAT CASE...

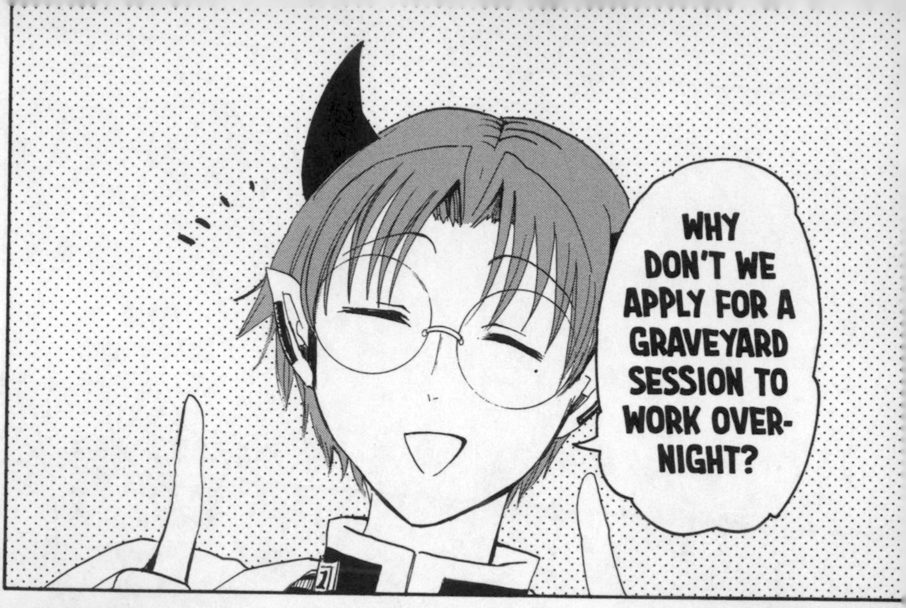
WHY DON'T WE APPLY FOR A GRAVEYARD SESSION TO WORK OVER-NIGHT?
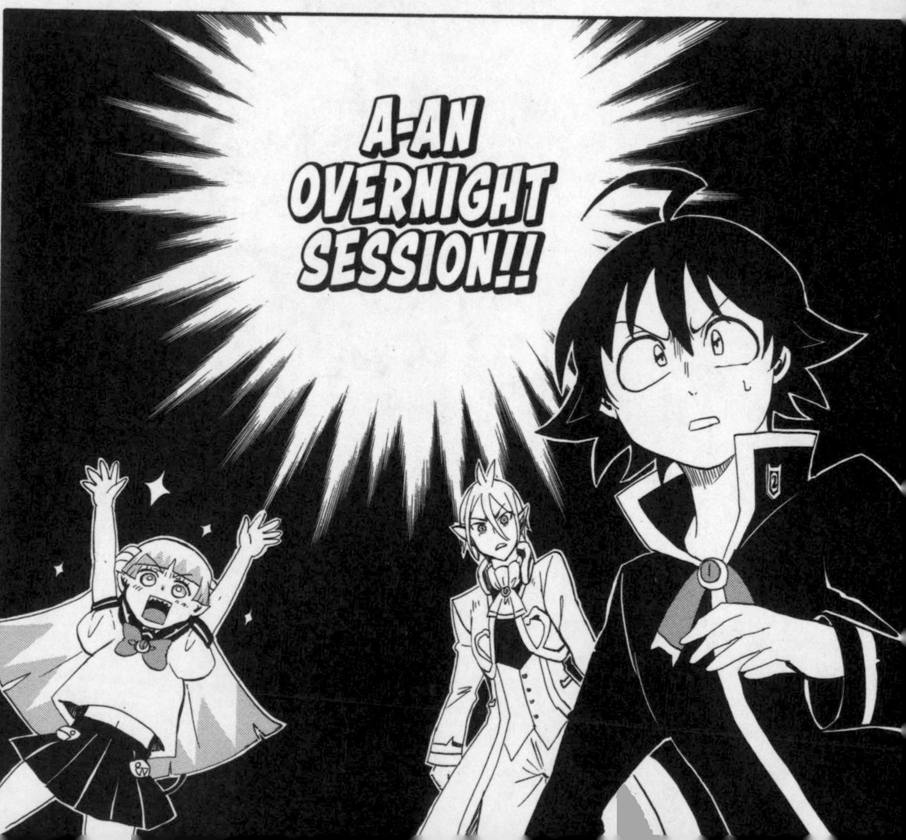
A-AN OVERNIGHT SESSION!!

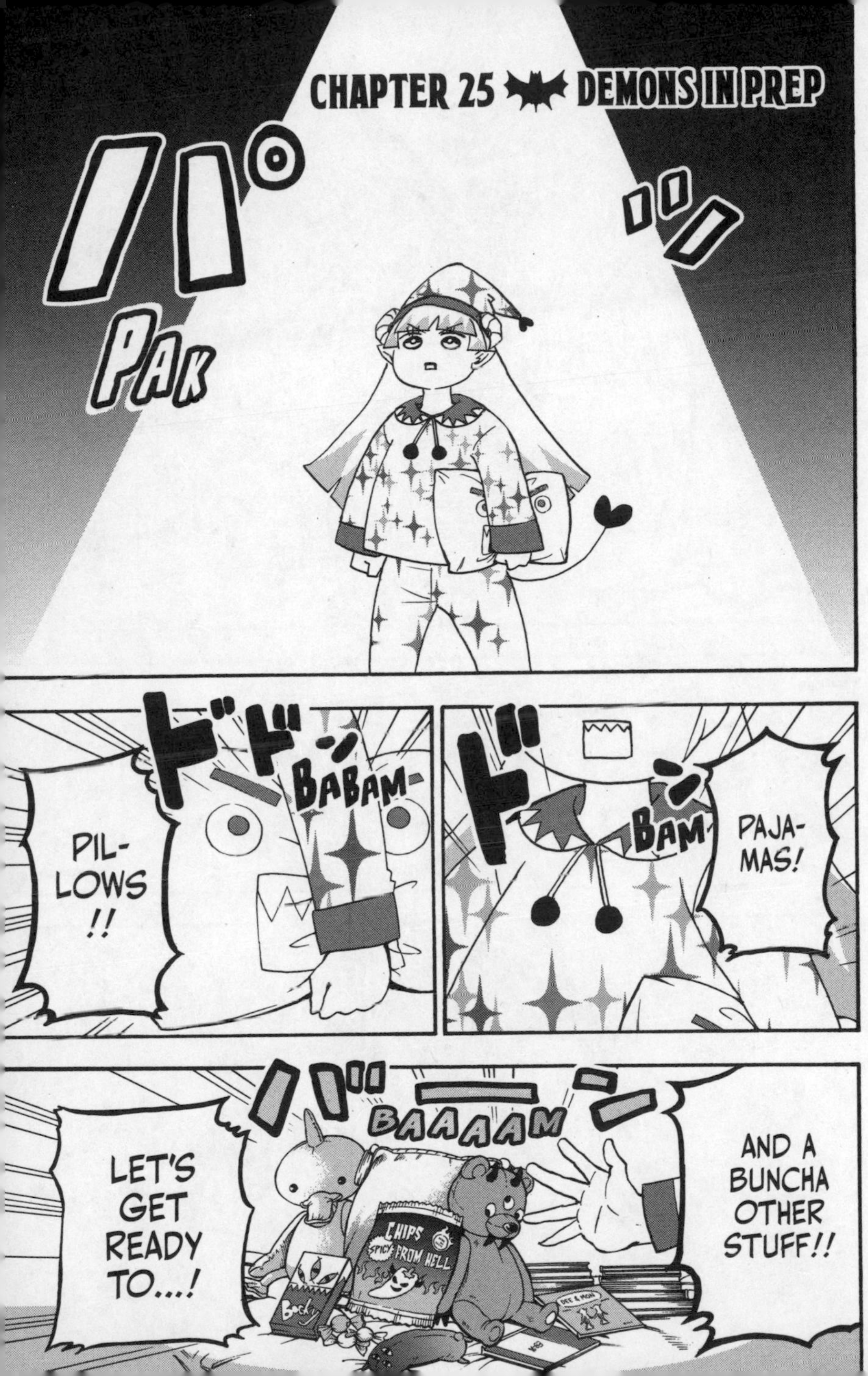
CHAPTER 25 DEMONS IN PREP
PAK
BAM
PAJAMAS!
BABAM
PILLOWS!!
BAAAAM
AND A BUNCHA OTHER STUFF!!
LET'S GET READY TO...!
CHIPS SPICY FROM HELL

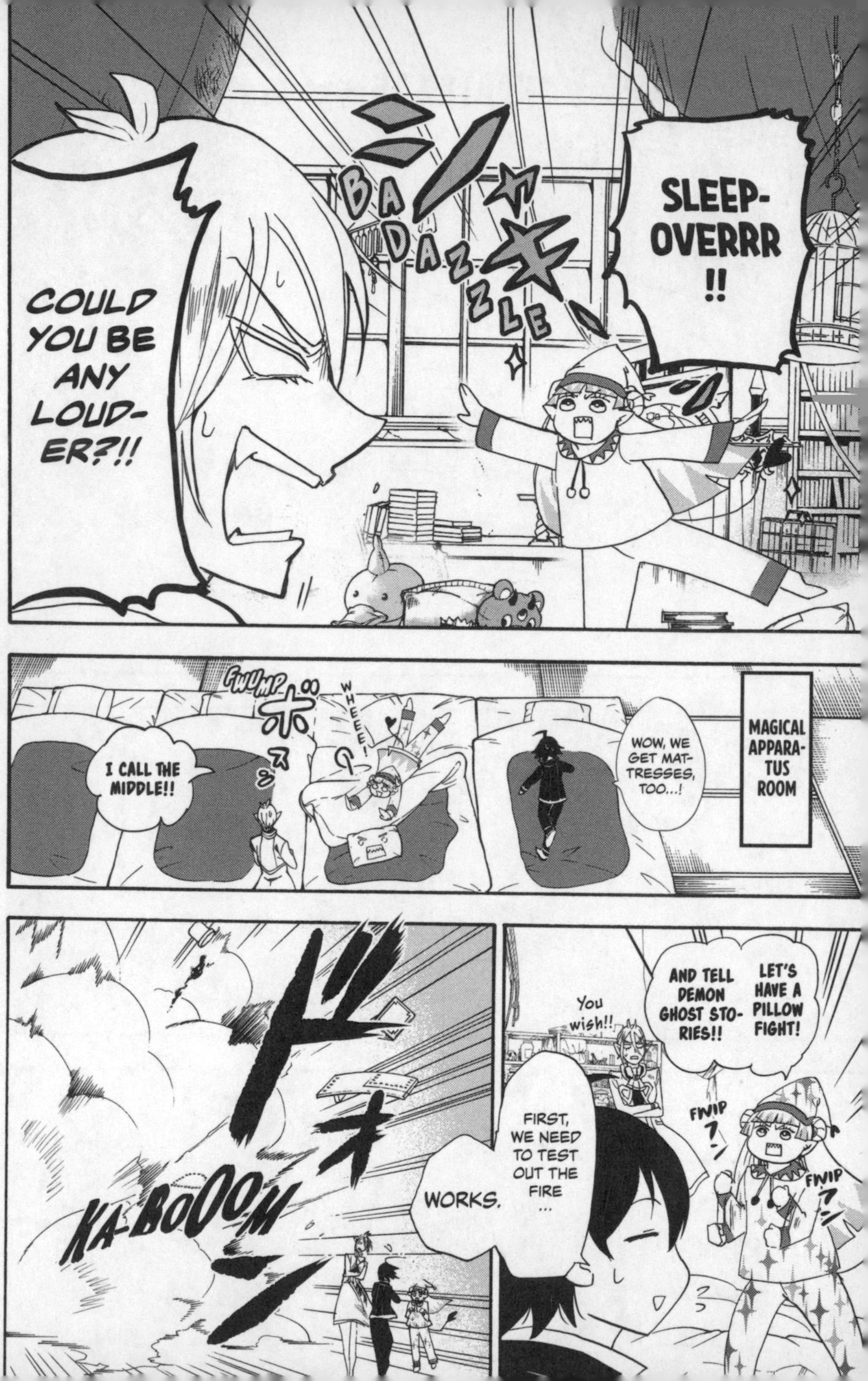
SLEEP-OVERRR!!
BADAZZLE
COULD YOU BE ANY LOUDER?!!
MAGICAL APPARATUS ROOM
WOW, WE GET MATTRESSES, TOO...!
WHEEE!
FWUMP
I CALL THE MIDDLE!!
LET'S HAVE A PILLOW FIGHT!
AND TELL DEMON GHOST STORIES!!
You wish!!
FWIP
FWIP
FIRST, WE NEED TO TEST OUT THE FIRE ...
WORKS.
KA-BOOOM

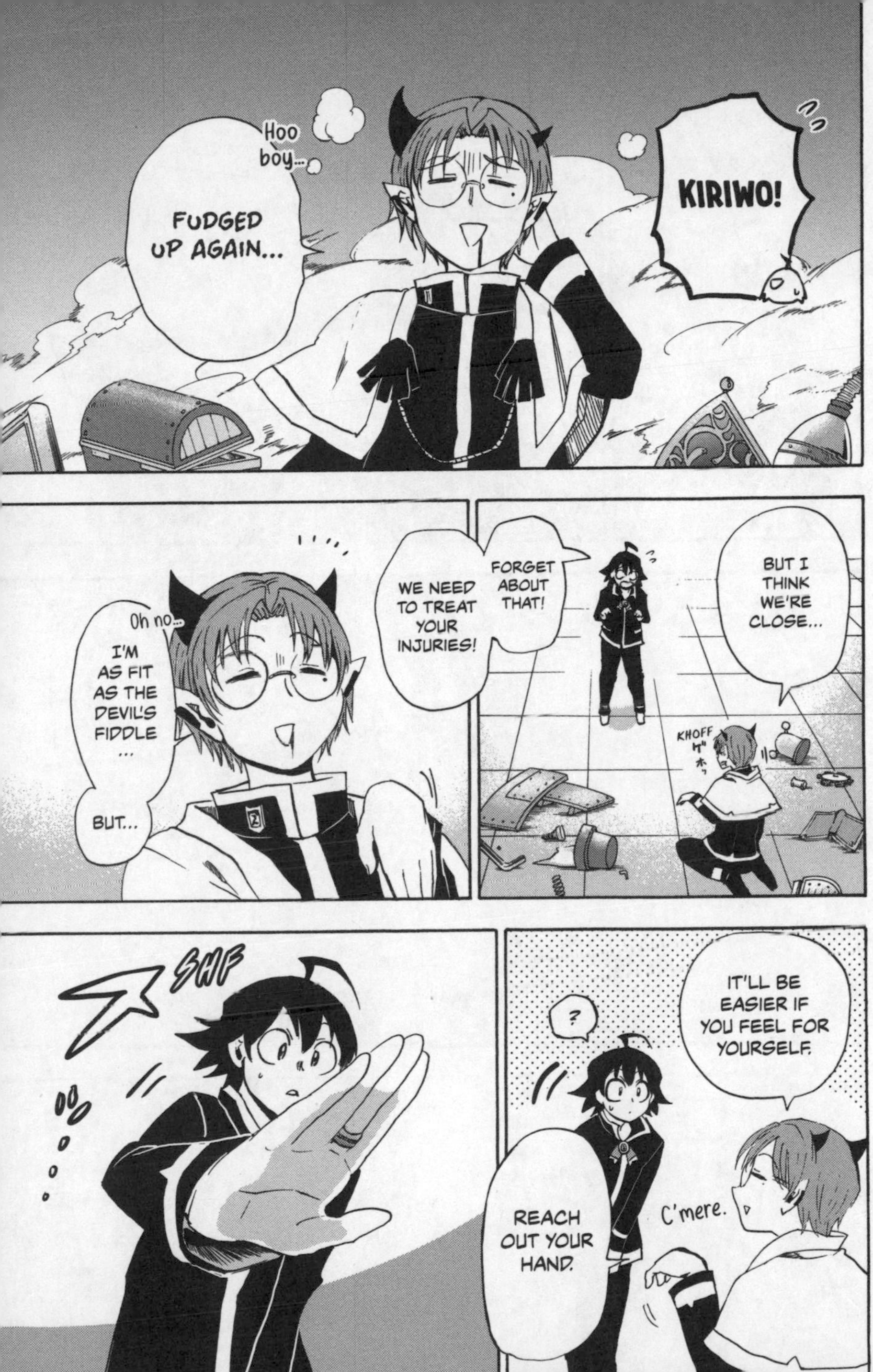
KIRIWO!
Hoo boy...
FUDGED UP AGAIN...
BUT I THINK WE'RE CLOSE...
KHOFF
FORGET ABOUT THAT!
WE NEED TO TREAT YOUR INJURIES!
Oh no...
I'M AS FIT AS THE DEVIL'S FIDDLE...
BUT...
IT'LL BE EASIER IF YOU FEEL FOR YOURSELF.
?
C'mere.
REACH OUT YOUR HAND.
SHF

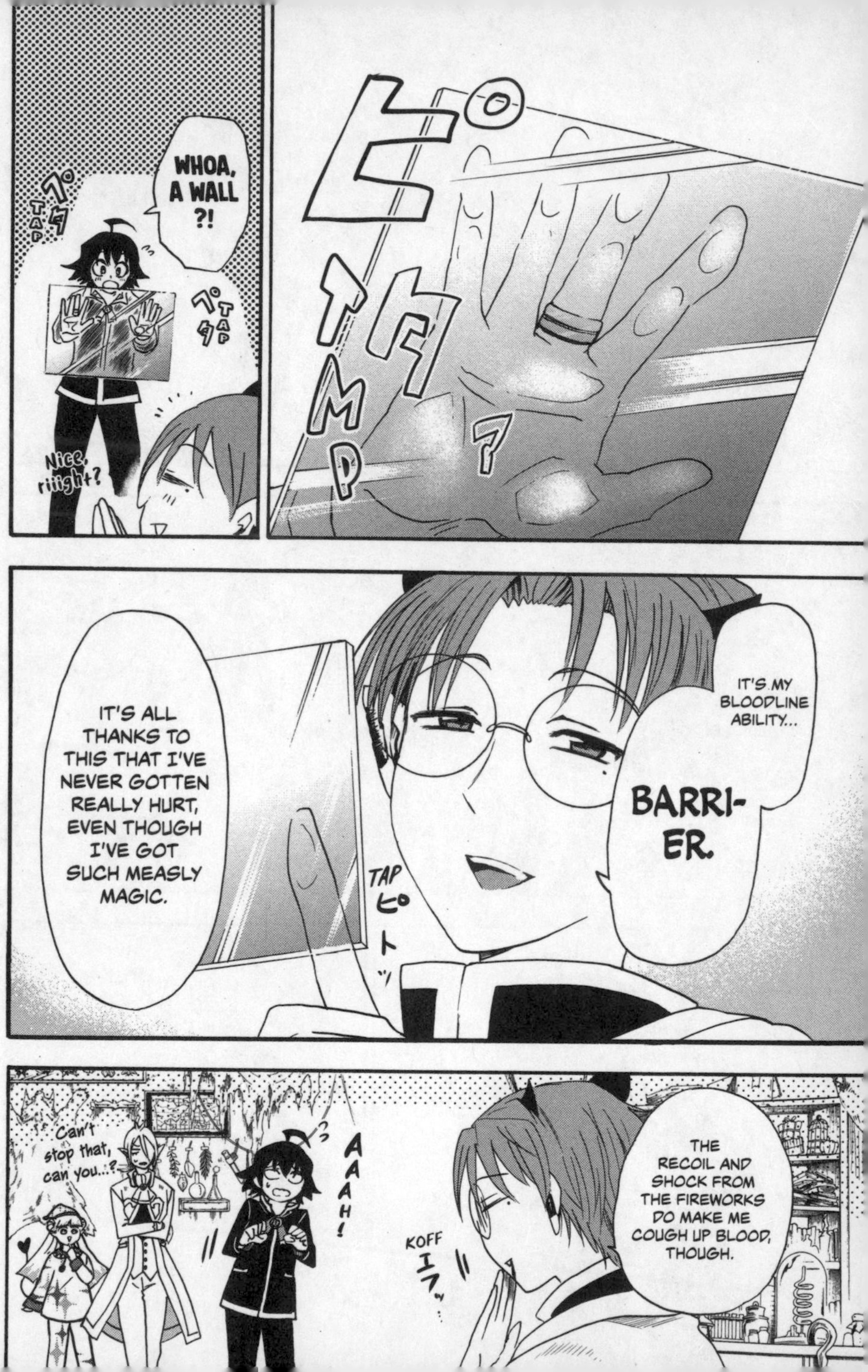
TMP
WHOA, A WALL ?!
TAP
TAP
Nice, riiight?
IT'S MY BLOODLINE ABILITY...
BARRIER.
TAP
IT'S ALL THANKS TO THIS THAT I'VE NEVER GOTTEN REALLY HURT, EVEN THOUGH I'VE GOT SUCH MEASLY MAGIC.
THE RECOIL AND SHOCK FROM THE FIREWORKS DO MAKE ME COUGH UP BLOOD, THOUGH.
KOFF
AAAH!
Can't stop that, can you...?

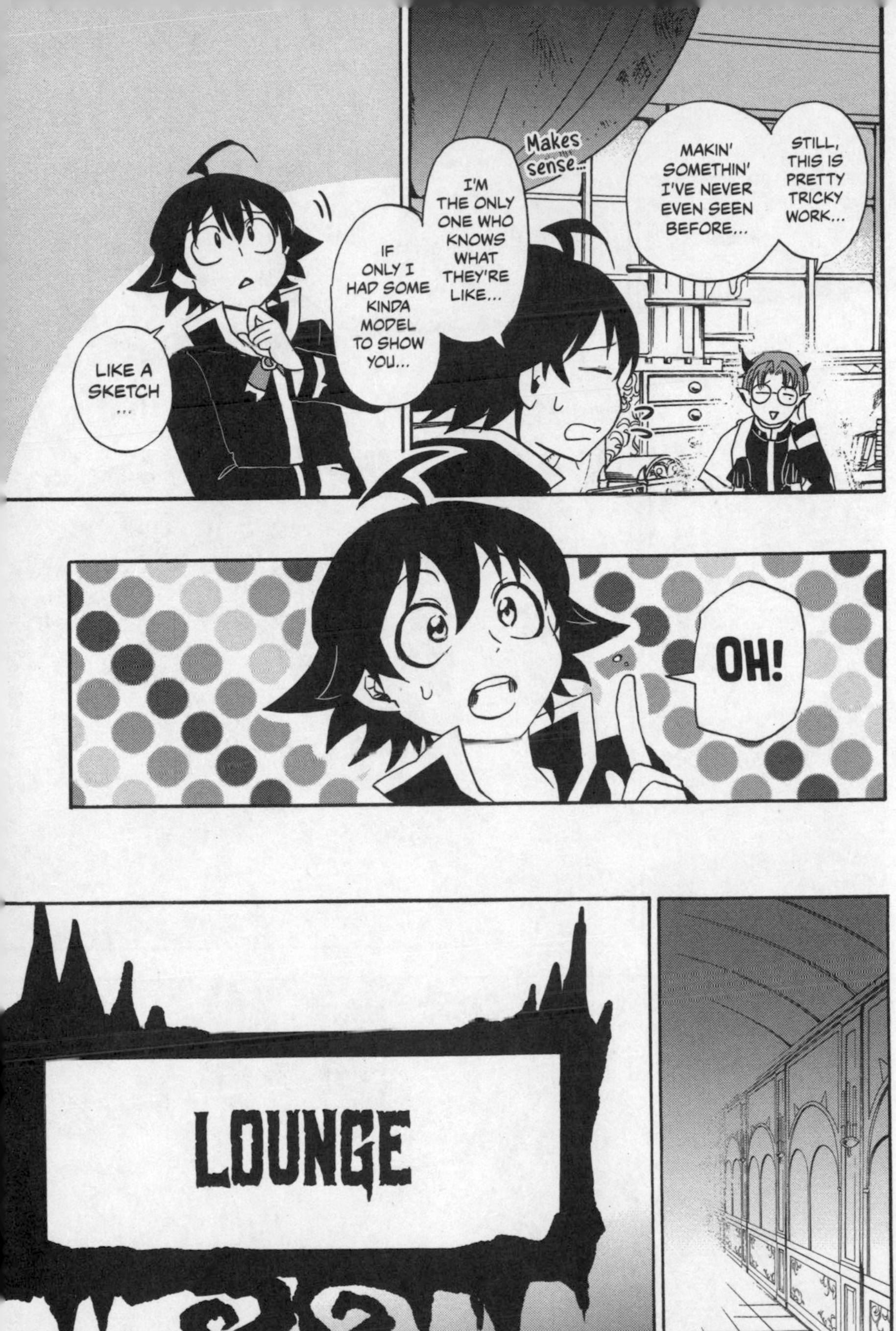
STILL, THIS IS PRETTY TRICKY WORK...
MAKIN' SOMETHIN' I'VE NEVER EVEN SEEN BEFORE...
Makes sense...
I'M THE ONLY ONE WHO KNOWS WHAT THEY'RE LIKE...
IF ONLY I HAD SOME KINDA MODEL TO SHOW YOU...
LIKE A SKETCH...
OH!
LOUNGE

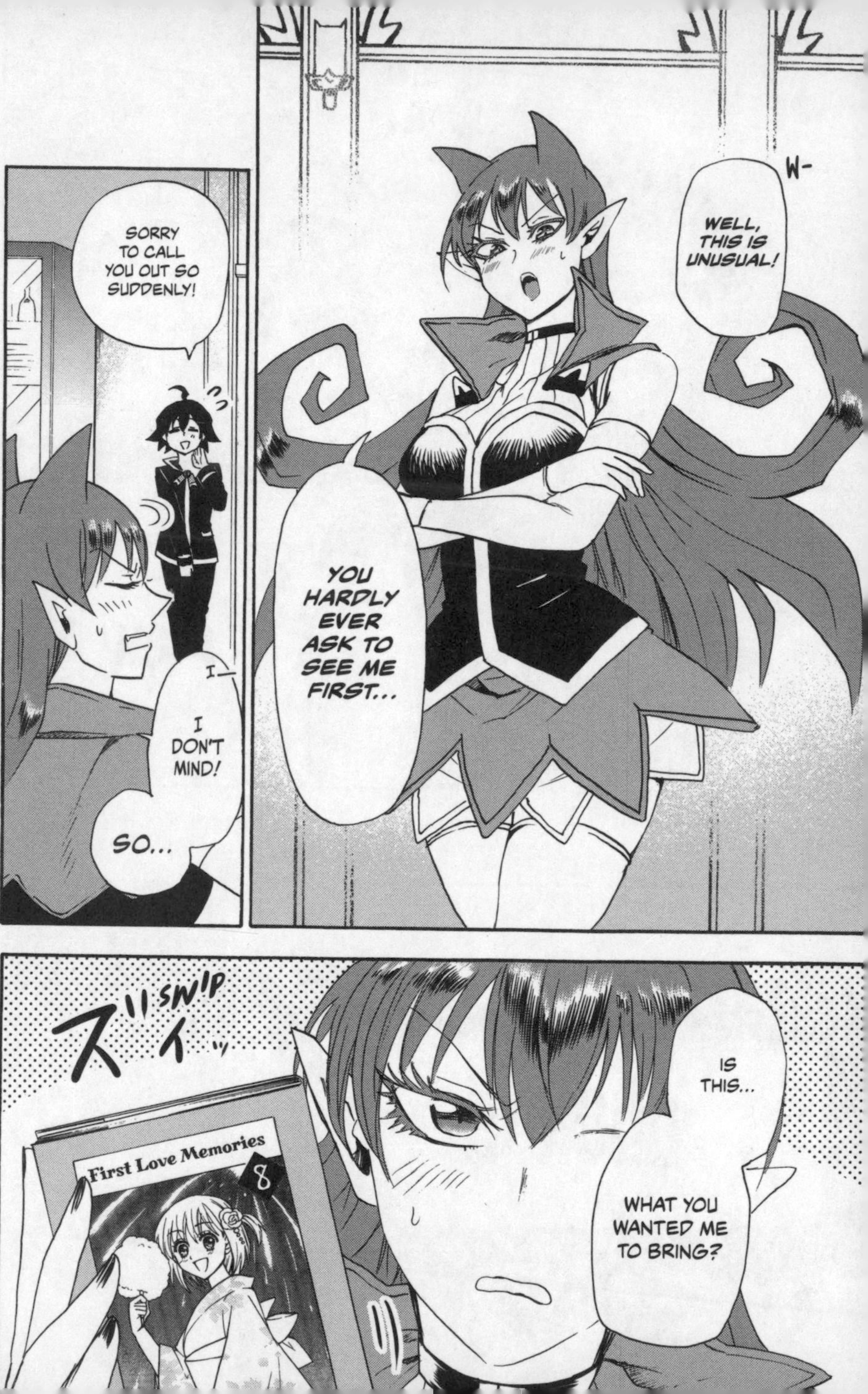
W-
WELL, THIS IS UNUSUAL!
YOU HARDLY EVER ASK TO SEE ME FIRST...
SORRY TO CALL YOU OUT SO SUDDENLY!
I—
I DON'T MIND!
SO...
IS THIS...
WHAT YOU WANTED ME TO BRING?
SWIP
First Love Memories
8

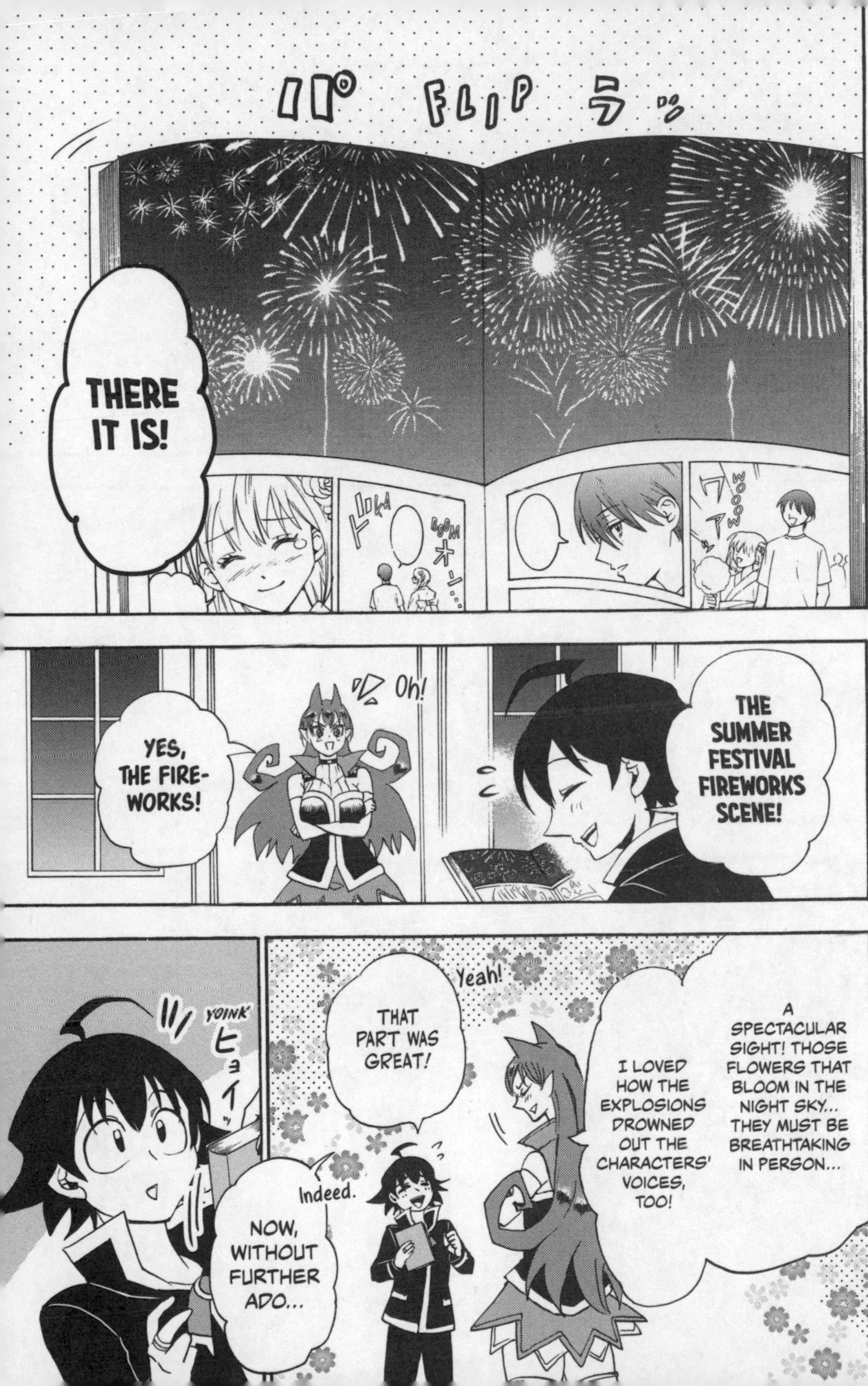
FLIP
THERE IT IS!
WOOOW
BOOM
THE SUMMER FESTIVAL FIREWORKS SCENE!
Oh!
YES, THE FIRE-WORKS!
A SPECTACULAR SIGHT! THOSE FLOWERS THAT BLOOM IN THE NIGHT SKY... THEY MUST BE BREATHTAKING IN PERSON...
I LOVED HOW THE EXPLOSIONS DROWNED OUT THE CHARACTERS' VOICES, TOO!
Yeah!
THAT PART WAS GREAT!
Indeed.
YOINK
NOW, WITHOUT FURTHER ADO...

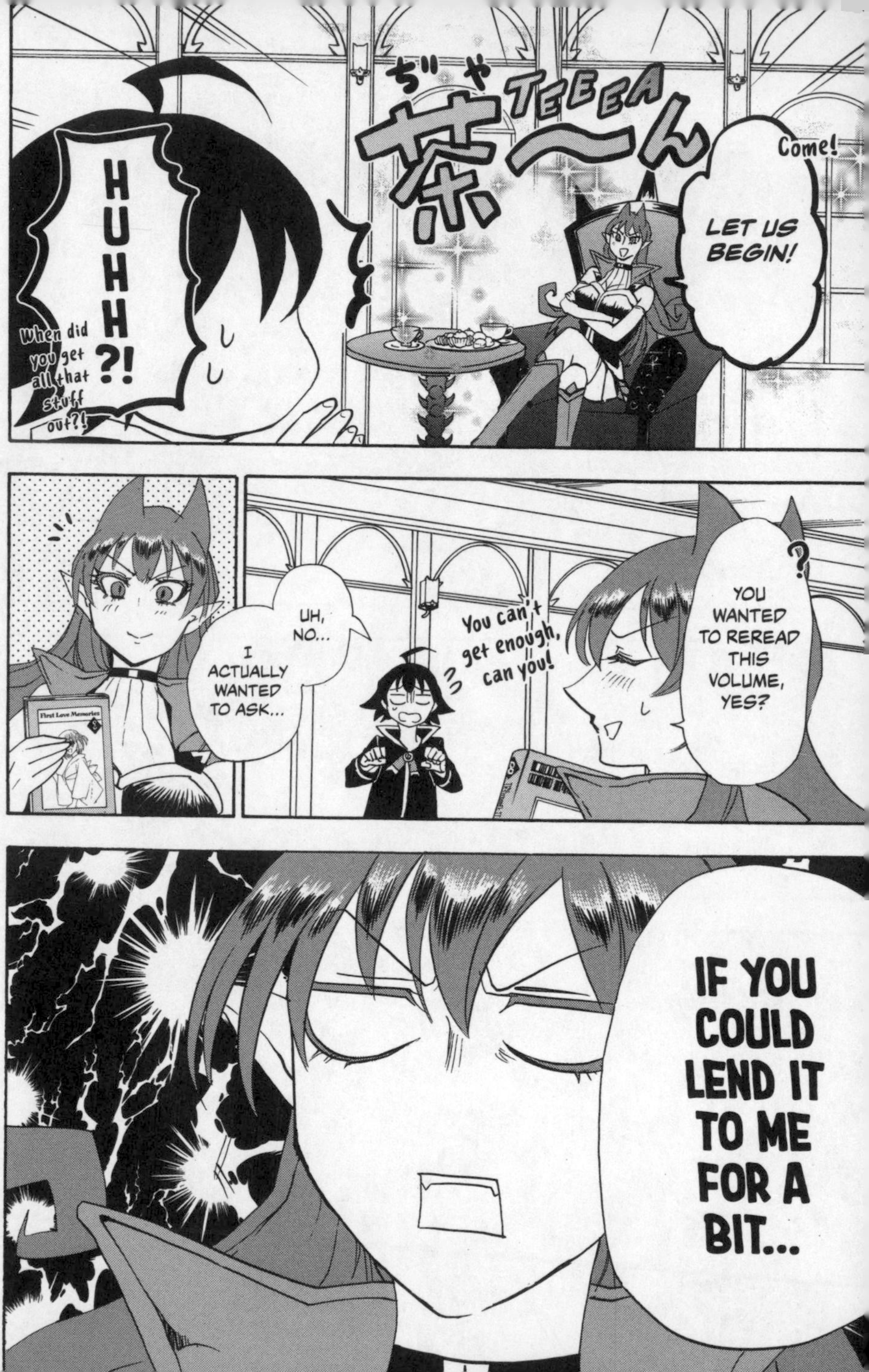
Come!
LET US BEGIN!
TEEEA
ぢゃ 茶〜ん
HUHH?!
When did you get all that stuff out?!
YOU WANTED TO REREAD THIS VOLUME, YES?
You can't get enough, can you!
UH, NO... I ACTUALLY WANTED TO ASK...
First Love Memories
IF YOU COULD LEND IT TO ME FOR A BIT...

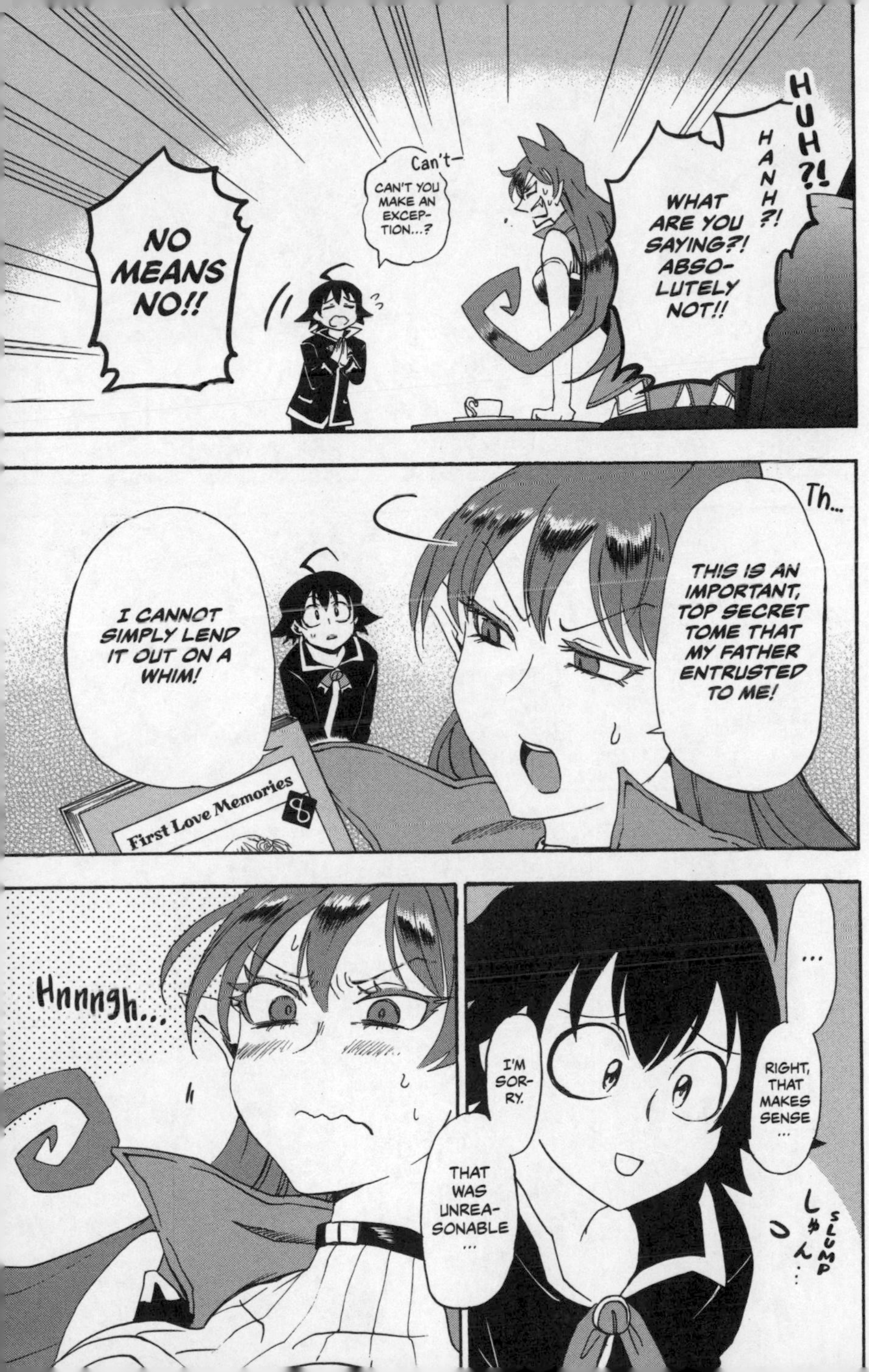
HUH?!
HANH?!
WHAT ARE YOU SAYING?! ABSO-LUTELY NOT!!
Can't—
CAN'T YOU MAKE AN EXCEP-TION...?
NO MEANS NO!!
Th...
THIS IS AN IMPORTANT, TOP SECRET TOME THAT MY FATHER ENTRUSTED TO ME!
I CANNOT SIMPLY LEND IT OUT ON A WHIM!
First Love Memories
...
RIGHT, THAT MAKES SENSE...
I'M SOR-RY.
THAT WAS UNREA-SONABLE...
しゅん
SLUMP
Hnnngh...

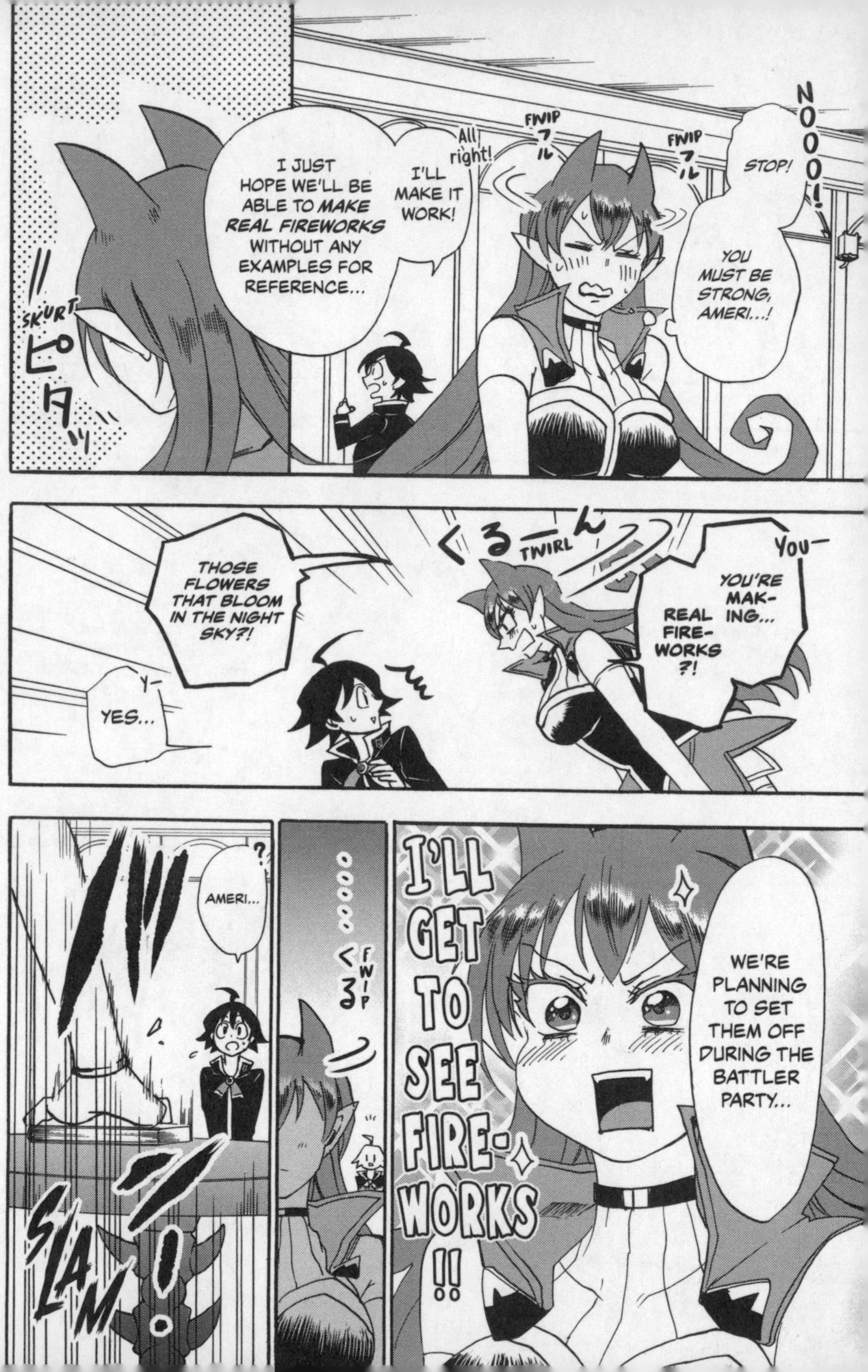
NOOOO!
STOP!
YOU MUST BE STRONG, AMERI...!
FWIP フル
FWIP フル
All right!
I'LL MAKE IT WORK!
I JUST HOPE WE'LL BE ABLE TO MAKE REAL FIREWORKS WITHOUT ANY EXAMPLES FOR REFERENCE...
SKURT ピタッ
You—
YOU'RE MAKING... REAL FIREWORKS?!
くるーん TWIRL
THOSE FLOWERS THAT BLOOM IN THE NIGHT SKY?!
Y-YES...
WE'RE PLANNING TO SET THEM OFF DURING THE BATTLER PARTY...
I'LL GET TO SEE FIREWORKS!!
......
くる FWIP
?
AMERI...
SLAM!

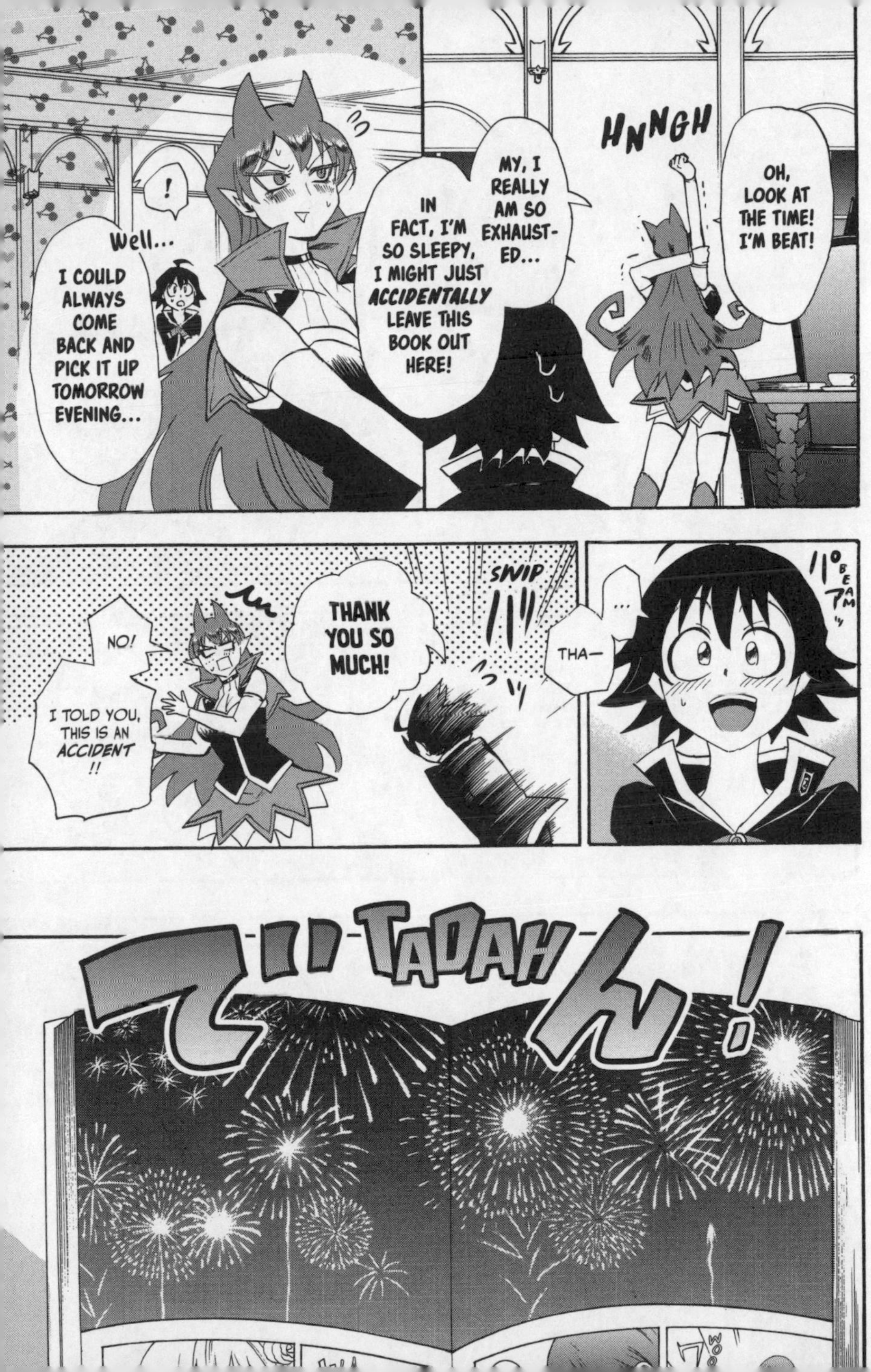
HNNGH
OH, LOOK AT THE TIME! I'M BEAT!
MY, I REALLY AM SO EXHAUST-ED...
IN FACT, I'M SO SLEEPY, I MIGHT JUST ACCIDENTALLY LEAVE THIS BOOK OUT HERE!
!
Well...
I COULD ALWAYS COME BACK AND PICK IT UP TOMORROW EVENING...
BEAM
...
THA—
SWIP
THANK YOU SO MUCH!
NO!
I TOLD YOU, THIS IS AN ACCIDENT!!
TADAH

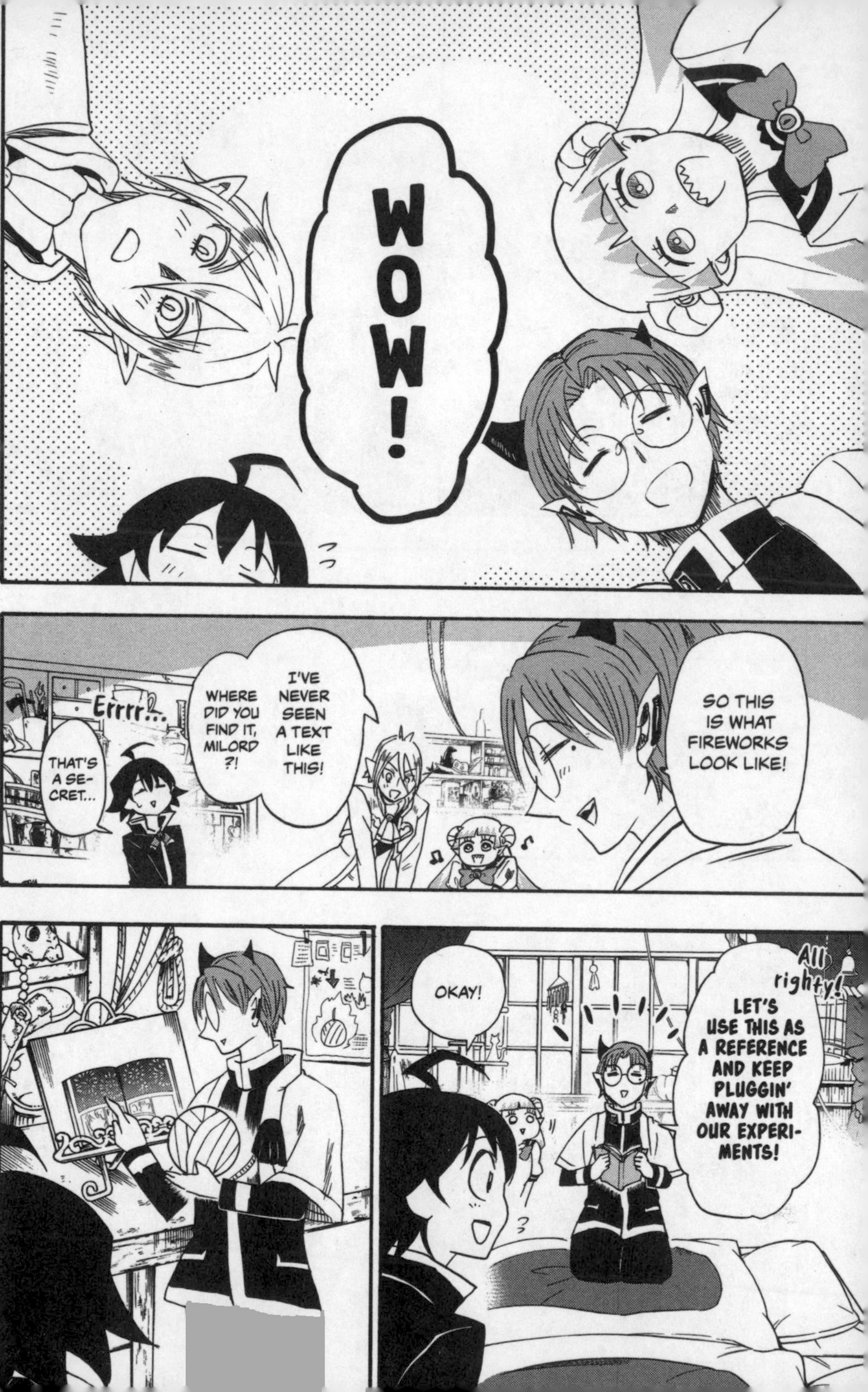
WOW!
SO THIS IS WHAT FIREWORKS LOOK LIKE!
I'VE NEVER SEEN A TEXT LIKE THIS!
WHERE DID YOU FIND IT, MILORD?!
Errrr...
THAT'S A SE-CRET...
All righty!
LET'S USE THIS AS A REFERENCE AND KEEP PLUGGIN' AWAY WITH OUR EXPERI-MENTS!
OKAY!

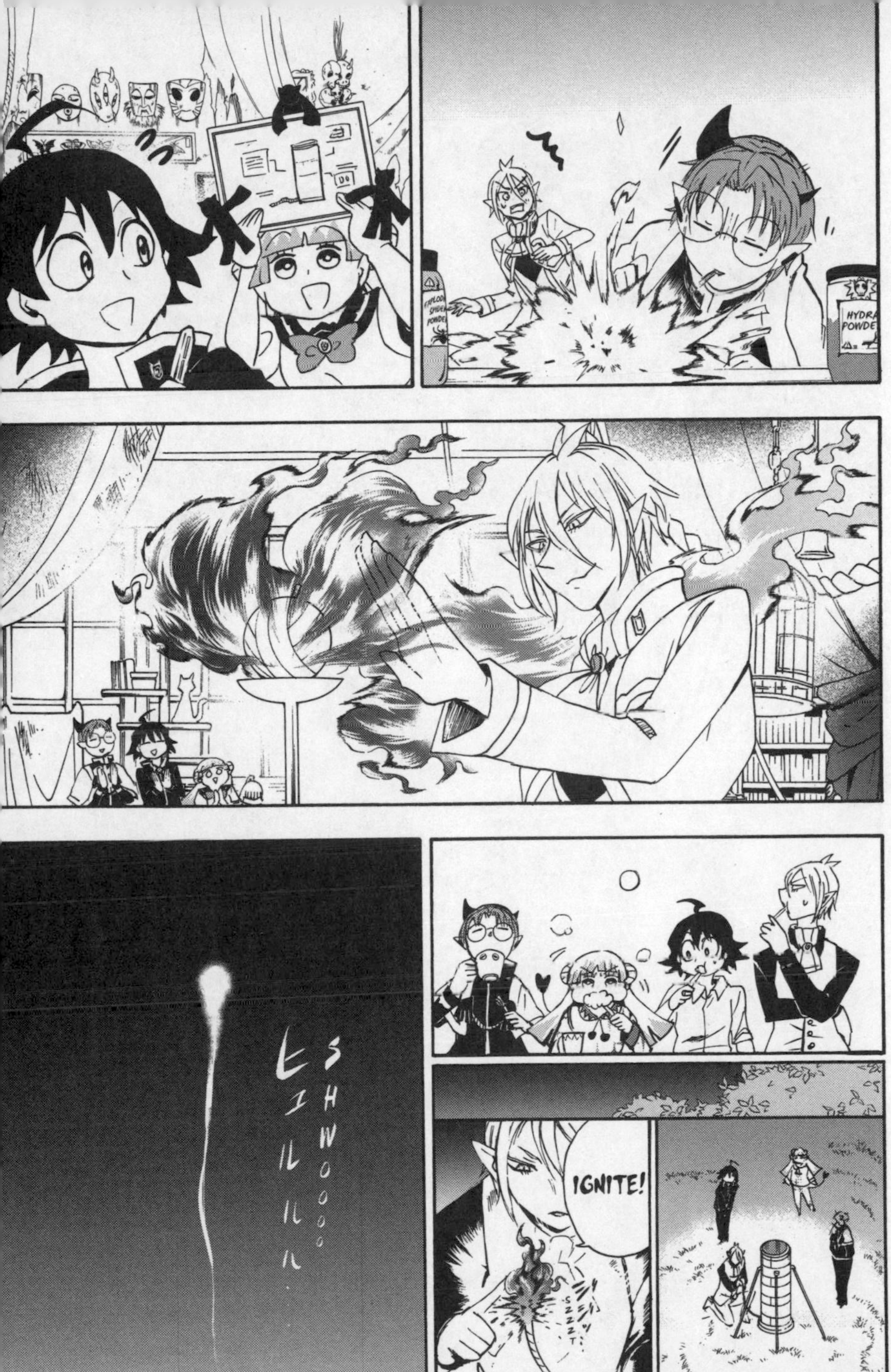
IGNITE!
SZZZT
SHWOOOO
ヒュルルル

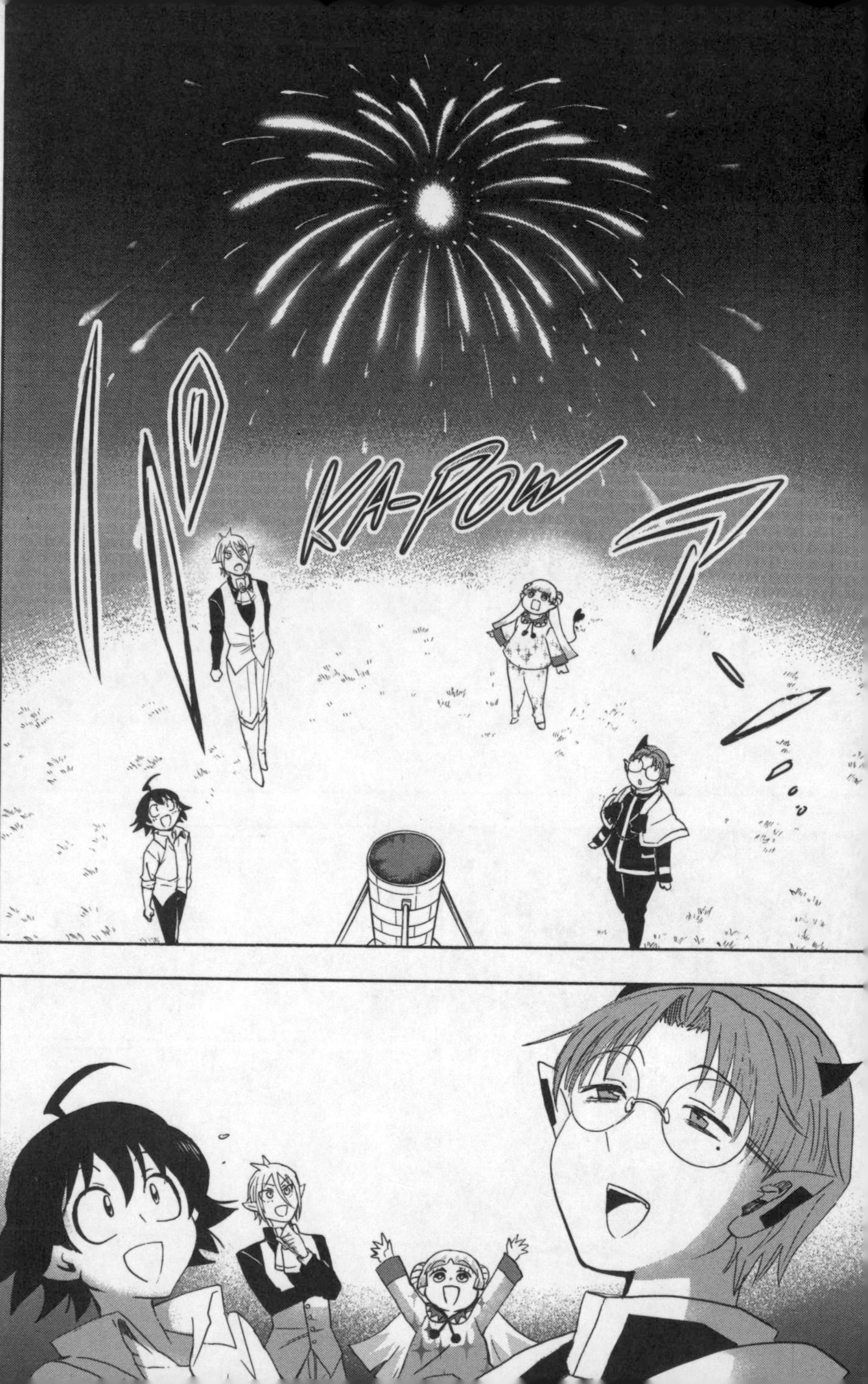
KA-POW

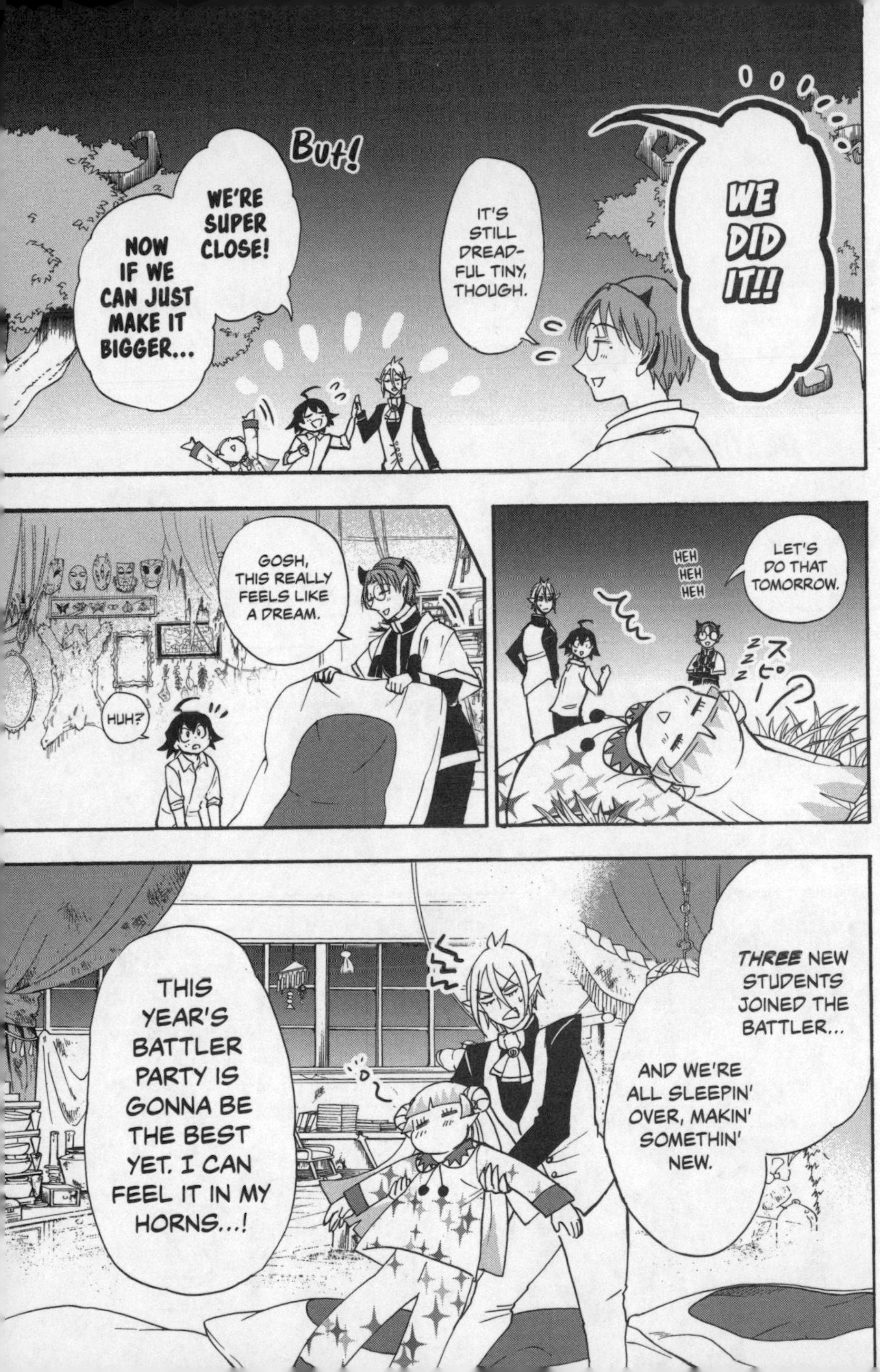
WE DID IT!!
IT'S STILL DREADFUL TINY, THOUGH.
But!
WE'RE SUPER CLOSE!
NOW IF WE CAN JUST MAKE IT BIGGER...
LET'S DO THAT TOMORROW.
HEH HEH HEH
スピー
GOSH, THIS REALLY FEELS LIKE A DREAM.
HUH?
THREE NEW STUDENTS JOINED THE BATTLER...
AND WE'RE ALL SLEEPIN' OVER, MAKIN' SOMETHIN' NEW.
THIS YEAR'S BATTLER PARTY IS GONNA BE THE BEST YET. I CAN FEEL IT IN MY HORNS...!

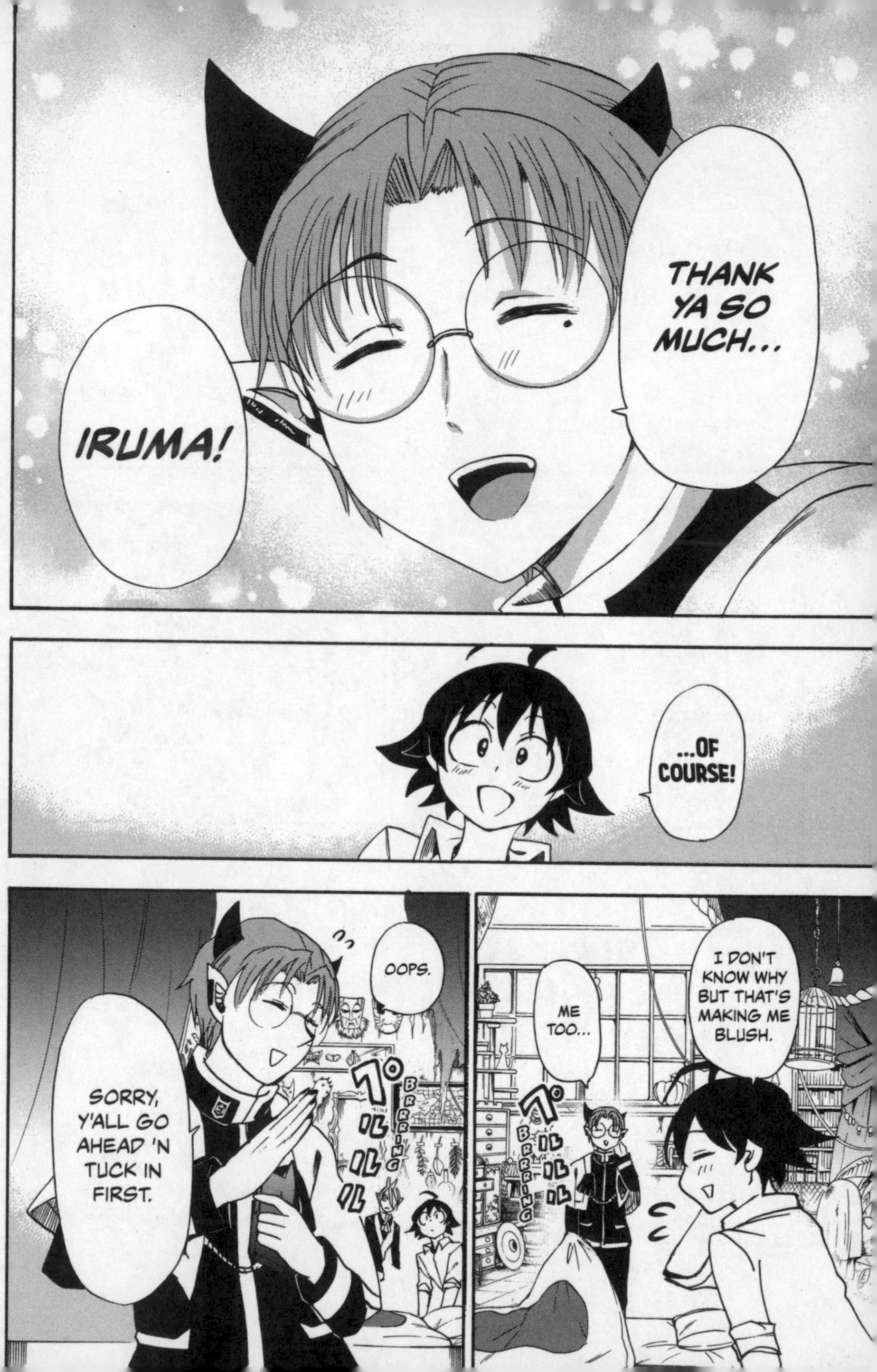
THANK YA SO MUCH...
IRUMA!
...OF COURSE!
I DON'T KNOW WHY BUT THAT'S MAKING ME BLUSH.
ME TOO...
BRRRING
OOPS.
SORRY, Y'ALL GO AHEAD 'N TUCK IN FIRST.
BRRRING

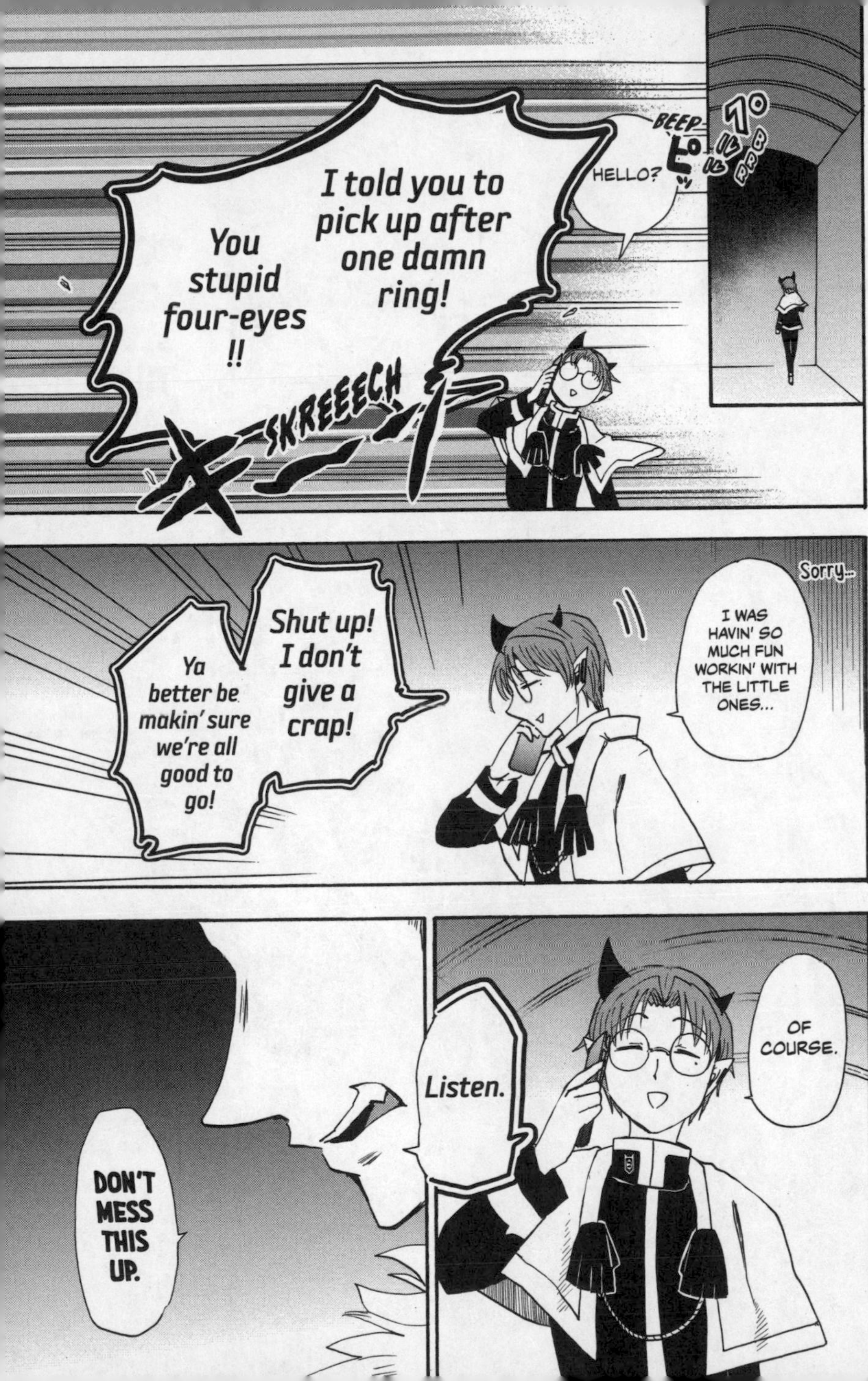
BEEP-
HELLO?
I told you to pick up after one damn ring!
You stupid four-eyes !!
SKREEECH
Sorry...
I WAS HAVIN' SO MUCH FUN WORKIN' WITH THE LITTLE ONES...
Shut up! I don't give a crap!
Ya better be makin' sure we're all good to go!
OF COURSE.
Listen.
DON'T MESS THIS UP.

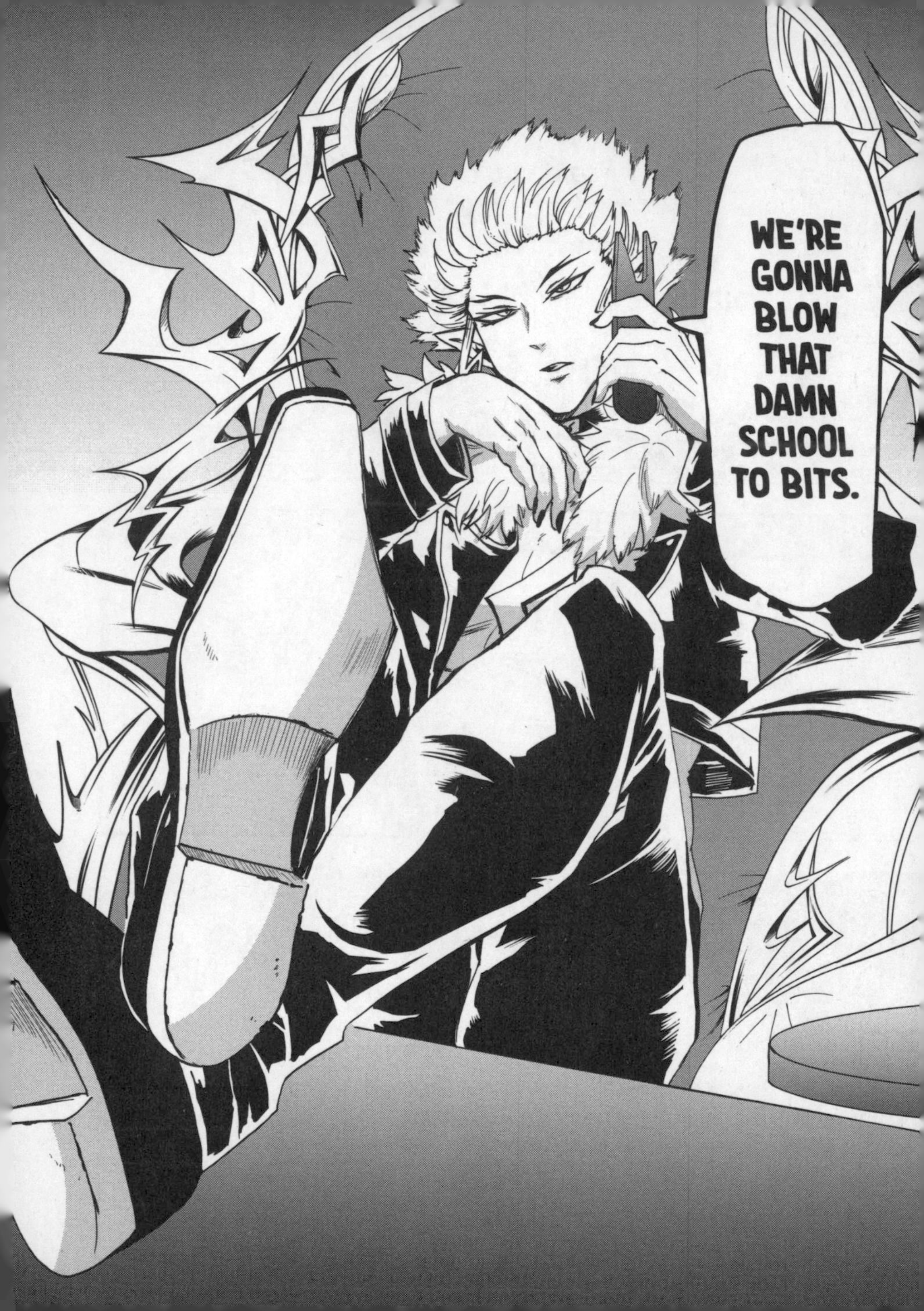
WE'RE GONNA BLOW THAT DAMN SCHOOL TO BITS.

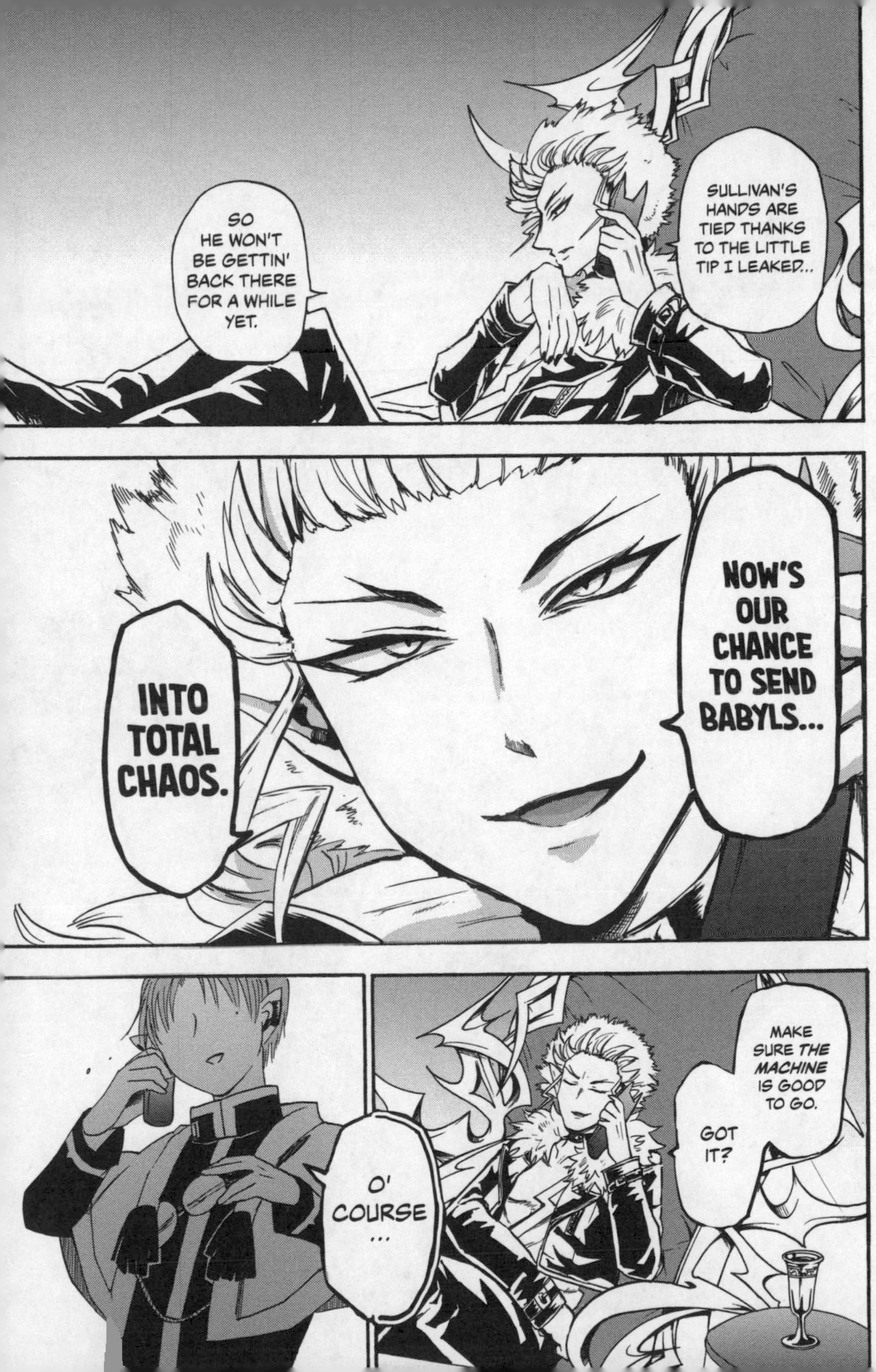
SULLIVAN'S HANDS ARE TIED THANKS TO THE LITTLE TIP I LEAKED...
SO HE WON'T BE GETTIN' BACK THERE FOR A WHILE YET.
NOW'S OUR CHANCE TO SEND BABYLS...
INTO TOTAL CHAOS.
MAKE SURE *THE MACHINE* IS GOOD TO GO.
GOT IT?
O' COURSE ...

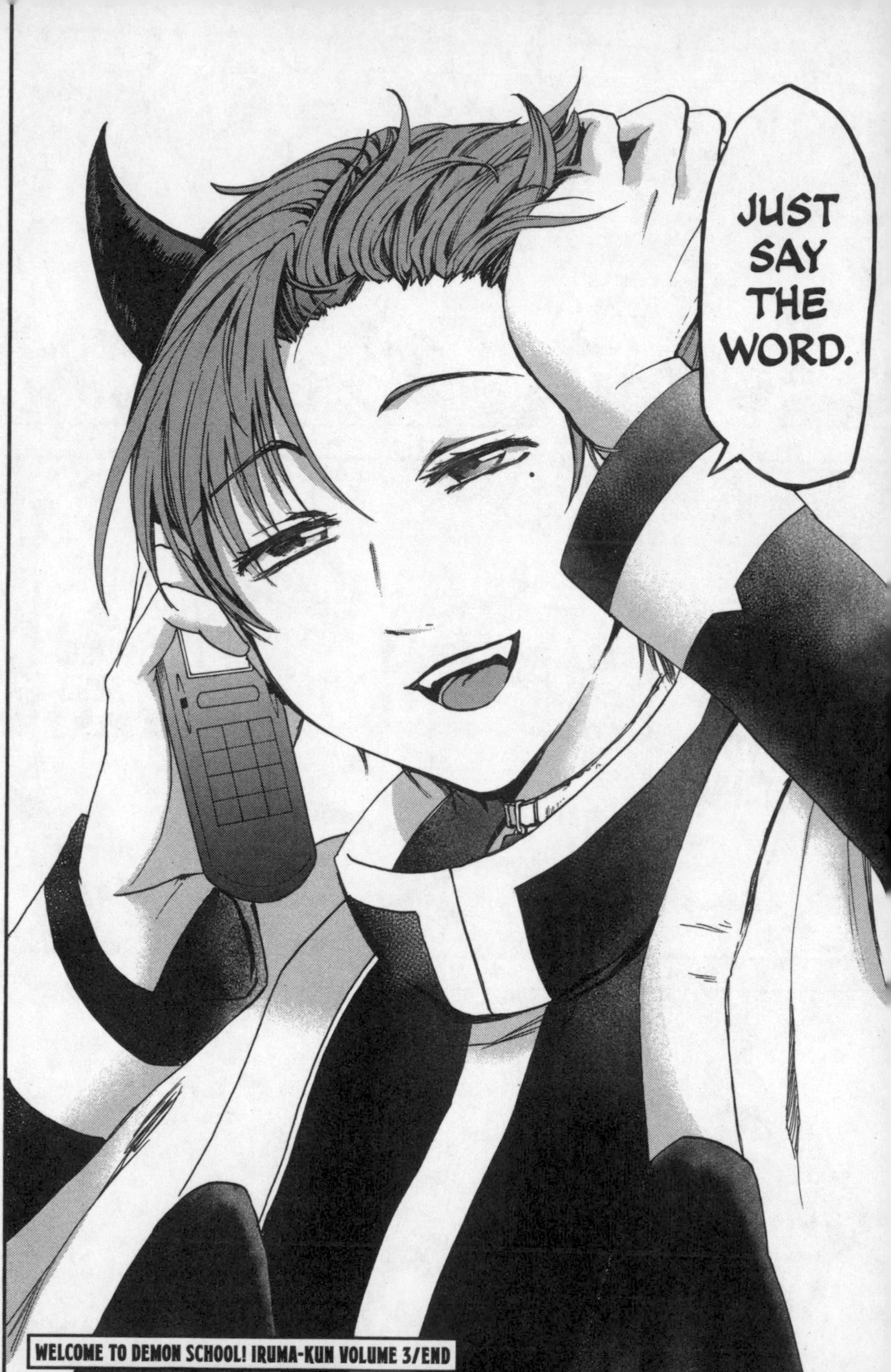
JUST SAY THE WORD.

WELCOME TO DEMON SCHOOL! IRUMA-KUN VOLUME 3/END

THE DEVILISH DETAILS OF EACH CHAPTER

DEVILISH DETAILS: CHAPTER 21

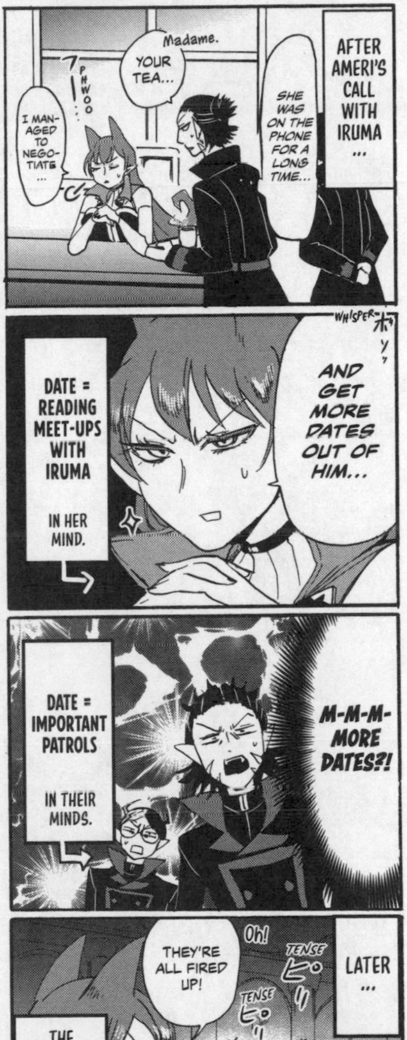
AFTER AMERI'S CALL WITH IRUMA ...
SHE WAS ON THE PHONE FOR A LONG TIME...
Madame.
YOUR TEA...
PHWOO...
I MANAGED TO NEGOTIATE ...
WHISPER
AND GET MORE DATES OUT OF HIM...
DATE = READING MEET-UPS WITH IRUMA
IN HER MIND.
M-M-M-MORE DATES?!
DATE = IMPORTANT PATROLS
IN THEIR MINDS.
LATER ...
TENSE
TENSE
Oh!
THEY'RE ALL FIRED UP!
THE STUDENT COUNCIL PATROLS GOT STRICTER FOR A SHORT WHILE.

DEVILISH DETAILS: CHAPTER 22

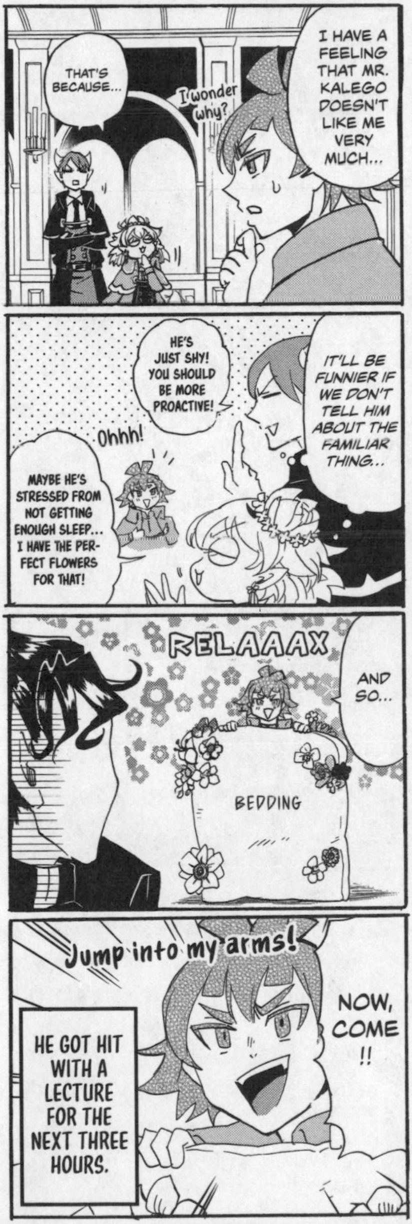
I HAVE A FEELING THAT MR. KALEGO DOESN'T LIKE ME VERY MUCH...
I wonder why?
THAT'S BECAUSE...
IT'LL BE FUNNIER IF WE DON'T TELL HIM ABOUT THE FAMILIAR THING...
HE'S JUST SHY! YOU SHOULD BE MORE PROACTIVE!
Ohhh!
MAYBE HE'S STRESSED FROM NOT GETTING ENOUGH SLEEP... I HAVE THE PERFECT FLOWERS FOR THAT!
AND SO...
RELAAAX
BEDDING
NOW, COME !!
Jump into my arms!
HE GOT HIT WITH A LECTURE FOR THE NEXT THREE HOURS.

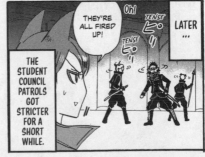

DEVILISH DETAILS: CHAPTER 22 PART 2

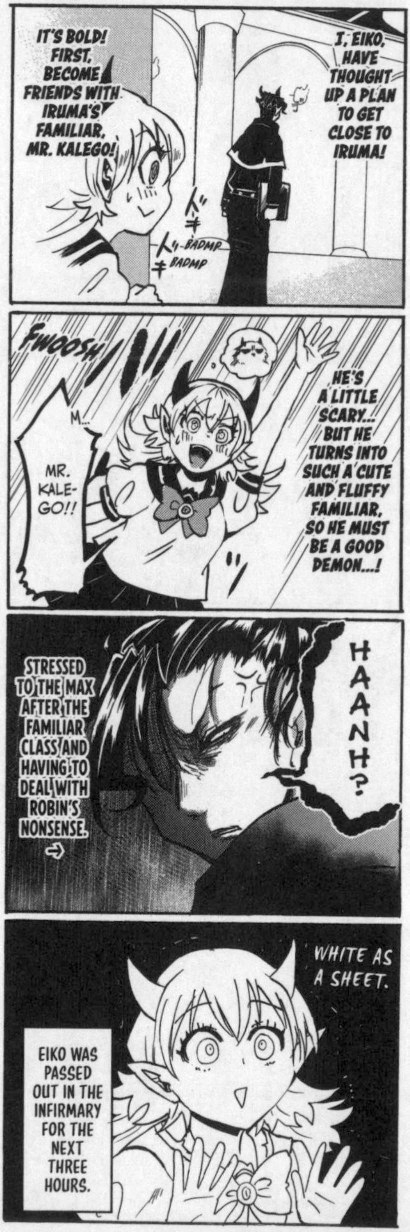
I, EIKO, HAVE THOUGHT UP A PLAN TO GET CLOSE TO IRUMA!
IT'S BOLD! FIRST, BECOME FRIENDS WITH IRUMA'S FAMILIAR, MR. KALEGO!
ドキドキ
BADMP BADMP
HE'S A LITTLE SCARY... BUT HE TURNS INTO SUCH A CUTE AND FLUFFY FAMILIAR, SO HE MUST BE A GOOD DEMON...!
FWOOSH
M...
MR. KALE-GO!!
HAAANH?
STRESSED TO THE MAX AFTER THE FAMILIAR CLASS AND HAVING TO DEAL WITH ROBIN'S NONSENSE. ⇨
WHITE AS A SHEET.
EIKO WAS PASSED OUT IN THE INFIRMARY FOR THE NEXT THREE HOURS.

DEVILISH DETAILS: CHAPTER 23

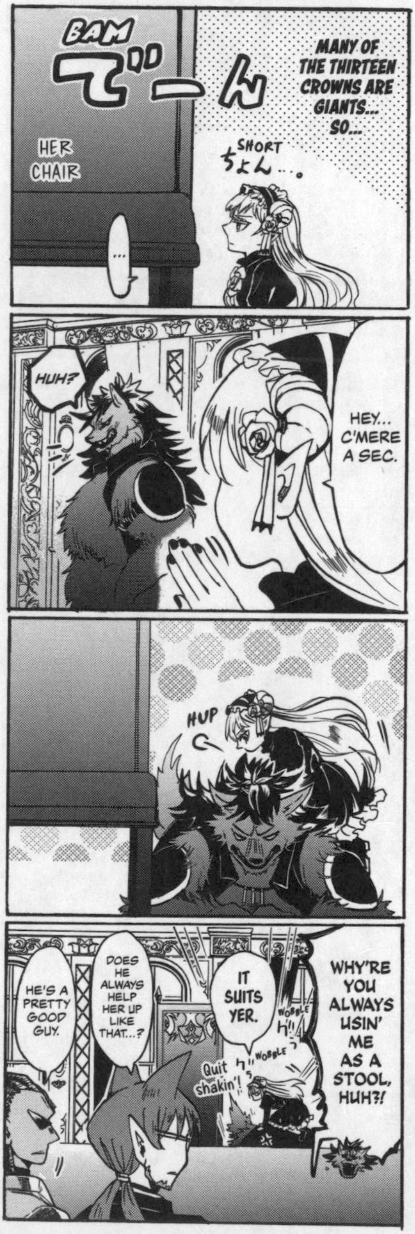
MANY OF THE THIRTEEN CROWNS ARE GIANTS... SO...
BAM
でーん
SHORT
ちょん…。
HER CHAIR
...
HEY... C'MERE A SEC.
HUH?
HUP
WHY'RE YOU ALWAYS USIN' ME AS A STOOL, HUH?!
WOBBLE
IT SUITS YER.
Quit shakin'!
DOES HE ALWAYS HELP HER UP LIKE THAT...?
HE'S A PRETTY GOOD GUY.

DEVILISH DETAILS: CHAPTER 24

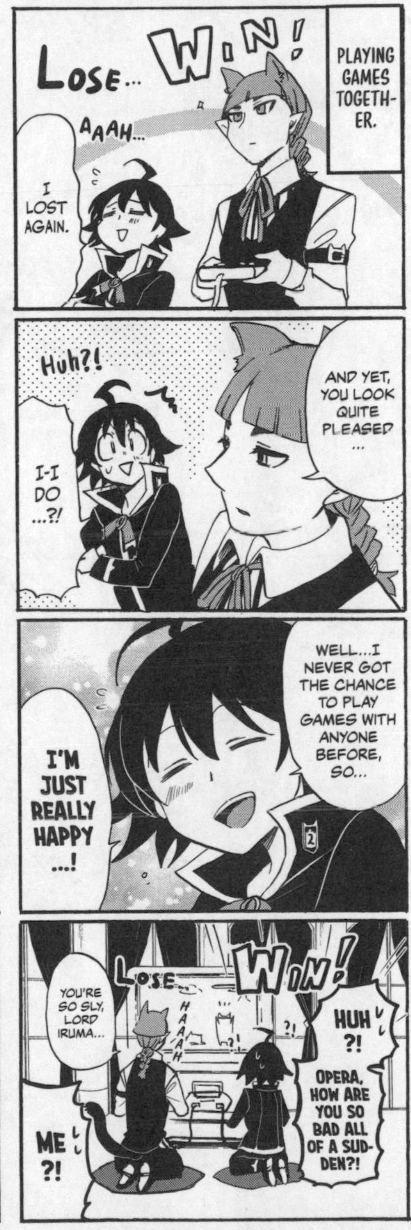
PLAYING GAMES TOGETH-ER.
WIN!
LOSE...
AAAH...
I LOST AGAIN.
AND YET, YOU LOOK QUITE PLEASED...
Huh?!
I-I DO ...?!
WELL...I NEVER GOT THE CHANCE TO PLAY GAMES WITH ANYONE BEFORE, SO...
I'M JUST REALLY HAPPY ...!
HUH ?!
OPERA, HOW ARE YOU SO BAD ALL OF A SUD-DEN?!
WIN!
LOSE...
YOU'RE SO SLY, LORD IRUMA...
HAAAAH
ME ?!

DEVILISH DETAILS: CHAPTER 25

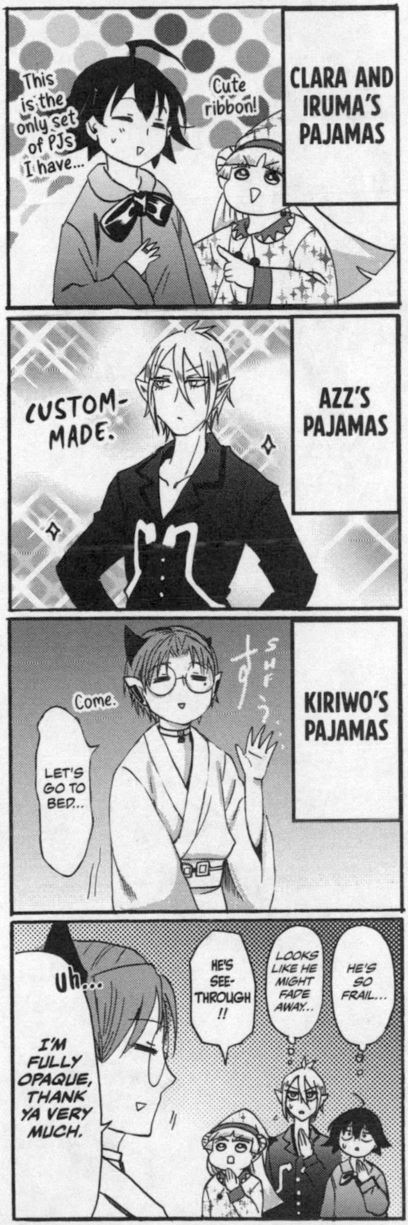
CLARA AND IRUMA'S PAJAMAS
Cute ribbon!
This is the only set of PJs I have...
AZZ'S PAJAMAS
CUSTOM-MADE.
KIRIWO'S PAJAMAS
SHFU
Come.
LET'S GO TO BED...
HE'S SO FRAIL...
LOOKS LIKE HE MIGHT FADE AWAY...
HE'S SEE-THROUGH !!
Uh...
I'M FULLY OPAQUE, THANK YA VERY MUCH.

WELCOME TO DEMON SCHOOL, IRUMA-KUN! REFERENCES

THE BOYS' UNIFORM

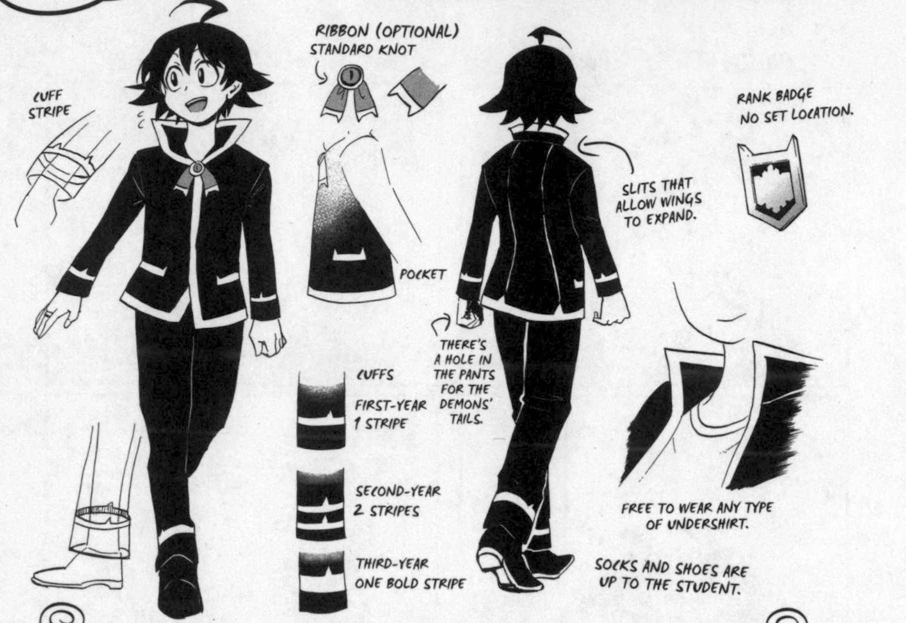

RIBBON (OPTIONAL)
STANDARD KNOT
CUFF
STRIPE
RANK BADGE
NO SET LOCATION.
SLITS THAT
ALLOW WINGS
TO EXPAND.
POCKET
THERE'S
A HOLE IN
THE PANTS
FOR THE
DEMONS'
TAILS.
CUFFS
FIRST-YEAR
1 STRIPE
SECOND-YEAR
2 STRIPES
THIRD-YEAR
ONE BOLD STRIPE
FREE TO WEAR ANY TYPE
OF UNDERSHIRT.
SOCKS AND SHOES ARE
UP TO THE STUDENT.

THE GIRLS' UNIFORM

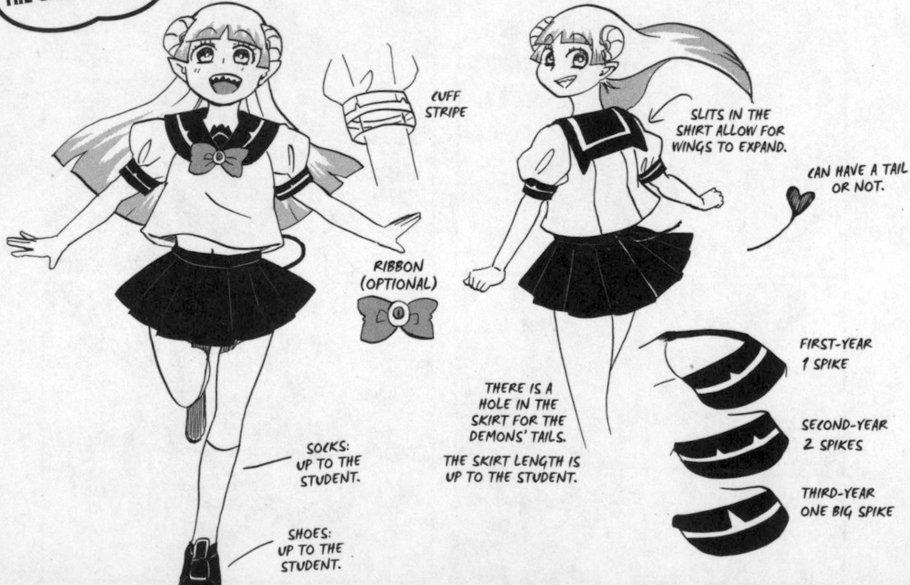

CUFF
STRIPE
SLITS IN THE
SHIRT ALLOW FOR
WINGS TO EXPAND.
CAN HAVE A TAIL
OR NOT.
RIBBON
(OPTIONAL)
FIRST-YEAR
1 SPIKE
THERE IS A
HOLE IN THE
SKIRT FOR THE
DEMONS' TAILS.
THE SKIRT LENGTH IS
UP TO THE STUDENT.
SECOND-YEAR
2 SPIKES
THIRD-YEAR
ONE BIG SPIKE
SOCKS:
UP TO THE
STUDENT.
SHOES:
UP TO THE
STUDENT.

THANK YOU FOR READING

CATCH YA IN THE NEXT VOLUME!

AFTERWORD

It's the third volume!

Hello, Nishi here!

Clara is a girl. She may be a mascot and a pet, but she's also a girl. That's what was on my mind when I drew the first chapter of this volume.

Clara's actions and speech may make her seem like a little child, but she's quite grounded, very attentive to those around her, and has a lot going on in her mind.

That might actually be why so much of what she does is very unnecessary—about 80%, in fact. Despite this, she's still bright and has the same worries as any other girl. Before I knew it, she'd turned into this→ That's pretty much her default look now. But she's still a girl who laughs and cries for Iruma. And this little Clara will keep running around and giving everything her all! Please keep cheering her on! Good luck, Clara!

Don't let Ameri beat you!!

Osamu Nishi

Thanks to my dependable

friends and staff

- Chu Kawasaki

- Makoto Sawa

- Haruna Nakazato

- Kota Nango

- Nishizawa

- Kazuki Nonaka

- Osai

THANK YOU VERY MUCH!

The person who gave me fried chicken

that day I had fried chicken for lunch

- My editor, Nishiyama

Lemegeton Clavicula
Irumanis

ᚴᛃ�ᛃ᛬ᛃᚾᚢᚢᛃ ᚼᛉᛈᛏᚢᛃᛇᚼᛦ ᚢᛏᛒᛒᛒᛉᛃᚢ�

Your key to the secrets of Babyls and the netherworld.

Culture and Translation Notes

The netherworld is about as foreign as you can get, and with this
new, strange land come customs and traditions—both in-world
and from the original language (along with some Latin and
esoteric Hebrew)—that may not translate well. The following are
a few items that you may have missed if you aren't adept in the
occultic arts (or Japanese):

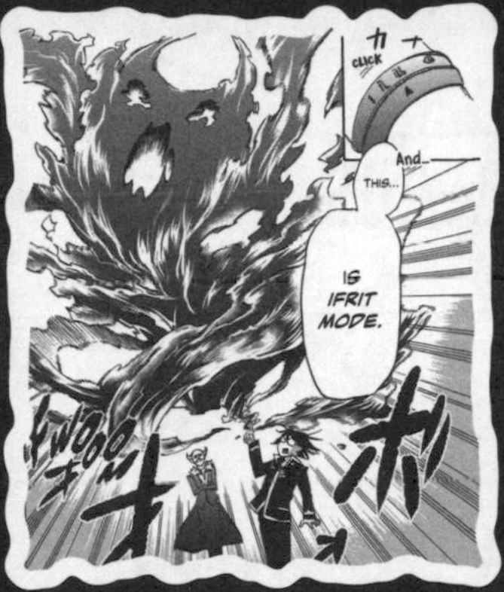
CLICK
And...
THIS...
IS IFRIT MODE.

小悪魔 = SMALL DEVIL
悪鬼 = EVIL DEMON
魔神 = DEVIL GOD

Ring of Solomon settings

- page 84 -

IRUMA'S RING GETS A MAJOR UPGRADE IN THIS VOLUME, WITH THREE NEW SETTINGS: DEVIL, DEMON, AND IFRIT. THE LOWEST SETTING, DEVIL, STARTS WITH THE CHARACTER FOR "SMALL" IN THE JAPANESE, INDICATING THE LOW LEVEL OF STRENGTH. THE SECOND, DEMON, IS A COMBINATION OF THE CHARACTERS FOR "EVIL" AND "DEMON." THE LAST, IFRIT, IS WRITTEN WITH THE CHARACTERS FOR "DEVIL" AND "GOD," AND IS DRAWN FROM AN EXTREMELY POWERFUL TYPE OF SPIRITUAL BEING IN ISLAMIC MYTHOLOGY OFTEN ASSOCIATED WITH THE UNDERWORLD AND SOMETIMES ALSO CALLED A JINNI OR DJINN.

Demon family names

MANY OF THE FAMILY NAMES FOR THE CHARACTERS IN THIS SERIES ARE BASED ON THE "72 PILLARS OF SOLOMON," BUT IN THIS VOLUME, WE'RE INTRODUCED TO A NAME BASED ON A DEMON OUTSIDE OF THE 72 PILLARS. HERE ARE BRIEF DESCRIPTIONS OF EACH NEW CHARACTER AND THE SOURCE OF THEIR DEMON NAME:

◇ ASTAROTH = DUKE ASTAROTH, A GREAT DUKE OF HELL WHO TEACHES OTHERS IN MATHEMATICAL SCIENCES AND CAN GIVE MORTALS POWER OVER SERPENTS.

◇ BELZEBUTH = PRINCE BEELZEBUB, ONE OF THE SEVEN PRINCES OF HELL AND LUCIFER'S CHIEF LIEUTENANT. THIS DEMON IS NOT AMONG THE 72 PILLARS OF SOLOMON.

WELCOME TO DEMON SCHOOL! IRUMA-KUN VOL. 3

CLARA AND FALFAL

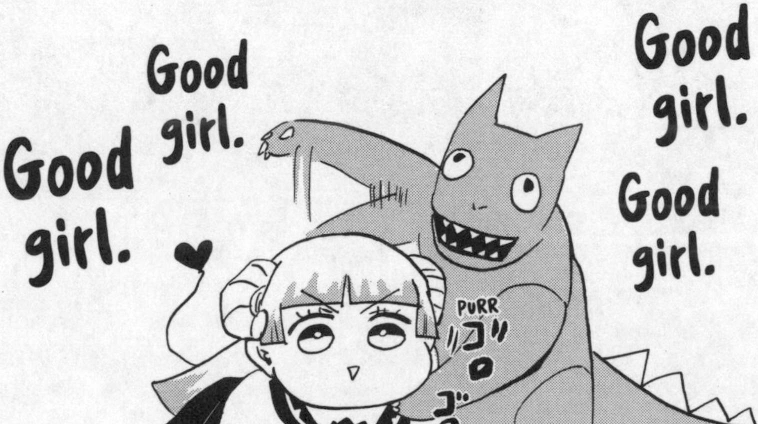
Good girl.
Good girl.
Good girl.
Good girl.
PURR
ゴロ
ゴロ
PURR

OSAMU NISHI

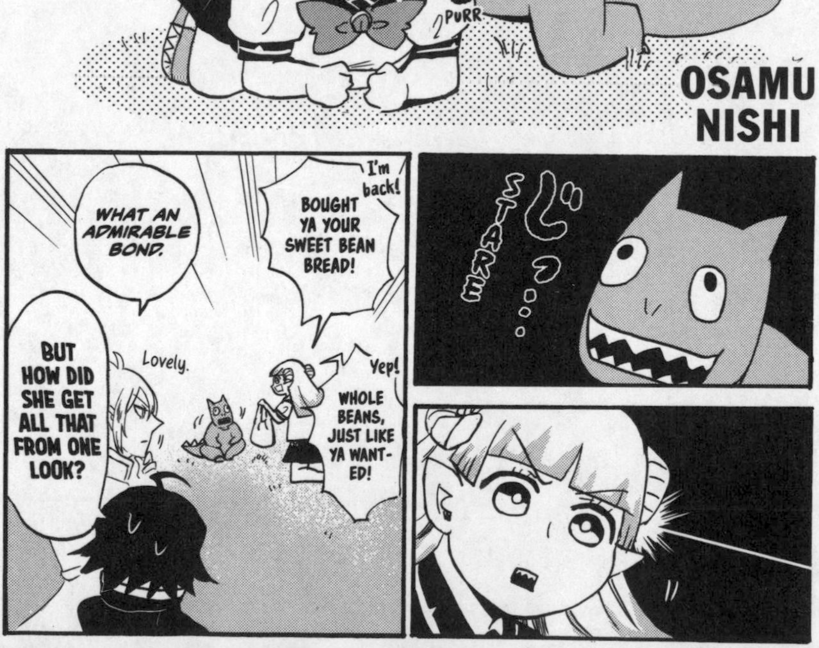
じっ…
STARE
I'm back!
BOUGHT YA YOUR SWEET BEAN BREAD!
WHAT AN ADMIRABLE BOND.
Yep!
WHOLE BEANS, JUST LIKE YA WANT-ED!
Lovely.
BUT HOW DID SHE GET ALL THAT FROM ONE LOOK?

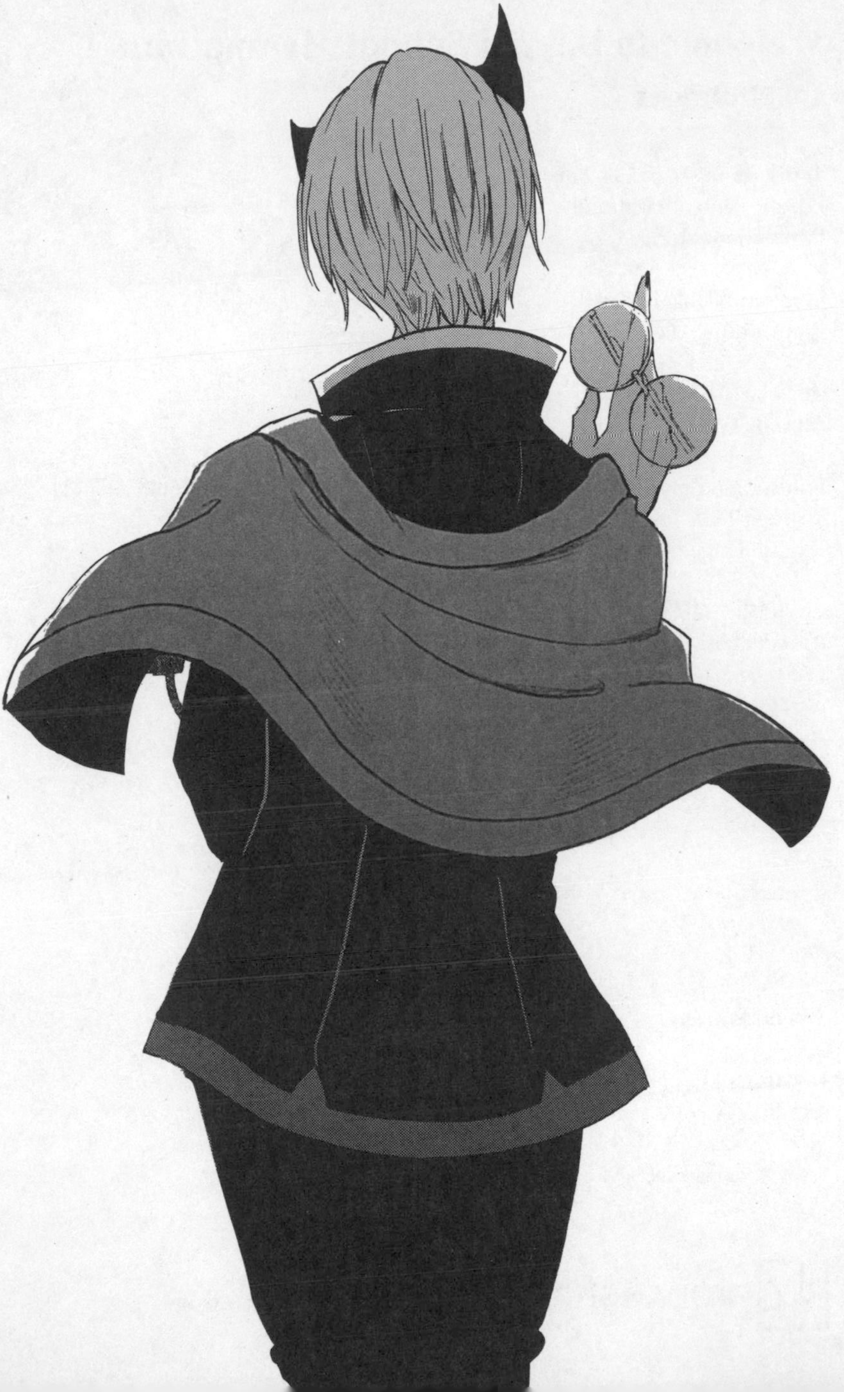

Welcome to Demon School! Iruma-kun 3

A VERTICAL Book

Translation: Jacqueline Fung
Editor: Alexandra McCullough-Garcia
Production: Shirley Fang
             Pei Ann Yeap
Letterer: Nicole Roderick
Proofreading: Kevin Luo

First published in Japan in 2017 by Akita Publishing Co., Ltd., Tokyo
Publication rights for this English edition arranged with Akita Publishing Co., Ltd.
through TUTTLE-MORI AGENCY, INC., Tokyo.
English language version produced by Kodansha USA Publishing, LLC, 2023

Originally published in Japanese as *Mairimashita! Iruma-kun 3* by
Akita Publishing Co., Ltd., 2017
Mairimashita! Iruma-kun first serialized in *Shōnen Champion Comics*,
Akita Publishing Co., Ltd., 2017-

This is a work of fiction.

ISBN: 978-1-64729-253-9

Printed in the United States of America

First Edition

Second Printing

Kodansha USA Publishing, LLC
451 Park Avenue South, 7th Floor
New York, NY 10016
www.kodansha.us

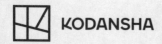

KODANSHA